01/2012

Elisabeth Schwarzkopf

By the same author

The Complete Gilbert and Sullivan Opera Guide

Delius
(Master Musicians)

The Glory of Opera

Inside the Orchestra

The Lieder of Strauss

The Life of Richard Strauss

Lotte Lehmann
A Centenary Biography

Der Rosenkavalier
(Cambridge Opera Guide)

Sir Thomas Beecham
A Centenary Tribute

Strauss
(Music Masters)

Elisabeth Schwarzkopf

ALAN JEFFERSON

VICTOR GOLLANCZ

LONDON

For N.C.B.-A.

non sum qualis eram bonae sub regno Cynarae

First published in Great Britain 1996
by Victor Gollancz
An imprint of the Cassell Group
Wellington House, 125 Strand, London WC2R OBB

© Alan Jefferson 1996

A catalogue record for this book is
available from the British Library.

ISBN 0 575 05278 3

Photoset in Great Britain by
Rowland Phototypesetting Ltd, Bury St Edmunds, Suffolk
Printed and bound in Great Britain by
St Edmundsbury Press Ltd, Bury St Edmunds, Suffolk

Contents

Foreword

Dame Elisabeth Schwarzkopf's many admirers in the musical world must often have wondered over the years at the absence of a substantial biography which this celebrated twentieth-century soprano demands. In 1990, I passed on to Dr Schwarzkopf, as she was then, the message from Gollancz that they would like to commission her autobiography or a biography. She was disinclined to accept the invitation, however, and one could only hope that as she had reached the age of seventy-five, some means of persuading her to alter her decision would be found. It would be regrettable if the details of this remarkable woman's life were not to become widely known after such a spectacular career on the opera stage, in the concert hall, the recital room and recording studio.

When living persons supervise the writing of their own memoirs, they are bound to have recollections and information unavailable elsewhere, especially concerning childhood and family matters, not to mention retrospective and mature views about their own formative years. On the other hand, nobody will want to divulge *every* past event or association, especially those of a deeply personal nature. A biography that is dependent upon the approval of the subject *may* reveal many obscure and important details; but it will almost certainly be highly selective.

In Dame Elisabeth's case, there is no established public archive relating to her life and career, although material is held in a dozen different opera houses, in city libraries and other collections. In going it alone, without the advantage of Schwarzkopf's help, I have been fortunate in receiving a great deal of willing assistance from outside sources.

The Schwarzkopf–Legge Society of London circulates useful information about her to its members; many newspaper and magazine interviews, minuscule biographies and a whole issue devoted to Schwarzkopf in the excellent *l'Avant-Scène l'Opéra* series have also been published. There is a fine book of photographs with brief but vital text by an Italian critic, and a short monograph with some family photographs, written by the music critic of a French newspaper in the 1950s. Then there is her own *On and Off the Record*, a tribute to Walter Legge that also contains a good deal about herself.

In the middle 1950s I spent a convivial day with the Legges. Then, during the last three years of Walter Legge's life, he and I met in London a number of times. In between these meetings, Legge and I frequently exchanged letters that covered all manner of musical subjects; but, less than a month before he died, he insisted that I destroy them. I have drawn on my memory to resurrect some of his views and anecdotes.

Many people have been unsparing in their time and experience in helping me with research, and I heartily thank them all. One of the pleasures of writing a biography is meeting and corresponding with people, sometimes for the first time, because of a shared interest in the subject. This book has proved no exception and the individuals and organizations named below have my sincere gratitude.

The following individuals greatly assisted me, on a personal basis, while I was writing this book: Thaddeus Crenshaw, Paris; Karin Heckermann, Berlin; Eliot Levin, New Barnet; Christopher Norton-Welsh, Vienna; and James Seddon, London, all of whose time spent in research on my behalf is very greatly appreciated.

Then to: Gale Andrews, Watford; Felix Aprahamian, London; Julian Budden, Florence; George Clare, Suffolk; Lord Donaldson, London; Mathias Erhard, Berlin; Niklas Frank, Hamburg; Michael Gasson, London; Guido Hausmann, Düsseldorf; John Hunt, London; Floris Juynboll, Nieuwegein; Frau Lotte Klemperer, Zollikon; Brian Lamport, Salzburg; Alfred Levy, Bournemouth; Isadore Lichtman, Chicago; Bernard Pallut, London; Ivor Pfuell, London; Henry Pleasants, London; Gerald L. Posner, New York; Dr Oliver Rathkolb, Vienna; Michael Scott, Rome; David Vick, Isle of Man and Dr Edward Wrzesien, Warsaw.

The following individuals and their organizations were most helpful, and deserve special thanks: Frau Edda Facklam, Pilz Music, Hamburg; Frau Karin Heckermann and Herr Curt Roesler, Städtische Oper, Berlin; Dr Dagmar Wünsche, Akademie der Künste, Berlin; Dr Peter Andry, Warner Classics International, London; D. Aubry, Société des Bains de Mer, Monte Carlo; Lisa Brant, Stratford Festival, Ontario; Christiano Chiarov, La Fenice, Venice; Mrs Chlebovcová, Poprad, Czech & Slovak Federal Republic; Jacques Davier, Geneva; Jürgen Gauert, Trier Theater; Melanie Leistner, International Music Festival, Lucerne; Koraljka Lockhart, San Francisco Opera; Sal Shuel of BAPLA; Dr Franz-Christian Wulff, Teldec Classics, Hamburg.

Also to the following archivists and librarians: D. Aubrey, Archives SBM, Monte Carlo; Christopher Baller, Basle; Jean-Jacques Eggler, Lausanne; Francesca Franchi and Jane Jackson, Royal Opera House, Covent Garden, London; Alfred Guindi, League of Nations Archive, Geneva; The Archivist,

Graz Opera; T. H. Jacobsen, Royal Library, Copenhagen; Ragnar Köhlin, Library of the Swedish Academy of Music, Stockholm; Paola Reverdini, City Music Library, Turin; Dr Lothar Schirmer, Theatre Collection, Berlin Museum; Siren Steen, Music Library, Bergen; Sabine Steinhage, University Library, Hamburg; Deirdre Tilley, late of *Opera* magazine, London; Robert Tuggle, Metropolitan Opera Archive, New York; Kirsti Turunen, City Library, Helsinki; Mrs Wischmann and Rosemarie Nief of the Wiener Library, London; the Librarian, Staatstheater, Oldenburg; and to Andrew Laycock and Staff of Plymouth City Library.

As well as to those solely connected with the cinema: Robert Hoffmann, Munich; Laurent Lyons, TPA, Wiesbaden; Wolfgang Theis, Stiftung Deutsche Kinemathek, Berlin; British Film Institute, London; Deutsche Institut für Filmkunde, Frankfurt; Friedrich-Wilhelm-Murnau Stiftung, Wiesbaden.

Extensive efforts have been made to contact photograph copyright holders; in a handful of cases this has proved impossible. The publishers would welcome hearing from owners of such material.

Alan Jefferson
Deviock, Cornwall
1995

Preface

To many lovers of fine singing over the age of thirty-five, Elisabeth Schwarzkopf in concert is still vividly recalled in the mind's eye, standing in a bright light beside a piano, the embodiment of femininity, gorgeously groomed and dressed. We remember how we applauded vigorously while waiting impatiently for her to fill the hall with her own special luxury of soprano singing. The programmes were always a skilful juxtaposition of the mournful and the contemplative, the cheerful and the humorous (and, just occasionally, the grotesquely comic), and they were always superbly delivered. In Elisabeth Schwarzkopf's heyday each event was a magnet that drew lovers of distinguished singing from all over the world.

Happily, much of Schwarzkopf's wide repertoire has been carefully preserved on disc, not only the Lieder, at which she excelled, but also her major operatic roles, which for two decades after the war she played on all the great stages of the Western world. Few London opera lovers under fifty will have seen Schwarzkopf there, for her last appearances at the Royal Opera House were as Strauss's Marschallin in 1959. As an opera singer she is still spoken of with reverence at the Vienna State Opera, at Salzburg and at La Scala, Milan. In the United States she is remembered more in San Francisco where she made her American début than at the New York Met, with which her relations were chequered.

Schwarzkopf's career was extraordinary because it involved so much travel, so many appearances: it was a quadruple life in the opera house, the concert hall, the recital room and the recording studio, from city to city and continent to continent. Her peregrinations are laid out in Appendix A.

From the mid 1960s onwards, Lieder recitals increasingly dominated her career, until she gave her farewell recital in March 1979, at the age of sixty-three. But she did not retire altogether. Masterclasses, private pupils, seminars and competitions continued to occupy her well past her seventy-fifth birthday in 1990. By then, she had received more honours and decorations than any other singer.

If one asks how all this came about, the answer lies in two words: talent and ambition. She grasped and nurtured the seed of a talent which had been born in her, willed it to flower through sheer, determined hard work, and sought no alternatives in life except those that would help it bloom even more richly.

Elisabeth Schwarzkopf faced few professional setbacks once she had passed a single audition to the Berlin Deutsche Oper during Holy Week in April 1938. There had been a disturbing passage with an inappropriate singing teacher at the beginning of her formal vocal training; but once that had been overcome and she found the right person to guide her, it was plain sailing, as she saw it. With Walter Legge, whom she was to marry, Schwarzkopf's style and technique underwent further changes. Opinions differ about Legge's effect on her singing; but his influence over Schwarzkopf between 1945 and 1964, over and above his vocal coaching, should not be underestimated. He could be compared to an efficient engineer, with superb equipment at his disposal. It was he who fine-tuned the precision instrument that was her voice and effected its smooth running.

Schwarzkopf's first professor of singing, though unsatisfactory, had already fostered her love of Lieder singing. At the same time, as a naturally gifted actress, Schwarzkopf knew how to project what was not a particularly large instrument to make it sound more than adequate in the opera house. History will never dub her solely a Lieder singer, because her operatic performances were gems of their own kind, planned and executed with consummate skill.

Apart from Walter Legge's support, including the resource of the Philharmonia Orchestra and his influential position at EMI, Schwarzkopf relied on Herbert von Karajan at first to give her encouragement and later on a great deal of work in Vienna and Milan during the mid 1950s when he often seemed to be making unilateral decisions. Whether they were the right ones or not, they all contributed to her fame and moved her to the top of her profession.

There are more than passing affinities in terms of character and career between Schwarzkopf and Karajan. They both suffered irritating delays after the war, when they were still politically suspect and the wheels of authority ground exceeding slowly. Through a mixture of patience and determination they both overcame the obstacles, thanks partly to Walter Legge. He had the wherewithal to accommodate them both in difficult times and to launch them as part of his grand musical plan, turning a blind eye to what some considered to be a misguidedly unpatriotic approach. His presence in both their lives immediately after the end of the war cannot be over-emphasized and was effectively the springboard from which these two artists emerged as world-famous stars.

In the 1950s and early 1960s the leading international sopranos, apart from the special category of the Wagnerians, were Maria Callas and Elisabeth Schwarzkopf, so different in every way that there could be no rivalry between them. Schwarzkopf was never one to make public scenes, to court the press or to walk out; she was totally professional, going about her job undemonstratively and producing a superbly finished product. This resulted in a far longer career than that of the tragic American–Greek diva, who burned herself out far too soon. When Callas in her decline was once asked 'Why don't you take up Lieder singing?' she replied, 'Because I don't know any Lieder.'

An outstanding Lieder singer has a distinct advantage over the opera or oratorio singer in that the whole focus of attention is upon her throughout the recital. There is no orchestra, no one to share the event and support her, no scenery, no resting while others take over. There is only the accompanist, in Schwarzkopf's case Gerald Moore or Geoffrey Parsons, both brilliant at their job, but none the less in her shadow. It is at her Lieder recitals that Schwarzkopf scored her greatest triumphs.

It is to be regretted that she did not have greater opportunities on stage to display more fully, and in a wider variety of stage characterizations, her sense of humour, more characteristically Viennese or English than Prussian. Fiordiligi and Alice Ford were her principal vehicles for comedy, though in rather different veins, and there is much evidence of humour in the four Johann Strauss operetta recordings as well as in the Lieder with which she used to end her recitals or give as encores, like Wolf's 'Mausfallensprüchlein', 'Ich hab' in Penna' or Richard Strauss's 'Hat gesagt . . . bleibs nicht dabei'. She was born a German, became a British subject by marriage, was granted honorary Austrian citizenship and was then admitted to the British establishment by being dubbed with the equivalent of a knighthood. Through all these cross–border travels her innate sense of fun and sparkle is unchanged.

PART I

I

Upbringing in the Weimar Republic
The Third Reich
1915–1938

Olga Maria Elisabeth Frederike Schwarzkopf was born on 9 December 1915. Her birthplace is given correctly in reference books as Jarocin near Poznán, Poland; but both her parents and all four of her grandparents were Prussian.

In 1871, Otto von Bismarck was instrumental in winning the Franco-Prussian War, and one result of the general slicing up of Poland was the return of former Prussian lands. Northern Silesia and Posen in the Prussian region were now renamed and administered by and for Germans, with former unpronounceable Polish cities and towns given German names. Opportunities soon arose for Prussian citizens, especially those in the professional classes, to resettle themselves and make a good living in Posen, on the border with Russia. Friedrich Schwarzkopf, a classics schoolmaster, went to work there, even though it meant that he might have to move to a different school in a different town every three years or so; his methods and abilities were apparently held in high esteem. He and his young wife Elisabeth (*née* Fröhling) were living in Jarocin, near Poznán in the north of Posen, when a royal assassination in Sarajevo turned Europe upside-down in August 1914.

In keeping with the rise in birth-rate that the war promoted, the Schwarzkopfs soon became the parents of another Elisabeth. In several respects, mother and daughter were to become much alike. There was the same distinguishing gap between the front teeth, the same shape of face and expression, the same strong-mindedness and determination.

Frau Schwarzkopf was the forceful member of the household, which was usually the way in Germany, and especially as Dr Friedrich was a kind, easy-going intellectual who liked the peaceful life. He adored his daughter and saw to it that she was brought up in conventional middle-class surroundings, where the stated form of worship was Evangelical, music and the arts were important, and material comfort was taken for granted, even during the rigours of the First World War and the depression that followed it. In career matters, Frau Schwarzkopf took charge.

In the summer of 1918, Emperor Wilhelm II left Berlin for neutral Holland,

and Germany was forced to surrender to the Allies. A large proportion of Germans were convinced that there had been a stab in the back from within, and the whole nation, especially the Army and Navy, believed they had been cheated. It was no wonder that various political parties, including extreme right-wing factions and an ever-growing number of Communists, felt that this was the moment to oppose central control of the old kind.

Numerous indignities were forced upon Germany by the vengeful Allies who took all her colonies and shared them out among themselves, demanding 132,000 million gold marks to be paid in reparation by 1988.[1] Everything possible was done, in fact, to ensure that Germany was prevented from waging war again in the twentieth century.

Northern Silesia, which had belonged to Prussia for the last 200 years, and Posen, which had been Prussian for nearly as long, were both returned to Poland. While these conditions doubtless affected the Schwarzkopf family in one way or another, they had become so accustomed to Posen, and Dr Friedrich was so firmly established there, that they stayed put.

The creation and unsteady progress of the Weimar Republic was an unhappy and unruly epoch following the Emperor's abdication, for Prussia had always had a King or Kaiser since the Hohenzollerns came to power in 1701. There was an immediate and frightening devaluation of the mark which escalated daily; strikes followed, then an unprecedented mutiny in the Navy, and growing street violence from the Communists. The young Elisabeth Schwarzkopf grew up in an atmosphere of uncertainty and change. She had known little else, but for those of her parents' age life must have seemed uncomfortable and unpleasant.

With inflation still rampant and worsening shortages of life's necessities, there was a pressing need for a new leader to inspire the German people and get the country back on its feet. Then, as in the next post-war phase of 1945, the 'unjust' war accusation rankled deeply, because the majority of Germans considered themselves to be entirely innocent.

In September 1923, when Elisabeth Schwarzkopf was not quite eight years old, the celebrated First World War strategist, General Ludendorff, lent his support to an Austrian ex-corporal and rabble-rouser called Adolf Hitler who, as head of the Deutsche Arbeiter Partei (DAP), had been campaigning for the working man since 1919.[2] Hitler operated from Munich where he enjoyed a fair degree of support, and it was here that his *Putsch* took place in an effort to seize power in Bavaria. It failed, Ludendorff was discredited and Hitler was imprisoned. He would not forget those of his followers who had stood beside him in Munich, 'the old Nazis', later rewarding them accordingly.

A Schwarzkopf family photograph taken at about this time shows a tubby little girl happily skipping along during a walk with her father.[3] He looks comfortably well built, the very picture of a successful educationalist. Elisabeth had no brothers or sisters but she got to know boys at school, where she was the only girl in her father's Greek and Latin classes. There were changes of towns and of schools, which Elisabeth took in her stride, keeping up her piano lessons and learning guitar, viola and organ as well, as if to counter a bias towards the sciences at the *Realgymnasium*. She was clearly devoted to music but she had to make her own because her family did not possess a gramophone.

Between 1922 and 1928 Friedrich Schwarzkopf's work meant that the family moved several times: from Liegnitz in Silesia to Breslau, then back to Liegnitz, which Schwarzkopf still refers to by its old name of Wahlstatt, and finally to Magdeburg, in 1928, within easy reach of the Prussian capital. By this time Elisabeth was already thinking in terms of music as a career, was becoming proficient at the piano and, more important still, had developed a naturally pretty, high voice which enabled her to take a leading part in her first opera, Eurydice in Gluck's *Orfeo ed Euridice*, at the Magdeburg school, where she was also in demand at concerts and local amateur performances. At one of the schools she attended, she played the glockenspiel in a marching orchestra. In 1931, her father was transferred to Cottbus, a twelfth-century city between Berlin and Dresden on the Polish border, and even closer to Berlin than Magdeburg, a mere seven railway stations away. The attractive countryside around Cottbus includes the River Spree with its lakes and the Spree Forest which used to border on the city itself. Frau Schwarzkopf recognized that if her daughter was to be properly trained as a musician, Berlin was the place, and the best institution was undoubtedly the Hochschule. She made inquiries and began to plan for the most significant part of Elisabeth's education.

At the time of their last move, to the Prussian capital itself in March 1933, Elisabeth was seventeen years of age. The Schwarzkopfs went to live at 8 Opitzstrasse in the Dahlem/Steglitz district of south-west Berlin. Elisabeth was entered for the Berlin Royal Augusta School and was at last in a favourable position to attend concerts and share all the excitements of the capital city. She finished off her schooling by gaining her Abitur in 1934 and immediately applied for entrance to the Berlin Hochschule für Musik or, to give its full name, Die Staatliche Akademie Hochschule für Musik in Berlin. Thanks to her pure, sweet singing voice, her proficiency on the piano, her familiarity with the viola and organ and her knowledge of musical theory, her attractively outgoing personality and her mother's determined support, she was awarded a place.

Political events in 1933 and 1934 offered welcome distractions for those Germans who recognized their salvation in the Führer. The leaders were highly visible, their voices were inescapable over loudspeakers and wireless, and the meetings and emotionally powerful parades, organized with great skill, drew tears of hope, joy and devotion. When the Führer addressed the nation, or Goebbels spoke, mass hypnotism and even hysteria took over. Although afterwards it was difficult for people to recall what had been said, it sounded marvellous at the time, with its oft-repeated main theme, hope for the German nation at last, in the full-throated, joyous *Sieg Heil!*

Even so, to others these events spelled a warning. The Jews had no doubts, and many Aryan Germans, in particular intellectuals and aristocrats, were anxious too, afraid of what the consequences might be under this new order. The generals were far from reassured by Hitler, whom they referred to as 'the corporal'. Yet the Nazi machine ran inexorably on, carrying the nation with it, and the longer the doubters remained, the more unlikely became their chance of reversing its progress.

In the Easter holidays of 1934, before beginning her musical training, and with a grant from the League of National Socialist Students,[4] Elisabeth left her parents in Berlin and took a cycling and camping holiday in England for the main purpose of learning the language. The late Deryck Cooke remembered seeing her in his home town of Leicester where, she has since said, she enjoyed her stay and acquired a good basic knowledge of English. At this time groups of German students were beginning to travel abroad, often to schools, as a 'goodwill gesture'. Their political motives were possibly questionable, but those who can recall the ebullience of these young Germans can vouch for their general good nature and friendliness. None the less, contemporary local newspapers reveal a generally anti-German attitude, showing very unflattering pictures of Hitler and Goebbels to emphasize an undercurrent of mistrust and unease felt by many people in England about what was going on across the Rhine.

After her holiday, Elisabeth Schwarzkopf took her place at the Hochschule and settled down to serious study. The school's overall director, politically appointed in 1933, was the once revered musicologist Professor Dr Fritz Stein who, in 1910, had discovered in Jena the manuscript score of a symphony which he optimistically attributed to Beethoven. Stein remained the school's director throughout the war: among the celebrated musicians on the staff of well over a hundred were Paul Hindemith for composition and theory; Carl Flesch and Georg Kulenkampff, violin; Edwin Fischer and Max Trapp, piano.[5]

The most famous professor in the vocal faculty was Frau Lula Mysz-Gmeiner. Now in her late fifties, she had been an adored mezzo and Lieder singer since her first Berlin recital in 1900, and the occasional concerts she gave were always sold out. Lula Gmeiner had been a pupil of Etelka Gerster in Berlin, of Lilli Lehmann (at Brahms's recommendation),[6] and also of the great singer and celebrated eccentric Raimund von zur Mühlen, in London. She had been so highly regarded by both Brahms and Hugo Wolf that, it is claimed, they accompanied her at the remarkably early age of nineteen or twenty in recitals of their own Lieder. In 1933 Elisabeth Schwarzkopf had been to a Mysz-Gmeiner recital at the Berlin Philharmonie. Although she disliked the hooting tone which the celebrated voice produced, her 'application of expression', according to Schwarzkopf, was the singer's more remarkable aspect, by which she means Mysz-Gmeiner's ability to colour and underline the songs' innermost meaning by purely vocal (and facial) resources. This certainly left its mark after the concert which Schwarzkopf attended.

With singing as her first subject and piano as second, Elisabeth was surprised and delighted to find that she had been assigned to Mysz-Gmeiner as her professor; but she was even more surprised and far less delighted when the great lady immediately became convinced that her new pupil, already vocally well equipped, would make another mezzo, and began training her accordingly.

Unless Gmeiner saw and heard in Schwarzkopf a familiar echo of her own youth, it is difficult to understand why she remained 'despotic to the point of blindness'[7] (or rather deafness) when the girl had such an entirely different voice. Fortunately this approach did not do any actual damage to her pupil's voice, a high, clear instrument with coloratura waiting to be brought out and a somewhat weak low register.

But while Elisabeth progressed happily with piano, her vocal classes were another matter altogether. She attended them as instructed, using the free and lovely top to her voice far less than before, but feeling that it was all wrong. Mysz-Gmeiner's name and aura of artistic respectability were such that most girls would have considered themselves very fortunate to be assigned to her, but Elisabeth complained constantly to her mother when she got home after singing lessons, feeling dispirited and worn out. At least she had to admit that when it came to interpretation and colouring of phrases, Mysz-Gmeiner could bring tears to the eyes; but often, in her lessons, the famous diva was close to bringing tears of anguish.

From the beginning of the summer term in April 1934, there had been a new requirement at the Hochschule. All students were ordered to assemble between ten and one on Sundays for political lectures, either 'In gratitude for the National Socialist Movement' or 'The principles of Party leadership'.[8] This signalled an upheaval among the Jewish students and staff who saw the danger signals all too clearly. A promising young Berliner on the Hochschule conducting course, who was a capable pianist, sometimes accompanied Schwarzkopf, as the more advanced students were required to do for the singers and solo instrumentalists. Suddenly he disappeared. When it became known that he had a Jewish mother, his fellow-students did not discuss the matter. His name was Peter Gellhorn and he managed to escape to England where he later took up a solid coaching and conducting career at Covent Garden and Glyndebourne.

In 1935, and now nearly twenty years of age, Schwarzkopf joined the students' association of the National Socialist Party at the Berlin Hochschule. For one term she became a Führerin of the National Socialist German Students' Association,[9] when she encouraged support from her colleagues in giving generously to the *Winterhilfe* ('Winter Aid'), one of the Party's favourite and continuing charities under the aegis of the Red Cross. Funds ostensibly went to poorer families in cold weather but, after the winter of 1941, demands for subscriptions were raised to help sustain soldiers on the Eastern Front. Another responsibility of a Führerin was to keep an eye on other students, to ensure that they pulled their weight and said nothing disparaging about the Führer or the Party. This move was endorsed by Frau Schwarzkopf, who felt that the political climate favoured dedicated supporters of the Party, and although Schwarzkopf's father was personally opposed to her joining, he was obliged to concur with his wife's decision.

Elisabeth was sometimes called upon to sing at public concerts with other Hochschule pupils, three of which were held towards the end of 1935. The first included two duets from Bach Cantatas, when her fellow-soloist was Carola Behr. They were performed to piano accompaniment. Then, in July, she sang third soprano in the Three German Folk Songs for Three Women's Voices by Brahms. At this concert, Lula Mysz-Gmeiner took the solo role in Schubert's *Ständchen* (the Serenade for Alto and Female Chorus), in which students from her singing class took part – Elisabeth included, no doubt. Another familiar name appears among the students at this concert: the soprano Gerda Lammers, who was to become a famous Elektra and Marie in *Wozzeck* after the war.

On 21 November 1935, Elisabeth sang Max Reger's *Vier schlichte Weisen* ('Four Simple Ditties') to Albert Busch's piano accompaniment in the first of two evenings of German Hausmusik by Professor Hans Mahlke's chamber students. Elisabeth, however, is clearly shown as belonging to Frau Professor Lula Mysz-Gmeiner's singing class, where she was still being taught as a mezzo.

After putting up with Mysz-Gmeiner's eccentricities, as she saw them, for more than a year, Schwarzkopf was at last able to convince her mother about the inadequacy of her training. It was now agreed that something was radically wrong, not least because of her lack of any real vocal progress.

Frau Schwarzkopf went to see Professor Stein and vigorously presented her case to him. The initial reaction was indignation. Nobody before had dreamt of turning down instruction from such a wonderful artist as Mysz-Gmeiner: it should have been an honour to sit at the Frau Professor's feet ... Thus ran Professor Stein's argument. But the determined Frau Schwarzkopf disagreed, and won the day.

There could be no question of Elisabeth's being transferred to another professor at the Hochschule for the time being; indeed, the situation had to be tactfully negotiated to avoid causing embarrassment to Frau Professor Lula. Yet some time between her last concert in November and another one before Christmas, Elisabeth acquired a new professor, as the programme makes clear.

On 20 December a large body of student singers accompanied by the Chamber Orchestra of the Hochschule and conducted by Professor Dr Fritz Stein performed Heinrich Schütz's *Weihnachtshistorie* ('Christmas Story') to commemorate the composer's 350th birthday. The first of the Three Shepherds was taken by Elisabeth Schwarzkopf. One of the basses on this occasion, Otto von Rohr, became a concert and opera singer of repute after the war.

It has always been assumed that, having secured her release from Mysz-Gmeiner, Elisabeth immediately started to study with a Dr Egonolf outside the Hochschule. But on 17 June 1937 she sang Schubert's Four Canzonets (D.688) accompanied by Professor Arthur Kusterer, to whose Lieder class, the programme states, she now belonged. Eventually, of course, Dr Egonolf became interested in her voice, concurred that she was no mezzo, and expressed confidence in her future as a coloratura soprano. He acknowledged the value of some of her former teaching, especially Mysz-Gmeiner's lessons in interpretation. But essentially Elisabeth was asked to submit to fresh instruction, and was only too glad to agree. From this point onwards her progress was rapid and the singing lessons went from strength to strength.

For some time now her sights had been set on one of the Berlin opera houses. The Deutsches Opernhaus in Charlottenburg was the most conveniently situated and seemed to be of a high standard, less reactionary, and under a more approachable management than that of the proud old Staatsoper. With this ambition in mind, she continued to take singing lessons from Dr Egonolf, who was undoubtedly the right teacher for her. Indeed, after passing all her musical examinations with merit and graduating in 1937, she became a member of the Hochschule's advanced course at their Opera School. Between November and the following April she appeared in its production of the 1930 Brecht-Weill children's opera *Der Jasager* ('The Yes-Sayer'), which seems a curious choice.

Both Brecht and Weill had been forced to leave Germany by 1933, and in that year Weill's music was officially banned as decadent Marxist rubbish. Nevertheless, their opera is about sacrifice for a cause, and begins with a static chorus intoning, 'Above all, it is important to learn consent.' Small wonder that Brecht and Weill followed it later with *Der Neinsager*.[10]

Besides becoming a member of the Opera School, Schwarzkopf joined the Favre Solistenvereinigung, a chorus of semi-professionals, music students and serious amateurs in Berlin founded by the opera singer Waldo Favre. They sang secular and sacred (but no Jewish) works. At about the time that Schwarzkopf joined, Favre had secured an engagement for them to sing the chorus in a recording of *Die Zauberflöte*. A tight budget may have demanded the recording company's use of such a body, less expensive to engage than either the Staatsoper or the Deutsche Oper, but well up to the task all the same.

The recording was due to take place in the rococo Beethovensaal of the Philharmonie in Bernburgerstrasse, conducted by the celebrated and eccentric English impresario, Sir Thomas Beecham, who brought a highly competent young man from London with him as his technical assistant. His name was Walter Legge. Schwarzkopf sang as a chorus first soprano in this famous recording, with three days of sessions in November 1937: it was an exciting experience and her first real engagement. Her eyes positively feasted on Tiana Lemnitz, Erna Berger and Helge Roswaenge, world-famous artists who were standing singing so close to her.[11]

On 1 March 1939, shortly before leaving the Opera School, Schwarzkopf was admitted as a member of Dr Goebbels' Reichstheaterkammer (RTK), part of the Reich Ministry for Public Enlightenment and Propaganda (ProMi). She was given the number 67784, a serious step towards joining the NSDAP and becoming what we would now describe as 'streetwise'.

2

Opera Singer in Berlin
1938–1940

Das Deutsche Opernhaus auf dem Bismarckstrasse was the official name of the Deutsche Oper when the twenty-two-year-old Elisabeth Schwarzkopf joined its company. On Wednesday, 13 April 1938 she attended an audition there before Wilhelm Rode, the General Intendant, Hans Batteux, his deputy and chief producer, and Artur Rother, the newly appointed First Kapellmeister (Director of Music). Schwarzkopf sang Agathe's scene 'Wie nahte mir der Schlummer . . . Leise, leise' from *Der Freischütz*, an ideal vehicle for displaying her legato at the start, and later showing off her top B. Egonolf, who had prepared her for this audition, knew exactly what he was doing.

The three executives were satisfied with Schwarzkopf's performance and told her that they were considering her for a part in a new production of *Parsifal*. Her début would be in the short but important role of Second Flower Maiden (First Group) in Act II. This was a demanding offer to someone who had never appeared on the professional stage before, especially on an opening night. The role involves solos interspersed among other sopranos' lines, and ensembles of great precision with stage movement by the whole chorus of Flower Maidens. Such roles were sometimes offered to test the more promising young singers in Germany and Austria; and although Schwarzkopf gathered that it was not an altogether unusual event, it was nevertheless a compliment to her. To the question, 'Can you sing this role? Do you know it?' the plucky, ambitious girl replied, 'Of course I do!'

Of course she didn't. There was a bigger snag.

'We are inviting you to sing it,' said Rode, 'but the first performance is on Good Friday, the day after tomorrow. You have only thirty-six hours in which to prepare – and Herr Rother will be conducting!'

Elisabeth went straight home and devoured the score. Her mother, ever ambitious for her daughter, was delighted. One piano rehearsal at the Opera House was followed by a run-through of her moves on stage which Elisabeth picked up at once, displaying the kind of determination that is one of her characteristics. On Good Friday she arrived at the Deutsche Oper in good time for the 18.30 performance. She whistled Wagner's tune as she went up to the dressing-room which she shared with the other Flower Maidens. Whistling in the theatre means bad luck, and little allowance for the beginner was made by the other superstitious girls, who looked as though they wanted to scratch her eyes out.[1]

Once on stage, Schwarzkopf held Artur Rother's eyes fast with her own, and got through the ordeal safely, enjoying her proximity to the American Wagnerian tenor, Eyvind Laholm, who was singing Parsifal. On that night, of 15 April 1938, Elisabeth Schwarzkopf became a probationary junior soprano in the Deutsch Oper, Berlin, with her name appearing on the programme and then on the artists' notice-board for forthcoming operas, all of which had to be learned immediately. The first was Wellgunde in both *Das Rheingold* and *Götterdämmerung*. Five more roles followed before the end of the season in August, and now the staff répétiteurs and coaches were on hand to help her.

This was a remarkable opportunity for such a young and inexperienced singer, because starting an operatic career in Germany usually meant a first engagement (if you were lucky) at one of the provincial houses of Chemnitz, Oldenburg or Stettin. But in one stride Schwarzkopf had arrived in Berlin's second opera house and attained status above that of a mere chorus member.

The Deutsche Oper had begun as the Charlottenburg Opera, in that western district of Berlin whose local council, funded by shareholders, had built the first private Berlin opera house. It held an audience of 2300 and opened as the Städtische (City) Opera in November 1912 with *Fidelio*. A resident company of reasonably good singers was inadequately supported by the artistic standards achieved, which neither the First World War nor the depression which followed it helped to improve. In early 1923, Otto Klemperer was invited to join the Charlottenburg as musical director so as to inject some vigour into the company, but he saw too many artistic and financial difficulties ahead and was put off by the building which was 'singularly lacking in charm but large and technically up to date'.[2] So he declined the offer.

On Christmas Day 1924 the Charlottenburg Opera was declared bankrupt and was immediately seized by the Greater Berlin City Council who owned the land on which the building stood. The Chief Burgomaster of Berlin had long wanted to establish an opera house with direct civic subsidy, in contrast to the established Staatsoper with its history of royal patronage, altogether at odds with the character of the present Weimar Republic. Heinz Tietjen, an outstanding conductor–stage-director–administrator from the Staatsoper, was appointed intendant, on the understanding that this would be a first step towards the creation of a new, overall *Intendanz* in Berlin under his control. Sensibly enough, the Charlottenburg now became known as the Städtische Oper (City Opera).

Being intimately acquainted with opera house business and personalities,

Tietjen knew where to go for the best artists and administrators. He imported Bruno Walter and Fritz Zweig to lead the music staff. At first Walter's genial approach to singers and musicians worked wonders, and he remained as principal conductor at the Städtische until 1929. Walter also introduced many new artists who helped elevate the standards there, but as a dedicated musician and practising Jew, he eventually became depressed and worried by the continuing political issues and Tietjen's endless machinations. Because all this eventually interfered with his work and was destroying his peace of mind and pleasure in it, Walter was only too glad to accept an offer from Munich. He was replaced at the Städtische Oper by the successful Austrian conductor, Fritz Stiedry, who left, again for racial reasons in 1933, to conduct the Leningrad Philharmonic.

The company achieved even greater artistic successes when Carl Ebert, from the Darmstadt Opera, was appointed General Director in charge of productions in 1931. He brought with him Rudolf Bing, his astute young general manager, whose ways, because he was thoroughly Viennese, were sometimes at odds with Prussian methods. But Ebert and Bing again raised the production standards, making them in many ways preferable to those at the Staatsoper, an unheard of state of affairs: *Stadt* versus *Staat*.

Unfortunately, some of the pride in achievement and good personal relationships among those who worked at the Städtische Oper lasted only until the beginning of 1933. In March of that year, brownshirted members of the SA (Sturmabteilung) forced their way into the Städtisches Opernhaus, manhandled Carl Ebert (who was not Jewish) because he had publicly refused to collaborate with the Party, and 'sent him on leave'. Bing, who was Jewish, saw the signs clearly enough and left Germany at once. Ebert was so thoroughly disgusted at the manner in which the new politics were controlling German art that he joined Bing and, together with Fritz Busch from Dresden, helped establish the Glyndebourne Opera in England.

During a period of uncertainty about the future of the Städtische, there was a strong possibility that the opera house might be turned into a centre for operetta to coincide with and support Joseph Goebbels' policies. Popular art was a valuable way of relaxing the public and making them more amenable to the propaganda which was fed into the entertainment: not quite a subliminal form of education but something like it. At all events, Goebbels saw the house as a valuable acquisition, not only for ministerial purposes, but also as a counter to his rival, Prussian Minister Hermann Goering, who had political control over the Berlin Staatsoper.

The Deutsche Oper's prospective new Intendant, Wilhelm Rode, was already on the payroll, having been principal Wagnerian bass-baritone there since 1926. He was now promoted on the recommendation of Hans Hinkel, SS Lieutenant General and Reich Culture Director in the Propaganda Ministry, who was also the guardian of Goebbels' filing system containing information on all artists in the Reich.

Evidently the negotiations over Rode's appointment had been going on for some time, and an unconfirmed story had persisted that it was during a train journey they made together that Hitler offered Rode the job. The Führer had often heard him singing Hans Sachs (forty-three times, Rode used to say); he had also been one of the finest Wotans at Munich in the 1920s, before he came to Berlin, and was greatly admired in his one *Ring* cycle at Covent Garden in 1928. It was only partly because of his contract with Munich, however, that he never appeared at Bayreuth Festivals.

Earlier in 1933, Rode had been seeking the strongest possible political support for himself by applying to join the NSDAP, which would seem to make sense if he was intending to curry favour with the Party and especially with the Führer. He was admitted on 1 April 1933, exactly one month before the 'closed season' for new members,[3] a move to achieve a contrived hierarchy. The Führer had ordained that this moratorium must last for four years, so Rode just squeezed in.

As soon as he had taken up his duties as general intendant of the Deutsche Oper, Rode discerned an atmosphere of greater intrigue in the house than had been evident when he was only a singer there; with Heinz Tietjen now the senior and overall general intendant in Berlin, such disquiet flourished. Rode strongly disliked Tietjen, who returned the antipathy and was the other reason why Rode never sang at Bayreuth; casting there was mainly in Tietjen's gift and he could always override other managements.

Nineteen thirty-three was the year when Schwarzkopf, a pupil at the Berlin Hochschule, 'first heard decent singing', according to Walter Legge.[4] She claims to have been only a very few times to the Berlin Staatsoper, where she heard Frida Leider and Dusolina Giannini. As early as November 1933, in his speech for the inauguration of the RKK (Reichskulturkammer) Dr Goebbels had explicitly declared what he was going to expect from all its members: 'No one, however high or low, has the right to use his personal freedom, and that applies also to all creative artists.'[5] And to the Hitler Youth in their official paper *Will und Macht*: 'Musical education is a political message to the whole nation, no longer the private business of the individual.'[6] Not very appealing statements, one would have thought, but they worked, and helped swell memberships of the junior, affiliated organizations to well over 50 per cent.

At this time, many first-class singers who were racially or politically unaffected by the new regime remained, or had since arrived, at the Deutsche Oper. Thanks to the experienced management, a good balance of voices had been maintained by the right kind of singers to fill all the roles in the house's repertory. Although the principal dramatic soprano, Elsa Lárcèn, was Swedish, the versatile lyrics and coloraturas were Aryans from the Greater Reich. Among them were four in particular with whom Schwarzkopf would soon be competing, in spite of her youth;[7] for although protocol was involved in the formal method of promotion based on age and length of service, it was sometimes possible to bypass one's seniors with sufficient protection and the kind of determination that Schwarzkopf already seemed to possess. Some of the tenors and baritones at the Deutsche Oper, such as the lyric tenor Walther Ludwig and the Heldentenor Gotthelf Pistor (whom Schwarzkopf greatly admired), had extensive guest artist contracts for the Berlin Staatsoper, and for Vienna and Bayreuth. Karl Schmitt-Walter, an elegant, light-voiced baritone, was later to be of enormous help and encouragement to Schwarzkopf. Of the two principal basses, Eduard Kandl had been a member of the company since its beginning and was also one of its few *Kammersänger*.

Schwarzkopf took her first step in the same direction as Rode when she joined the NSDAP a month after arriving at the Deutsche Oper. She had to sign a form stating that she came from an entirely Aryan family and had never been in any way connected with the Jewish faith; then, eight days later, she made another detailed declaration about the racial purity of her parents and grandparents, completed in her presence by a Party official at the Deutsche Oper.

It took two years before she was registered as a full member of the German Nazi Party,[8] and that was not ratified until nine months later, in December 1940, when she was sent her Berlin Party number[9] and her *Arbeitsbuch* (a kind of Party log-book) that had to be deposited at the Opera.

The Opera House contracts normally ran from 1 August until 31 July of the following year; but with only three months to go before the end of the season, the agreement with Schwarzkopf covered only the forthcoming 1938–9 season. Schwarzkopf's contracts were all annual until the one due to begin on 1 August 1943 which was for three years, but she never signed it.[10] In April 1938 she became a 'Soprano (Beginner)' in the Deutsche Opernhaus, Berlin, to receive 2400 RM a year paid monthly (about £12,000 in 1995 purchasing power) with an extra 2.50 RM (a comparable £15) if she sang twice in one day. She was obliged to give up to four performances a week 'as cast', which meant singing any role the management chose to give her, but the payment for a second performance was stingy, because if that were the normal going rate, she would have to sing eight times a week. Schwarzkopf had been engaged as a soprano, rather than as a chorus member, so she was entitled to some consideration in the distribution of parts. From her first full season of 1938–9, which began in August, she had to sing far more than four times a week and in a variety of small roles, some of which were desirable cameos.

The management did not force her at the outset of her career, and required her to learn only one new role a month. After her Wellgunde Schwarzkopf was already expecting to be given more named roles, but her third one was a Rag Picker in *Evangelimann*. It cannot have suited her because she somehow managed to drop it and never appeared in Kienzl's opera again. Two other assumptions were quite good ones for a beginner: Esmeralda, the pretty Circus Dancer in Act III of *The Bartered Bride*, who has two decent duets (and whose dress was to make a totally unexpected appearance five years later); and Adele's 'Schwester Ida' in *Die Fledermaus*, which Schwarzkopf positively hated because Ida has no solo line. There is only dialogue, and all Ida can do otherwise is to sing along with the chorus. From the start, Schwarzkopf had her eye on the far more worthwhile Adele.

Her last role before the season ended was a rather spectacular one as Marie, the heroine in Lortzing's light opera *Der Waffenschmied* (*The Armourer*). Obviously she was being tested by the management to see how she might respond to the forthcoming season when she would be put through her paces. Nineteen performances in her first twenty-eight weeks was below the usual average for an attractive young soprano at the Deutsche Oper. Naturally, though, she was busy learning other roles in preparation for advancement.

In the following season of 1938–9 she progressed at great speed with sixteen new parts, of which the first important one was Frasquita in the trio of gypsies from *Carmen*. The policy at both Berlin houses was for all operas to be sung in German, making for easier comprehension by the audience and for national pride in their language. Hence Schwarzkopf's second important role was the extrovert Musette (Musetta) in *Die Boheme*, who moves from her impossible flirtations in Act II through the bitter quarrel with Marcello in the next act to tender sympathy at Mimi's illness and death in Act IV.

The First Noble Orphan in *Der Rosenkavalier* was Schwarzkopf's baptism in a Richard Strauss work, although it was going to take nine years before she reached Sophie, and seventeen before she undertook the Marschallin. The Orphan was one of Schwarzkopf's 'quick home' roles of short duration in performance. The sopranos taking the three Orphans in Act I are sometimes called upon to change to terrified Faninal maidservants pursued by the Ochs retinue in Act II, and among Annina's tormentors of the Baron in Act III, but Schwarzkopf's contract specified 'soprano', not chorus member.

Likewise, the Duchess of Mantua's Page in Act I of *Rigoletto* has a vivid, short solo engaging everybody's attention; and, rather later, the Woodbird's Voice in *Siegfried*, which is sung offstage, did not even require her to change into costume. In all these cases, Schwarzkopf was able to leave the theatre early in the evening and, because they are all decent little roles, it seemed thoroughly indecent to her rivals that she was being favoured with them when she had been in the company for so short a time. This is all part of the business of survival in an opera company. Other singers, especially the less favoured, are always quick to spot such advantages by one of their colleagues; and when that more talented (or more favoured) artist is considered to be on the same rung of the ladder, the more jealous the others become, female of female, male of male.

An ever-widening variety of roles laid a firm foundation of Schwarzkopf's future successes, although at the time some of their musical and dramatic significance seemed negligible, if not rather tiresome, like the First Squire in *Tannhäuser*, although she was sometimes given the Shepherd in Act III as well, and that was always worthwhile. There was the other First Squire in *Lohengrin*, the unimportant Pepa in d'Albert's verismo shocker, *Tiefland* (popular with the Führer) and the minute role of Inez in *Il Trovatore*, waiting woman to the principal soprano.

They nevertheless became the means by which Schwarzkopf accustomed herself to quick study, to continuous changes of makeup and characterization, while it was sometimes necessary for her to make adjustments in her own role when singing opposite different colleagues. All this is the stuff of being a performer in a busy organization running at fever pitch and with human temperament in abundance.

In 1936 Norbert Schultze's *Schwarzer Peter*, subtitled 'An Opera for Young and Old People', from a story based on an old German folk-tale, had first been given in Hamburg. *Schwarzer Peter* is the name of a German card game equivalent to Old Maid, where you must avoid being left with the named card, and the opera is a light-hearted work with clearly drawn, fantastic characters, ideal for Christmastime and a welcome change from *Hänsel und Gretel*. Now, in December 1938, the opera had its Berlin première and performances continued intermittently until March.

Lore Hoffmann first sang Erika, a rich king's daughter and the heroine, which Schwarzkopf then took over for three nights. She has one delightful aria, 'So schönen Blumen hast du' ('You have such beautiful flowers') and a love duet with Roderick, a poor king's son. Schultze conducted a few performances himself.[11] A few months before coming to the Deutsche Oper, he had composed a sentimental song that was hardly noticed at first but, in 1941, was broadcast from German-occupied Belgrade and immediately caught on, travelling round the world wherever there were soldiers of any nation and soon becoming the internationally best-known of all wartime songs: 'Lili Marlene'.

Early in her operatic career, Schwarzkopf exhibited many of the traits that were to become characteristic of her professional behaviour: full concentration on the matter in hand; absolute seriousness during rehearsals; intolerance of vulgarity; consideration for the conductor and director, but sufficient presence and determination to state her own case and argue it when given instructions that she considered unreasonable. This applied particularly to her contract, her salary and leave of absence, all of which became of such vital importance that they led her, for a while, to throw overboard some of her main attributes as a well-behaved member of the Deutsche Oper.

When Schwarzkopf first joined the company, political events were moving towards Hitler's territorial demands being satisfied through threats, bullying and conquests. The Berlin man in the street was transfixed by his Führer's power and success, by the personal hypnotism and persuasive oratory constantly being delivered by Hitler and Goebbels, by the extraordinary massed parades, the torchlights and bonfires, which amazed everybody, even on cinema news-reels, and in general by the way in which the country had been transformed from the misery of Weimar to the present flush of prosperity and intense optimism. Unless the man in the street was Jewish, of course.

After the sham of Munich in 1938, Hitler stormed into Poland in August the following year and conquered that troubled country in a matter of weeks. Britain and France issued a joint ultimatum for him to stop and withdraw, but it was ignored. So at 11 a.m. on 3 September 1939, a state of war existed with Germany, not because Britain and France had declared it, but because there had been no reply from Germany.

The next day was a Monday, when the sun rose on the first of more than 2,000 days that were to dawn before the end of the war in Europe left the 'Thousand Year' Reich in ruins. On that rather special morning, 4 September, Elisabeth Schwarzkopf made her second recording of four duets from operetta with the popular Hamburg radio tenor, Rupert Glawitsch. It was a single 12-inch disc of a potpourri from Franz von Suppé's *Boccaccio*. Another selection, from Lehár's *Paganini*, displays her voice as exceptionally strong and pure, at this stage in her career, and with the character emerging vividly. Her short solos and the duets are pretty, light and agile, but without the last degree of finish to the phrases. On top notes at ends of numbers the intonation is slightly suspect; but one instantly recognizes that Schwarzkopf is the more interesting of the two artists, even though Glawitsch was a minor star and his operetta tenor's bright voice is by no means to be despised.

Such recordings exemplify one of the methods deployed by Goebbels of jollying along the German people. Competing record companies tended to use celebrated tenors like Herbert Ernst Groh, Walther Ludwig, Marcel Wittrisch or Richard Tauber, whose voices outclassed those of their respective sopranos. But on her début disc Schwarzkopf, not yet twenty-four, was Glawitsch's equal.

Schwarzkopf began her first full season at the Deutsche Oper with the new role of Bertha in Weber's Gothic opera *Euryanthe*, a useful part in an awkward work that is somewhat out of fashion today. Then, after further developing her characterization of Marie in *Der Waffenschmied*, she sang the other Marie in Lortzing's *Zar und Zimmermann* with Hans Wocke as Tsar Peter the Great. Disguised as a carpenter, he discovers how other nations build their ships. It is a pleasant work and hers is an attractive role.

The First Boy in *Die Zauberflöte* was Schwarzkopf's introduction to a Mozart opera, a part she held on to for as long as she remained at the Deutsche Oper, in spite of the fact that she generally avoided *Hosenrollen* (breeches parts). Then, in December 1939, she was cast as Barbarina in *Figaro*, a first step towards Susanna and the Countess. *Figaro* and *Die Zauberflöte* were so close to Artur Rother's heart that he conducted practically every performance. Likewise, he took almost all the *Parsifal*s and *Ring*s in which Schwarzkopf was now singing Ortlinde, second voice among the warrior maids in *Die Walküre*.

In the spring of 1940 she sang Lauretta in *Gianni Schicchi* with Hans Reinmar taking the old rogue's part. Lauretta has the only 'hit number' in this one-acter: 'O mio babbino caro', which Schwarzkopf was to record in 1949.

On 1 May 1940 there was a significant piece of casting, from her point of view, when she was at last given Adele in *Die Fledermaus*. It was ideally suited to her vocal lightness and agility coupled with her flair for comedy. She was delighted at having been given it to sing at last, because the personal cachet attached to the character had become a sensitive issue and Schwarzkopf now hoped that her name was going to occur far more frequently on the Adele roster. Evidently the management thought otherwise, because the Idas kept returning to her far more often. She was to sing Adele only three more times, with a final score of 22 to 5.

3

Rising Star
1940–1942

The Berlin Staatsoper and Deutsche Oper fulfilled their quasi-political functions under Goering and Goebbels respectively, and each vied with the other in producing works that appealed as much to their individual Party bosses as to the public. Hitler still involved himself with Bayreuth and continued to give the Wagner family all his moral and financial support. The Bayreuth singers, in that hot summer of 1940, were drawn exclusively from the Staatsoper thanks to Tietjen, whose Prussian operatic parish extended that far.

The avidly pro-Hitlerian Jaro Prohaska, a fine bass-baritone, was a member of the company: his neurotic wife, whose inclinations followed her husband's to excess, generally had to be carried out of the room in a faint if the Führer was present. The baritone Herbert Janssen once asked her why she had a golden swastika on one hand, fastened by chains to her fingers and thumb. 'That is where the Führer kissed me!' she replied coyly, to which the normally courteous Janssen retorted: 'A pity he didn't kiss you on the mouth!'[1]

By the end of the 1939–40 opera season in August, Schwarzkopf had sung a total of thirty-seven different roles (see Appendix A) and was becoming recognized as one of the most promising young sopranos at the Deutsche Oper. In the few rather unimportant roles that she sang, her star quality shone through, and, if her acceptance at short notice into the company can be regarded as the first break in her career, an even greater one now followed. She was sufficiently well regarded by the end of her first full season to be cast as Zerbinetta in a new production of Richard Strauss's *Ariadne auf Naxos*.

The role was written into her contract for 1940–41, justifying an increase in salary to 9,000RM for the year, duly authorized from Goebbels' office.[2] In a short space of time she had been handed a plum part that others have waited years to try to catch. Zerbinetta is a flighty member of a Commedia dell'Arte team, the only woman among four men, who believes in taking as many lovers as possible and getting as much out of them as she can before dropping each in turn when she tires of him. The vocal role parallels and parodies this philosophy in stratospheric coloratura, and demands absolute precision in the acting and an artful sense of humour. Zerbinetta is a delectable little minx. To succeed in the role, the singer must focus all the attention on herself whenever she is on stage, even to the exclusion of Ariadne, the prima donna.

This requires star quality, which you either possess or you don't. Schwarzkopf did. She achieved a public success but confessed, much later, that 'it was a dreadful indiscretion' to have attempted it. After the first and second performances on 28 and 30 September, a short announcement rather than a review, as was the custom, appeared in the *Berlin Lokal-Anzeiger* of 1 October:

> Richard Strauss's *Ariadne auf Naxos* is now in the repertoire of the Deutsche Opernhaus. The main parts in Hans Batteux's new production of this most charming chamber opera are taken by Bertha Stehler as Ariadne, Elisabeth Schwarzkopf as Zerbinetta, Henk Noort as Bacchus and Karl Schmitt-Walter as Harlekin. Musical direction is by Artur Rother.

Maria Ivogün, the most famous portrayer of Zerbinetta since Selma Kurz, its creator in the opera's second version, was in the audience that night. Ivogün had first joined the Deutsche Oper in 1925 but retired from the stage in 1933 to teach in Berlin. She was married to the celebrated accompanist Michael Raucheisen, the Gerald Moore of Germany.

Karl Schmitt-Walter came to the Deutsche Oper in 1935 as a leading baritone with a light, musical voice and very clean production; he was on good terms with Rode, who protected him against pressure to join the Nazi Party, which in fact he never did. Before singing Harlekin opposite Schwarzkopf in this *Ariadne*, Schmitt-Walter had been impressed by her voice and personality and by her generally professional manner. He also came to the conclusion that her vocal technique could and should be greatly improved, and it is likely that he had already prepared the ground for what he was going to say to her after the performance:

'Look, my child, you have a good voice, and are gifted. That's obvious. But you are going to need to learn how to sing all over again. I'm going to introduce you to Madam Ivogün!'[3] This was a name to conjure with, especially for a young singer; and when Ivogün heard in Schwarzkopf all the necessary requirements and ability for Lieder singing, she agreed to take her on as a special pupil providing she was willing for her voice to be taken apart and rebuilt, note by note, in the right way. Otherwise the great teacher would only be wasting her time. Many years later, in 1987, shortly before Ivogün died, Schwarzkopf asked her what this first Zerbinetta had been like. The celebrated singer answered, 'Simply terrible! Here was a girl with great talent and no knowledge of technique at all.'[4]

Schwarzkopf agreed willingly to the proposition, though again there was the need for extra funds to pay for these singing lessons, but strings were pulled and they were soon authorized by high authority in the Reichstheaterkamme.[5]

It cannot have been easy for her to go on singing at the Opera as usual, while taking lessons which often contradicted what she had already been taught and was still doing.

Schwarzkopf sang even more Zerbinettas between then and early December, with a guest artist replacing her for one other performance: apparently no other soprano in the company was able to sing the role. She then gave a single performance the following March which turned out to be her last in Berlin. She was a very ambitious girl. Even before her first audition, she realized that the Deutsche Oper would serve as a useful platform from which to jump into lucrative recitals, films and recordings whenever she had free time. Her attractive personality and appearance, coupled with a certain magnetism and a truly professional determination, all contributed to her swift rise from the ranks; but Wilhelm Rode was disturbed because she was always pestering him for more important roles.

An interesting vocal relic of Schwarzkopf's Berlin days exists on CD, singing the Second Rhine Daughter, Wellgunde. It comes from a broadcast perform- ance of *Das Rheingold* from the Deutsche Oper on 24 May. In the excerpt heard, Alberich's voice is omitted altogether, making it a potpourri of the Rhine Daughters' trios in the first scene. Hilde Scheppan, First Lady in the Beecham *Zauberflöte* recording (when Schwarzkopf was a chorus-member), and the mezzo, Marie-Luise Schilp, make up this trio. It is a fine performance in which the orchestra of the Deutsche Oper plays extremely well under Artur Rother.

She now began to aim even higher in her determination to reach the top in the shortest possible time, taking her successes calmly in her stride, striving, even pleading to be cast in roles that she felt she was well able to tackle, even though her senior colleagues were convinced that they were rightfully theirs. In her own mind, Elisabeth Schwarzkopf was on course to becoming a prima donna and she was not going to let anyone stand in her way, least of all those who abided by opera house protocol.

Unfortunately, this attitude was not universally accepted; nor did it endear her to other sopranos, especially Irma Beilke, Konstanze Nettesheim and Lore Hoffmann. They were all older than she, and, having reached an intermediate rung of the ladder before Schwarzkopf's arrival, were naturally vexed that she had so suddenly bobbed up, almost from nowhere, to compete with them. And when she was obliged to take the unimportant roles, known as *Wurzen*, three or four other young sopranos in this category, like Ruth Jahncke, also resented her.

The singers in an opera company, while they still have a chance of promotion, are always striving for attention, advancement and popularity in competition with those of their own *Fach* at least, and, for the sake of peace, a delicate balance has to be kept in relations between them all. The maintenance of this balance is generally in the hands of several members of the management from the intendant down to the stage manager and the wardrobe mistress and dressers, many singers' confidantes. In less than a year, Schwarzkopf had managed to upset this equilibrium among the sopranos with whom she worked because she wanted immediate results, whereas most of the others were prepared to plod on in the hope of gradual advancement. During rehearsal one day, a female singer in the company, who was carrying a property riding whip, slashed at Schwarzkopf's legs because she was dominating the rest of the cast by standing too far downstage.[6] One wonders whether this may have been more than a lone individual's public protest.

In October 1939, when Schwarzkopf considered she had become sufficiently established in the company to do something original, she appeared barefoot on stage as the Young Shepherd in *Tannhäuser*, instead of wearing the footwear provided.[7] There were ructions over this, but Schwarzkopf innocently replied that she had done it before and felt more comfortable with bare feet. She was given both verbal and written reprimands by *Oberregisseur* Dr Batteux, who fined her 100RM, a substantial sum for a first offence – Rode reduced it by half.[8] In the following season she was also often in trouble. On one occasion she was late back for a *Fledermaus* speech rehearsal with the excuse that she had run all the way from the film studios at Babelsberg (that was indeed a very long way!) and had to get bandages for her feet because they were so sore.[9]

A goody-goody who keeps quiet and always does what she is told in an organization like an opera house, especially one with political affiliations, is not likely to attract much notice. She will merely be taken for granted and may not even be thanked for her loyalty. Schwarzkopf was determined to be noticed as often and by as many people as possible, and she certainly achieved this intention. Yet the Deutsche Oper always had first call on her and, for the time being, she knew she must not endanger her security there.

Her first ambition was to be cast as a middle-ranking soprano at the far more prestigious Berlin Staatsoper, although Tietjen had rejected her one indirect attempt to approach him. She also had aspirations to appear annually as a guest at Bayreuth, with all that that involved; but the determined attitude which she displayed towards her female colleagues, coupled with her casual manner towards the intendant, inevitably resulted in decisive action being taken against her. Whether it was a case of her having arrived twenty minutes late in the Opera House (fine 20RM) or having left a rehearsal early and without permission, Schwarzkopf was still bothering Rode, and his disquiet at her apparent immunity from his control[10] is clear from letters in the RTK file. Nor did he misread the situation, which amounted to a good deal of interference over his head, allowing Schwarzkopf to enjoy support from highly placed persons in the Reich Ministry, constantly undermining his authority. Rode's anxiety over Schwarzkopf is revealed in his correspondence with Ernst Keppler, *Leiter* (Chief) in the Theatre Division of the RKK, when he tried to save face by asking for support from somebody senior to himself in the Reich Ministry, though not in highest authority.

Although Rode may have displayed some weakness by admitting his inability to control Schwarzkopf, he insisted upon taking credit for having instantly spotted her talent at the only audition she gave them, straight from the Hochschule. Thereafter he had nursed her along and put up with her behaviour because, he admitted, he had great faith in her ability.

Rode told Keppler officially how he had made it clear to Schwarzkopf that, for the time being, she must go on singing the smaller roles although she was being groomed for several of the more substantial ones. There were, after all, other sopranos to consider, but Schwarzkopf had decided to ignore this. So Keppler interviewed her in order to put over this point forcibly and directly; the fact that he got no further than Rode had done seems to indicate that Keppler was equally impotent when it came to disciplining Elisabeth Schwarzkopf.[11] She maintained afterwards that this had nothing to do with politics; rather, that she understood how to get round Rode (and apparently Keppler too) in order to further her career in the acquisition of roles and contracts that would secure quicker promotion.

On 7 June 1941 Schwarzkopf and others took part in a benefit concert for Marie von Bülow in the Berlin Meistersaal. Hers was the major contribution, and included Frau Fluth's aria from *The Merry Wives of Windsor*, Johann Strauss's 'Voices of Spring' and three groups of Lieder. There were five songs by Schubert, six by Schumann and, most importantly, for the first time in public, she sang five of Hugo Wolf's Eichendorff Lieder. She was accompanied by Michael Raucheisen.

Germany's military successes in Europe had led to the fall of France in 1940. There was a need for some appropriate publicity in the occupied countries to demonstrate the established musical culture of the German people. In addition to those in Belgium, Holland and elsewhere, one of the most substantial was in May 1941 at the Paris Opéra, when the pro-German dramatic soprano, Germaine Lubin, sang Isolde to Max Lorenz's Tristan in an otherwise German cast, conducted by the young and brilliant Herbert von Karajan who was to be seen in Paris from time to time, directing either opera or concerts. On this occasion he played the *Horst Wessel Lied* before the opera's *Vorspiel*. Wilhelm Furtwängler, his senior, refused to participate in such highly charged missions. The *music*, he maintained, must come first, not competition with his rival, about whom he was so paranoid that he was able to refer to him only as 'that man K'.

Previous Goebbels-sponsored musical tours and reciprocal events in Italy were not nearly as lavish as the three-week so-called 'goodwill visit' to Paris by a total of 400 artists and staff in several prestigious works from the two Berlin opera houses. There was fierce competition among the singers, not only for selection but for roles. *Die Fledermaus* was scheduled to open the tour with seven performances; its farcical Viennese plot and marvellous score would appear lighthearted, charming and not provocatively *deutsch* at all. That was the thinking behind the choice of opera, but it was scarcely reassuring to the vanquished population of the French capital.

Far from being impressed with Goebbels' public relations exercise, the Parisians were highly indignant when they found out that *Die Fledermaus*, billed in German, would be sung in German and that audiences were to be restricted to local German civil and military personnel. Worst of all, it was to be staged at the Palais Garnier, the Opéra, one of France's proudest cultural bastions, which had been commandeered for the occasion. The event could not have been intended to woo the French through art, as a terse comment in *Le Figaro* on the day before the première made clear: '*La Chauve-Souris* de Johann Strauss va être donnée à l'Opéra. C'est bien la première fois qu'on entendra une opérette au Palais Garnier.'

The first night, on 17 September 1941, was in the presence of the German C-in-C in Paris, General von Stülpnagel, with Ambassador de Brinon representing Vichy (German occupied) France. Walter Ludwig, the graceful Mozartean lyric tenor from the Berlin Staatsoper, sang Alfred, and Schwarzkopf was cast as Adele. She should have considered herself very fortunate indeed, especially as her chief rival, Irma Beilke, had taken the role when the production opened at the Deutsche Oper in 1938.

Schwarzkopf always took great care of her stage appearance and, on this occasion, she intended to be seen at her very best. Before leaving for Paris, she applied to the Opera House wardrobe for seven pairs of stockings, a corset and two pairs of slippers, one black and one white, to take with her. The paperwork involved in these negotiations is comical in its complexity, with at one end the name of Reichsminister Joseph Goebbels, proclaimed as authority for the trip; and a bureaucrat from the state department dealing with leatherware, at the other. In the end, all they allowed her was one pair of black pumps.[12]

This Paris *Fledermaus* was to be an impressive occasion and an opportunity for several artists from both houses to appear in an exchange of roles on successive evenings. On the second night, Walther Haller from the Deutsche Oper and Margarethe Slezak (Leo Slezak's daughter), took the leading roles, while Irma Beilke returned to sing Adele. No French critics were invited so there were no French reviews, but the German services newspaper *Das Reich* praised the second performance (not Schwarzkopf's) in a short comment two days later. It is difficult to believe that cast changes were not announced some time in advance, or that Schwarzkopf was expecting to sing all the Adeles, but she has confessed to being furious at her 'demotion' to the non-singing role of Ida on subsequent nights and made her feelings abundantly plain by kicking off a shoe that made a hole in the cyclorama,[13] the huge, curved canvas screen at the back of the set. Lit to represent the sky, and used for projected images like moving clouds, or for Valhalla in *Das Rheingold*, for example, it must of necessity appear to be in one piece, and any visible tear or hole will ruin the seamless illusion and is extremely expensive to repair.

Schwarzkopf admitted somewhat ruefully that the cyclorama was damaged at 'an important state occasion',[14] which may either have been in Paris or, more likely, at the Deutsche Oper, when the entire cast had returned to Berlin a month later for a State Gala Performance of *Die Fledermaus* in October to celebrate the fifteenth year of the inauguration of Gauleiters.

Schwarzkopf was called before a disciplinary committee charged with sabotage, and was penalized by being forbidden to sing at the Deutsche Oper under her own name. By her own account she was relegated to the smallest roles under the pseudonym of Maria Helfer and she claims that the situation was so serious that the famous accompanist Michael Raucheisen and her father were called to defend her; Raucheisen pleaded for her release on artistic grounds to perform for the troops and to sing Lieder for his Berlin Radio programmes.

The pseudonym order for Ida in *Fledermaus* and First Page and a Flower Maiden in *Parsifal*, was evidently revoked quite soon. Certainly the name of Maria Helfer occurs in Deutsche Oper programmes, for example, but inconsistently and only as a means of identifying Schwarzkopf in a less dominant role when she is singing two small parts in the same performance. It is intriguing that she was allowed to use two different names in the same performance. No similar device has been discovered anywhere in connection with a singer, which seems to give Schwarzkopf a unique place in operatic history. She achieved the new role of the Woodbird's Voice in Act II of *Siegfried* amongst a clutch of her usual roles, such as Ännchen, Serpetta and Lola, which continued as usual.

Schwarzkopf gave another Liederabend in Berlin on 9 May 1942, at 19.30 in the Beethovensaal, accompanied by Professor Michael Raucheisen who was referred to as the 'living encyclopedia of German song'.[15] Their programme was entitled 'On Spring and Nightingales', and the concert was sold out. An announcement appeared in the *Nachtausgabe* newspaper (one of the few to make reference to artistic matters), but no review, because it was not usual then for adverse criticism to be directed towards artists: 'the emphasis of the critic was always on saying what was good'.[16] In this case he said nothing at all. In an interview nearly half a century later Schwarzkopf spoke warmly of Raucheisen:

> He was our greatest accompanist at the time, not only for Lieder but also for chamber music . . . he was . . . head of classical music of Berlin Radio. So when I was halfway ready, they grabbed me and said, 'We have two hours in the studio, and we can take this and that, and just do it.' I just sang them, I didn't know it was a recording, it was just once through, I was too naïve to think 'Is this a recording, or what are they doing?' I hadn't the faintest idea, I just did my two hours of singing and left it to Raucheisen to choose whether there was anything good in it.[17]

Schwarzkopf was not the only one to be dragged unexpectedly into the recording studio, and consequently these contemporary voices became known as the Raucheisen Collection. It is valuable for many reasons, especially because it gives some insight into the Lieder which she sang in those early days and, what is more, how she sang them. The inclusion of Lieder by lesser-known composers, like Richard Trunk of Munich with his *Four Cheerful Songs*, indicates a view of their being considered representative of the best in wartime. Some of this material has surfaced from behind the old Iron Curtain since 1991, issued either on LP or on CD, under the title 'Raucheisen Lied Edition', probably not the name by which it was originally known. Raucheisen is believed to have planned the series himself, and normally to have accompanied the singers too, although his style is self-effacing by comparison with his contemporaries Paul Ulanowsky and Gerald Moore, and the younger Geoffrey Parsons.

The singers in the series, between 1941–43, were chosen from among the most eminent of their time and, although criticism has been levelled at the quality of interpretations because the performances sometimes took place during air raids, it is small wonder if the artists sound uneasy. Sometimes, too, it is apparent that the Lieder are not yet fully lodged in the singers' repertoire, perhaps having been learned specially for the occasion, as Schwarzkopf implies. That is understandable if the idea was to create a 'bank' of German Lieder as Reich-time was running out.

She seems to have been devoting more time to Lieder than to opera because, concurrently with her preparations for the recital and shortly afterwards, she had been missing rehearsals at the Deutsche Oper, delaying signing her contract and generally behaving in a capricious manner. As a result, Rode was driven to write to Keppler again. He had lost all patience with her and, because Keppler had been unable, unwilling or even prevented from persuading Schwarzkopf to change her ways, Rode now had no alternative but to offload any possible criticism of his own inactivity by directing it against his Party boss.

The following is taken from a letter marked 'Urgent – Confidential. To the Security Council Direction'.

> I must declare my strong recommendation that Fräulein Schwarzkopf be sent before the proper authority and be punished according to the evidence. Herr Keppler, Dr Lang and others in even higher positions must bear responsibility for encouraging the undisciplined behaviour of this beginner, who relishes her acquaintanceship with them.[18]

Schwarzkopf seemed unperturbed, and went on writing to Rode solely about matters affecting her career, which he continued to take politely and seriously, with copies as usual to the Reichstheaterkammer's main filing system. This 'Hinkel File' was on the upper floor of the director's office at Schlüterstrasse 45, not far from the Deutsche Oper.[19] Although disciplinary incidents involving her were being recorded and filed, Schwarzkopf still managed to keep her most cherished roles, and to acquire more money and more favours. On two occasions there were notes on her contracts to confirm that the President of the Reichsmusikkammer himself, Joseph Goebbels, authorized extra payments above the standard maximum for each grade of singer, despite an official stop order on increased salaries. While Schwarzkopf made Rode the object of her official correspondence, he had no alternative but to accede to many of her requests, because he knew that she was 'politically safe': probably more so than he was.

4

Opera, Cinema and Adversity
1942–1943

Schwarzkopf had several confirmed enemies among her colleagues in the Deutsche Oper and, in spite of protection from on high, she did not get her own way all the time. After her first striking success as Zerbinetta, she sang only six new roles during the rest of her engagement with the Deutsche Oper. The penultimate one, which she gave only twice, was the heroine, Leonore, in Flotow's *Alessandro Stradella*, whose plot is 'a mild and comic extract from the turbulent life of the seventeenth-century Italian composer'.[1] The opera is rarely performed today; but it is melodious and gives the singers several outstanding opportunities, not least Leonore in her exacting recitative and aria 'So wär' es denn erreicht'. Walter Ludwig as Stradella and Eduard Kandl, a bandit engaged to assassinate him, were the principal tenor and bass in this melodramatic piece.

Schwarzkopf's first performance in her latest role, the desirable Susanna in *Figaro*, had been in the previous February. She sang five Susannas altogether in Berlin between February and mid-May 1942, appearing as a brunette. She had appeared in twenty performances as Barbarina since December 1939, the last only a month before, and she must indeed have led a charmed life to have acquired such an important role when unflattering reports on her behaviour were still current.

This was a well-established, well run-in production of *Figaro* with Elisabeth Friedrich, who had been at the Deutsche Oper since 1930, as the Countess, Karl Schmitt-Walter as the Count, and Ludwig Windisch as Figaro. They were all very experienced singers and actors, well used to working together in the Mozart idiom, so that for the first three performances the newcomer Schwarzkopf was at a disadvantage.

In May 1942 the case of Schwarzkopf's nightdress became something of a *cause célèbre* in Berlin's opera world – and in the Reichstheaterkammer. A special morning *Figaro* ensemble rehearsal had been called for 14 May, but it was abandoned when Schwarzkopf failed to arrive. A run-through cannot get very far without Susanna and, as scheduled that evening, it was only her fifth performance in the role. This was an emergency and at Rode's urgent request a house report from the staff manager, Lorenz, landed on his desk before midday:

14 May 1942

At 10.10 this morning, Frl. Schwarzkopf telephoned to ask whether she had a rehearsal. I replied that at 10.30 she had a *Figaro* ensemble rehearsal to which she answered, 'I can't get there until 11, I'm still in my nightdress!' This rehearsal had been called at the express wish of GMD Rother, and Frl. Schwarzkopf had asked for it too. The other soloists, who were all on time, considered this to be disgraceful behaviour for such a young singer, and Herr Kandl did not mince his words. It must also be noted that Frl. Schwarzkopf was informed of the rehearsal yesterday at lunchtime . . .[2]

This memorandum, with copious notes and remarks written on it in several hands, was circulated to conductors, singers and theatre staff, among whom the buffo-bass Eduard Kandl (singing Dr Bartolo) made the following observation:

It is disgraceful that such a young singer permits herself to keep her elder colleagues waiting, especially as I had an important role last night (Falstaff);[3] but in spite of that I came to the rehearsal. I spoke my mind to Frl. Schwarzkopf and would ask the General Intendant to take suitable measures because she often turns up late – we are used to that. I need to add that this rehearsal was really called for her benefit because the last time we sang *Figaro*, she gave an inadequate performance.[4]

Kandl was a Bavarian of the old school and of a generation accustomed to courtesy, which is why he found Schwarzkopf's behaviour especially intolerable. He had every reason to be outraged for, as a founder member of the then Charlottenburg Opera, he had been singing on that stage since 1912, three years before Schwarzkopf was born.

She immediately wrote two letters to Rode. In the first, she made excuses about missing the rehearsal but ended with an apology. The second letter, concerning the contract conference of the previous month, is *brutta figura* and worth quoting in full:

Dear Herr General Intendant,
        From our talk on 27.04.42, I am sorry to have to conclude that I will be superfluous to your House in the coming season, so I ask you kindly to be allowed to take the consequences thereof. Of course I shall in future be at your disposal for any solo parts such as:

Zerbinetta	Konstanze	Blondchen	Susanna
Sophie	Gilda	Traviata	Frau Fluth
Rosina	Adele	Nedda	etc.

Kindest greetings
        Heil Hitler!
                Your very obedient servant   Elisabeth Schwarzkopf[5]

After she had written and delivered these letters, Schwarzkopf sang her last Susanna with the Deutsche Oper. Rode expressed astonishment at her attitude, never having implied, let alone stated, any form of dismissal. In his reply, he accused her of being at fault by allowing more than three weeks to pass before coming back to him with her argument for, in his absence on business, she had been instructed to see his deputy, Dr Maeder. She reported sick.

Schwarzkopf returned to Maeder's office in the middle of June and told him that in future she had decided to give preference to her concert work and, as he noted:

> this was because of the many complimentary offers she has received, and the possibility of being artistically successful in this field. Naturally she would be quite happy if it were possible for both occupations to be combined, but the number of offers she has already received, and others still to come through her contacts in the concert world, persuaded her that she might be better off elsewhere.[6]

This was a new tack altogether, and may well have been influenced by her shadowy agent, Hermann Rudolph Gail. He stood to gain more commission from finding her concert dates than from her standard salary at the Deutsche Oper on which she had no need to pay him anything unless he had negotiated on her behalf with Rode, which seems unlikely. She was managing very well on her own.

Schwarzkopf complained bitterly and, to the impartial observer, somewhat unreasonably, about Irma Beilke and Tresi Rudolph, her seniors in age by a dozen years, who had been at the Deutsche Oper far longer than she had and seemed to deserve preference in the solo roles she wanted for herself. For some time Beilke, Rudolph and others had been asking Rode why young Schwarzkopf was being unduly favoured. Rode could only sympathize with them, yet was powerless to intervene. Irma Beilke was particularly indignant at the preferential treatment granted 'this beginner with the pretty face'.[7]

Then Schwarzkopf put forward a new suggestion. She would be prepared to be taken on under a guest artist's contract 'for a series of evenings . . . because there are so many candidates for the parts under discussion'.[8] Rode was absent on business again, and once more he handed Schwarzkopf over to Maeder for him to deal with her. Maeder retained his composure and told her plainly that, as a young singer, she had got to take the small roles now, but that she 'would gradually grow in seniority alongside the other artists. In any case, guest contracts are not given, on principle, nor is it the intention of the Reichsminister to institute them.' He quietly reminded her of the statutory term of leave for her concerts, or, if the number exceeded that, subsequent absence without pay might be negotiated. He asked to see her list of confirmed concerts for the coming year, not merely the pencilled bookings.

Schwarzkopf's letter gave a list of dates when she wanted to be away between September 1942 and May 1943, ranging from five to twenty-three days, though where the concerts were, whether the bookings were open for her and how many were confirmed, was revealed only in part. These dates disposed of 130 days, according to Maeder's calculations, with another one and a half months to come. He saw no possibility of confirming such a contract with her, but agreed to refer it to the Intendant on his return.

To Maeder's intense surprise, when Rode came back to Berlin and read Schwarzkopf's letter he wrote in the margin: 'A guest contract, providing she restricts her opera singing in Berlin to the DO. I don't expect there to be more than 20–25 evenings in the DO. OR?' (His 'OR?' was not explained, and evidence of direction from higher authority does not show up in the file. The decision was probably reached by telephone.)

Schwarzkopf's reply did not express the sense of obligation that might have been expected. Somebody, probably Maeder, has written across the top in longhand: 'ungrateful and lacking respect'.

This was Schwarzkopf's ultimatum:

1. On the basis of my promised commitment it has emerged that I will be at the disposal of the DO only for a guest contract of approximately 15 evenings.
2. Because of my loyalty to the DO, I am prepared, in this case, to agree to whatever fee is offered.
3. Casting decisions would have to accord with my artistic prestige: mainly considering my *Fach*.
4. There is one misunderstanding which I would like to put right. It is not my wish only to sing concert guest performances in the coming season. This resulted from talks on 27 April with Herr Rode, from which I had to conclude that the roles required for my artistic development cannot be guaranteed.

In spite of Maeder's belief that 'guest contracts are not given, on principle', Schwarzkopf got one, with everything in her favour, and in which clause 2 (below) is not only revealing, but amazing:

CONTRACT
Elisabeth Schwarzkopf, formerly a full and exclusive member of the Deutsche Oper between 1.8.38 and 11.7.42 –
1. Is available for the Deutsche Oper season 1942–43 as a member, especially for a series of 15 appearances and if necessary for further appearances, providing there are no other commitments.
2. She also contracts herself to rehearse, so far as her other commitments permit.

3. She is to receive a yearly income of 7500RM, payable by equal sums on 15th of each month.

4. She contracts, during the duration of this agreement, to make no appearance in any other theatre in Greater Berlin. Exceptional participation in such guest appearances will need special permission.

5. Employment by the Deutsche Oper will be according to the agreed rules.

6. For all other matters connected with this contract, the normal contractual ones apply.

(sd.) Maeder for Rode, and Schwarzkopf 23 Sept. 1942[9]

Another contract on her file was issued retrospectively, in January 1943, for 'official' (i.e. Party) engagements which Schwarzkopf undertook after her guest contract had been signed. They were for December 1942, when she joined a Berlin Artists' Tour with two concerts in Prague and two for the Waffen SS on the Eastern Front. She received only 375DM in cash for them all, a paltry figure which would suggest generous expenses. But this was now of secondary importance to her because she and her agent were already quietly negotiating a contract with the Vienna State Opera.

Karl Böhm was about to become the Director there for the 1943–44 season, and was already talent-spotting. An Austrian from Graz, he had been appointed to the Dresden Opera in 1934, in succession to Fritz Busch, and had turned in nine successful years as musical director. The new appointment was made by Goebbels, and Böhm was probably the right man to direct the Vienna Opera at that particular time. 'Böhml' had all the necessary qualifications on and off paper: solid musicianship and successful experience of precisely the right kind. As far as the Viennese were concerned, he also possessed an appearance of compliance in the face of authority, a willingness to turn a blind eye towards it when necessary, and an ability to suggest, convincingly and frequently, that black was white. He was not every musician's friend, indeed many singers found it well-nigh intolerable to have to work with him. Irmgard Seefried was an exception. She and Böhm had been close friends since he conducted her first appearance in Vienna as Eva in *Die Meistersinger* at the exceptionally early age of twenty-four. Her remarkable career in principal Mozart and Strauss roles was considerably helped by this association which continued long after her marriage to Wolfgang Schneiderhan, co-leader of the Vienna Philharmonic Orchestra.

When Böhm was guest-conducting in Berlin, he had not needed much persuasion from Hermann Rudolf Gail, Schwarzkopf's agent, to hear her as Blondchen because Gail was also his agent. Böhm was impressed, as Gail assured him he would be, and she was invited to give two guest performances at the Vienna State Opera in October and November 1942. Böhm wanted talent, and Schwarzkopf obviously had it.

★　　★　　★

Schwarzkopf's talent was not limited to singing. She was a good actress too, and soon after arriving in Berlin she began to look at possibilities for herself in the cinema. This was a vital part of Berlin's artistic life as well as being in the mainstream of Nazi propaganda. Three experienced German actresses of these years have all emphasized, in post-war television films, that casting for any new picture at Babelsberg was in Goebbels' gift. They were the actress–director, Leni Riefenstahl; Margot Hielscher; and the Czech Lina Baarova. Goebbels was so infatuated with the gorgeous Baarova, his long-term mistress, that he seriously contemplated giving up his family, and his career as Propaganda Minister, to become German Ambassador to Japan and take her with him. Hitler put a stop to that, however.

'His influence was endless,' said Hielscher of Goebbels.[10] Had he once shaken his head, neither Schwarzkopf nor any other attractive artist would have been able to appear in the medium. Schwarzkopf always seems to have had an eye for the main chance, rarely overlooked an opportunity to further her career; and as early as January 1939 she was in demand from the film company UFA, though not for any of their important pictures. Of the five she is known to have made there, only the first has survived, called *Die Drei Unteroffizieren (The Three NCOs)*. In this she appeared as a popular Berlin singer, including a short extract from Bizet's *Carmen*, but six years later it was proscribed by the military occupation forces in Germany as sheer propaganda for the Gestapo.[11]

All Goebbels' cunning films with a message, and Schwarzkopf's more modest pictures too, were filmed in UFA's huge studios, far larger than Elstree, at Babelsberg in West Berlin. In 1926, Fritz Lang had made *Metropolis*, his silent black and white masterpiece, there. A genuine 'family' atmosphere was said always to exist at Babelsberg, with everybody working harmoniously and happily, without any of the normal professional barriers.

Schwarzkopf was in a further four pictures up to 1944, by which time Germany's enemies were approaching Berlin from two directions at once. Goebbels was so emotionally involved with the cinema that the shooting of his last picture, the historical colour extravaganza, *Kolberg*, was being completed in 1945 while elements of the Red Army were already in the suburbs of Berlin. According to one of his attachés, Wilfred von Oven,[12] Goebbels had withdrawn over 100,000 soldiers from the front line to take part in the film, knowing full well that the war was nearly over, and that it was far better for them to be fighting Napoleon in the studio than losing their lives to Stalin in the Unter den Linden.

From the few surviving cinema stills of Schwarzkopf it seems possible that, had a number of events in her life turned out differently, she might have made a successful film career. Her unusual combination of acting, singing and piano-playing was already being exploited in the medium, as demonstrated by two very different shots from *Der Verteidiger Hat das Wort* (*Counsel for the Defence May Speak*). They show her versatility, and the trick shot is effective.

All this appealed to her ambitions and meant that she was certain to be seen by Joseph Goebbels, whose obsessive passion for the big screen led him to create movies that were primarily entertaining and purposely refrained from giving the audience any impression that they were being targeted, as Leni Riefenstahl's pictures always did. Goebbels aimed to please and relax the audience, putting the viewers into the right frame of mind to receive his propaganda messages, insidiously planted in apparently innocuous material. This worked like magic.

The attractive women who appeared in his pictures, and at his say-so, often willingly became short-term mistresses. His taste was exclusively for brunettes. 'Of course many submitted to him,' said Hielscher. 'He was not only charming and attractive but he was a man of history. How could they resist?' Adjoining his main office in the ProMi was a comfortable extra *Zimmer*, or private room, fitted with a bed and wash-basin. By a system of signals on a bell, Goebbels' adjutant knew exactly what was expected of him when the Minister was occupied.

Each of Goebbels' three Berlin houses had a properly equipped private cinema and he spent much of his spare time in one or other of them, watching new and old films, from home and abroad, far into the night, sometimes encouraging the Führer to be there with him.[13] Hitler and the National Socialists had cheated their way 'in a democratic manner' to political victory in 1933 – 4, thanks to Goebbels and his propaganda machine. As a result, they had become the rulers of Germany and their voices, methods and political objectives had become those of the Third Reich and its people.

Elisabeth Schwarzkopf has always shrugged off personal questions about her wartime political affiliation, however obliquely they were put to her; and in any case, there has been an understandable disinclination among former artist-members of the National Socialist Party to admit that it was of much importance, especially when people remote from events in the Reich point an accusing finger. This also applies to 'non-political' singers and musicians who are disinclined to tell tales about old colleagues out of professional loyalty. For anyone wanting promotion, whether artisan, artist or an Elisabeth Schwarzkopf, there was no better way of achieving it than by joining the NSDAP. Viewed from within the Reich this was an obvious move, although it was *not* the same as joining a trade union. It is wrong to assume it was essential for members of national theatres and orchestras in the Reich to join the Party; for by no means everybody did so. When Furtwängler led the Berlin Philharmonic Orchestra, only eight out of the 110 players were Party members.[14]

Clemens Krauss was one who tried to play both ends against the middle and came to grief. His wife, Viorica Ursuleac, frankly admitted that they had miscalculated and lost their considerable fortune as a result.[15] So far as other singers were concerned, there were one or two who stood out as dedicated Nazis. Jaro Prohaska, already mentioned, was one; another was Tiana Lemnitz, a wonderful artist who had become so accustomed to supporting the National Socialist regime from its inception that as late as 1981 she said of the Berlin Wall, 'Shame, that the Jews have divided our city!'[16]

The *Gottbegnadete Liste* in Appendix C is not one of dedicated Nazis only, because others were artistically qualified to enter the Party's hall of fame. Hans Hotter, for instance, kept a very low profile in Vienna and Munich during the war; Paul Schöffler did likewise, but with greater difficulty because his English wife and their son were in Britain for the duration. Goebbels made it very clear that he did not like Schöffler's attitude, and was angered by his refusal to agree to his family being enticed back to Austria via Switzerland. The famous bass–baritone was imprisoned, only to be let out in a matter of days when Karl Böhm threatened to cancel those performances at the Vienna State Opera in which the singer's presence was essential. Life in Berlin was harder than this, however, and although there were artists who preferred to ignore all but minimal obeisance to the Party, the police and Gestapo were always busy in the Reich's capital.

Rode's relationship with Goebbels had been deteriorating badly, for Rode had the Führer's support, to a certain extent, and had been able to use it to circumvent unwelcome moves by Goebbels and Tietjen, both of whom he detested. Rode was courageous, outspoken (which was dangerous) and knew his own mind: he was not going to stand interference from anybody in the running of his Opera (even though he had lost out on Schwarzkopf).

Then one day in October 1943, when the Führer was otherwise deeply engaged in conferences about the disastrous state of the Russian front, Goebbels struck at Rode and unseated him. He sent Dr Rainer Schlösser to the Intendant's office, uninvited and unexpected, together with three men whom he introduced to Rode as Dr Hans Schmidt-Isserstedt, the Opera Director (an entirely new post), Dr Günther Rennert the régisseur, and Leopold Ludwig the GMD (General Music Director).[17]

Rode took the insult magnificently. He greeted his three 'colleagues' politely, noted that Dr Maeder would remain as Deputy and then left the Opera, never to return. For a successful artist and administrator, this was too much.

Over the years of air raids on Berlin, the Deutsche Oper had suffered substantial damage, but none as serious as that on the night of 22/23 November 1943 when it was completely destroyed. So was Rode's flat opposite, and with nothing further to keep him in Berlin he went back to Bavaria, although he remained General Intendant of the Deutsche Oper in name. Because he was politically unacceptable when the war ended, Rode severed all his connections with Berlin and opera administration by joining the Regensburg Opera for guest performances, in his former capacity as leading Wagnerian bass-baritone.

The Berlin Deutsche Oper continued to play wherever there was still a stage and an auditorium; at first they shared the Theater des Westens in Kantstrasse with the Volksoper and, from February 1945 until closure of all theatres in August, they were at the Admiralspalast opposite the Friedrichstrasse Railway Station.

Three months after the House was destroyed, Schwarzkopf went back to Berlin on sick leave for a few days to visit her mother who had been bombed out. Partly out of curiosity, and a certain sentimentality, she went to see the remains of the building where her career had begun and where there had been so many successes for her, so many wrangles. As she approached what was left of the open stage door, she was amazed to see nearby, hanging from a shattered tree, her own costume for Esmeralda in *The Bartered Bride*.[18] This macabre vision hastened her return to Vienna.

5

Vienna, Sweet and Sour
1943–1945

Schwarzkopf 'left Berlin for Vienna with precious little in her suitcase – it was all in her head, the projects and the requirements.'[1] This was in early October 1942, as she went to sing her début guest performance of Zerbinetta in that world-famous opera house, so closely associated with Gustav Mahler and Richard Strauss. The opera was carefully cast with the heroic-dramatic soprano Gertrud Rünger as Ariadne, and the Swedish *Heldentenor*, Set Svanholm, in sweet voice and entirely credible as the young god Bacchus, despite his short stature.

Schwarzkopf knew that her critics would be acute and demanding, and her first performance was well received. The Vienna Straussian Dr Roland Tenschert wrote:[2]

> In the recent performance of *Ariadne auf Naxos*, conducted by Rudolf Moralt, Elisabeth Schwarzkopf presented herself to advantage. She portrayed and lived her role completely in the spirit of Zerbinetta: the delicate figure, graceful movements in dancing and acting, every aspect underlined with elegance and charm, all combined to make this a very promising start indeed. The voice possesses a warmth that is rarely met with in singers of this type, so that her scene in the Prologue which leads to the splendid duet [with the Composer] was both ardent and most convincing. In her coloratura, the soprano favours a legato binding of the individual notes in the finely chiselled musical figures, so that the great aria was not just a brilliantly polished showpiece but, instead, sounded full of emotion and temperament. In sum, a very remarkable achievement which arouses a lively interest in her portrayal of other roles.

Schwarzkopf was accepted, that was the main thing, and, after going back to Berlin for her penultimate performance at the Deutsche Oper in *Alessandro Stradella*, she returned to Vienna in November to rehearse and sing Blondchen in a new production of *Die Entführung* conducted by Karl Böhm. One hears more about Schwarzkopf's reliance on Böhm in Vienna than on the General Intendant, Lothar Müthel, who had been appointed by Goebbels in 1938.

In this *Entführung* production, the dashingly handsome thirty-year-old leading actor, Curt Jürgens, took the speaking part of the Pasha, while Maria Cebotari sang Konstanze. The performance seems not to have been reviewed but, much later, Anton Dermota remembered Schwarzkopf clearly:

> She was both clever and beautiful with a fascinating voice, a truly blonde Mädchen. She had sung a single Blondchen, as guest artist for a repertory performance in the middle of the war, at the Opera House on the Ring, when I was the Belmonte. Böhm conducted . . .[3]

We shall never know exactly how it sounded, because no recording of Schwarzkopf's Blondchen was made, or survives from a live performance. All that imagination can do is to combine her Zerbinetta and Susanna.

After that she went back to Berlin and sang at four troop concerts in December, organized by ProMi, and then gave her last performance with the Deutsche Oper. This was as the contentious Adele in *Die Fledermaus* on New Year's Eve, a particularly good role and an ideal occasion for her send-off. The company was not aware of this, but it was certainly her intention.

Thereafter she was involved with smaller concerts that had been arranged by her agent: there is no evidence of anything spectacular apart from a request from the Breslau Opera, on 9 March 1943, to sing Galatea in Handel's masque at the end of May. This offer did not reach Schwarzkopf in time for her to act on it because the stage doorman at the Deutsche Oper held on to the telegram for nearly a fortnight,[4] for which he was later taken to task.

So Schwarzkopf went back to Vienna, having been offered four roles in what was left of the season. The first was Blondchen, when Konstanze was sung by the attractive Italian soprano, Alda Noni, who was usually considered a *leggiera* and thus more suited to the role of Blondchen herself. Other *leggiere* also included the fascinating Hungarian, Esther Réthy, who has left this memory of Schwarzkopf:

> . . . she was very clever, and her ambition, combined with an iron will, put her very rapidly in the front ranks. I never found her performances moving – too cerebral for my Hungarian nature – but they were perfect, not a comma missing.[5]

Réthy was about to graduate from Musetta to Mimi, and so was Maria Cebotari, who had been at Dresden with Böhm before the war, singing Konstanze there.

Then there were the 'heavies'. Anny Konetzni had been her younger sister Hilde's teacher, so they preferred to appear together as little as possible. Hilde sang Donna Elvira and they both sang the Marschallin but, as yet, Schwarzkopf was not even singing Sophie. Maria Reining, a statuesque and versatile Viennese, another Marschallin, as well as Ariadne, Arabella and Eva, was also well established.

A much younger soprano, Irmgard Seefried, had just made her début as Eva, having come from Karajan's opera in Aachen. She was to remain in Vienna until 1976, singing a relatively small number of roles, among which were her famous Susanna, Fiordiligi, Marzelline and the Composer in *Ariadne*. Sena Jurinac had a richer, darker timbre than any of the younger sopranos and was a wonderful Cherubino and Octavian, but she also sang Mimi and a sympathetic Elvira. This, then, was the state of the 'opposition' when Schwarzkopf became established in Vienna: an assembly of mainly youthful soprano talent that has never been equalled. And Lisa Della Casa was yet to arrive.

After Schwarzkopf's experience in Berlin with fifteen or so Musettes in *Die Boheme*, she fitted easily into the role in Vienna with her new colleagues Maria Cebotari and Anton Dermota as Mimi and Rudolf. Matthieu Ahlersmeyer, the veteran baritone from Dresden, sang Marcel, and Rudolf Moralt conducted. Schwarzkopf followed this with the new, for her, role of Rosina in *Der Barbier* (in those days often sung by a light soprano), with Dermota as Almaviva and Alfred Jerger as Dr Bartolo. Gustav Oeggl, a powerful but dramatically wooden Swiss baritone from the Volksoper, was singing Figaro and, as he was not up to the standard of the rest of the cast, Schwarzkopf's Rosina attracted most of the audience's attention. This was precisely the kind of part she had been demanding in Berlin – it was on the list she had given to Dr Maeder.

In 1943 there was a struggle over Schwarzkopf between Wilhelm Rode of the Deutsche Oper and Karl Böhm in Vienna. She was being called to account for having overstayed her run of guest performances and Berlin insisted they 'owned' her, so Böhm procrastinated with the negotiations because he wanted her to stay in Vienna, as did she. The many differences with Rode had of course begun in 1941/42 and now, when the critical nature of this argument reached Goebbels' ears, he ordered that Schwarzkopf, as a German, must without question return to Berlin and resume her career there, instead of remaining in Vienna. This was an uncomfortable situation, especially as it looked as though it might interfere with her plans.

An important Lieder recital with Raucheisen in Berlin, early in March 1943, was tied to more broadcasts and recordings for Berlin Radio; then, towards the end of April, Schwarzkopf sang solo soprano in a performance of the St Matthew Passion there. A few days later, she was taken ill.

Schwarzkopf's lung complaint was brought about, she believed, by having spent too many hours in damp air raid shelters during bombing raids on Berlin,[6] where she made good use of the time by studying her scores.[7] As things turned out, it could not have happened at a more propitious time because a complete rift with Berlin would not come amiss, especially as she had been accepted as a member of the Vienna State Opera, a fact she had already made public with a small announcement in the *Charlottenburger Zeitung* of 13 April.

Even though she was no longer under full contract to the Deutsche Oper, they were not prepared to let her go altogether but expected the usual arrangement of joint membership of both houses. There were a number of the usual obligations on both sides, and, for their part, the Berlin management honoured theirs by paying her salary in full for three months after she was admitted to a sanatorium. This was Dr Gühr's clinic in Tatranská Polianka, high up on the Czech side of the Tatra Mountains and 100 kilometres from Krákow on the other side of the mountains in Poland, a convenient place for treatment of 'respiratory diseases and neurosis'[8] now that the Swiss health resorts were unavailable to all but the most affluent or influential German families.

From the end of August 1943, and for another month, Schwarzkopf remained on full salary, but this was reduced to half for the next six weeks;[9] and although payments from the Deutsche Oper then ceased, she was able to stay at the clinic, thanks to funds from an unknown source which were made available to her in October. In that month, her father, Friedrich Schwarzkopf, now a captain in the Wehrmacht and on leave from the Russian Front, visited her at the clinic and reported favourably on her progress to the Deutsche Oper. No sign of the tension between the opera house management and his daughter is evident in Dr Maeder's charming reply.[10]

It was remarkably fortunate that she had the benefit of such an effective *Kur* whereby her bronchial trouble, and all its possible complications in those days before antibiotics, was prevented from interfering with her subsequent career. She emerged from the clinic in sound health, having missed the worst of the air raids on the Reich, and went on sick leave in February 1944 before resuming her career, not in Berlin, but in Vienna.

This recommenced with a Blondchen in *Die Entführung* on 15 April. Then, on 2 May, she sang Rosina again in a new production, conducted as usual by the imperturbable Rudolf Moralt. The Viennese critic and minor composer, Fritz Skorzeny, wrote:[11]

> Although possessing flowery freshness, beauty of voice and a secure technique which mastered the sparkling coloratura, this was not her main concern. In her overall charming attitude, gestures and rich, more inward-looking facial expression, deeper than usual in this trilling and twittering doll in love, she was less dependent on the traditional brilliant effect. Very characteristic, in this respect, was her choice of the insertion in Act II of Handel's serio-comic aria, 'Il penseroso' (with flute obbligato), instead of the usual sort of cold, decorative fireworks.

'Il penseroso' is, of course, 'Sweet Bird', one of Schwarzkopf's early and favourite arias (recorded after the war) and which she most likely requested of Moralt that she be allowed to sing. Then it was Ännchen in *Der Freischütz*, which she had last sung at the Deutsche Oper in November 1941, and also Musette: she gave eight performances of these four roles before the end of the season in June.

At first she kept clear of Berlin and, because she wanted to see her mother again, they arranged to meet in July 1944 at Marienbad, just over the Czech border on the way to Pilsen, where she stayed at the Stern Hotel under her mother's maiden name of Fröhling.[12]

In that month, a desperate group of German generals bungled an assassination attempt on the Führer at a conference in his East Prussian headquarters at Rastenburg. Frantic with rage, Hitler intended to make as many people suffer as he possibly could. All places of entertainment were closed (except the Bayreuth Festival Theatre and those cinemas still standing) and their employees ordered to the armament factories by 1 August. Schwarzkopf had received these instructions but, in the early autumn of 1944, she was ignoring them and staying put. In September she was cast as Konstanze in an Austrian Radio production of *Die Entführung* and her voice was heard again in the city after an absence of seventeen months. This early account of her Konstanze, conducted by Moralt, has fortunately been preserved and displays her fresh young voice to perfection; while the instrument is not especially large, it is well produced and projected with great ease in the coloratura. The recording has no dialogue and also omits Konstanze's first aria, 'Ach, ich liebte', which Schwarzkopf never committed to disc.

The removal of her name from the God-favoured List did not prevent her from broadcasting and recording, thanks to the protection of Hans Erich Schrade, business manager of the Reichstheaterkammer,[13] who obtained her dispensation from the *Arbeitsdienst* in a classic example of the Nazis' multiple standards. He reminded Rainer Schlösser, leader of the theatre division in ProMi, of her much admired loyalty: 'I would be very pleased if you could forget, or let be forgotten, the E.S. affair. My opinion of this talented artist and special person is shared by your colleague Dr Lang.' Now there was even more of a need for Schwarzkopf to keep up a dialogue, however remote, with the Deutsche Oper, because of the undesirable interest that was being expressed in her by lesser officials in ProMi.

She sent Rode three lists of operatic roles, those which she had sung, those which she was ready to sing, and those which she was in the course of studying. Noticeably absent are a few, like Zerbinetta, which she had clearly put behind her, because she was beginning to concentrate upon more substantial characters.

Three more, evidently considered suitable, were added in another hand. Suggested new roles were Zerlina in *Don Giovanni*, which in fact she never sang, and Marzelline in *Fidelio* which she did, and quite soon, with great success. (This list is included in Appendix B.)

Viennese life depends upon opera and theatre to a large extent, so an intense feeling of depression followed the closure of Staatsoper, Volksoper and Burg-theater. Those obliging Viennese doctors who, as patrons of the arts and espe-cially of the opera, had in the past taken it upon themselves to help singers by signing pessimistic medical reports, were no longer available; nor could an important singer or musician be classified as belonging to a 'reserved occupa-tion'. Even so, a few artists got round the regulations, either because they were old, truly infirm, or of sufficient substance to bribe the bureaucrats into allowing them to remain in Vienna. The system throughout the Reich was becoming more and more corrupt as the futility of the war unmistakably showed through the cracks of Goebbels' persistent, though increasingly less credible, propaganda.

It is typical of the Viennese character that despite the 'Führer Order' banning public entertainments, including opera, a makeshift outdoor production of *Der Barbier von Sevilla* was put on for a couple of weeks in August 1944 'especially for the KdF' (*Kraft durch Freude*, or Strength through Joy Movement). It was produced by the Staatsoper baritone Alfred Jerger in the Heldenplatz at the back of the Hofburg in Vienna. Among the many listeners was a man inside that august building, Baldur von Schirach. As Gauleiter of Vienna, he lived and worked there.

Schirach was a musical amateur and a strong supporter of the opera. His appointment had been approved on artistic grounds by Goebbels in 1940 because it fitted his theories of Party propaganda through easy entertainment, whereas Hitler had put von Schirach there 'for the express purpose of driving the Jews and Czechoslovaks out of Vienna'.[14] Schirach had established himself luxuriously in the former Viennese Royal Palace of the Hofburg, where he behaved to the manner born. Such an ostentatious and indeed insufferable manner gave him the local sobriquets of 'the Viennese Pompadour' and 'Emperor Baldur'. The grand title, Gauleiter of Austria's Capital City, had gone to his head so severely that senior, and usually very busy, members of the Party from Berlin, quite often only passing through the city, were obliged to report to him in his palace, while an underling was sent to meet other prominent visitors. Schirach only deigned to journey to the railway station or the airport in person when there was a head of state to be made welcome in his capital.

He was nevertheless sympathetic to artists deserving protection from the excesses of the regime and was especially indulgent towards Richard Strauss, whose enchanting String Sextet introduction to his last opera, *Capriccio*, was first played in Schirach's music room at the Hofburg. Strauss also received protection from Hans Frank, the governor-general of Occupied Poland, who normally lived and worked in Krákow, but Frank kept clear of Berlin, as far as possible, for his own good reasons. He used Vienna as a power base and kept a suite in the Imperial Hotel, made available to senior Party members whenever they visited the city.

Frank, another 'old Nazi', was very musical, and one of the most cultured members of the Party as well as a senior one, but he did not have nearly as much clout as his title suggests. As head of the Reich's legislature before the war, he had argued with Hitler and tried, but failed, to curb some of the Führer's more barbarous acts which were outside any acknowledged legal code. Thereafter Hitler demoted him from his post as chief of the Justiciary and, in 1939, sent him to Poland, where his new task was to superintend the Final Solution. Besides doing what was demanded of him, albeit half-heartedly because the job technically belonged to the SS, Frank formed a symphony orchestra and small opera company in Krákow and invited celebrated German and Austrian musicians to appear in concerts and performances, irrespective of the cultural ban elsewhere in the Reich.[15]

In Vienna, the State Opera's director, Karl Böhm, should have been planning his next season but, not knowing whether there was ever going to be another, instead gave a few concerts for soldiers on leave or convalescing, and made some recordings in the Musikverein. It was during one of these sessions, shortly after 11 a.m. on 12 March 1945, that the air-raid sirens sounded. Artists and staff, including the musicians in the Musikverein, obediently filed down to their designated area in the shelters below the front of the opera house, 'one of the safest in the old city, on account of its depth'.[16] A few American aircraft flying northwards over the city dropped a stick of bombs. Böhm believed that 'the excuse that they had not wanted to hit the Opera but rather the North-West railway station really does not hold up'.[17] The bombs went through the roof of the Staatsoper, landed on the stage, and in moments the beloved building was ablaze.

Böhm has vividly recalled how 'the iron curtain had in fact been lowered as a precaution, but the first bomb – containing high explosives – fell right on to the stage and the incredible blast from it pushed the safety curtain out into the auditorium'.[18] The next bombs were both explosives and incendiaries so that fire engulfed the whole building, except for the foyer and the staircase, which protected those in the shelter below, all of whom survived. Seven years before, to the day, all the Nazis in Vienna had turned out to greet Adolf Hitler, Austrian-born Führer of the Thousand Year German Reich and their self-styled saviour; now, thanks to him, the lovely Staatsoper, one of Vienna's most prized possessions and focal point of the city's culture, was a charred ruin.

Schwarzkopf has already confirmed her place in operatic history because today there are very few people left alive, artists or artisans, who worked in the old Vienna State Opera. She walked the same corridors as Gustav Mahler, Franz Schalk and Richard Strauss had done; she appeared on the stage where Maria Jeritza, Lotte Lehmann and Richard Tauber had all been part of that house's glory before they were obliged to leave Austria in the 1930s.

On 13 April 1945, three weeks before the total collapse of the Third Reich, Soviet troops arrived in Vienna and took over the romantic capital city of the nation they considered to be a firm ally of their deadliest enemy. The easy-going Viennese had already been alerted by the SS about Russian treatment of conquered peoples, and were prepared for a rough time.

On the first day, however, the strange new visitors from the East behaved so well that the advance warning was taken as scaremongering, and the Viennese began to relax again. Schwarzkopf, however, was prudent enough to listen to advice and arranged to leave Vienna before she was prevented from doing so. She got through the cordon that was being put round the city and made for the relative safety of the Salzburg area, too far to the west to be reached by the Russians.

What happened to the citizens of Vienna during the first twenty days of 'liberation' could not possibly have been imagined or foreseen. It began with a vengeance: drunkenness and lawlessness by Russian soldiers; men beaten up and murdered; women and children raped; property looted and senselessly smashed. Stalin had given the Red Army carte blanche in Germany, to pay back the enemy for their bestialities in Russia during 1941/42; Austria was in the Reich, Austrians had fought in the Wehrmacht, and to have been a common soldier, remote from the SS, was no excuse. And as far as the Russians were concerned, there was no difference between Austrian, Hungarian or German women. What was going on in Vienna hardly seemed possible: it was like some dreadful nightmare, a retribution for their compliance with the Nazi regime, so they were told. But how could that have been avoided? After all, Austria had not invited Germany's invasion in 1938, her Jews had suffered severely from the start, and now she was becoming a repressed nation all over again.

Doctors were overwhelmed by the number of hysterical or dangerously withdrawn female patients from the age of eleven (or even younger) into the sixties (or older), crowding into their waiting rooms. The main concern was not so much whether the youngest were pregnant; far more alarming was venereal disease, which was rampant in the Red Army where it was not considered a stigma, as in all Western armed forces.

When Stalin called his troops to order, some two and a half weeks later, the 'Ivans' suddenly behaved with discretion; if any of them reverted to the free-for-all which had previously been encouraged, they were summarily executed by their own officers. For the Austrians, however, the damage had been done and the invading – never 'liberating' – Russian troops were regarded with permanent hatred and mistrust.

On 27 April, the Austrian Republic was restored when Dr Carl Renner, a former chancellor in 1918, and now working closely with the Russians, became

Chancellor of Austria for a second time. Three days later, on 30 April 1945, Hitler's suicide was announced, and by 8 May hostilities in Europe were over.

The Russians' monstrous behaviour in Vienna in the first weeks of occupation makes it clear that Schwarzkopf did the right thing in leaving the capital when she did. The prettiest girls were often collected off the streets for the Russian brothels which, for most of them, was literally a fate far worse than immediate death. Yet the 'Ivans' did all they could to encourage the resumption of opera, theatre, and cinema because 'under the Soviet system, culture and politics were reverse and obverse of the same propaganda coin'.[19]

The two generations of *Weltklasse* European singers in Vienna in 1945 made it the focal point for an immediate rebirth of supreme European singing and opera, keener and of a quality unknown anywhere else in the world. The Viennese had only one thought: to help restore the vanished glory of their opera. This was motivated less by financial considerations than by the artistic urge to find their own building and resume performances. Because the Staatsoper building was in ruins, the principal opera company had to be resited immediately; the Volksoper was undamaged and, to begin with, the single stage was shared by the two companies. Alfred Jerger became temporary director of the Vienna Staatsoper, as his rising company was resolutely calling itself, and 'was largely responsible for its being able to perform *Figaro* as early as 1 May 1945',[20] a week before the war was officially over.

Franz Salmhofer was then appointed full-time director and, determined to provide the company with their own stage and supporting staff, he set about his job vigorously, examining with his technicians a number of likely sites, among the most hopeful of which was the Theater an der Wien. They found it in 'an advanced state of dilapidation',[21] housing only rats and a crop of mushrooms on the stage, which the caretaker was cultivating for profit. Salmhofer soon settled for the famous building and displayed his own brand of Viennese humour by engaging the old woman on the spot as the company's permanent lavatory attendant.

6

Red Soldiers and Red Tape
1945–1946

Once it had been established that the Theater an der Wien could be restored to its proper use, considerable refurbishment was essential. Members of the State Opera Chorus formed a willing workforce and got down on their hands and knees, with scrubbing brushes and without salary, to provide their company with a stage, an auditorium and artistic freedom once more. In spite of a critical shortage of all necessary materials from cleaning rags to paint and timber, they brought the old place back to something like its pre-war condition.

This generous spirit was symptomatic of a determined intention to reinstate the Vienna State Opera without delay. A big draw was the offer of support from the Vienna Philharmonic Orchestra, whose instruments and library had remained intact, for every opera performance. The Volksoper, on the other hand, with a fully equipped building, had to raise its own orchestra, but the decision seemed a fair one.

The Theater an der Wien had been built by Emanuel Schikanaeder, Austrian theatre manager, author, composer, actor, singer and Mozart's first Papageno, who had earlier commissioned Beethoven to write a new opera for him. Nothing came of this to begin with, but after Schikanaeder moved his company to the an der Wien, Beethoven felt himself bound to honour the commission. He began work on *Leonore*, moved into the theatre and saw the work through to its first performance there in November 1805. So it seemed highly appropriate when, on 6 October 1945, the same opera (in its final form as *Fidelio*) was chosen by the new Wiener Staatsoper to begin its life again.

The Russians had demanded entertainment, so they willingly assisted the company in its greatest need: electricity. There was none until the theatre's mains intake was connected to the priority supply of a Soviet-run hospital, in exchange for seats in the directors' box at every performance, a very satisfactory arrangement on the face of it, except that the Viennese were unprepared for certain extravagances in Russian behaviour. They often stood up, waved, and exchanged comments with their friends in other parts of the auditorium during performances; they were also extremely fond of anything which was, or resembled, gold, such as the property chairs in *The Marriage of Figaro* which disappeared one by one.

The Viennese simply looked on these Slavonic caprices with good-natured patience: it was all part of the game which they felt they had already won, with the Wiener Staatsoper Company once more in action. There are also many stories about the typically Viennese ploys to achieve results during the first, extremely hard six months of the peace. The Allies had plenty of food and fuel, so hijacking it for the company was a frequent occurrence, regarded by the Viennese as fair game. If soldiers pulled up in a lorry and left it standing outside a house of dubious reputation, there was always intense sympathy for them when they lurched out to find their vehicle empty – or gone.[1]

The black market thrived. Virtue was cheap, musical instruments, gramophone records, books, china, pictures and other works of art were willingly bartered for a little coffee or some cigarettes with any of the occupying troops who had an eye for such things. But amidst the luxury of opera and concerts by the Vienna Philharmonic Orchestra there were others, too proud to yield to moral defeat, who died of starvation or exposure.

Opera in Vienna normally was, and still is, a daily event throughout the year, although not every night produces a performance of Festival standard, as can usually be expected in Salzburg, the mountain city that glorifies the memory of Mozart every summer. The Salzburg Festival began in 1920, and remained free of any political stigma until 1938, when the first of six festivals under Nazi domination was held. Then, in early May 1945, US troops walked into the undefended fairy-tale city as liberators rather than conquerors, and within a fortnight, discussions were taking place about restoring the Salzburg Festival that very year, with a limited number of performances, even though there were only three months in which to plan and prepare for them. The Salzburgers expected Baron Heinrich Puthon, their former Society President, with nineteen years of experience, to resume this duty, but the Americans, always accustomed to command any bi- or multi-national operation in which they are involved, nominated Otto von Pasetti instead. He was to be general manager of the 1945 Salzburg Festival, with the Baron as chairman in name only.

Aristocratic and urbane, 'Puthon did not participate in artistic planning for the Festival; instead he devoted all his subtle and diplomatic skills to dealing with artists, composers, politicians and local dignitaries alike.'[2] Pasetti, by contrast, was a small-time Viennese singer, who had lived in Austria and Italy before the war. Karl Böhm referred to him as 'a frustrated tenor who had actually sung Parsifal before the war in Graz'.[3] Pasetti was something of a Lothario too, for 'in 1933 [he] had seduced Lotte Lenya away from Kurt Weill;'[4] afterwards, when they had been reunited, he followed them to America.

Pasetti joined the Army when the United States entered the war and in 1945 came to Salzburg as a multilingual lieutenant with every qualification, in the American view, for running the Festival. Its financial success, until immediately before the *Anschluss*, had been partly due to the support of American and other foreign visitors, and it was anticipated that this would continue.

Pasetti was determined to set up his Festival between 1 and 31 August and make it a success, as much for his own sake as for Salzburg's. The Americans saw it as a way of competing with the Russians on the cultural front after the successful Soviet enterprise in supporting the revived Vienna State Opera. The first post-war Salzburg Festival began, a little later than planned, on 12 August. 'For the first time artists, administrators and local dignitaries mingled with the Americans over drinks; up to that point there had been an official "non-fraternization order".'[5] The charming light soprano, Esther Réthy, sang the Csárdás from *Die Fledermaus* and some other familiar numbers by Lehár and Johann Strauss, very appealing to the large number of US troops who made up two-thirds of the audience. Austrians were allowed to buy the remaining seats, although at the inaugural performance guests from among the other occupying powers were present as well.

Plays, concerts, choral works and opera made up the bill, but because usable scenery in Salzburg was confined to that of the 1939 production of *Die Entführung* by Robert Kautsky, there could be only one choice of opera: at any rate it was Mozart, and a magnificent cast was available, with principals from Vienna.

Maria Cebotari sang Konstanze, Ludwig Weber Osmin, while Belmonte was taken by Julius Patzak who, although Viennese by birth and familiar at Salzburg Festivals since 1938, had been leading tenor at the Munich Opera for most of his career: he had finally come home as a distinguished member of the Vienna State Opera. The fact that these singers, and most of the other Festival artists, had sung in Salzburg during the Nazi regime was comfortably over-looked, and Karl Böhm was engaged to conduct *Die Entführung*. He and his wife were staying at Attersee, in the Salzkammergut, 60 kilometres from Salzburg, where they were accommodated in the outhouse of a large and imposing property belonging to the actress Käthe Dorsch. This was in a room above the chicken shed which was only unpleasant, Böhm recalled, 'in so far as we were always woken by the chickens early in the morning'.

When Böhm arrived in Salzburg, a disturbed Baron Puthon met him: 'We are such old friends – it's so awful – I know your position – but the Russians insist . . .'[6] On account of his besmirched political record, Böhm was forbidden to conduct and, utterly dejected, made his way to his home town of Graz in the British Zone rather than back to Vienna.

With the well-placed assistance she was able to call on, Schwarzkopf and a companion (whom she said was her mother)[7] also made for the relative safety and calm of Attersee, carrying a few basic necessities, walking most of the way and existing on potatoes and any other food they were able to find en route. They too were glad to accept Käthe Dorsch's 'accommodation for touring artists' (the tenor Max Lorenz and his wife had been there before then), and in spite of the noisy poultry it was there that Schwarzkopf awaited developments, artistic and political.

There was an initial going-through-the-motions by the authorities in Austria, when all citizens known to have had connections with the Party were given *Fragebogen* (questionnaires) to complete. Schwarzkopf was on the Salzburg register of National Socialists, because she was living in that district when the war ended. On 4 July 1945 she too was given a *Fragebogen*.[8]

Had her answers been found acceptable, she would have been allowed to return to the stage and concert platform, but when she handed in her form to the American Intelligence Officer, the same Otto von Pasetti, he immediately realized that many of her answers were untrue. The paper was destroyed. The following day she filled out another,[9] and although what she wrote this time, with regard to her membership of the Party, was not altogether accurate either, Pasetti accepted it.

At the beginning of the first post-war opera season at Graz that September, Böhm was lending as much anonymous help as he could, and persuaded the three principals from the recent Salzburg *Entführung* to sing there, although he had to appoint Rudolf Moralt to conduct. Maria Cebotari was taken ill after her first performance on 16 September, and so Moralt consulted Karl Böhm about a replacement. Remembering Schwarzkopf from Attersee, but perhaps forgetting that she had only sung Blondchen, Böhm, who was still director of the Vienna State Opera, if only in name, used his influence to surprising effect. He persuaded the Americans in Vienna to collect Schwarzkopf from Attersee and convey her to Graz to sing there because 'no other suitable singer was available'. This phrase would soon become an operatic cliché. Schwarzkopf was collected in a jeep by a US officer, Lieutenant Albert van Erden who, like Pasetti, had returned to Europe with American rank. He drove her the 250 kilometres to Graz[10] where she sang Konstanze on 21 September with Patzak as Belmonte and Ludwig Weber as Osmin.

That afternoon, the three of them were to be seen driving about the city in a battered old motor-car, looking for somewhere to get their costumes ironed.[11] There was a repetition of *Die Entführung* on 7 October and it is more than surprising to see Schwarzkopf's name enhanced with the title of Kammersängerin on both programmes. This cannot have been acquired from Berlin or bestowed in Vienna before the end of the Reich; rather, it was a way of

Elisabeth Schwarzkopf's stage début at the Deutsche Oper, Berlin, on 15 April 1938, as a Flower Maiden in Act II of *Parsifal*. She is third from left in the front row, head bowed, left foot forward (*Deutsche Oper, Berlin*)

Schwarzkopf's début as Zerbinetta in a new production of *Ariadne auf Naxos* at the Deutsche Oper (*Deutsche Oper*)

Sonnabend, den 28. September 1940

NEUINSZENIERUNG

Ariadne auf Naxos

Oper in einem Aufzuge nebst einem Vorspiel von Hugo von Hofmannsthal (Neue Bearbeitung). Musik von Richard Strauß op. 60

Inszenierung: Hans Batteux   Musikalische Leitung: Artur Rother   Bühnenbilder und Kostüme: Günther Krause

Personen des Vorspiels:

Der Haushofmeister	Edwin Heyer	Ein Lakai	Wilhelm Lang
Ein Musiklehrer	Hanns Heinz Nissen	Zerbinetta	Elisabeth Schwarzkopf
Der Komponist	Constanze Nettesheim	Primadonna (Ariadne)	Bertha Stesler
Der Tenor (Bacchus)	Henk Noort	Harlekin	Karl Schmitt-Walter
Ein Offizier	Ernst Franke	Scaramuccio	Rudolf Schramm
Ein Tanzmeister	Hans Florian	Truffaldin	Ludwig Windisch
Ein Perückenmacher	Georg Rahtjen	Brighella	Reinhard Dörr

Personen der Oper:

Ariadne	Bertha Stesler	Zerbinetta		Elisabeth Schwarzkopf
Bacchus	Henk Noort	Harlekin		Karl Schmitt-Walter
Najade	Tresl Rudolph	Scaramuccio	als Intermezzo	Rudolf Schramm
Dryade	Marie-Luise Schilp	Truffaldin		Ludwig Windisch
Echo	Hilde Scheppan a. G.	Brighella		Reinhard Dörr

Technische Leitung: Kurt Hemmerling   Pause nach dem Vorspiel

 Bei Fliegeralarm: Den Anordnungen der Logenschließer ist unbedingt Folge zu leisten; die Garderoben bleiben geschlossen; Kleidungsstücke werden nicht ausgehändigt.

Anfang 18.30 Uhr   Runde I   Ende 21 Uhr

As Esmeralda in *The Bartered Bride* at Deutsche Oper, June 1938,
wearing the dress that would later reappear unexpectedly
(*Deutsche Oper*)

Right Schwarzkopf's contentious Susanna in *Figaro* at the Deutsche Oper, February 1942 (*Deutsche Oper*)

Below Schwarzkopf (left) in her single performance as Susanna at the 1947 Salzburg Festival, with Maria Cebotari (Countess), Hilde Güden (Cherubino)

Left 'Sweet Idleness' from the UFA film *Nacht ohne Abschied*, Berlin 1943 (*Trouble Pictures Archiv*)

Below Double-take: Schwarzkopf accompanying herself in the wartime film *Der Verleidiger hat das Vort* (*Trouble Pictures Archiv*)

As Blondchen in *Die Entführung aus dem Serail*, with Herbert Alsen as
Osmin, Vienna State Opera, April 1944

As Marzelline in *Fidelio*, Salzburg, August 1950

Above With
Michael
Raucheisen
after their
recital in Berlin,
May 1942

Left Wilhelm
Furtwängler,
c. 1937 (*Wilhelm
Furtwängler
Society UK*)

Schwarzkopf entertaining von Karajan at Legge's house in Hampstead

Wedding picture, 19 October 1953; Schwarzkopf, Walter Legge, Ernest Newman, Jane Withers

Left As Mélisande in Act III of Debussy's opera at La Scala, May 1953

Below Lohengrin at La Scala, January 1953. Left to right: Wolfgang Windgassen (Lohengrin), Herbert von Karajan, Schwarzkopf (Elsa), Otto Edelmann (King Henry), Josef Metternich (Count Telramund)

making herself appear of equal importance to Maria Cebotari and the two Kammersänger with her in the cast.[12] Schwarzkopf did not retrace her steps to Attersee but returned with van Erden to Vienna, where she decided to remain.

Towards the end of October 1945, Schwarzkopf had to fill in her third *Fragebogen*; again her answers were incomplete and evasive and differed from those she had previously declared. This time she stated she had applied for membership of the NSDAP 'only once in 1939 but received no answer'; that she had been a Student Führerin at the Berlin Hochschule for one term; and that she had left the NSDStB. (Association of National Socialist German Students) in 1936.[13]

Why, one may ask, did someone as intelligent as Elisabeth Schwarzkopf resort to these clumsy methods of fudging her past? The main reason was probably fear for her career, which had progressed very satisfactorily so far; but we do not know exactly what lay at the core of this fear, what precisely she was trying to hide or attempting to obliterate, if it was more than just her Party membership.

Colleagues and others have spoken of Schwarzkopf's 'protector' in the highest ranks of the Party, but while two names in particular have been mentioned with some confidence, this does not constitute evidence. During post-war investigations into her past, Schwarzkopf's defence partly rested upon the differences she had experienced with Rode and also with Keppler who, she maintained, had pushed her into joining the Party in return for recommending her promotion at the Deutsche Oper.[14] In fact, the intervention of Keppler came more than a year after 1940, when she had already been accepted into the NSDAP. But when she denied her membership of the Party, this was something that concerned only herself, and seems like a panic measure. She was trying to clear her political image as quickly as possible in order to take full advantage of an important opportunity to resume her career. It had always been her resolve to get to the top, and she did not hesitate to take every measure she considered necessary to do so. As in love and war, both of which she had experienced, all's fair in an opera house.

Among the Allies, it was principally the Russians who regarded Austria as an aggressor and an enemy nation, although many Austrian citizens and immigrants were under general suspicion because of their political pasts. This applied equally to the former members of Goebbels' Reichstheaterkammer, performing artists of all kinds in the Third Reich, who had been obliged to join the RKK (*Reichskulturkammer*). Individual files had been opened on their career and behaviour, with copies of every letter they wrote to superiors and every letter or memo in reply.

There were also copies, when warranted, of other memoranda addressed to officials more senior than the subject's immediate superior. This huge file of a quarter of a million index cards had been held and administered by Hans Hinkel, and was captured intact by the Russians in Berlin on its way to destruction in 1945. In their search for more valuable loot, however, they left it complete in its three lorries, and by good fortune the hoard was discovered and its immense importance recognized by British Intelligence who returned it all to the old RKK headquarters, now in the British Zone of Berlin, at 45 Schlüterstrasse, where it had accumulated daily since that department was set up.[15] Officially, the 'Hinkel File' was for reference by all the four Occupying Powers, and it yielded some devastating information.

Schwarzkopf's personal file runs to almost 200 foolscap pages and logs every political move she made after joining both junior branches of the Party until her full membership. It charts her swift and brilliant career at the Deutsche Oper and details her aggressive behaviour towards Rode, laid out in the correspondence between them. She was probably unaware that the Allies possessed all this damning evidence, but now that she was back in Vienna, brazening it out by singing at the State Opera in spite of threats and arguments against her, she showed determination and a fearless spirit at odds with her occasional lapses in self-control.

Some operas continued to be mounted by the Vienna State Opera at the Volksoper, and Schwarzkopf made her first, entirely unauthorized, post-war stage début there in a new production of *Bajazzo* (*Pagliacci*) with the Greek tenor, Peter Baxevanos,[16] as Canio. Her assumption of Nedda confirmed a change in her voice, but her first appearance at the Theater an der Wien on 10 January 1946 as Mimi, a truly lyric part, sung in German, required a different kind of vocalism from any of her previous roles.

The political climate began to move against certain artists in Vienna when the Austrian police expressed strong opposition to all Germans living there. However, they did not exert any real pressure when their unwelcome residents overstepped the law until March, and then only after some behind-the-scenes discussions. The Austrian Cultural Society had booked Schwarzkopf to take part in a commemorative concert of the US Intelligence Services' First General Assembly on 10 March. Two days before, the Americans cancelled this invitation and told her that she was not at liberty to sing for them.

Strictly out of courtesy, the American delegate informed his Russian counterpart, Colonel Epstein, of the decision.[17] He was a cultured and sensitive man who was unable to forget the appalling sight of ground moving over buried bodies in a concentration camp his men had overrun. This had made him more violently anti-German than most Russians and consequently he instantly concurred with the Americans about Schwarzkopf, who was now strictly forbidden to perform in Vienna. Only four days later, she was given the opportunity to sing Mimi in *Die Boheme,* one of her current seven roles, and did so, apparently out of sheer defiance.

Dr Egon Hilbert, the new General Intendant of all Viennese theatres, attempted to regularize her position with the Allies by putting forward a strong case to Epstein. Hilbert stressed that if she was forbidden to sing at the Theater an der Wien, there were going to be times when no other soprano was available to take her roles, thus placing the scheduled performances in jeopardy. Special allowances should be made, Hilbert added, because this kind of restriction was making life impossible for him in his endeavour to present daily performances of opera in accordance with the Allies' requests.

'*Niet!*' was Epstein's reply, but he added a curious corollary. He was prepared to alter his view on the matter only 'if ordered to do so by a superior officer',[18] which seemed to indicate an impending change in Russian policy over Schwarzkopf. Meanwhile, the Americans reinforced their ban on her appearances because of the conflicting statements in her three *Fragebogen* and other information that had come to light in Berlin.

The Russians did change tack, as Epstein's remark suggested, and they supported Dr Hilbert's argument to allow Schwarzkopf to perform again in *Die Entführung.* The Americans raised no further objections and at last there seemed to be agreement, although the British and French were not intervening; in any case, delegates representing the four powers had to be in complete accord before any decision could be fully implemented.

Then, after a unilateral nocturnal discussion, and as if deliberately intending to cause international dissent, the Russians performed a *volte-face.* They telephoned their American counterparts in the middle of the night following their meeting to inform them that they were banning Schwarzkopf from the Opera. This turned out to be no more than a temporary spanner in the works because a week later the Russian C-in-C, Marshal Koniev, gave his personal permission through General Lebedenko, the Russian commander in Vienna, for Schwarzkopf to appear in *Rigoletto* 'because no other soprano was available'. So she was cast to sing four Gildas – and one Mimi as well.

Baffled by these ups and downs, the Americans next proposed three conditions under which Schwarzkopf's official position might once and for all be settled. If there was no other singer to take a specified role; if all the Allies agreed and the Russians stuck to their agreement, then she would be allowed to sing in order to save the performance. In this event, the name of Schwarzkopf was not to be printed on the theatre programme or playbill.

Yet the arrangement was not entirely foolproof. While another singer's name might be announced for a certain night without there seeming to be the least intention of Schwarzkopf or anybody else taking her place, the management regarded itself as fully covered by Marshal Koniev's formula with a verbal announcement to the effect: 'We regret to announce that Fräulein XYZ is indisposed, but we have fortunately been able to secure the services of Frl. Schwarzkopf, who has kindly agreed to step in at the last moment to save the performance.' It is an old dodge, and it always works.

'"Popular" artists were being allowed to perform on an exceptional basis, while lesser ones were banned,'[19] confessed Lieutenant Henry Alter, representing the US Information Control Division in Vienna. Meanwhile, the Allied Council had been asked to deliberate on the Schwarzkopf case so as to avoid any more uncertainties or contradictions, and in May 1946 she had to complete a fourth *Fragebogen*.

This time she nearly came clean, admitted to having joined the Party 'in 1940 or 1941', but still maintained that she had not been allocated a Party number.[20] Allied Intelligence had only to refer to her RKK file to see that this was untrue, and so the delegates got tough with her.

The British, French and Americans (echoing Colonel Epstein) unanimously proposed that because Schwarzkopf was a German citizen and a former National Socialist, she must not be allowed to perform any longer. The French went further, with contingency plans for arresting and repatriating her to Germany if she as much as showed her face again on the stage of the Theater an der Wien. The British, with a typical desire for compromise, thought this was going too far because of her 'artistic quality' that merited her eventual return to the Opera, but certainly not at present. The Russians remained implacably silent.

Austria was now permitted to restore her own democratic institutions, so the Allies considered it preferable, and certainly less time-wasting, for the Austrians henceforth to take charge of their own denazification process. It was not working satisfactorily under the Four Powers, although they must still retain the right of veto so long as they remained in overall control. The Austrian government appointed their Minister of Education, Dr Felix Hurdes, to head the Commission which bore his name. He was a true Austrian patriot who, like Dr Hilbert, had survived Dachau.[21]

When Schwarzkopf's case came before the Commission they questioned her argument that she had initially joined the Party in order to be able to sing at the Deutsche Oper; and that there had never been a 'deal' with Keppler. At last she admitted that her statement about such a bargain had been untrue. Rather than punish her, the Commission noted that her misdemeanours in making false statements might now be regarded as 'active regret'. This was very favourable to Schwarzkopf, and almost amounted to clearance, so she went on singing roles in Vienna which 'could not adequately be filled by another' until there was a total degree of impatience all round.

In early June 1946 the Austrian State Theatre Administration ordered Elisabeth Schwarzkopf's deportation.[22] The Viennese police took action accordingly, but they botched it. Their letter was addressed to the British, French and American delegates to forward to Hurdes, who alone now had the power of enforcement, but the Occupying Powers were bound to reject it when no similar letter had been sent to the Russians. The intention became null and void.

By mid-June 1946, the Inter-Allied Commission admitted that no decision had yet been reached 'concerning the cases of Wilhelm Furtwängler, Herbert von Karajan and Elisabeth Schwarzkopf'. Schwarzkopf was adopting precisely the same attitude as Karajan recommended: do as much as you can, don't upset the authorities by resisting them, play it gently, maintain your dignity, time is on our side. Both Schwarzkopf and Karajan had contracts to take part in the 1946 Salzburg Festival but, after extensive rehearsals of three operas in Vienna – Schwarzkopf was to have sung Susanna in *Figaro* – they were both prevented from appearing.[23]

The wheels of the Allied Denazification Bureau continued to turn slowly until, at the end of October 1946, a full summary of all Schwarzkopf's peccadilloes in the four *Fragebogen* was circulated. Her membership of the junior National Socialist organizations at the Berlin Hochschule and donations to the *Winterhilfe* seemed, at this juncture, to weigh rather heavily against her.

Her lawyer did his best to extricate his client because (he wrote) she thought her NSDAP pink card implied only 'Party candidate'. This was not received with very much credence, so then the lawyer admitted on her behalf that she had knowingly falsified the statements made on the first two *Fragebogen*. She remained blacklisted.

At the end of 1946 determined opposition to Schwarzkopf declined and the reason for this is plain. The Nuremberg Trials were over, verdicts on the twenty-one principal Nazis had been returned and implemented, and the British, French and Russian lawyers, putting the whole unsavoury business behind them, had all gone home, leaving it to the Americans to sort out the lesser Nazi fry. Beside the real villains, for whom there was no sympathy at all in Austria and little in Germany, musicians seemed charismatic personalities with very special gifts; they had given pleasure to thousands of people in the past, and should be allowed to do so again.

By the beginning of 1947 it was the Hurdes Commission's responsibility to disentangle the Schwarzkopf case but, to judge from the meagre number of papers turned over to the State Archive once the Commission had been dissolved, it can only be concluded that either they kept indifferent minutes of their meetings, or else they destroyed far more than have survived. So without further evidence, it is impossible to say exactly how the Schwarzkopf case was closed.

She continued to receive welcome support from Egon Hilbert and from a number of unidentified colleagues who declared: 'She was Pg.[24] but not a Nazi'. Then, in February 1947, 'assisted by the advantages of her extraordinary popularity in Vienna, and the general inclination to allow most artists to resume their activities, she was cleared . . .'[25] Fortunately for her, Elisabeth Schwarzkopf still had some useful friends, although it was an Englishman, on the point of entering the forbidden city of Vienna in search of talent, who would do much more for her than anyone.

⁓ 7 ⁓

Walter Legge

Walter Legge came into Elisabeth Schwarzkopf's life before she had been politically cleared, when she was playing the provocative game of 'Now you see me, now you don't', as described in the previous chapter. She already had a following of her own in Vienna, but pressure on her to stop performing, even to return to Germany, had still not been removed. She needed an ally, someone who was politically neutral in Vienna and possessed enough personality and thrust both to shield her and to further her career. He materialized in the form of Walter Legge and she gladly seized the opportunity.

Harry Walter Legge was born on 1 June 1906 in Shepherd's Bush, London. Accounts of his early life come from sources which sometimes lack precision of detail, like his chapters in *On and Off the Record*, but they are always full of interest and colour. It has always been thought that he was Jewish, but there is no reason to suppose he was other than Gentile.

He was only seven years old when his father took him to his first opera. Cavaliere Francesco Castellano's Italian Company were celebrating the centenary of Verdi's birth at the Coronet Theatre, Notting Hill. The 'specially engaged Rumanian Nightingale', Signora Georgescu, was the star soprano, with 'the great Italian tenor', Signor Elvino Ventura:[1] a stunning experience for the young Walter.

Walter Legge said that by the age of eight he could strum opera tunes on a piano from the score and he also began to collect gramophone records. He left school when he was sixteen, and continued to live at home, listening to his records, going to concerts and the opera, singing from scores with his sister and getting to know the standard works at first hand.

Ten years later, while queuing for the gallery at the Royal Albert Hall where Frieda Hempel was giving a recital, Legge was heard to remark that one day he would marry the most beautiful singer in the world.[2] About this time, too, he also attended the first post-war Grand Opera Season at Covent Garden. Until then he had heard no Wagner or Strauss operas, and found them both new and fascinating in their depths, for it was his feeling for things German, the

German language, German music and poetry, German people, which motivated him; French and Italian culture held far less attraction.

Greatly struck by Ernest Newman's reviews in the *Observer*, Legge began searching out his books. Newman's 1907 biography of Hugo Wolf changed his life. To his surprise, he found that not a single gramophone record of Wolf's Lieder was available and so, with the aid of scores, he began to learn the songs, guided by Newman's notes and soon by Newman himself. The older man was impressed by Legge's keen desire to learn everything he could about music, and took him up. However, Legge's letters to record companies, suggesting it was about time they considered Hugo Wolf's Lieder, achieved no result beyond polite thanks for what they evidently considered a senseless and uneconomic proposition.

After a trial job at HMV, which lasted far less than the probationary six months because of his caustic manner, Legge somehow managed to get back into the company as the sole member of a new Literary Department, writing all album and analytical notes. He did this for the first complete Bach B minor Mass on 78s in 1929, and what he wrote is worth reading today for the insight he displays about the life and works of a composer not normally associated with him. The job at HMV was of great importance to Legge because it finally gave him access to the hitherto forbidden studios and the chief recording manager, Fred Gaisberg. The real live recording side of the business fascinated him far more than its administration.[3]

Until then, the only recording principle had been to capture – even to snatch – sound on wax, to gather as much of it as possible in the scheduled time. Legge's conception was entirely different. He intended to put artistic excellence on a par with commercial considerations.

Far from being put off by the ignorance of record company spokesmen with regard to Wolf's Lieder, Legge was being far-sighted. He and Newman were among the few musicians in England to appreciate their genius. Legge intended to educate the public with the help of a few fine Lieder singers, although he would have preferred to find a soprano of his own choosing to be their champion. This, he knew, was not going to be an easy matter; but a few years later, in a sudden moment of intense gratification, he was to find her in Elisabeth Schwarzkopf.

In the summer of 1930 Legge persuasively floated an original idea to the HMV board for the production of an album of 78 records devoted to unfamiliar, even esoteric works, and proposed, to start with, a collection of Hugo Wolf's Lieder because they were unrepresented in any catalogue. It was to be paid for in advance on a subscription basis. And so began the first of many albums of Society recordings for the specialist collector.

Legge's position in the record industry was greatly enhanced. His increasingly wide and detailed knowledge continued to project his influence into the general music field and brought him into contact with most of the international conductors, instrumentalists and singers. The eccentric landed country gentleman, John Christie of Glyndebourne, had built a small opera house adjoining his seventeenth-century family house in the Sussex Downs. His idea of staging *Der Ring* there was a forlorn ambition fuelled by a pro-German attitude, which extended to the adoption of *Lederhosen* at home, as well as personal acquaintanceship with Bayreuth and the Wagner family.

By 1934, Christie had settled for Mozart instead of Wagner, and three joint promotions with HMV followed. The first was a highly praised Society recording by David Bicknell of *Le Nozze di Figaro*, for which Legge was co-opted to write the notes, as well as those for *Così* and *Don Giovanni* which followed. He heartily disliked the use of a piano for recitatives; disapproved of the way in which Fritz Busch handled the scores; felt the absence of musical decoration to be stylistically wrong and considered that some of the Glyndebourne singers were inadequate. In fact it was none of his business because his province was in the sister company, Columbia, but he did not like Bicknell in any case. He gleefully, and publicly, suggested the wording for a notice to be placed over the stage door at Glyndebourne: 'Ladies must remove their *apoggiature* before entering'.[4]

The fourth Glyndebourne Opera recording, scheduled for 1937, was to be *Die Zauberflöte*, but Legge was shocked by the inadequacy of a performance he heard at Glyndebourne that summer and, having now become sufficiently influential to gather support with the board, vetoed Christie's casting.

HMV particularly wanted to include *Die Zauberflöte* in their album series of the four greatest Mozart operas, and Legge not only agreed wholeheartedly that it must be included, but insisted that it would be a far better proposition were they to record the opera with the right conductor and in Berlin rather than Glyndebourne. To him, Sir Thomas Beecham seemed the right choice. After some discussion, Legge's proposal was accepted, the finance agreed, and Electrola in Berlin authorized to take care of the technical side. The board then formally invited Sir Thomas Beecham to conduct, and he graciously consented, with the proviso that Walter Legge accompanied him as his artistic assistant and record producer. They had both worked it all out this way in advance.

Naturally, Legge's realignment with HMV infuriated the Bicknell faction, who provided such a ridiculously small budget for the whole *Zauberflöte* production, including travel, hotel and living expenses, as to smack of sabotage. Beecham was known to travel, reside and dine only under first-class conditions, and *Die Zauberflöte* is a substantial opera. The whole Beecham–Legge enterprise was regarded by the Glyndebourne Opera as a snub to them, and their manager,

Rudolf Bing, still probably remembered this slight some quarter of a century later.

Beecham and Legge wanted Alexander Kipnis for Sarastro and Herbert Janssen for the Speaker of the Temple, but the one was Jewish and dared not go to Berlin, while the other was 'politically undesirable' and unlikely to be allowed to take part. After auditions of many basses, they were forced to settle for Wilhelm Strienz as Sarastro and Walter Grossman as Speaker, less famous, but vocally acceptable. Current rigidity in the German political system was causing all kinds of unexpected artistic difficulties such as these.

Tamino was to have been sung by Richard Tauber, an Odeon artist under contract to Parlophone, part of the HMV-Columbia (EMI) Group in Britain. There should have been no internal complications in signing him up, only the racial consideration as to whether his safety in Berlin might be guaranteed. However, hostile strings were pulled at headquarters in Hayes and, at the last moment, Parlophone declared Tauber to be 'unavailable' to HMV. So the second-choice leading tenor, Helge Roswaenge, was engaged instead, making up in ardour what was lost in Tauber's beauty of tone.

Beecham took it all very coolly. He told his partner to fly at once to Berlin, to make all necessary arrangements for them both, and to begin casting the principals. He would follow. 'The idea was to produce a *Zauberflöte* recording of such excellence that it would last for a very long time and be acceptable everywhere'[5] – which is why it consisted only of the music, because extended dialogue was always unacceptable on 78s.

There was nobody in Berlin who remotely resembled this dapper, super-confident and eccentric English conductor. Sir Thomas Beecham, Bart. immediately attracted attention because he was so very different. He even played the fool sometimes, but only to improve the atmosphere at a rehearsal or in the recording studio. This was a very unGerman thing to do, especially where music was concerned, and at first such behaviour was regarded with amazement and disapproval. However, Beecham knew Mozart's score by heart, was adept at getting exactly what he wanted by way of full co-operation from the artists, and secured the finest performance from singers and orchestral players alike.

At this time – November 1937 – Walter Legge looked serious, inscrutable and somewhat owlish in his thick spectacles; he always carried a walking stick and seemed far older than his thirty-one years. His intense concentration gave him a complete grasp of the proceedings and consequently, although unusually for him, he was far too preoccupied to scrutinize the female members of the Favre Chorus[6] among whom, altogether unperceived by him, was a young high soprano, almost twenty-two years old and very beautiful, called Elisabeth Schwarzkopf.

The opposition at HMV may have drawn first blood over Tauber, but they were totally unprepared for Beecham's resourcefulness. He had been able to add considerably to the meagre budget from a variety of perfectly legal sources in Germany, thanks to one of Legge's few dependable friends at Hayes, the chief accountant.[7] This enabled Beecham to continue working and living in his usual manner, in which Legge was delighted to join him.

When the recording was finished and everything paid for, there was enough cash left to buy the Berlin Staatsoper sets for both *Elektra* and *Die Entführung* at a knock-down price, which would prove an important asset for his 1938 Grand Opera Season at Covent Garden. Although Heinz Tietjen had an enormous state subvention for his opera houses, he was only too relieved to be able to dispose of those sets because the designer, Paolo Aravantinos, had recently become *persona non grata* with the regime.

Having worked with Sir Thomas and observed how that individual invariably managed to persuade others to go his way, Legge adopted many of the same tactics while assuming a degree of familiarity with the maestro. Beecham regarded this as tiresome, and referred to 'young Legge' as 'a mass of egregious fatuity'[8] for attempting so blatantly to ape his behaviour.

Beecham was prone to fits of temper, but often they were contrived. Legge's towering rages, on the other hand, were only too real: he did not have Beecham's finesse or engaging manner. He also lacked his Lancastrian wit, though none of his acerbity; and while Beecham's jokes live on, real or apocryphal, Legge's jibes are unprintable.

After the Second World War began in 1939, Legge initially remained with Columbia; but when his exceptional talents were fully recognized he was appointed to a job with Basil Dean, the successful West End stage director with responsibility for ENSA's[9] Drama Department. He was also overall Director of Entertainment. Dean was at ENSA's HQ in Drury Lane Theatre one morning, wondering how he was going to respond to a call demanding more 'good music' for the troops, when Walter Legge arrived.

> Providence blew a stormy petrel into my office, with a cigarette drooping from its mouth and waving a walking stick, a creature of uncertain temper with a supreme indifference to the feelings of those who sought to hinder its unerring flight . . . Ultimately it was mainly to him that ENSA's outstanding achievements in taking the finest music to millions of men and women in the Forces and the factories was due.[10]

Legge liked to think he was head of ENSA's music, but in fact he was only in charge of its Classical Division. Long before he had arrived, a certain Gerald Walcan-Bright was appointed chief, and he remained so, at least on paper, for he and his band had got a more popular kind of music swinging as early as 1940. He was universally known as Geraldo.[11]

Legge's first task was to send gramophone records to service units, the simplest and most effective way of getting music to the troops when there was little possibility of its being presented to them live, and, of course, this boosted EMI's wartime sales quite considerably.

As soon as France had been liberated, Legge took himself to Paris, uncomfortably – and unsuitably – dressed in khaki ENSA uniform, ostensibly to arrange concerts for the troops. This was his means of entrée and his efforts were very successful, but his principal reason for being there was a head-hunting expedition for European recording artists on behalf of HMV and Columbia.

In early January 1946 he threw away his uniform and travelled to neutral Switzerland where there was a recording company affiliated to EMI. To Legge's mind, it was being extraordinarily inactive, given the opportunities that existed in post-war Europe. So taking the matter in hand, he renewed pre-war contracts with the pianists Edwin Fischer and Wilhelm Backhaus within a fortnight, and also discovered the brilliant young Dinu Lipatti in Geneva, whom he also signed up.

As a British subject, Legge was not allowed to travel to Austria, nor was he permitted to conduct any business there, but he could act on behalf of the Swiss company which had neutral status. Even so, he was finding all his plans blocked by the authorities, because he held a British passport, not a Swiss one. There then occurred one of those rare, chance meetings. In his Zürich hotel, wondering how he was going to get to Vienna, Legge found himself next to an American, apparently some kind of movements officer, at the bar. After a substantial number of drinks, the stranger gratuitously handed over to Legge all the necessary permits and railway ticket for entrance to the forbidden city, including a first-class sleeper berth for that very night, all made out in somebody's else's name. But that did not deter Legge.

The following day, 16 January, refreshed and finally in Vienna, he got in touch with his pre-war amour, Hilde Konetzni, who invited him to escort her to a party at the Hofburg that evening. Now that its recent tenant had left, Emperor Franz Josef's Royal Palace was occupied for a month in rotation by each chairman of the four occupying powers, and on this occasion the Russian Commandant in Vienna was in residence.

Legge had not yet found Furtwängler, whom he knew to be there somewhere; but on his way to the party along the unlit streets, he nearly bumped into a very tall, thin man with an oversized head, arm in arm with two women, all laughing, talking loudly and steering an uncertain path. It was Furtwängler and two occasional companions. He was delighted to see Legge again for the first time since 1938 and gave him his telephone number, whereupon the trio went on their merry way, stumbling between pavement and gutter.[12]

In the congenial though unfamiliar surroundings of the Russian party, Legge renewed another pre-war acquaintance in Dr Egon Hilbert, the new chief of all Austrian State Theatres, from whom he sought information about his next quarry, Herbert von Karajan. The conductor was under a severe political cloud because of his attachment to the regime, and had been forbidden to appear in public, although he had given two concerts in Vienna during the previous week, on 12 and 13 January. Legge had been told about them by several people who had been there, and he was determined to seek out this interesting young man whom on Tiana Lemnitz's recommendation he once went to watch conducting at the Aachen Opera in 1938. Karajan was said to be living in reduced circumstances at a secret address in Vienna, but only two days after his arrival, Legge got hold of the number, called him, and suggested that they met.[13]

'If you want to see me, you must come here,' was the typical reply from a communal telephone. 'Here' was up many flights of stone steps into a shared room without electric light where Karajan's bed and table were curtained off from those of a complete stranger. Karajan was particularly depressed because his next post-war concert, due to have taken place that very evening, 18 January, had been banned by the Russians; but after he and Legge had been talking together in German for only a short while, he became far more animated and approachable.

Legge was certain that once the political clouds had cleared away Karajan was going to become highly significant to European music, to Columbia, later to EMI, and to him personally. He was such an important property that Legge hardly liked to let him out of his sight until he had been persuaded to sign an exclusive conducting contract with Columbia Records. This he did in full faith and without demur.

Another Karajan concert, planned for 2 March, had also been cancelled by the Russians, but the following day Legge, who was still in Vienna, told him that he was going to hear a performance of *The Barber of Seville*. Karajan was very much aware of what was going on among musicians, and not only in Vienna. He was shortly to begin rehearsals for the 1946 Salzburg Festival operas and had already cast his Susanna for *Figaro*. He had her in mind when he told Legge: 'There's a new soprano for Rosina tonight, just about the best singer we've got, if not the most promising in Central Europe today. Her name is Elisabeth Schwarzkopf.'[14] Neither she nor Karajan had, at that time, been politically cleared.

Walter Legge was certainly intrigued by Schwarzkopf in the Theater an der Wien that evening. She had a captivating personality and a remarkable voice, but he was certain she was singing Rosina in entirely the wrong way. A week or so later, she was at a house concert *chez* Baron Otto Mayr, where Legge immediately recognized her as the promising Rosina and, after a short conversation, offered her a recording contract. She replied firmly that she could not possibly accept such terms. Evidently she had quickly summed Legge up, for she insisted that he give her a proper audition, otherwise he might be buying a pig in a poke[15] and she didn't want that to happen. By 'a proper audition', she meant one which lasted for at least two hours.

Legge was startled. This girl was extraordinary! Nobody had adopted such an attitude towards him before: he had always been the one who made the conditions, and if anybody was fortunate enough to be auditioned by him and offered a contract, he dictated the circumstances. With all his commitments, Legge could not hear the disturbingly self-possessed young person for several weeks, but he told her that when he was able to arrange a general audition, she must apply and would be heard.

When this happened, in late March 1946, Schwarzkopf was invited to meet Legge at the Café Mozart beforehand; because of the occasion and what she had been advised, she wore a hat especially for the 'English gentleman', whose name nearly everybody in Vienna pronounced 'Leggé'. After this rendezvous, he took her across the road to the Musikverein for the delayed audition which Karajan had been asked to attend. He would be certain to know some of the voices, and his advice would be useful.

Schwarzkopf was heard first. She offered a number of her own selected items, after which Legge asked her to sing Wolf's Lied 'Wer rief dich denn?' from the *Italienisches Liederbuch* (*Italian Song Book*). Its very words suggest that Legge was trying to get his own back by being provocative:

Wer rief dich denn?	Who called you?
Wer hat dich herbestellt?	Who sent for you?
Wer rief dich kommen wenn es dir zur Last?	Who said you could come when it was awkward for you?
Geh' zu dem Liebchen, das dir mehr gefällt!	Go to your lover, who pleases you far more!
Wer rief dich denn?	Who called you?
Wer hat dich herbestellt?	Who summoned you here?

He made her go on and on, particularly with the last phrase, colouring it in different ways, encouraging her to find the best expression, not letting up himself nor allowing her to rest. Eventually Karajan could bear it no longer. He accused Legge of being a sadist, adding, 'I told you weeks ago that she is potentially the best singer in Central Europe,' and left in disgust.[16]

Legge worked on the Lied with Schwarzkopf for another hour because she was being so marvellously responsive to all his requests and suggestions. This was far too important an occasion for him to let pass, especially as he had been searching fruitlessly for his ideal Wolf singer for twenty years. Now, at last, he believed that he had found her. It had been a test of strength for Schwarzkopf, and she showed still more spirit – if not daring – by staying on after her ordeal to accompany the other singers, by sight or from memory, who had been waiting for hours to be heard. One wonders how much interest Legge took in them or if he had only called them in to make it look like an open audition, or to test Schwarzkopf's musicianship further. If it was indeed his sadism that had irritated Karajan, then Legge was perpetuating it by forcing Schwarzkopf to go on singing until he was totally satisfied. At the end of the gruelling audition and Wolf lesson, he was elated.

By the time Schwarzkopf signed her exclusive contract with Columbia Records, Legge had already told her she must regard herself, from now on, as a lyric soprano, a direction in which she had already begun to move. This was where her career lay and Legge was certain she should be singing Pamina, Donna Elvira, Eva and the *Figaro* Countess instead of Blondchen, Zerbinetta and other such scheming coloraturas with whom he had no musical or intellectual sympathy. He considered Olympia in *Tales of Hoffmann* to personify 'the very negation of human intelligence'.[17] Dolls did not appeal to Walter Legge.

Schwarzkopf had been listening to him carefully. It was a great triumph for her, musically, artistically, personally. Telefunken, for whom she had made four 78 rpm records in 1940, were taking time to recover from the war and the ravages of invading troops. There had been no new offers from them and, in any case, there might not be anybody still there who remembered her. On the other hand, the names of HMV and Columbia were famous world-wide. Legge knew and was known by all the leading European musicians, most of whom now had post-war contracts with him, and she would be joining them: Casals, Cortot, Fischer, Furtwängler, Gieseking, Klemperer, Schnabel – and Karajan. Schwarzkopf was well aware that she had bested Legge at the audition, which few others could claim. But he seemed to be taking her over completely, there and then. Whether Schwarzkopf thought that to be a good idea or not, she denies that she fell in love with him on the spot.[18]

According to Alec Robertson:[19]

> After the Second World War, Walter became in effect an impresario, ruthless in criticism, careless of popularity, fanatical about the maintenance of the highest standards, insistent on intensive rehearsal. These last were valuable qualities and with them went a passionate desire to be creative which he could only exercise through influencing the interpretations of others.

Having achieved a coup in Vienna, Walter Legge returned to England like a modern Autolycus, to display his tray of fine wares to his directors. They were naturally impressed by his achievements and he told them he wanted to get back to Vienna as soon as possible, to record both Karajan and Schwarzkopf, whom he praised highly.

Although, at the time, both artists were still politically suspect, Legge brushed that aside, got his sessions agreed, and set them up between September and November in the Brahmssaal and the Musikvereinsaal. Diplomatic strings were pulled at the Foreign Office to enable him to return to Austria legally, but meanwhile he was busy at the Abbey Road Studios in London rehearsing and recording Ginette Neveu, Artur Schnabel and Elisabeth Schumann, although he had already carefully planned an interesting and varied recording programme for that other E.S., his favourite new, young and very beautiful soprano in Vienna.

PART II

The Great Partnerships
1946–1948

It had now become easy for Schwarzkopf to resume her career without opposition or aggravation from the authorities. First of all, her voice, her main asset,
was being promoted by Walter Legge, groomed for Lieder and a different range
of operatic roles. He had planned a fine 78 rpm recording programme for her
under his direction, intending to make this a new and substantial aspect of her
career. Separately from these exciting developments, and outside Legge's direct
control, lay her establishment as a valued soprano of the Vienna State Opera,
with a growing number of fans and general delight in her appearances. If things
did not turn out as she hoped within Legge's empire, she still had her contract
with the Theater an der Wien.

On 23 October 1946 she made her double-first recording: with Columbia
Records and under Karajan's baton. It was Konstanze's 'Martern aller Arten'
from *Die Entführung*, never issued on 78, but released on LP and subsequently
on CD. It shows her well and truly in the coloratura mode, managing a top D
with ease but then finding the B below middle C rather unconvincingly. Her
only other studio recording from this opera was the 'Traurigkeit' aria made a
week later, which was not considered suitable for release. There was also a
particularly delightful pair of Schubert Lieder, 'Seligkeit' and 'Die Forelle'; light
and joyous, the 10-inch disc sold by the thousand when it first came out. In
addition, Bach's Cantata 208, some Handel, including 'Sweet Bird', and more
Mozart under Krips made up this early batch of records.

Schwarzkopf's career was reformed once she came under Walter Legge's
direct influence. She became the instrument which he intended to remould
and make into a perfect creation for the opera stage and the recital room. She
was a conscientious worker, of which he wholeheartedly approved; she was
strong and had a proud nature, which appealed to his masculinity because
he intended to remain the master, however much she gently opposed him.
Schwarzkopf had put herself into his hands to discover exactly how she was
going to respond to his direct and personal production in a new and different
style of vocal production. Was his advice going to be right for her in the future
as well as now? And was it likely to conflict with that of Josef Krips, musical

director at the Theater an der Wien, who was taking a great interest in her voice?

Herbert von Karajan, as we have seen, already knew and admired Schwarz-kopf's artistry, and was to play an important role in her life during the Karajan–Legge–Philharmonia enterprise, so it is fascinating to reflect upon how she might have fared had she remained at the Theater an der Wien and not been lured to England, however willingly. She probably did the right thing professionally by allowing herself to be snatched away from Vienna, the cradle of major post-war operatic talent, and although her progress might have been less accelerated, she would not – could not – have failed to achieve her ambition.

Walter Legge had more than five years' direct experience of continental musicians before the war; his name was universally known in the business; and, from 1947, he expected and found many doors obligingly held open for him, partly because he was in uniform and spoke fluent German, and partly because if he felt the situation required it, he could nonchalantly dangle a Columbia recording contract in front of him and get exactly what he wanted.

The Vienna Philharmonic was willing to play and the singers were longing to sing for him, while the EMI directors at Hayes were eagerly watching to see what else was forthcoming. What he had managed to achieve so far was phenomenal, and he was not the kind of operator likely to fall on his face, even in these treacherous circumstances, a fact that his enemies regretted. He was also depending a great deal on Karajan's future successes, although in 1946 the utterly self-contained and infuriatingly patient little man was biding his time while forbidden to conduct in public. But was a recording session public?

Legge decided to put it to the test, and so he let it be known that Karajan and the Vienna Philharmonic Orchestra were booked for a session the following day. A terrible commotion followed the news,[1] with an immediate telephone message from the Committee of the Vienna Philharmonic to say they felt the session could not possibly take place and urging Legge to come at once to their office. When he arrived, Karajan was already there. The Americans, whose turn it was to be installed in the Hofburg that month, had unequivocally forbidden him to conduct.

Legge took it calmly and forcefully. He had already checked with the British military authorities who confirmed that, as he already believed, the ban applied only to public concerts. The Americans were told so firmly, and Legge made it quite clear to them that he intended to go ahead as planned because a recording session was in an entirely different category. He was in the kind of mood which brooked no argument, especially as he was certain of his facts and the American spokesman might go to hell. In fact, as Legge reported: 'At the first session we did not get a note recorded – he was really out to show what he could do with the Vienna Philharmonic . . . We took an enormous time to get his first record out of him.'[2] That was of less importance than the very significant fact that the ban on Karajan was removed in the privacy of the recording studio and he could work with an orchestra again. Legge kept him well occupied until – and long after – he was politically cleared in October 1947.

Early in 1947, Schwarzkopf assumed two new roles. Walter Legge had been urging her to sing Donna Elvira in *Don Giovanni*, which she did for the first time at the Theater an der Wien where alternative sopranos in the role were Hilde Konetzni, Esther Réthy and Maud Cunitz. (Konetzni had sung this and other roles in London before the war, when Legge was Beecham's assistant at Covent Garden.) Schwarzkopf's début as Donna Elvira in Vienna on 19 January 1947 was not reviewed because it was a repertory performance. Paul Schöffler sang the Don; Helena Braun, Donna Anna; Hugo Meyer-Welfing, Don Ottavio; and Irmgard Seefried, Zerlina. Then, just over a month later, Schwarzkopf sang her first Violetta in *Traviata* under Josef Krips, who was championing her to the extent of persuading her to sing Zerbinetta in his new production of *Ariadne auf Naxos*. This was not in line with Legge's plans for her and, although she did it to please Krips, it was definitely the last time that she appeared as the Commedia dell'Arte flirt.

The Paris Opéra company had been to Vienna at the end of 1946 on a goodwill visit, when their conductor, Roger Desormière, had been inspired by hearing the Vienna State Opera's own performance of Mozart. He had managed to persuade the French cultural authorities to grant an exchange visit and so, in March 1947, the entire Viennese company – orchestra, staff, scenery and costumes – were conveyed by military train to Nice and Paris, so as to avoid any intermediate complications or civil objections that might ensue if they travelled in the normal way. Some French people were very touchy about 'allies' of the Third Reich.

David Webster, the general administrator of the new Covent Garden Opera, soon heard about the Vienna State Opera's plans, and invited them to sing in London. Their response was very positive, and although there were to be difficulties and opposition, not least from the Musicians' Union, Webster booked the company for September, bag and baggage. As Marcel Prawy, the Viennese writer and broadcaster, put it: 'By a curious paradox, it was the four-power occupation of Austria that was largely instrumental in re-introducing Austrian art and culture to the world at large . . .' by means of these early post-war tours.[3]

Webster was an astute Scot, and a sensitive man, despite his pugnacious features. He had learned his opera before the war among audiences of the great European houses; but it was his intimate knowledge of big business that got him the job at Covent Garden in the face of opposition from those with more artistic backgrounds.

The Royal Opera House was the first properly founded and financed British national opera in England, but it was too soon for Webster's organization to become fully established or its productions to be regarded highly abroad because of the many teething troubles involved in having to start an opera company from scratch.

From the start, Webster was sniped at by critics often impatiently and unfeelingly demanding immediate improvements, among whom Ernest Newman of the *Sunday Times* was the most sarcastic. To say that there was no competition in London with the Royal Opera House was not exactly true. The Carl Rosa Opera Company, which spent the majority of the year touring, and the Sadler's Wells Opera in Islington both operated on a modest scale and performed in English.

The London Music, Art and Drama Society, on the other hand, posed more of a threat. The company performed nightly at the Cambridge Theatre, Seven Dials, between June 1946 and May 1948,[4] and was owned by Jay Pomeroy, a Russian-born impresario with a passion for opera. In 1944 he had failed in his bid to obtain a lease for Covent Garden, but now he was promoting some splendid nights with Margherita Grandi and Mariano Stabile in *Tosca*, with Stabile and Martin Lawrence in *Don Pasquale*; Alda Noni, Marko Rothmüller, Italo Tajo; Stabile as Falstaff and the Don, Ljuba Welitsch as Donna Anna.

These were the highlights, and they offered severe competition with Covent Garden in spite of the old-fashioned, stock sets, and productions of the stand-and-deliver kind. But there were also too many performances that fell short of the best, and Pomeroy eventually went down for £250,000, a huge amount of money in the late 1940s. He was unlucky because his last season at the Stoll Theatre might have saved him from complete disaster had not Wagner and a heatwave intervened to keep the public away.[5]

The major London operatic attraction that summer of 1946 was the first post-war *Ring* at Covent Garden, after which Pomeroy disappeared from the scene and went back to his former lampshades business, according to current rumour.

In early 1947 the politically liberated Schwarzkopf was free to sing and to take part in that summer's Salzburg Festival where she was given one performance only: as Susanna in *Le Nozze di Figaro* under Krips. But it was a start. Then on to Lucerne, which is an ideal place for a festival and, being in neutral Switzerland, it meant that the directors had few qualms about employing musicians who were still not 'authorized' by the Allies as, indeed, had been true of Schwarzkopf,

Hotter and Furtwängler when their bookings were made. Furtwängler had been going in and out of neutral Sweden and Switzerland during the war, and was still welcome there.

The Allied authorities in Austria did not regard the matter in this way and were very angry with the Lucerne Festival Administration for inviting Furtwängler whose position was doubtful. But the Russians said that two such politically sensitive artists whose names had often been linked with Karajan's should not be paraded at an international festival. Neither the Swiss nor Furtwängler or Schwarzkopf cared in the least: it was a proper invitation to a neutral country, and the musicians could do what they liked there. And what they liked doing best was making music.

Furtwängler gave a deeply felt performance of the Brahms Requiem in which Schwarzkopf made her début in the soprano solo on 20 August, finding it a joy to work with him. Something of his unique gift as a conductor is captured in these words from the timpanist of the Berlin Philharmonic:

> One day I was sitting beside my kettledrums while a guest conductor was rehearsing . . . Suddenly the sound changed. There was warmth and intensity as if everything were at stake. Astonished, I looked up from my score to see if some new baton acrobatism had brought about this miracle. But it was still the same conductor. I looked at my colleagues. They were all staring at the door at the far end of the hall. There stood Furtwängler. His mere presence had suffered to draw those sounds from the orchestra.[6]

If he was able to kindle hardened orchestral musicians like this, it is small wonder that Schwarzkopf should have found him so inspiring. She sang Mozart's *Exsultate, jubilate* at a subsequent concert, a work she occasionally revived in the late 1940s.

In September she returned to London with the Vienna State Opera for their short season. Their very professional productions, costumes and singing gave younger members of London audiences their first opportunity to witness international opera performed to a standard far higher than anything else in London – just the kind of artistic inspiration which the struggling residents of Covent Garden needed. Some of the singers were not welcome in France or London: Esther Réthy and Schwarzkopf did not sing in Nice or Paris; Maud Cunitz sang the four Donna Elviras in France but not in London; and Réthy did not sing in London at all.[7]

Josef Krips opened the season with *Don Giovanni* when Schwarzkopf appeared in what was only her ninth Donna Elvira: she was to sing four more there against two different Donna Annas: Maria Cebotari and Ljuba Welitsch. She also sang a charming Marzelline in *Fidelio*, for the first time in her career, and five more performances with the star cast of Hilde Konetzni, Julius

Patzak, Paul Schöffler and Ludwig Weber, conducted by Clemens Krauss.

Schwarzkopf received an enthusiastic response from public and critics alike: 'She had the temperament and fire for Donna Elvira and sheer beauty of phrasing', wrote the *Times* critic.[8] Later on, at a Sunday charity concert, she sang two operatic arias, as did Richard Tauber, now an adopted Londoner. But it was Schwarzkopf, the *Times* critic again enthusiastically wrote, who 'once more showed that the human voice can be as fine an instrument of phrasing as the violin'.[9]

The last *Don Giovanni* of that London season was an historic performance, when Anton Dermota generously stepped down so that Richard Tauber might appear again as Don Ottavio among his former Viennese colleagues. He had last sung the role in June 1939 at Covent Garden, and now performed as though he had been singing it regularly ever since. His achievement was all the more extraordinary because one of his lungs had been removed.

Schwarzkopf has described her excitement during their scene together, when she found herself on stage facing the man who had been one of the most stylish of Mozart singers since she was a girl, a great tenor from another age. His voice and presence had a remarkable effect upon her, of course, but it was a unique experience for everybody in the theatre that night. Although they did not know it, Tauber was making his farewell to the stage: it was his last public performance; and it was also the last time Schwarzkopf sang Donna Elvira at Covent Garden, although she was often to be heard in the role at Milan, Vienna, Salzburg and elsewhere, with a challenging variety of singers and conductors.

Schwarzkopf recorded Donna Elvira's 'In quali eccessi . . . Mi tradì' under Krips in London, making it a testament of her vocal accomplishment at the time and her stage successes led to an invitation from Webster to join the Covent Garden Opera Company as leading lyric soprano. Hans Hotter, now associated almost exclusively with Wagner's music, was heard for the first time in London as a Mozart singer, but was asked back for Hans Sachs in *The Mastersingers*, Wotan in *The Valkyrie*, and King Mark in *Tristan and Isolda*, all initially in English.

This kind of operatic cross-pollination had already occurred the previous year when the Italian baritone, Paolo Silveri, moved to Covent Garden after first appearing there with the San Carlo Opera Company. Because Schwarzkopf had also expressed the wish to live in England whenever her Viennese commitments allowed, Walter Legge, acting as honest broker, put forward a persuasive argument to David Webster.

Meanwhile, she continued to be one of the stars in Vienna and, soon after her return there in mid-November, after the tour, she sang Agathe in *Der Freischütz* for the first time, under the very experienced Hans Knappertsbusch from Munich. But after a second performance a month later, Schwarzkopf never sang the role again.

Walter Legge affirmed that Schwarzkopf had reached a breakthrough in her international career by 1947 'on a broad front',[10] when she sang the Brahms Requiem, with Hotter and Furtwängler; but because the only other foreign visit she had made that year was to Salzburg, it seems to have been more a display of what she was about to show the world than an international achievement. In his statement, Legge may have been counting on contracts already signed for performances not yet undertaken, such as the impending Covent Garden appearances, the following year's Salzburg Festival, and a visit to La Scala by the Vienna State Opera which was to include her; but they had not yet happened.

Even so, a wider audience was already beginning to know Schwarzkopf's voice from the sale of her 78s; and at the end of 1947 she first recorded the solo soprano role in Beethoven's 'Choral' Symphony under Karajan in the Vienna studio, with the three finest contemporary singers for this work: Elisabeth Höngen, Julius Patzak and Hans Hotter. Schwarzkopf's pure, youthful and unaffected singing contributed to the success of the recording.

Legge also engaged Karajan to conduct the Brahms Requiem and make the first complete recording of the work using the same forces that had performed for Furtwängler in Lucerne. It may have been out of mischief or *Schadenfreude* on Legge's part, or perhaps Furtwängler wasn't free to conduct in Vienna; but the elder conductor's disappointment was intense. Nor was it the last time that this same set of circumstances occurred. Legge found Karajan easier to work with than the unpredictable Furtwängler.

Legge had convinced Schwarzkopf that she need not consider herself to be under an exclusive contract to Vienna, and should defer to Webster's beckoning. Krips was appalled when he heard what she was intending to do, not only because they would lose her, but because this wise little man, a wonderful musician, conductor and trainer, considered it would be undesirable for her at that important stage in her career. Further, he wished to help her during her transition from lyric coloratura to lyric soprano.

Consequently another rift ensued which upset Dr Hilbert and Josef Krips who took it personally. After all, Böhm had protected Schwarzkopf from the Deutsche Oper in 1945, she had been nursed by the Vienna State Opera after that and had been promoted to singing exactly the kind of repertoire she had been demanding in Berlin. Krips had gone to a great deal of trouble to prepare her for a number of new roles such as Agathe, and again the management considered her attitude to be both casual and ungrateful. They tried to persuade her to stay by saying that 'if she left their theatre for even three months a year she would lose her voice and be useless to them. But she and her voice survived it.'[11]

Negotiations were concluded between London and the reluctant Vienna State Opera up until the end of the 1948/49 season, and Schwarzkopf worked out her remaining contractual performances as a guest artist. As things turned out, she made only a few subsequent appearances in the Theater an der Wien and did not return to sing in Vienna until September 1957, two years after the Staatsoper had been rebuilt. As one who had sung principal roles in the old house, she was not there for its palingenesis.[12]

Vienna was one thing, Columbia Records was another, and nobody had any doubt or argument over Schwarzkopf's binding and exclusive contract with the record company for a substantial programme: Legge had seen to that. Her records would promote her popularity, and the British public, having bought them, would want to come and hear her in the Opera House. So ran one of Legge's many arguments in favour of her joining Webster. Legge and Webster never cared for one another, any more than Beecham and Webster did, but they agreed about Schwarzkopf. The wily Scot welcomed the support of such a highly experienced and industrious singer for £60 a week (worth about £900 today). Legge made certain that she was going to be cast as lyric heroines: Mimi, Pamina and Massenet's Manon, all of which he regarded as her real future, as well as in roles like Sophie and Susanna which suited her to perfection. She was being considered, too, for Gilda and Violetta because of her clean coloratura.

Webster's new young opera company was trying to establish its first season of 1947/48 with twelve productions, while the successful Sadler's Wells Ballet, eventually to become the Royal, and already streets ahead of the Opera in experience and finish, was sharing the stage to satisfy its public, to create programme variety and to allow time for the opera singers to rest and rehearse.

Once Schwarzkopf had settled in London, she was treated to a course of vocal interpretation from Walter Legge. He was astonished to discover that she had never owned a gramophone, which was incomprehensible to him because his life had been controlled by one; furthermore, by this time, his collection of records was approaching the size of a national archive – something Britain did not yet possess.

Legge has written[13] that he made his pupil listen over and over again to Rosa Ponselle for her timbre and line; to Nina Koshetz for her brilliance; and to the glorious Meta Seinemeyer who, as a fellow Teuton, knew how to make her voice sound Italian. Schwarzkopf also listened carefully to Lotte Lehmann's 'all-embracing generosity'; to Frida Leider's dramatic intensity and to Elisabeth Schumann's silvery charm and sprightliness. From Melba's recorded output on 78s, Legge chose only one word: 'Bada' from Mimi's 'Donde lieta uscì' in Act III of *La Bohème* because of the sudden freshness she puts into the word at this poignant moment in the story. The significance of John McCormack's marvellous A flat octave leap, and the following phrase, all in a single breath, towards the end of 'Come my beloved' from Handel's *Atalanta*, were further pearls from Legge's vast operatic knowledge.

Schwarzkopf certainly learned all she could from her eminent predecessors and, in addition, heard records of Fritz Kreisler and Artur Schnabel, whose inspired instrumental playing could be made to sound like singing. This taught her a great deal about legato, phrasing and sheer beauty of sound. Many years later, she confirmed to her own pupils the importance to singers of listening to the violin:

> stringed instruments are the only ones which can give you the fluid sound
> . . . It can really show what a legato is, which is very different for singers
> because it isn't second nature. You have to want to do it all the time, and if
> your concentration wanders and you are not listening to the legato, you lose
> it, because the other way of singing is so much easier.[14]

~ 9 ~

Covent Garden, London
1948–1950

By mid-January 1948 Josef Krips had put aside his disappointment over Schwarzkopf's severance from Vienna and saw her well coached before directing her first performance of Pamina in German at the Theater an der Wien. 'She is a lively, more human and sympathetic Pamina who also sang her part fluently and appropriately,' said one of the Viennese critics.[1]

Schwarzkopf was due to sing *The Magic Flute* in English, three weeks later, for the first time as a resident member of the Royal Opera House. Hans Hotter was to be the Speaker of the Temple. When she arrived for rehearsals, one of the first people she set eyes on was Peter Gellhorn, now a staff conductor. It was Gellhorn who had suddenly disappeared from Berlin, during her early days at the Hochschule, where he had sometimes accompanied her. Those times were too painful for him to have had any memories of the young blonde soprano. But she knew him at once[2] and addressed him as one Berliner to another. Gellhorn 'was very knowledgeable and very hardworking; unlike Reggie Goodall he had an excellent stick technique but nothing he could do as a conductor was ever right for the Press'.[3]

Schwarzkopf and he were to work together on several performances of *The Magic Flute*.

> In the matter of English words, it was to be noted that Mme Schwarzkopf, who sang the part of Pamina most beautifully, had no difficulty either in speech or song and that Mr Hans Hotter . . . might have passed for an English singer. She was a great success.[4]

So reported the *Times* critic, and Schwarzkopf continued to be so every time she sang Pamina at Covent Garden. The occasion gained an entirely new dimension as soon as she appeared because of that star quality which she had brought with her from Berlin and Vienna and which was so rare in post-war London's repertory performances.

At that time the casting of many of the smaller roles, and some of the larger ones, too, was far from ideal. The singers often got away with too much that was sub-standard and, too often, Covent Garden was palmed off with inferior guest artists from abroad, especially in an emergency, when they demanded exorbitant fees or a year's contract.[5] It became uncomfortable for David Webster, as he woke up morning after morning to find that his singers and often he too had been flayed by the critics, and especially, when Wagner was concerned, by Ernest Newman who spared none of his powerful though often witty castigation. Part of Webster's strength lay in his policy of appearing to be doing nothing when he was up against difficulties of any sort. This earned him from his board colleagues the initials, AP (Arch Procrastinator) or AD (Artful Dodger).[6] While many people outside the Royal Opera House found him exceedingly difficult to deal with, he maintained a paternal and in many cases affectionate relationship with those inside the organization and he seems to have had an especially soft spot for Schwarzkopf, whose professionalism he admired. It was becoming obvious in London that Schwarzkopf had a distinct advantage over other British and American sopranos who were singing the same roles. Because she was also performing some of them in German, at the Theater an der Wien, she was able to provide greater depth of knowledge and characterization.

Her practical introduction to *Der Rosenkavalier* had been as the First Noble Orphan in March 1939 at the Deutsche Oper, but when she finally sang Sophie, a role to which she was very well suited, it was in English at Covent Garden in February 1948. She easily attracted the audience's full attention whenever she was on stage, simply by being the most interesting person there. Unfortunately there remains no complete recorded performance of her Sophie, but her advance Vienna studio recording in 1947 of the Presentation Scene is a wonderful memento.

It begins at the approach of Octavian in Act II, with Schwarzkopf gasping in astonishment and anxiety (cries of 'Rofrano!' omitted), and then the Presentation, with Irmgard Seefried as a lightweight Octavian. (They never sang these roles together on stage.) Schwarzkopf is excellent in placing those top Bb s and Bs as Elisabeth Schumann once did; she is altogether the heroine, especially in duet, although the insufficient differentiation in timbre with Seefried is noticeable. When they are left together after the ceremony of chairs, Schwarzkopf's prattling and cheeky attitude is done to perfection, and the continuous excerpt ends immediately before the Baron's arrival. The Vienna Philharmonic play beautifully, and Karajan conducts, although his name could not be printed on the record label at the time.

On stage, Schwarzkopf displayed her youthful vigour and strong character as Sophie in the more aggressive moments towards the end of Acts II and III with a voice to match, making the audience wonder how – and for how long – Octavian was going to fare as her husband. The *Times* critic particularly welcomed her Sophie:

Mme Schwarzkopf has already shown us that she can sing effortlessly, purely and affectionately. Her sure high notes now put the final touch of beauty to the concerted music . . . her characterization is dramatically true in that she conveys in succession the ingenuousness, the spirit and the sweetness of the girl.[7]

David Franklin was her first Ochs, a painful characterization, and the horse-play which she had to accept from him was crude in quite the wrong way, but he did not prevent Sophie from becoming one of Schwarzkopf's more affecting creations, of which she gave only nine performances in London.

She had been singing Violetta at the Theater an der Wien, and was preparing it in English for London. Verdi's tragic heroine makes widely varied vocal and emotional demands, and it came as no surprise that Schwarzkopf's interpretation sharply divided audiences.

'Too cold by far,' said some; 'Quite unsuitable,' said others. *The Times* considered her more favourably because she: 'added to her laurels for sheer, dramatic power in carrying the main burden of the opera with the same ease as she shows in the phrasing and the vocal mastery of her singing'.[8]

The conductor, Reginald Goodall, was a Furtwängler disciple, and his pre-ferred repertoire was German; as Geraint Evans put it, 'singers loved to learn with him'[9]. Schwarzkopf was well supported in the pit, and on stage by Kenneth Neate as her lover and, especially, by the well-sung, sympathetic father of Paolo Silveri. The slightly quirky production was by Tyrone Guthrie, who had reverted to Dumas' French names in the novel, so we had Marguérite, Armand and Duval. The sets, by Sophie Fedorovich, were most effective in their sim-plicity.

Geraint Evans, then a beginner at Covent Garden, has recalled how, when Violetta collapses on a chair in the gambling scene, 'we men were always eager to cluster round and comfort her, as we were supposed to do, so that we could catch a glimpse of that lovely bosom as she caught her breath and the bodice stood away from it'.[10] (Presumably this stage business was not in the prompt-book.)

'Collapse' is a word not usually associated with Schwarzkopf, but during a performance of *Die Entführung* at the Theater an der Wien on 21 June 1948, something remarkable occurred. One keen Viennese opera-goer who heard her as Konstanze on that occasion vouches for the fact that she cracked on a top note, lost her nerve and ran off in tears.[11] Unhappy as it may be to record this, it is symptomatic of the strain and pressures to which even the most assured and experienced artist is sometimes forced to submit under opera house conditions and personal stresses.

Schwarzkopf's next major assumption was in August 1948, when she went back to Salzburg and sang the role of Blessèd Spirit in Gluck's *Orpheus und*

Euridike, which was an unusual credit. Elisabeth Höngen and Maria Cebotari were the lovers and Sena Jurinac sang Amor. Karajan, now released from all political restrictions, was at last able to conduct at Salzburg, much to Furt-wängler's disgust. The tall man was back for *Fidelio* in which the up-and-coming Swiss soprano, Lisa Della Casa, sang Marzelline.

Schwarzkopf was being groomed by Karajan for the *Figaro* Countess, and she sang it five times during the festival amongst a distinguished cast that included Seefried as Susanna, Jurinac as Cherubino and Giuseppe Taddei as Figaro. Not much has been said about this performance but Karajan, who was very keen for Schwarzkopf to undertake it, booked her for two more performances at La Scala, at the end of the year. He supported her so vehemently that she put everything she had into it but, as will be seen, his theoretical casting was sometimes more successful than the practical result.

Schwarzkopf went on to Lucerne for two performances of the 'Choral' Symphony with Furtwängler, which was a welcome rest after the exertions of Salzburg. At the beginning of the international opera season in September, she divided her time between Vienna and London and took on the new role of Eva in *The Mastersingers*. There was a purpose in this which would not have been apparent to the Covent Garden audience at her single performance on 23 November under Karl Rankl. Apart from the Swiss tenor, Franz Lechleitner, baffled by the English text, it was a local cast and a homespun production in pre-war sets, although Murray Dickie excelled as David.

Then came Schwarzkopf's participation in the Vienna Company's visit to Milan. This was only her sixth *Figaro* Countess, which she was presenting to the knowledgeable and highly critical audience at La Scala as her début there. She was safe in Karajan's hands and the cast was almost the same as at Salzburg, which reassured her. Seefried and Maria Cebotari, a former Countess, alternated as Susanna in the two performances.

In December, Schwarzkopf began rehearsing for a new production of *Figaro* in English at Covent Garden, with real fireworks in the last act. This was to be directed by Peter Brook, an extraordinarily gifted man of the theatre, but less successful in the opera house because, like Tyrone Guthrie, he seemed unable to reconcile his innate sense of drama with the demands of the music.

Geraint Evans was cast as Figaro in this production, a new role for him, with Schwarzkopf as Susanna rather than the Countess. As they were going to play many important scenes together, she suggested that they put in some work on them, 'together with Walter Legge'. Evans had not heard of Walter Legge, nor of his association with Schwarzkopf; so he was not aware that Legge was known in Vienna as the *Schallplattenkönig* (Gramophone record King), or that their proposed rendezvous, 'an old Victorian house in Abbey Road', was EMI's main recording studio.

But one thing was very clear to Evans after the three of them had been rehearsing together for a short time.

> . . . the way he sometimes spoke to her in front of me was no way to talk to a lady, and one day when she was out of the room I said as much. I ventured to tell him I thought he was humiliating her, as well as embarrassing me.

Legge moderated his language but, annoyed at being criticized, did not cast Evans in any of his future recordings.[12] The production went ahead as planned and the *Times* critic made the following assessment of Schwarzkopf's Susanna:

> [She] never forgot that she was a lady's maid. Articulation of words was creditable from almost all – Mme Schwarzkopf's being an example to many an Englishborn soprano, and Mr Hans Braun, new from Vienna, as the Count, to foreigners who are willing to essay a role in English. Mme Schwarzkopf is such a Susanna as Mme Schumann once was. Every vocal inflexion is touched with significance and the gesture that accompanies it is invariably apt: words, tone, action, phrasing, all work together.[13]

Eric Blom held the minority and unsubstantiated opinion that she failed as an actress with her Susanna.[14]

Now that she had become established in Floral Street, Schwarzkopf was broadening her scope and her repertoire, and the news that she was making London her headquarters raised many eyebrows internationally. Here was a stunning young soprano, already a favourite on the Opernring in Vienna and singing at Salzburg, an annual visitor to the prestigious Lucerne Festival and becoming increasingly familiar through her recordings. Yet she had to go to London, of all places, where it was true that there was a lovely opera house, but what a company! After her operatic education in the efficiently run Deutsche Oper, whose standards remained high even in wartime, what could she think of Covent Garden's *Schlamperei?* She was seen as being amongst a group of beginners – or dug-outs – murdering Mozart in English. Can it have been the promise of a huge recording programme with a 'family' orchestra and enormous influence in the musical world that made her do this?

There was another matter that would not go away. In 1941, Walter Legge had married the mezzo-soprano Nancy Evans. Their daughter Helga grew up in Chalfont St Giles with Legge's mother and sister. The marriage was not a success, and the couple's inability to agree on important questions had damaged Legge's ego. When Nancy and Helga went to live in London after the war, he was not welcome there; and while he seemed to be doing all he could to bring the family together again, his main motive was to prevent the total collapse of the marriage, for the idea of any personal failure was anathema to him. Nancy had a very sunny and loyal disposition, in marked contrast to Walter's, and the main differences between them can be accounted for by his character and habits. Nancy found it impossible to put up with him any more; and although she was still legally Mrs Legge, she had many friends and well-wishers as Nancy Evans, the highly attractive singer who had scored successes at Glyndebourne and with the English Opera Group. Legge had put this marital tangle out of his mind as far as he could, for there were pressing and important matters to attend to with Schwarzkopf and her career.

William Walton had been commissioned by the BBC to compose a major opera as a national contribution to the proposed Festival of Britain scheduled for 1951. His librettist was the poet Christopher Hassall, and after spending some time searching for a suitable subject, they agreed on *Troilus and Cressida*. Walton, who had known Legge for some time, asked for Schwarzkopf to take the leading soprano role of Cressida. Legge applauded the compliment, for it fitted well with his plan to raise Schwarzkopf's international status, always providing the opera was of the kind that travelled, and he agreed. So Walton began the composition of Cressida with Schwarzkopf's voice in his mind.

As he and Hassall progressed, the poet had been agreeing amicably with all the composer's requests by making considerable revisions. Walton used to point to the shape of lines at certain places in Italian libretti, as examples for Hassall, until they were both entirely satisfied, but there were many changes and the third act proved to be the most complicated.

In March 1949 Schwarzkopf rejoined the Viennese company as Susanna for a visit to Paris, where she gave all four performances under Karl Böhm, with Maria Reining as the Countess; then she sang a single Susanna with the Covent Garden Opera Company on a short provincial tour to Birmingham. Tours were unpopular, but her name was a draw, so she agreed to go in order to gain further experience in singing a second Eva there as well. An agreement would also soon materialize for her to sing Eva in *Die Meistersinger* under Karajan at the Bayreuth Festival of 1951. She now had some experience of it, though in the wrong language and ambience.

Schwarzkopf has remarked on the problems which ensue when a singer has to change from one language to another:

> The difficulty is that every language has its own vowel sound and you cannot sing German opera with an Italian vowel sound. Nor can you do German opera with an English vowel sound, nor vice versa . . . even though they told me at Covent Garden that my pronunciation was clearer than that of the English singers, I was very conscious that it wasn't really a very English sound.[15]

The Susannas continued for a while in London, matched – and matchless – against several singers of the Countess, among whom only Sylvia Fisher seemed to know what she was doing. Schwarzkopf stayed on in London, contributing ten invaluable roles to the company between 1948 and 1951 and bringing authentic international class to everything she undertook, even to Madam Butterfly which did not exactly suit her.

Schwarzkopf and Otto Klemperer had seldom worked together, but in September 1949 she accompanied him on a tour to Australia. They did three concerts of Handel and Bach in Sydney, then another three of Mozart and Mahler in Melbourne; Schwarzkopf also sang in the Mahler Fourth Symphony, a work she was later to record with Klemperer. She returned to the Royal Opera House for the start of the 1949/50 season in October to sing Susanna yet again.

Karajan never conducted at Covent Garden, although he occasionally dropped in quietly for performances or, more often, parts of them, in order to hear singers. He was inclined to despise London's stage and concert hall lighting equipment (much of it pre-war), fancying himself as a modern lighting expert, for whom only the best would do. Since the destruction of Queen's Hall in 1941, and before the Royal Festival Hall was built as part of the South Bank complex in 1951, the Royal Albert Hall was the only auditorium in London of any size – and what a size! However, in November 1949 Karajan conducted a remarkable performance of Beethoven's 'Choral' Symphony at 'the Albert', when Schwarzkopf gave a breathtakingly beautiful account of the soprano solo.

The *Times* critic called it a 'coherent and convincing interpretation', stressing its musical power and lyrical beauty. The lightning response of all concerned, including Rudolf Schock (replacing the announced Walter Ludwig at short notice) and Boris Christoff, went a long way to achieving a memorable performance of the great work, which Karajan controlled by remaining 'firm but modest'.[16]

At the beginning of January 1950, entirely unprompted by Karajan, Schwarzkopf experimented with a new operatic character. She had ventured into the Oriental with Liù in *Turandot* (but only twice) in Vienna under Böhm; now it was the still more demanding role of Madame Butterfly whom she sang seven times at Covent Garden in a new production by Robert Helpmann. This outstandingly talented man of the theatre had danced the principal noble and comic roles with the Sadler's Wells Ballet before, during and after the war, and had choreographed four ballets. He was also a straight actor, who had played Hamlet and other major roles in the West End and at Stratford-on-Avon; he had appeared in films, too, and was now turning his hand to opera production.

Madam Butterfly was conceived with skill and in exemplary taste, aided by Sophie Fedorovich's imaginative sets. Monica Sinclair, an appealing young contralto who was already making her mark in the Opera Company, sang Suzuki with great style and passion. This *Butterfly* was moderately successful although the performance did not reach out far enough to achieve the grandeur of tragedy. When this is allowed to happen in a Puccini opera, we are all too often left wallowing in sentimentality. Schwarzkopf's offstage voice for the Entrance was magical, however; her dignified bearing and conception of the role were just right, and she put into it all her experience and effort, avoiding the temptation to caricature which so often leads the unwary Western soprano astray. Yet surprisingly for Schwarzkopf, it didn't really come off: she seemed too cool in her association with Kenneth Neate as Pinkerton, and altogether out of sympathy with Puccini's fragile heroine. So although it was certainly no failure, afterwards Schwarzkopf wanted to shake off memories of the role – but in a career of such magnitude as hers, not every one can be a winner, as was soon to be brought home to her still more forcibly. Having been indisposed and off for one of the scheduled performances, she was suddenly obliged to sing another *Butterfly*, in place of a cancelled *Rosenkavalier*. Near the end of the first interval, she walked slowly to the prompt corner, picked up the stage manager's score left open ready for the next act, looked carefully at the page she wanted, then closed the bound volume, put it back, and now, fully in character, walked with tiny steps on to the stage to begin Act II.[17]

On one of her rare visits to the Royal Albert Hall, between *Butterfly* performances, Schwarzkopf sang the *Exsultate, jubilate* in an all-Mozart concert conducted by Rafael Kubelik. It was a sparkling performance and something of a relief from the last three symphonies (Thirty nine, Forty and the 'Jupiter'), whose individual characters, to this listener, seemed to have merged into one. Fortunately, Schwarzkopf has recorded the *Exsultate*.

Schwarzkopf's next new role at Covent Garden was as Manon in Massenet's opera. The caprices of this flighty creature seemed to suit her well but, as in the case of her Butterfly, warmth and tenderness were lacking. *The Times* welcomed the revival of this sugary operatic confection, generally considered the finest of Massenet's operas. It always makes excellent entertainment, and Schwarzkopf was described as: 'good dramatically as well as vocally. She shows Manon in states as a silly goose, a weakling fool, a hard-boiled good-timer and a pathetic failure.'[18] Walter Midgley was her partner in this sensible production by Frederick Ashton, another former principal dancer and choreographer from the Royal Ballet. He saw to it that 'they both seized all the opportunities going. The words were more intelligible than usual.' When Victoria de los Angeles took over Manon in a few performances, it seemed an altogether different opera, although she did no disservice to Schwarzkopf's interpretation.

From 1945 Dr Ernst Roth of Boosey & Hawkes, London, became Richard Strauss's new publisher. The German branch of the company had taken over a large slice of the copyright from the bombed-out Fürstners in 1943. After the war, Dr Roth established a strong personal contact with the composer and obtained his permission for performance of his latest work, *Four Songs for Soprano Voice and Orchestra*, on the understanding that they were given by a first-class singer and conductor. Strauss had not specified any particular orchestra, but its excellence was taken for granted, and the Philharmonia was engaged. Then Legge got the bit between his teeth and, while they were both in Milan, approached Wilhelm Furtwängler. Although he had engagements in Buenos Aires during April and the first half of May, he agreed to conduct the new work in London on 22 May even though rehearsal time was going to be limited. The soprano was to be the Norwegian Kirsten Flagstad, also in Milan at the same time and of whom one of her biographers wrote: 'it had been the composer's wish that she sing them in their first public performance'.[19] The *tessitura* of 'Frühling' makes this unlikely: Legge persuaded Flagstad to sing all four Songs, thus raising expectations of a rush for every seat in the Royal Albert Hall. A substantial Wagnerian item would make up the programme.

Schwarzkopf was not directly concerned, because she was singing in repertory at Covent Garden and also had a Lieder recital with Gerald Moore immediately before the great Strauss event. She had read the Songs with interest but without any immediate view to performing them; they were not then known as *Vier letzte Lieder* (*The Four Last Songs*) as they are now.

Schwarzkopf knew Flagstad well and was able to give her some moral support with a task that was proving far more demanding than the soprano had imagined it would be when she agreed to sing. Walter Legge was worried about the whole business. He felt that Strauss, with his indifferent hearing in old age, had very slightly miscalculated the orchestral texture for what was always going to be a performance from the platform rather than with the orchestra in the pit and the singer on the stage.[20] Nor did Furtwängler's or Flagstad's performances at rehearsal convince Legge. The Songs may have operatic affinities, but they are still essentially concert pieces, and Flagstad's own concern about her ability to do them justice was evident. Schwarzkopf sat in at the last rehearsal, listening and observing, but because she was singing Pamina that evening she had to miss the Strauss event at the Royal Albert Hall.

Furtwängler's handling of the new and very sensitive work understandably took up most of the three hours of rehearsal, with the rest of the familiar programme being left until evening. The Maharajah of Mysore, Patron of the Philharmonia Orchestra, asked for acetate discs of the Songs to be taken for him at the rehearsal. Legge was agreeable to this but the orchestra was not, and demanded, and got, a session's payment in advance. It is believed that three sets were taken of which one was for the Maharajah, and one for Legge.

In *The Times* of 13 May there had been an announcement on the concerts page: 'Four Orchestral Songs – Strauss. World's First Performance', but a week later, and only two days before the concert, it had been changed to 'Three

Orchestral Songs – Strauss'. This uncertainty was resolved on the night, when Flagstad sang with the music in her hands.

There was no note in the printed programme about the Songs' provenance, let alone their character, words or scoring: it was very much a world première of a brand-new, unknown composition. Several pirated versions of this performance are available on disc mainly in very poor sound; the best one to be found was published in 1994.[21]

On subsequent occasions when Flagstad gave the Songs – though never again in London – she dropped 'Frühling' altogether; nor would she record any of them commercially.

Lisa Della Casa was the first to record the *Four Last Songs* in the studio under Karl Böhm's direction. It was not long before Schwarzkopf was persuaded to sing them and, having done so, she became one of their most celebrated interpreters, due both to her recordings and to the infrequent concerts in which she included the Songs.

A week after this world première, the Russian composer Nicolas Medtner was given a concert at the Wigmore Hall, mainly at the request of the Maharajah of Mysore who was his patron also. Schwarzkopf sang some of Medtner's songs and they were later recorded, but she does not seem to have enjoyed the experience of working with him. When asked about it much later, for a biography of Medtner, she would say nothing at all about him.

Medtner seems to have been a curious character. Two visitors called by appointment one day to see him in London, and the conversation went smoothly until one of them mentioned his fellow Russian, Rachmaninov. Medtner went bright red in the face, his wife stood up and unceremoniously showed the visitors the door, saying to them as they left the room, 'Nobody must ever mention another composer's name in my husband's presence.'

In 1950, the bicentenary of J. S. Bach's death, Karajan chalked up a total of five performances of the B minor Mass in Milan, Vienna and Perugia, and Schwarzkopf sang in all of them. Legge began a recording with the Vienna Symphony Orchestra, in connection with a concert, and seized the opportunity of engaging Kathleen Ferrier in the alto role, but time passed and her final illness and death prevented it from being finished. Three movements, two featuring her and Schwarzkopf together, are now available on CD, because Legge allowed the tape machines to be kept running during a rehearsal, and so the unique combination of their two voices was captured.

In the summer of 1950, Schwarzkopf sang three different operas, for the first time under Wilhelm Furtwängler, two at Salzburg and the third at Lucerne. The first was *Don Giovanni*, in which she presented her ever-developing Donna Elvira, with gratitude to the conductor for his deep knowledge of the work and his careful guidance. Furtwängler then gave his famous *Fidelio* with Kirsten

Flagstad, Julius Patzak and Paul Schöffler, which had been heard at Salzburg the previous summer when Irmgard Seefried sang Marzelline. Now Schwarzkopf repeated the role which she had first sung so successfully with the Vienna State Opera on their visit to London three years before. One of these 1950 performances is available in good sound on CD, giving a valuable indication of Schwarzkopf in the complete role.

She always sang Marzelline convincingly and winningly. One especially remembers her look of disbelief, and then horror, when she realizes that her beloved 'Fidelio' is in reality a woman more completely feminine than herself. Furtwängler gave the five performances 'a warmth and impetuosity highlit by the vigour of the soldiers' march in Act I and the immense joyfulness of the last scene' in Günther Rennert's apt and gripping production. The *Gazette de Lausanne* critic, in comparing like with unlike, certainly intended to be complimentary towards both ladies, when he curiously declared that Schwarz-kopf was 'magnificent, equal to Kirsten Flagstad'.[22]

Lucerne that year saw a performance of Berlioz's *Damnation de Faust*, in which Schwarzkopf sang Marguerite for the first time. Furtwängler rarely conducted French music,[23] and this is the only Berlioz work he ever did. Schwarzkopf sang it in concert performances spasmodically during her career.

It was in 1950 that Schwarzkopf appeared for the first time at a Promenade Concert at the Royal Albert Hall. This was during the last week of the season when she sang Schubert's 'Der Hirt auf dem Felsen' ('The Shepherd on the Rock'). Liszt was a great embroiderer of Schubert and, on this occasion, the LPO gave his orchestral version of the *Wanderer Fantasie*, as expected. The audience was not prepared, however, for his inflated arrangement of the delicate voice–clarinet–piano original of 'Der Hirt auf dem Felsen', with Basil Cameron conducting an (admittedly small) orchestra that replaced the keyboard instrument. Schwarzkopf's voice came over beautifully in this enchanting com-position which, regrettably, she never recorded.

The last time she had sung at the Albert Hall had been with Karajan the previous year, but his career had now taken wing. With his appointment as musical director of La Scala, Milan, he was to make his first major step as an impresario, which would soon take him to Vienna, Salzburg and Berlin. Herbert von Karajan possessed endless patience and was prepared to wait for years if necessary to achieve his objectives: there was something feline about him; indeed he had observed and copied the methods of Siamese cats, which lie stretched on the floor to relax completely, and adopted this position himself while learning his scores.[24] Now he was poised and waiting for the moment to pounce, because he saw himself as the only logical contender for the Berlin Philharmonic Orchestra, once death had removed Furtwängler from that par-ticular podium.

He was also waiting for the opportunity to replace Böhm, Krips and Krauss at the Vienna State Opera and to take artistic control there, along with the Salzburg Festival. When that happened, he intended to combine forces with La Scala, in the certain knowledge that he was going to be supremo there as well. Then the productions and casts would become interchangeable, a refinement of the grand scheme once proposed for opera houses in the Third Reich by Joseph Goebbels. Karajan had the next twenty years mapped out for himself, and although some of this did not materialize quite as he intended, a great deal eventually did. He evidently did not believe that the fickle Viennese were either strong or determined enough to remove him against his will, or anticipate that outside forces might become a danger to his supremacy.

But it soon became apparent that another Austrian superman in Europe, whether a painter *manqué* or a musician, was going to be undesirable, and especially one as independent and self-willed, lacking any control from one of the recognized power groups.

In Milan, Karajan was able to offer his choicest singers a variety of interesting roles and ample rehearsal time. Rehearsals were not at all conventional. Sometimes they lasted for ten hours at a time, with Karajan giving the singers all of his considerable support. Schwarzkopf has often stated that she demanded three weeks to rehearse a new role. Her request met, she would then put on a magnificent show and pull in full houses – a great asset to any management. Karajan recognized this, and Schwarzkopf was only too willing to help him put La Scala firmly back on the map as one of the two leading houses in Europe. As she had already become a great favourite of the Milanese public, he continued to mount a wide variety of works from the standard repertoire, casting her as one of his leading Mozart and Strauss sopranos. So far, so good.

10

Callas, Wagner and Karajan
1951

Antonio Ghiringelli as sovrintendente (artistic director) and Herbert von Karajan as musical director both began new careers at La Scala, Milan, in 1948, after the departure of the Fascist sovrintendente, Gino Marinuzzi. 'My first big step was La Scala in Milan,' Karajan recollected later. 'They had always wanted me. I had conducted a single concert there in 1936. They had told me later on, when I was in Milan after the war, that the moment all the occupation business was finished I should come back. So I did and began a long and happy association with them.'[1]

The artistic directorship at La Scala, like those of lesser opera houses in Italy, is always a political appointment of prime importance, in which the Mafia are said to exercise considerable influence. Ghiringelli was a self-made man of humble origins[2] who had a great love for the theatre without having received any musical training. He was an astute businessman and an elegant wheeler-dealer but also a bully, full of his own importance and a predator of young ballet and chorus girls. He used to tell them firmly: 'Going to bed with me gives you no hope for a better part. Understand that? *No hope.* But if you don't go to bed with me, you have the *certainty* of no better part.'[3]

He and Karajan knew exactly how they stood vis-à-vis each other, so they managed to co-exist; but it is not surprising that Callas and Ghiringelli conceived an instant and mutual dislike: she was as earthy and tough as he was. Schwarzkopf came to La Scala thanks to Karajan and so virtually bypassed Ghiringelli except for the contract, which needed careful negotiation because of what appeared to be conflicting requirements from Covent Garden where she was still a principal soprano.

Karajan had asked for, and was given, the opportunity to direct *Tannhäuser* with Schwarzkopf as Elisabeth of Thuringia in what was only her second principal Wagnerian role. At the very end of December 1950 and into the New Year, there were five performances. She looked lovely but the voice was not entirely adequate to Wagner's demands, as comparison with other eminent portrayers of the role makes clear. Although this *Tannhäuser* was an expensive Preetorius production with the strong male support of Hans Beirer, Hans Braun and Gottlob Frick, it was not reckoned a success. All the same, Schwarzkopf regarded it as important to her career because it was her proper entrée to La Scala as an individual guest artist, rather than as a member of a visiting opera company. She had appeared there in 1948 once, as the *Figaro* Countess with the Vienna State Opera when they came to Milan; but now she had her foot well and truly in the door, especially as Elisabeth was to be followed by Donna Elvira.

In keeping with Italian newspaper reviews on opera, the distinguished critic Franco Abiati delivered a lofty diatribe, making a direct comparison between *Tannhäuser* and Verdi's *Otello*. He then complimented Karajan for using the first (or what is generally known as the Dresden) edition of the opera, and mentioned the designer; but there was absolutely no discussion of the singers.[4]

After the fourth performance of *Tannhäuser*, Schwarzkopf had to risk a winter flight to London to sing Violetta at Covent Garden under Peter Gellhorn, in accordance with her English contract; then she returned to Milan for her last Elisabeth and the following day sang Elvira in a lavish new production of *Don Giovanni*. This had sumptuous sets by Wilhelm Reinking, Karajan conducted and Victoria de los Angeles sang a Donna Anna remarkable for sheer beauty of sound and impassioned acting. Schwarzkopf, who valued the Spanish soprano's technique and ability more than those of almost any other contemporaries, afterwards declared her admiration for de los Angeles in these words: 'She is quite astounding. She sings with miraculous ease and her legato is unsurpassed. Once in 1952 (or so) I heard her as Violetta and I decided not to sing it again. [She also said this about Callas.] I have not got a great voice. That is why I do not sing all the roles in opera.'[5]

After the last Elvira on 28 January, Schwarzkopf again flew back to London for another Violetta the following day, but by then her Scala performances were over for the time being. She was to sing many more Donna Elviras but only one Elisabeth, and that was to be in Vienna, again under Karajan's baton, but a long time afterwards. It seemed a curious resurrection and received this even more curious, retrospective review:

> Elisabeth Schwarzkopf sang Elisabeth and took pains to present a well-balanced view of the role, which of course is not for her. A few years ago, also under Karajan, she had no real success in *Tannhäuser* at La Scala.
>
> Memories of that production indicate that this sensitive artist was suffering acutely from nervousness. Her large voice did not seem able to adapt to Elisabeth's cantilena in the course of the evening, and even the Prayer lacked that inner peace which one had a right to expect.[6]

At some time 'early in 1951', according to Schwarzkopf and Legge,[7] they were staying in Rome and, one evening when she was resting before a concert, he went to the opera to hear Maria Callas in person for the first time. He had been thrilled by her early 78s for Cetra, but was quite certain that she would record far better under his direction and was determined to capture her for Columbia.

On this particular occasion Callas was singing Norma, and after the first act Legge was so delighted with what he had heard that he telephoned Schwarzkopf and urged her to join him at the opera house immediately. To his great surprise, she refused. Nobody, she replied, not even he, was going to prevent her from listening on the radio to the marvellous soprano voice of one Maria Meneghini Callas as Norma. It is a good story and only a pity that it does not fit with the facts. Are we to suppose that Schwarzkopf was unaware that Legge had gone to the opera that evening or of who was singing there? The dates do not fit, either.

Callas sang Norma in Rome for five performances in late February and early March 1950, when Schwarzkopf was in London. And when Schwarzkopf was preparing for her only Italian Lieder recital in three years, on 5 March 1950 in Florence, Callas was in Mexico City. They were all together in Milan a year later, however, when Callas was singing Norma between performances of Schwarzkopf's first Marschallin; and it is impossible to believe that Callas's voice was unknown to Schwarzkopf and Legge at that late date. The point of the story is not about conflicting dates, but about Legge's business methods.

He pursued his prey with immense skill, but she did not intend to submit easily. Difficulties were piled in his way by Callas herself, by her industrialist husband, Giovanni Battista Meneghini, by constant delays, as well as by their cavalier and totally unBritish treatment of contracts. Only after a long time, heated arguments and less than honourable dealings did Callas become a Columbia artist, and in July 1952 Legge at last jubilantly exclaimed – as Scarpia does in *Tosca* – 'Finalmente mia!'

It was in 1952 that Maria Callas broke out of the smaller Italian opera house circuit and spread her talents wider. Owing to the perspicacity of David Webster, to whom she was forever grateful, she appeared first at Covent Garden and then at La Scala, on the brink of international fame, when she became the most acclaimed soprano of her time due to her appearance, her aura, her voice and gripping, magnetic personality on stage. In both her private and professional life she made marvellous material for the paparazzi.

Schwarzkopf was no less fine a singer, though of a completely different kind. She was a person who rarely presented a story to the press, let alone a hot one. Legge admitted that he was 'rather late on the Callas bus' because, apart from his collaboration with Karajan at La Scala and recordings with Boris Christoff, Italy was not regarded as Legge territory. When he had finally got Callas under contract, many things changed.

Once the haggling was out of the way, there was not a great deal to prevent Schwarzkopf and Legge and the Meneghinis from enjoying each other's company and appearing together in public. Schwarzkopf always looked extremely elegant in her diaphanous gowns in the evening, or in beautifully tailored doeskin leather jacket and skirt in the daytime, but she had no need to act the Tosca, the prima donna incarnate. Callas was all this, although analysis of her features and physique revealed that she was not beautiful in a conventional sense. But why analyse when the whole was so gorgeous? Maria Callas had to be at the centre of things, an astonishingly vibrant personality who dressed to be noticed by royalty, presidents and millionaires.

Schwarzkopf, on the other hand, appeared so attractive and well-proportioned on the platform that nobody had reason to consider the balance of her facial and physical attributes. Her features had a regular, classical beauty. But unlike Callas, she often kept in the background, deliberately under-dressing so as not to be noticed. The late Harold Rosenthal described how he had once been invited to listen to a promising young singer at one of the smaller Italian opera houses and, taking his seat in a box after the lights had gone down, found an unknown woman already there, very ordinarily dressed, without makeup and with unruly hair. Even when the lights went up at the interval he failed to recognize her until she asked, 'Don't you know me, Harold?'[8]

Between February and March 1951 Schwarzkopf was in London, taking part in various performances connected with the Festival of Britain. They included *Fidelio* at the Royal Opera House, again with Flagstad and Patzak, with Karl Rankl conducting. The *Sunday Times* critic waxed enthusiastic:

A rare 'Fidelio' at Covent Garden
Nobody who saw *Fidelio* at Covent Garden last Wednesday is likely to forget the performance. The first act unwound itself rather stolidly, although Miss Elizabeth [sic] Schwarzkopf's Marcelline was wholly delightful, and Mme Flagstad's Leonora [sic] magisterial, to say the least . . .

The *Times* critic was generally less convinced:

There was fine singing from the much praised Patzak, Flagstad and Miss Elisabeth Schwarzkopf in German. In bearing as in song, Miss Schwarzkopf was an enchanting Marcelline; Howell Glynn and Tom Williams were adequate but there were bad performances from the English singers, from the orchestra and from Karl Rankl.

In April 1951, when the Royal Albert Hall's monopoly as the only large London concert hall had virtually ended, the Polish conductor Paul Kletzki conducted the Philharmonia Orchestra there in a programme of great interest to Straussians. Schwarzkopf sang the 'First performances in England of [Final]

Scenes from Richard Strauss's Operas "Dafne"[9] and "Capriccio" ', as stated in the programme.

The words were given in German and English with translations and succinct notes by Walter Legge, to underline the importance he attached to the occasion. The concert began with Hamilton Harty's arrangement of Handel's *Water Music*, and then Schwarzkopf sang the closing scene from *Capriccio*, whose music would have been known only to those members of the audience who had been abroad, or who had the pre-war record of the scene sung by its creator, Viorica Ursuleac. *Capriccio* was to be heard in several houses in Germany and was presently in rehearsal for the first post-war production at the Theater an der Wien. As there were no means of assessing Schwarzkopf's performance, it was accepted wholeheartedly as an absolute delight which her complete recording, three years later, was to confirm.

Then followed the Metamorphosis of Daphne with its high tessitura, brilliantly executed by Schwarzkopf. Again, this was a delightful novelty that made the listener want to hear more of Strauss's self-confessed favourite among all his operas. Mahler's Fourth concluded the programme, with Schwarzkopf singing the child's song in the last movement. It was altogether a perfect display of Legge's enterprising and energetic programme-building as well as Schwarzkopf's ability to thrill and delight.

In May she had a major choral engagement, repeated for the opening of the new Royal Festival Hall in London during the Festival of Britain. It was presided over by Sir Malcolm Sargent and the work in which she sang was Beethoven's 'Choral' Symphony. At the opening performance, the orchestra was composed of representatives from all the London Five,[10] which occasioned many difficulties: there were sulky looks and not enough cohesion, a state of affairs which Sargent did nothing to alleviate. It was not repeated when the London Philharmonic played alone at the second performance. The untamed acoustics of the new Hall produced a cold string tone and emphasized the cannon-shot sound of the timpani in the Scherzo. Schwarzkopf's companions among the soloists were British, and they sang in English with voices that did not blend happily.

The following day she was in Vienna, singing Strauss under Kletzki again, this time for her maiden performance of Strauss's *Four Last Songs*, which curiously, she was not to sing again until 1954. Far more significant, at the end of this exceptional month of May, was when she sang the soprano solo in Verdi's Requiem for the first time, with Sir John Barbirolli and the Hallé Orchestra. Despite her un-Italianate timbre, she was to have notable success with this work.

Nineteen fifty-one was to prove a crucial year in propelling Schwarzkopf to the top of her profession. When she was at the Deutsche Oper, one of her ambitions had been to sing at Bayreuth. At that time Heinz Tietjen was the Festival's guiding spirit, thanks to his influence over Frau Wagner, and he had rejected any personal contact with Schwarzkopf,[11] so she never got there during the Third Reich. Nine years later, however, in 1951, the doors of the Festspielhaus were opened wide to welcome her.

The Wagner Festivals and Frau Winifred, the English-born widow of Richard Wagner's son Siegfried, and their children, had attracted Hitler long before events of the mid-1930s in Germany had stamped Bayreuth as Nazi with a capital N. Frau Winifred's name had often been coupled with Hitler's during the Weimar Republic, and when he came to power the Führer regarded Bayreuth and the Wagners with special affection. The children still called him 'Wolf', from the time when he was a political refugee in the 1920s and used to tell them bedtime stories, showing them the pistol he always carried.[12] As a result of this close relationship, three of the four grown-up Wagner children were probably the only people in the world who dared to tease and cajole Hitler. Friedelind Wagner, the second child, was the family exception. She hated Wahnfried, their Bayreuth house, and was so violently opposed to her mother and the way things were going in Germany that she fled to Switzerland in 1939 and then to the United States.

As soon as the war was over in 1945, there had been special difficulties with Winifred Wagner, and in 1947 she had been condemned as a major Nazi collaborator, forbidden to have any control over future Festivals, even though the entire Wagner estate belonged to her in law. Eventually she was forced to resign all rights in favour of her two sons, Wieland and Wolfgang, and once the veto had been lifted they announced their intention of promoting the first post-war Wagner Festival on the 'Green Hill' in the summer of 1951.

The Wagner brothers had less than adequate funds at their disposal and Bayreuth was in the American Zone of Occupied West Germany. The Festival's opening was going to depend to a large extent upon dollars, as well as on support from the emerging West German industries and the town of Bayreuth itself. As ever, Wahnfried was a hotbed of intrigue, jealousy and unending squabbles worthy of the Wälsungs, Gibichungs and Niebelungs combined. 'Beware!' Frida Leider advised Martha Mödl as she set out for Bayreuth in 1951. 'Unless it is much changed, I know by experience that vipers abound there.'[13] And it was not much changed.

Walter Legge had met the Wagner brothers before the war when they were youths, and again afterwards through Karajan's introduction. Legge once observed pensively[14] that Wieland became as good a friend as was humanly possible in his case; but he did not at all care for Wolfgang Wagner. Legge had been using his experience and knowledge of European artists to advise the brothers when casting singers and orchestral players during the auditions which had begun in 1949.

Kirsten Flagstad was the only pre-war singer to be invited back, but she declined, partly because the Americans strongly disapproved of her husband's wartime connections in Norway. She still thought well enough of Wieland Wagner to recommend, in her place, the Swedish-American soprano, Astrid Varnay, who was known at the Met.[15] Purely on the strength of Flagstad's recommendation, Varnay was booked by Wieland Wagner for all six Brünnhilde performances without a Bayreuth audition, even though, from a practical-musical aspect, the Festspielhaus acoustic plays tricks with certain voices that one would expect to be heard clearly, but are not. Elisabeth Schwarzkopf's was, however.

At the laying of the foundation stone for the Bayreuth Festspielhaus in 1872, Richard Wagner had directed a performance of Beethoven's 'Choral' Symphony. Now, to commemorate that event for a new kind of beginning, Furtwängler was to conduct the Symphony for the post-war reopening, and Schwarzkopf accepted his invitation, endorsed by the Wagner brothers, to sing the soprano solo with three artists who were taking part in the Festival: Elisabeth Höngen, Hans Hopf and Otto Edelmann.

The work was also going to be recorded, and as Schwarzkopf had sung in it for Furtwängler at three consecutive Festivals in Lucerne, it seemed an honest *sequitur*. Furtwängler had last appeared at Bayreuth in 1944, and Wieland Wagner had been counting on the fact that, after the inaugural Beethoven Symphony, his boyhood hero would conduct the first *Ring* cycle. After the usual protracted deliberations about his place in the continuing history of Bayreuth Festivals, however, Furtwängler announced that he would conduct only the Beethoven Symphony.

His reason was twofold. First, he had decided to improve his political image by no longer being regarded as *the* Wagner conductor; and to this end he had already appeared at Salzburg with *Fidelio* and, for the first time, two Mozart operas. But when Furtwängler heard that Karajan was to be at Bayreuth for the *Meistersinger* production, he could not bear the thought of the hated 'K' being about the place.

As a result, the Wagner brothers were forced to revise their planned conducting schedule. Hans Knappertsbusch was to have been in charge of *Parsifal* and the second *Ring* cycle but now, in Furtwängler's absence, he became the senior conductor for the operas, with the vacant place on the podium for the second cycle now occupied by Karajan. He was Knappertsbusch's junior by twenty years, and neither had conducted at a Bayreuth Festival before, although Karajan had given a Wagner–Bruckner concert in the Festspielhaus in May

1950, to raise funds for the 1951 Festival. Knappertsbusch had always been prevented from accepting an invitation there because he was at Munich where their Summer Festivals clashed with Bayreuth's. He was a real character, with a wickedly censorious and lavatorial humour who 'aroused Wieland's intense admiration. "Do you know why I love Kna?" he once said. "He *does* nothing – he just *is*." '[16]

While Knappertsbusch was sufficiently traditional in outlook to regard the call to Bayreuth as an honour, the financial reward was more important to Karajan.

> Younger conductors, who now had the choice of several summer festivals, were liable to raise the question of fees. For all his rebelliousness, Wieland was in this respect an old-fashioned Wagnerian. He was shocked and from the start he regarded his second conductor with a certain amount of reserve.[17]

There were two British recording teams in the Festspielhaus. The twenty-seven-year-old John Culshaw, who had been at Decca for only five years, represented them with a senior recording engineer, Kenneth Wilkinson. The very experienced Walter Legge, who led the Columbia crew, had secured a far better recording position by getting there first. The Decca technicians regarded their opponents with considerable awe: John Culshaw even referred to Legge as 'legendary'.[18]

Decca had superior microphones and equipment, and were thinking in terms of LP; both teams were using magnetic tape and had many opportunities for letting the machines run during rehearsals as well as for multiple performances of *Parsifal* and *Die Meistersinger*. Legge and the Columbia label had the franchise for Karajan's *Die Meistersinger* but the two cycles of *Der Ring*, with identical casts, were an unknown quantity. Decca were not intending to record anything from *Der Ring*, but Legge kept an open mind, although neither company ever had the intention of recording a complete cycle: 1951 was too early for such a colossal venture, especially as Columbia were still marketing 78s.

Parsifal under Knappertsbusch was a combined project between Decca, London, and the German company Teldec, which would lead to great difficulties when both wanted to bring it out on CD many years later. Legge considered Karajan to be a far better commercial proposition, not only because his 78s were already bought in large quantities, but also because 'Kna' lacked an equivalent recording personality in spite of his formidable experience with Wagner in the opera house. With measured tempi he attained a massive grandeur; and in the ideal acoustics of Wagner's opera house, with its wooden auditorium, the results were astonishing.

When John Culshaw heard the unique 'Bayreuth sound' for the first time that summer, during *Parsifal* rehearsals, he was so bowled over that he immediately sought and obtained permission to make some trial recordings of the first *Ring* cycle. Perhaps the perceptive Culshaw realized that an operatic revolution was about to erupt from Bayreuth, for the 'new look' undoubtedly influenced all *Ring* productions, and many others throughout the world for the next forty years, although largely in terms of the staging and presentation.

Legge fully realized the importance of Elisabeth Schwarzkopf's place in this Festival for which rehearsals began at Bayreuth in May 1951. She was going to be appearing there on the crest of a wave, for the opening concert, for a Lieder recital on the rest day of the first *Ring* cycle, two performances each of Woglinde in *Das Rheingold* and *Götterdämmerung*, with seven Evas in *Die Meistersinger*. It was an arduous programme.

Furtwängler and Karajan were being diplomatically kept well apart. During one of his rehearsals for the Beethoven symphony, however, Furtwängler caught sight of Karajan sitting alone in the gloomy recesses of the auditorium. In a fit of temperament he threatened to withdraw altogether from the Festival unless his *bête noire* was removed. The offending conductor instantly stood up and walked out in silence.[19]

During the last week of July Bayreuth was *en fête*, with some of the visitors arriving early, intent on enjoying themselves. There was plenty of food – far more than was available in Britain at the time – and an abundance of light German lager, especially in *Die Eule* (The Owl), an establishment frequented by the singers. Because Bayreuth was in the US Zone of Occupation, their troops were always in evidence round the town.

The opening concert on 29 July was recorded live. Here was real *schöne Freude*. Furtwängler's first movement was truly monumental and Schwarzkopf's voice – as can still be heard – rings out in the jubilant choral finale. This was the way Furtwängler interpreted the work at the time and its effect that very special day was overwhelming.

The performance greatly moved the many elderly members of the audience. Surprisingly, most of the men still had dinner jackets, gone a bit mouldy due to having been put away for more than a decade but now brought out in celebration of the great event. Afterwards they forgot their reservations and joined in the general jubilation with everybody else: their Festivals were at last being resumed in spite of major opposition, and Wagner was to be heard in Bayreuth again after six years' silence.

Schwarzkopf was not in *Parsifal*, the opera with which the Festival proper opened on the afternoon of 30 July, but Knappertsbusch set the standard in orchestral playing. He found the orchestra very much to his liking but thoroughly disapproved of the sparseness in Wieland Wagner's staging: no swan, no dove, no spear for Klingsor.

When asked reproachfully by guardians of the old Bayreuth tradition why he had consented to conduct this disgraceful production of *Parsifal*, he replied that he had imagined during the dress rehearsal that the stage decorations were still to come . . .[20]

A typical piece of Knappertsbusch cynicism.

David Harris, then opera manager for BBC Radio, reviewed the Festival for *Opera* magazine and wrote: 'The orchestral playing under Hans Knappertsbusch was the highlight of the whole festival – broad and dignified.'[21]

Those who attended that opening *Rheingold* of the first cycle under Knappertsbusch on 31 July 1951 were privileged to see the first stage 'saucer' and Schwarzkopf's face dimly visible with those of her two Rhine sisters in the depths. Extreme contrasts of light and darkness were elemental features of *Der Ring* and *Parsifal*, suggesting both Gordon Craig and Adolph Appia.

A calm and spiritual kind of singing was evident in most of *Parsifal*; but in *Der Ring* the more savage and brutal moments seemed underplayed, as though to give them full rein might still have had unpleasant connotations. Consequently it seemed dramatically a shade pale, especially as the stage settings were so stark. Musically, a granite splendour prevailed under the sixty-three-year-old Knappertsbusch's powerful control, although Bayreuth's vocal casting, made a year or more beforehand, was, here and there, slightly below the standard that both record companies might have chosen.

When it came to *Götterdämmerung*, Schwarzkopf's presence was far more substantial, and her mocking words to Siegfried (Bernd Aldenhoff), coupled with a sensuous coquetry, remain in the memory. The disappointingly feeble collapse and fire of the Gibichung Hall, at the end of the cycle, seemed to indicate that the budget had run out in Act II, but it hardly mattered in view, of the marvellous sound which Knappertsbusch conjured up. From the Funeral March onwards, the orchestra played as if possessed, and the result was thrilling.

John Culshaw knew at once that this *Ring* had all the necessary sonic attributes for publication. Columbia had not recorded it, Decca had and, full of enthusiasm, Culshaw progressed as far as making a master-tape. Then he was ordered by his managing director in Switzerland to stop immediately.

Culshaw was stunned. He argued and protested at the waste of what he considered to be a masterpiece in his hands, but the order stood without explanation. The 1951 *Götterdämmerung* under Knappertsbusch has remained unissued and the reason is very simple: Elisabeth Schwarzkopf! Walter Legge was never going to allow his intended wife's voice to be heard in a solo role, however small, on a competing label.

Knappertsbusch's *Parsifal* was soon issued on LP, but the CD version was delayed until 1993. None of his *Ring* seems to have survived, Culshaw's master-tape of *Götterdämmerung* is said to have been lost; and of the Karajan *Ring*,

Rheingold and *Siegfried* have been unofficially issued, with Act III of *Die Walküre* put out on CD in 1993. This, EMI claim, is all the material that exists from their 1951 Karajan cycle.

On 3 August 1951, two days before the first *Meistersinger* that he was to conduct at Bayreuth, Karajan went to hear a rather special Lieder recital at the Margrave's opera house. With its interior decoration in royal blue and gold, carried out by the Bibiena brothers in 1748, it is one of the most beautiful little baroque theatres in the world, with an equally glorious acoustic. Elisabeth Schwarzkopf's Lieder recital in aid of the Friends of Bayreuth was the only non-Wagnerian musical event during the Festival and took place on the evening after the first *Siegfried*, traditionally a night off for everyone. A few days beforehand, tickets for quite good seats were easily available at 2 DM each (with 12 DM to the pound for British visitors) and the little house was sold out.

Afterwards Legge gave a reception at which Schwarzkopf, heroine of the evening, reappeared in a dirndl and carried round refreshments, chatting to musicians and other discerning guests who had been at her recital. Walter Legge was deep in German conversation, so she waited until he had finished his sentence before speaking. Then he turned to her slowly and said audibly, 'You sang that last Wolf Lied like a pig!' She continued on her way, unmoved.

The third production of the 1951 Festival was *Die Meistersinger*, which the Wagner grandsons chose because it

> shares with the *Ring* the reputation of being the most politically suspect of Wagner's works. It was therefore an astute move on their part – whether deliberate or not – to entrust the production of it to an outsider: to Rudolf Hartmann of Munich, who staged it in the traditional realistic way.[22]

Wieland Wagner declared in the 1951 Bayreuth Festival Programme Book that it

> calls for a certain naturalism (imposed by a historically fixed time, a geographical place and human beings of flesh and blood). *Parsifal*, on the other hand, requires mystical expression of a very complex state of the soul, rooted in the unreal and grasped only by intuition. To present both works in a similar way, as seemed natural in earlier days, appears to us neither possible nor even remotely desirable. The gap between them arises from the innermost core of their differences, and it cannot be bridged.[23]

A large section of that 1951 audience had been looking for Wagnerian conservatism, but they certainly did not get it in *Der Ring* or *Parsifal*. Other considerations apart, it assisted the general pressure on Festival coffers, when a traditional, brightly lit production was first revealed.

This *Meistersinger*, which had naturalistic scenery by an anonymous artist and period costumes borrowed from the Nuremberg Opera, was in the joint hands of Rudolf Hartmann and Herbert von Karajan. Pictures make it appear more *passé* today than any of the other productions that year. An anonymous German critic, quoted by Geoffrey Skelton, wrote:[24]

> How much Bayreuth stands in need of a new approach and of experiment in order to remain significant and effective was shown by the production of *Die Meistersinger*. Excellent as the performance was in its individual parts, balanced as it was as a whole, there was nothing exceptional about it and certainly nothing unique. It was not itself of the stuff of which festivals are made.

Perhaps it was for reasons of economy that this production was repeated the following season (when Trude Eipperle sang Eva), but it was Bayreuth's last presentation in Wolfgang Wagner's era to use naturalistic scenery.

Schwarzkopf's Eva was delightful: her singing was eloquent and her characterization was beautifully poised under Hartmann's direction. By contrast with some of the other performances that year, she displayed true star quality. Her scene with Sachs (Otto Edelmann) and the shoe in Act III was especially affecting; and that magical moment in the opera's last scene is still to be heard on the last of the four CDs when, with a beautifully placed trill, she crowned Walther (Hans Hopf) with the victor's laurel wreath. Gone were the pre-war Wagnerian giants like Leider, Melchior and Schorr (Hotter was not yet singing at Bayreuth), but Schwarzkopf would not have been out of place among them.

Before coming to Bayreuth, she had sung Eva twice, in English, with the Covent Garden Company. Now, in the hallowed precincts on the Green Hill, singing in German, Schwarzkopf had all the support of trained Bayreuth répétiteurs and of the experienced Rudolf Hartmann. Her presence in the Festival had marked her as a fully fledged international soprano, and her performances, especially in the 'Choral' Symphony and *Die Meistersinger*, had confirmed her appealing personality and technical panache. As for her vocal suitability for Eva, she said afterwards, somewhat defensively, that nobody had ever questioned that her voice might be insufficiently ample for the role.

Schwarzkopf sang Eva fewer than fifteen times in her career. Having achieved her old ambition of appearing in a major role at Bayreuth, and conquered the Festspielhaus audiences *cum laude*, she had no desire to return there. Hopes were expressed by some of her fervent supporters that she was to become one of the new Bayreuth sopranos for Elisabeth and Elsa, even for Sieglinde, which she had studied ten years before in Berlin, in spite of the fact that the role lies too low for her. All such hopes were dashed by her declaration that she was not going back. The continuing (and apparently unavoidable) Wagner family domination of the Festival created a cloying, secretive atmosphere; and while there was certainly a cachet in working there, once was enough for Schwarzkopf.

Nor was Karajan in the least thrilled. He 'hated Wieland Wagner's staging conception to the extent that two Bayreuth seasons were all he could stand. The egocentricities of the two men clashed as well.'[25]

Karajan was not one to assume a senior conducting position in an opera house with rooted family control. He had other, far more desirable plans to cultivate, where he intended to be his own master in spite of whatever local committees were already in place.

Stravinsky, Tippett and Karajan
1951–1953

Schwarzkopf and Karajan left Bayreuth after the last *Meistersinger* for the altogether fresher air of Lucerne, where they took part in two performances of the B minor Mass on consecutive days. He returned to Milan, while she went to Venice to begin rehearsals for the leading role in the world première of Stravinsky's new opera, *The Rake's Progress*. The composer had become attracted to the subject after seeing Hogarth's prints at a New York exhibition. It is his only three-act opera, set in eighteenth-century England and representing him in his most neo-classical vein. *The Rake's Progress* has an amusing and cleverly written libretto in English by Wystan Auden and Chester Kallman, fairly freely based on Hogarth's eight engravings.

Although Schwarzkopf's musical education and experience had been German, Austrian and, latterly, British, Verdi's Requiem was comfortably within her powers. A week after Lucerne, and with *Rake* rehearsals between, she was in Milan for a very special performance of the Requiem conducted by Victor De Sabata. It was to commemorate the fiftieth anniversary of Verdi's death (albeit seven months late) and otherwise with all-Italian forces. The vocal soloists were Ebe Stignani, Giuseppe di Stefano, Cesare Siepi – and Elisabeth Schwarzkopf. Renata Tebaldi might have been the obvious choice, but no. It was a great compliment to Schwarzkopf and, having acquitted herself nobly, she was on the stage at La Fenice three days later, singing Anne Trulove in the main international musical event, now that the first post-war Bayreuth Festival was over. Singers can expect such a chance as this perhaps once in a lifetime, all things being equal, which in Venice they so often are not.

Legge always wanted Schwarzkopf to create the principal role in an operatic world première, and, through the agency of La Scala and Boosey & Hawkes (the composer's publishers in London), his persuasiveness resulted in her being cast as the faithful heroine; Stravinsky, although most widely revered of living composers, seems to have had little or no say in the details of this production. He did suggest Otto Klemperer, whom he much admired, as conductor, but that did not materialize. There was no official invitation for Klemperer, and in any case he was immured in the United States where his passport had been withdrawn because of a previous association with the Budapest Opera.[1] These were the McCarthy years.

Nearer the time, Stravinsky asked for Igor Markevitch, but La Scala refused. So the question of conductor was left temporarily in abeyance. Stravinsky suggested Eugene Berman as designer, then John Piper, but neither was approached. The Russian artist, Nicola Benois, son and pupil of Diaghilev's designer, Alexandre, was finally placed in charge of sets and costumes, although he does not seem to have studied Hogarth very hard.

Both Schwarzkopf and Jennie Tourel (Baba the Turk) had been 'engaged' as late as 6 July, and the arrangements proceeded very slowly. David Webster made a logical bid for the première at Covent Garden, but by then Stravinsky had promised it to Venice without consulting Boosey & Hawkes. He seems to have taken this independent action because he had still been paid nothing for the score, and the Italians were offering him 20,000 dollars to conduct the first night. Ernst Roth, chairman of Boosey's, was indignant and wrote to Stravinsky: 'in Venice you will find yourself in a turmoil of disorganization which requires improvisation in the smallest matters . . . the situation for us is extremely awkward.'[2]

All administrative arrangements for the Venice première were negotiated and effected by Stravinsky's old friend, the Russian-American composer Nicolas Nabokov, while the stage production was in the hands of Carl Ebert. In spite of his strong credentials from Reinhardt's company, the Deutsche Oper Berlin, Glyndebourne and elsewhere, Ebert failed almost entirely to convince with this opera.

> The preliminary rehearsals took place in Milan . . . Stravinsky lived in the Duomo Hotel, but since the librettists had neglected to make reservations, they were obliged to reside in a bordello where, they said, 'The girls were very understanding, but the rooms could be rented only by the hour and so were terribly expensive.' Auden came to rehearsals in a white linen suit, polka-dotted with Chianti stains.[3]

Auden was supposed to be coaching the chorus and advising on the scenery, but because he disagreed so violently with the sets and the production, he ignored this part of his duties. 'It could hardly be worse if the director were Piscator and the singers were climbing and descending ladders,' he said. The luxurious Trulove house in Act I led him to conclude that 'the Rake would have been better off marrying the daughter right away and forgoing his "Progress" '.

There are two important, creative aspects of the libretto and score of this opera that should not be overlooked. 'Wystan Auden's devotion to Chester Kallman was the most important fact of the poet's personal life, as well as the real subject of the libretto (the fidelity of true love) . . .' and the composer was likewise motivated:

Stravinsky's feelings for *The Rake* were intensely personal . . . he had never written love music before [except for the berceuse in *Perséphone*] and now, at nearly seventy, he was inspired for the first time to do so by a text. He identified the love of Tom and Anne . . . with that of himself and his wife . . . written for her first of all, and only then for 'the world'.[4]

So beneath all the political and artistic hazards of this première lay two romantic strands which can scarcely have been perceived either by the protagonists on stage or, least of all, the audience. Tom Rakewell was played by the American tenor Robert Rounseville, and his evil mentor, Nick Shadow, by the Czech-born baritone Otakar Kraus.

When asked whether she had worked much with the composer, Schwarzkopf replied, 'Fortunately not. He was no conductor and looked into his score for the whole evening . . . You cannot sing that music without help.'[5] Ferdinand Leitner, the deputy conductor, soon became aware of this and when Stravinsky was on the rostrum for rehearsals, Leitner stationed himself behind the composer so that he could give cues to the singers, which the Master was not doing all the time. Then it all went much better. After the final dress rehearsal, Leitner took an extra rehearsal on his own initiative, which did much to pull the opera into shape. On the first night, though, Stravinsky had to be there alone, to earn his 20,000 dollars, but Leitner conducted the remaining two performances in Venice, and in December, when the production was transferred to Milan, he was in sole charge.

La Scala had originated and backed *The Rake's Progress* as part of the XIV Biennale Musicale, and now it was to be performed in Italian as *La Carriera d'un Libertino*. There were several changes of cast round Schwarzkopf, but she sang all four performances, making a total of seven *Rakes*. After that, she never again sang Anne Trulove on the stage.

Anne's first aria, or *scena*, forms Act I, Scene 3, and begins 'No word from Tom', followed by the quaintly worded first line of the aria, 'I go, I go to him!' This needed all Schwarzkopf's resources and is the strongest moment in the opera for the pure and faithful Anne, who always displays resolve within herself, though never against others. She handled this heroic aria beautifully, receiving applause each time she sang it.

An illuminating essay by Jonathan Keates, in the Glyndebourne programme book, contains references to the three female characters in *The Rake's Progress*. Baba the Turk is 'in her own eyes . . . as much the *grande dame* as the Marschallin in *Der Rosenkavalier*'. Certainly Baba's is a far more spectacular role than Anne's. Even with a soprano of Schwarzkopf's status for the mild heroine (thought to have been Kallman's creation), Baba dominates the scene whenever she and Anne are on stage together.

In the front-cloth scene of Act II, Tom has just married Baba, who is arriving at his house with her chattels. Anne's accidental presence, Tom's horror at seeing her there, and the lukewarm confrontation between the former lovers make Anne seem pure and honest, thoroughly out of place in dissolute London and convincing in her arguments. But as soon as Baba's head emerges from the sedan-chair window, it is she who again controls the scene and Tom is forced to pacify her by saying (*'ironically'*) that Anne is 'Only a milk-maid, pet/To whom I was in debt.'

Anne's most fetching scene is the last one, where she plays Venus to the mad Tom's Adonis. Her aria, 'Gently, little boat', with choral interruptions by other inhabitants of Bedlam between the three verses, was ideally realized by Schwarzkopf's languorous legato.

This is not quite the end, however, because the opera closes with an echo of the moralizing finale of *Don Giovanni*, when the main singers address the audience. Here the moralizing is more acerbic than with Da Ponte and Mozart, in keeping with the flavour of the whole work.

If Schwarzkopf had expected Anne's music to have been specifically tailored to her voice, she was disappointed. Stravinsky's angular, parodistic lines do not always lie comfortably for the soloist. Schwarzkopf found that she had to adapt herself to him – and to Auden and Kallman as well.

Though she was ambivalent about the role of Anne Trulove, she subsequently sang three of Anne's arias successfully at concerts; and, over forty years later, she was prepared to consent to a release of the first-night recording. The switch to Italian for the second run of performances of *The Rake's Progress* at La Scala was generally welcomed. Spike Hughes emphasizes this obliquely in an article about Glyndebourne's later production of the opera:

> The English language, teased and worried as it is by the Russian Stravinsky in *The Rake's Progress*, is the native tongue of no singer on earth. The composer's whimsical treatment of the stresses, accents, cadences and sense of English virtually forces all who sing it to tackle it from scratch as a language they have never known before.[6]

It seems that John Christie did not much care for *The Rake's Progress* either. While the opera was in rehearsal at Glyndebourne for its British première at the Edinburgh Festival by his company, he encountered two strangers in his garden.

'What are you doing here?' he asked them and, because they looked surprised and were initially at a loss for words, he demanded, 'Well, who are you?'

The elder one replied, 'I am Wystan Auden, and this is Chester Kallman . . .' Pause, and no response, so he persisted, 'We wrote the libretto, you know.' Still no glimmering. '*The Rake's Progress*,' he added proudly. Christie's face fell and, sadly shaking his head, the promoter of pure Mozart turned away: 'You shouldn't have done it, you shouldn't, you know . . .'

★   ★   ★

Before the last Milan performance of *The Rake*, Schwarzkopf was preparing for a production of *Der Rosenkavalier* in which she was going to make her début as the Marschallin. Karajan told Schwarzkopf in 1951 that she would be singing this coveted role in his new production at La Scala, scheduled for January 1952. Schwarzkopf trusted his judgement and Legge backed it.

Two days after Christmas 1951 all the *Rosenkavalier* principals went to Milan for an intensive month's rehearsal under Karajan's musical and stage direction. The cast had a strong Viennese slant, with Lisa Della Casa as Sophie, Sena Jurinac as Octavian, Erich Kunz as Faninal and Otto Edelmann as Ochs. As usual in the Karajan–Legge sphere, both together or separately, they always waited until they could assemble what they considered, at the chosen time, to be the best possible cast available anywhere. Robert Kautsky had gone back to Alfred Roller's last sketches for the set designs and costumes, and Karajan believed he had shorn the work of its usual excesses and vulgarity. His rehearsals sometimes continued for up to ten hours a day under the conditions which he most enjoyed: complete charge of stage as well as pit, with everything going his own way. It must be said, though, that Karajan was not quite the brilliant stage director he imagined himself to be, and was also open to criticism for the planning and execution of stage lighting, however much he understood and enjoyed its technicalities.

In spite of the claim that Karajan had 'a highly developed visual sense', the conductor-turned-director was undoubtedly less of an *Augenmensch* in this sphere than Serge Diaghilev had been in his own era of more primitive equipment, for the Russian impresario had a profound understanding of how stage lighting could also be made to colour the scene.

Walter Legge was at La Scala, being protective of Schwarzkopf and planning their corporate future. He got on famously with the Italian director Antonio Ghiringhelli, which is more than Callas and her husband were doing at the time. Legge was delighted when he managed to come to an arrangement to record *Der Rosenkavalier* at La Scala. Having got in all the sound-machines, his plan was thwarted by the orchestra whose demands were excessive.

When Legge came round to recording the opera in London five years later, he had the benefit of the Philharmonia Orchestra, a better bet at the time than the Scala players would have been. As it turned out, Legge gained an advantage in Milan, worth far more than *Der Rosenkavalier* in the long run, of an exclusive contract for EMI to record at La Scala, which is where he was to make all the Callas operas.

Legge's view about the superlative quality of Schwarzkopf's first Marschallin did not seem to be generally shared by managements and she established herself in the role only gradually, as she did with Mozart's Countess.

★　　★　　★

Interspersed with three solid blocks of operatic work in 1951 – Bayreuth, *Rake's Progress* and the *Rosenkavalier* rehearsals – was a variety of Lieder recitals and concerts, among which Bach's Cantata No. 51, *Jauchzet Gott in alle Lande*, under Eugen Jochum in Munich, was repeated by Ernest Ansermet in Geneva where, in addition, Schwarzkopf sang scenes from *The Rake's Progress*.

She sang them in London under Harry Blech at the Royal Festival Hall in March 1952, making much of the *scena* at the end of Act I, 'I go to him!' Blech was also in charge of one of the two early Mozart oratorios, given extremely rare performances, in which Schwarzkopf sang. These were *Betulia Liberata* in Turin in May 1952 under Mario Rossi, and *Die Schuldigkeit des ersten Gebotes* (*Obligation of the First Commandment*) at the Royal Festival Hall, London, in July.

Die Schuldigkeit des ersten Gebotes is in three parts, of which only the first is by Mozart – the second and third are by Michael Haydn and Anton Adlgasser respectively. It requires two tenors and three sopranos, in this instance Schwarzkopf, Adèle Leigh and Jennifer Vyvyan. According to *The Times*, it was a stylish, well-voiced female trio in a performance commemorating ten years of the BBC Third Programme. Although it was broadcast, there is still no indication that it has been saved for posterity. But the *Betulia Liberata* has been on CD, displaying Schwarzkopf in fine, strong voice in her two florid arias.

She found time in October for an important recording as Belinda to Flagstad's eponymous heroine in Purcell's *Dido and Aeneas*. Flagstad had first sung Dido in September 1951 at Bernard Miles's Mermaid Theatre when the Belinda was Maggie Teyte.

Nineteen fifty-two was the year the Philharmonia Orchestra went on its triumphant European tour. Legge and Karajan had brought them to such a pitch of excellence that they both knew it was time these skills were displayed in cities where the resident orchestras all thought they had little to fear from competition.

In Milan, Toscanini listened to the Philharmonia on the radio and was astonished. His subsequent visit to London that year was the direct result. At a supper after the Milan concert at La Scala, given by Victor De Sabata, Walter Legge was taken aside by the enthusiastic conductor who said to him, 'Your orchestra is the most wonderful English virgin. All she needs to achieve the ultimate perfection is to be raped by a hot-blooded Italian. I will do that for you.' Legge adds, in parentheses, that 'unfortunately his ill-health deprived the orchestra of that enriching experience!'[7] Schwarzkopf met Toscanini but never sang for him; in gaining De Sabata's favour in the Italian field during the previous year, however, she had done the next best thing.

Salzburg was waiting for her, after a year's absence, with five performances of the *Figaro* Countess scheduled to be conducted by Furtwängler; but after a few rehearsals he became ill and could not continue. Rudolf Moralt carried on and saw the performance through, at first attempting to follow Furtwängler's often slow tempi, which severely taxed the singers. It was an exceptional cast, with Irmgard Seefried as Susanna, Hilde Gueden as Cherubino, Erich Kunz a marvellous Figaro and either George London or (for one performance) Alfred Poell as the Count. These singers were more experienced in their roles than Schwarzkopf who, since the beginning of 1949, had gone back to singing Susanna in London. However in all future *Figaros* she was always going to take the role of the Countess.

De Sabata had kept his promise to Schwarzkopf that she should sing the soprano solo for him in the Verdi Requiem at Salzburg, which she did in two performances on consecutive days. Dermota and Josef Greindl took the lower voices, and the choir was formed of choruses from the Vienna State Opera and Salzburg Cathedral, leaving the mezzo, Fedora Barbieri, as the only Italian voice in the entire production.

There was no Furtwängler at Salzburg that year, and no Karajan either, so Clemens Krauss tried – unsuccessfully – to regain his former kingdom of Salzburg over which he had ruled during the war years, installed in Max Reinhardt's Leopoldskron Palace and greatly acclaimed by the traditionally right-right-wing Salzburgers. Now he presented Strauss's last opera to be staged – *Die Liebe der Danae* – in its acknowledged première.[8] It failed to gain the kind of approval that would ensure immediate productions elsewhere, as it might have done had Krauss lived long enough to reshape the score, as he was intending.

As usual, the Lucerne Festival followed Salzburg, but Furtwängler was still on the sick-list, and Schwarzkopf sang in *Messiah* instead of the usual 'Choral' Symphony. Neither Furtwängler nor Karajan espoused Handel's masterpiece, which Schwarzkopf only sang three times in concert and once in a studio recording. This was the first of these performances, in French as *Le Messie*, under the eminent Swiss composer and conductor, Robert Denzler. A local chorus and orchestra supported Schwarzkopf, and three other strong voices made up the solo ensemble.

One newspaper critic wrote:

> In the quartet of soloists, Mme Schwarzkopf adopted a magisterial presence; and I think it is needless to emphasize here once more the charm which lies in her voice. It is of such perfect purity and exceptional musicality that she is able to reach every kind of listener with equal success.[9]

Furtwängler recovered in early November and resumed his orchestral recording programme in Vienna. Schwarzkopf had a similarly heavy schedule in London that had lasted from early September until the end of November, mainly consisting of songs: Bach, Mozart, Wolf and the successful Christmas album. To crown the sessions, there was Bach's B minor Mass under Karajan, with whom she had not worked since February. This recording divides critics in our authenticity-conscious age; but it was highly praised on its appearance. Because it was only the second choral work which Karajan had committed to disc, it was described by Alec Robertson as 'a landmark in the history of the gramophone record'.[10] Desmond Shawe-Taylor concurred: 'The entire performance is magically beautiful as sheer sound.'[11] Schwarzkopf's singing in the *Laudamus Te* is especially notable for her impeccable line, her breath-control and the unexaggerated 'face' to her voice.

In 1953 Schwarzkopf seemed to be entirely under the artistic control of Karajan, who encouraged her to learn operatic roles which were to take only a temporary place in her repertoire. There were five leading soprano roles entirely new to her, and a sixth in an unfamiliar language although she had often sung it in German or English. Altogether there were twenty-six performances: four were staged, another was given in concert performances, and the sixth was in the broadcasting studio.

The new roles were interleaved among other well-tried characterizations and came in two groups of which this was the first:

Jan.   Elsa in Wagner's *Lohengrin* (6)
Feb.   Orff's *Trionfi*, principal soprano in two 1-act operas (4)
May   Mélisande in Debussy's *Pelléas et Mélisande* (5)

Elsa in *Lohengrin* was at La Scala, and Schwarzkopf looked lovely in a long blonde wig. She had strong support from a cast that included Wolfgang Windgassen as an ideal Lohengrin; Martha Mödl a terrifying, malign Ortrud and Gustav Neidlinger a prowling, consumed Telramund. Karajan conducted all six performances, but Schwarzkopf did not sing Elsa again. She was uneasy in the role, partly because it did not lie comfortably on her voice; and partly because she found Elsa, like Strauss's Ariadne, too passive and naïve a character for her to identify with fully.

Interspersed among these performances were five Elviras under Karajan's acutely responsive direction, then it was immediately on with the next new one, Carl Orff's triptych, *Trionfi*, parodying the Renaissance masque but using his own distinctive repetitive rhythms and highly coloured orchestration. The best known and most frequently performed of the three pieces is the *Carmina Burana*, to a libretto based on erotic Latin and Greek verses, in which she did not sing. The *Catulli Carmina* is also done in concert, but less frequently. The third opera, first performed on 13 February, was *Trionfo di Afrodite*, with the role of the Bride specially written for Schwarzkopf, and with Nicolai Gedda, Legge's new and greatly prized lyric tenor, as the Bridegroom.

Legge was perturbed by the constant repetition of verses when he attended the last rehearsal of *Afrodite* and gently suggested to Orff that he might consider a few cuts. 'I know the effect of my rubber-stamp music,' he replied.[12] Schwarz-kopf was the leading soprano in two of these works, on four occasions, in special performances at La Scala, but she did not sing them again.

Immediately after the first two performances of this doubtful Orffian enter-prise she appeared, for the only time in her life, in Michael Tippett's *A Child of Our Time*. Herbert von Karajan conducted the RAI Chorus and Orchestra of Turin, making it as surprising a choice for him as it was for her. Probably he had been under some pressure from Walter Legge, who the previous year had been unsuccessful in persuading Tippett to take up the post of chorus master for his new Philharmonia Choir, and may now have been having another try.

'There had been so many chorus rehearsals [in Turin] that there was not very much for Karajan to do, save conduct the performances.'[13] (Tippett uses the plural, but there seems only to have been one.) Mario Petri, the bass, gave the composer a lot of trouble, and consistently failed to get the recitatives right. The other soloists, apart from Schwarzkopf, were the Swiss mezzo Elsa Cavelti, and Nicolai Gedda: a potentially strong line-up for the performance, which was being broadcast. Exceptionally for him, Karajan 'was deliberately late'[14] in arriving at the hall for the performance, although he was staying in the same hotel as the principals. Consequently there was a delay in starting the concert and the Italian radio engineers had to fill in with records. When the maestro eventually turned up he asked Tippett, who was anxiously waiting backstage, having got there in plenty of time, whether he would mind if there was an extra, unscheduled interval in the second half of the work (after the second spiritual), adding, 'I think it would be more effective.' Tippett replied, 'I would mind very much, but I can't stop you.'

Karajan went on to the platform but then took his interval without giving any warning to the hall management, the radio engineers, the audience or the performers.[15] This was totally uncharacteristic and, apart from the professionally immaterial consideration that he was not attuned to the work, it was arrogant and inconsiderate behaviour from one established musician to another. Karajan had probably timed the extra interval so that he could telephone his current *amour* Eliette Mouret. Hence, also, his late arrival at the hall. Mlle Mouret was a French model working in London whom he eventually married; during the Coronation season of 1953, her glamorous picture was on the back cover of every Covent Garden programme book advertising haute couture for a well-known Knightsbridge store.

Schwarzkopf had now sung sixteen performances in four different works, all inspired and conducted by Karajan, in the short space of five weeks, beginning with Elsa. She then made a short tour of Italy with three Lieder recitals and Giorgio Favaretto as her accompanist, with the last *Trionfi* (Karajan), sandwiched in between.

Such was Schwarzkopf's work schedule that she flew back to London in April in order to record the complete *Land of Smiles* under Otto Ackermann at Kingsway Hall with the tailormade cast of Emmy Loose, Nicolai Gedda, Erich Kunz and Otakar Kraus; then back to La Scala for rehearsals of a new production of *Pelléas et Mélisande*. The Debussy opera had a mainly French cast and was conducted by Victor De Sabata. Neither Karajan nor Legge showed any interest in the work.

Mélisande is usually thought of as a young girl, frail, pure and apparently terrified of everything, most of all men. Schwarzkopf's Mélisande, by contrast, appeared to have all the assurance in the world, and far more eroticism than is normally associated with the role. It may be latent in Mélisande's character, but Schwarzkopf overlaid her characterization with uncalled for sophistication, even in the opening scene in Act III, where her presence at the window seems confident, knowing and enticing. Nor was she entirely at home in the French language.

Schwarzkopf was on surer ground for her next operatic engagement, returning to Covent Garden as a guest artist for four performances of *Die Meistersinger* in July 1953. The *Times* critic wrote:

> The Eva of Miss Elisabeth Schwarzkopf is full of youthful charm, rather consciously applied, no doubt, for the quintet was spoiled by a failure in natural directness, though everywhere her liquid tones were pleasant on the ear. Clemens Krauss made the overture sound superficial and the opera had a lighter gait than usual.[16]

These were the only performances which Schwarzkopf had sung under Clemens Krauss's baton since London and Vienna in 1947/48, and the only time in her career when she was produced by Heinz Tietjen who she considered had been so unhelpful in 1942 by refusing to see her in Berlin. Now he was obliged to come face to face with her at last, though under very different circumstances. He remained as impassive as ever.

That Coronation summer in London, the public rushed to hear *Die Meistersinger*, with Schwarzkopf as Eva, Paul Schöffler singing Sachs for the first time in London, Hans Hopf his mellifluous but wooden self as Walther, while Murray Dickie, a Scot who had recently become a permanent member of the Vienna State Opera, made an endearing David.

When the Salzburg Festival came round again, Furtwängler was very much in evidence after his enforced absence of the previous summer. Schwarzkopf sang five Donna Elviras with a few newcomers in the cast, including Elisabeth

Grümmer as Donna Anna and Erna Berger as Zerlina; and she had four *Figaro* Countesses with more or less the same wonderful cast as ever in 1952, but this time the opera was in German.

Paul Czinner was preparing to make a colour film of *Don Giovanni* in the Felsenreitschule (Rocky Riding School). Schwarzkopf sang all five stage performances, but when the film came out Lisa Della Casa was Donna Elvira. Schwarzkopf declined to take part in it, and because most of the filming was being done during performances, all the Elvira scenes had to be reshot and patched in. Legge spread it about that Furtwängler, who was unwell at the time (he was to die in November 1954), had conducted only the overture.[17]

Nineteen fifty-three was the fiftieth year since Hugo Wolf's death, and with the power that Legge then wielded in Salzburg he persuaded the Festival authorities to set down an entire Wolf recital with Schwarzkopf as soloist. Because the pre-war Lieder concerts had not been resumed, a place for the recital was found in August among the chamber concerts. It became an extraordinary event with Schwarzkopf accompanied by Wilhelm Furtwängler.

The Schwarzkopf–Furtwängler partnership came about in a surprising manner. Schwarzkopf recalls that she was dining with Furtwängler after they had given a performance of Beethoven's 'Choral' Symphony in Turin at the end of the previous year. He shyly asked whether an accompanist had yet been booked for the planned Wolf recital the following August. A little surprised at the question, she told him that as far as she knew none had. Schwarzkopf always found Furtwängler's quiet charm particularly disarming and was astonished when he humbly requested to be allowed to play for her. As he was going to be conducting opera at Salzburg in any case, his offer was gladly accepted, and that summer, when Schwarzkopf arrived at the village outside the Festival city where most of the artists stayed, Furtwängler could be heard practising his fiendishly difficult Wolf accompaniments as industriously as a music student before an important examination.[18]

Legge was in Milan recording Callas in her first *Tosca*, and missed both rehearsal and recital, but afterwards he was most annoyed to hear that Furtwängler had insisted on having the piano lid fully open, spoiling the balance from some seats in the auditorium, and tending to drown Schwarzkopf's voice[19] – though this is not evident on the CD that emanates from the Austrian Radio recording.

After Salzburg, Schwarzkopf went alone to Lucerne to sing in the Verdi Requiem which, between 1951 and 1958, became an annual event. The conductor was Antonino Votto, who had been one of Toscanini's assistants at La Scala, and all singers trusted him implicitly. The *Gazette de Lausanne*'s critic confessed to having exhausted most of his superlatives:

Madame Schwarzkopf possesses all the virtues which one could possibly hope for in a singer. Her solo in the 'Libera me' will long be remembered in Lucerne, for in it this prodigious interpreter reached the limits of human subtlety.[20]

Her companions in the quartet were again the magnificent Oralia Dominguez, Giuseppe di Stefano and Cesare Siepi, and this indisputably glorious occasion was the penultimate appearance which Schwarzkopf made as an unmarried woman. Her last London appearance was with the Prommers at the Royal Albert Hall on 9 September when, for the first and last time under the austere but very reliable baton of Sir Adrian Boult, she sang Mozart's *Exsultate, jubilate,* 'not just as a showpiece,' said the *Times* critic, 'but for an exceptional voice, first and foremost as a living piece of music . . .' The second and third movements showed 'many refreshing, imaginary touches of insight in her phrasing so it was no surprise that the vast audience recalled her time and time again'.[21]

~ 12 ~

Herbert von Karajan Supreme
1953–1954

There had been many favourite ladies in Walter Legge's life, a good few of them singers, and for years he had sworn he would marry the most beautiful of all. Elisabeth Schwarzkopf was exceedingly beautiful; he took good care of her on both professional and personal levels. He needed to be certain that she was looked after, whether he was with her or not, and so when they were apart, he telephoned her every day, wherever she might be. In fact he used the telephone to propose to her from London when she was in Australia.[1]

In October 1953, after sharing his house in Acacia Road, Hampstead for several years, entertaining with him there as a couple whenever she was in England, and appearing everywhere with him, Elisabeth Schwarzkopf became Mrs Walter Legge. She was unmarried, but he was divorced, so there could not be a church wedding even if she had wanted one, nor was there an announcement in *The Times*. Their names had been coupled for some considerable time and they were married quietly in the Register Office at Epsom on 19 October with Jane Withers, manager of the Philharmonia Orchestra, and Ernest Newman as witnesses. Afterwards they went back to Tadworth where Mrs Newman provided the wedding breakfast.

More than a few of the Legges' acquaintances were surprised, even alarmed, that Elisabeth Schwarzkopf had chosen to commit herself to marrying Walter. He was renowned as a womanizer in England, Germany, Austria and even France. Perhaps he was no Don Juan, but he is noted for having notched up many sexual conquests. Just as Donna Elvira was well aware of Don Giovanni's activities, so must her sometimes *alter ego*, Elisabeth Schwarzkopf, have been aware of Don Walter's numerous successful amatory escapades.

For all the dislike Legge aroused in business circles, his musical achievements were held in higher esteem than ever when, in September 1953, he concluded an important new agreement for EMI in the United States with Dario Soria, an Italian who now launched Angel Records after having sold his Cetra-Soria company in New York. The new company took its name from the Recording Angel trademark which had always appeared on the blank side of single-sided Columbia acoustic 78s. Luxuriously designed, presented and marketed, Angel

Records were drawn from the UK Columbia list and strongly appealed because they had what their new public called 'a touch of class'. This was accurate as far as their intrinsic quality was concerned, and Schwarzkopf's picture on many of the record sleeves helped to introduce her to the United States.

Her first engagement after the wedding was her US début in a Lieder recital at Town Hall, New York, on 25 October 1953, with the Hungarian pianist, Arpád Sándor as accompanist. He was put through several gruelling days of rehearsal under Walter Legge's vigilant eye and ear and played a crucial role in the success of the recital. Afterwards, the American media made much of their erroneous belief that Schwarzkopf would be learning the role of Beethoven's Leonore in *Fidelio* during her return flight to Europe. This was nonsense, of course: she had been working on it for much longer, and although she may have been a quick study, this would have been asking the impossible. Three days later, on 28 October in Basel, she sang the role for the first time, in a concert performance, with the Vienna Symphony Orchestra and *Singverein* under Karajan. The star cast included Lorenz Fehenberger as Florestan and Josef Metternich as Pizarro. Ludwig Weber, who should have sung Rocco, was ill, and his place was taken by Theodor Schlott, a good alternative choice.

> The combination of Fidelio, the Vienna Orchestra, von Karajan and Elisabeth Schwarzkopf (the principal magnet) became a great attraction, so that the auditorium and the adjacent foyer were packed with a delighted audience. It had been sold out for two months before ... As Leonore, Elisabeth Schwarzkopf impressed with her vocal beauty and eminent skill, as well as her vivid shaping [of phrases]. Nevertheless, the wonderful voice did not seem as free and flexible as usual and also sometimes sounded markedly stifled.[2]

The work was repeated in concert, in Geneva and Zürich, with much the same response; but it was not until a year later that Schwarzkopf returned to Leonore, recording the Act I *scena* 'Abscheulicher!' on 78. Having been excluded from LP, this aria has re-emerged on CD, revealing Schwarzkopf as somewhat ill at ease, forcing her naturally lyric voice and using an unfamiliar, covered timbre, perhaps the same 'stifled' tone remarked on by the Basle reviewer. In the tender passages, however, such as the *Farbenbogen* (rainbow) phrase in the recitative, she sings beautifully. And those bugbears for most dramatic sopranos, the high Bs, and the G octave leaps, come easily to Schwarz- kopf, while she manages the last, cruellest six bars perfectly, catching the two horns on their upward flight in one of the cleanest, most accurate accounts on disc.

No more is known to have been preserved of Schwarzkopf's Leonore, and this uncharacteristic role heralded the second phase of new ones under Karajan's direction, which also included Pamina in *Il Flauto Magico* in December 1953 and Marguerite in *Faust* in February 1954.

Karajan maintained his faith in Schwarzkopf as Leonore to the extent of seriously considering a production of *Fidelio* when his Salzburg Easter Festival had become established.[3] As we know now, he decided in favour of Wagner, and when he did come round to mounting *Fidelio* at the 1971 Salzburg Summer Festival, it was too late for Schwarzkopf to be considered.

Karajan rounded off 1953 by persuading her to sing Pamina in a broadcast for RAI Milan of *Il Flauto Magico*, which his Milanese public insisted on hearing in their vernacular. Fortunately for us, the performance has been preserved and is the only opportunity of hearing Schwarzkopf singing a complete Pamina, one of her radiantly successful roles in London and Vienna. All that exists on CD of her German-language Pamina is the aria, 'Ach, ich fühls,' and the 1947 Karajan-conducted Pamina–Papageno duet 'Bei Männern' with Schwarzkopf and Erich Kunz, the supreme Papageno of the day. The Italian CD set is thus of great importance in Schwarzkopf's recorded heritage. Her voice is in excellent shape and, with an actress to speak her dialogue, she vividly captures Pamina's growth from innocence to awareness. After working in the ambience of La Scala, the Italian language posed no problem to Schwarzkopf, any more than the language-change in *The Rake's Progress* had done two years before.

As neither Karajan nor Legge was particularly interested in French opera, with one exception, these works were left to other conductors: De Sabata for *Pelléas* and Rodzinski for *Faust* in Italian. Schwarzkopf agreed to join Boris Christoff as Mephistopheles and 'Giuseppe di Stefano, undoubted star of La Scala; but the role of Faust was actually sung by a mediocre Gianni Poggi who pleased Schwarzkopf not at all'.[4] As Walter Legge put it, preferring future oblivion on the matter, 'she, like Goethe, sank without trace'.[5]

The one exception just mentioned was the complete *Pelléas* studio performance Karajan made for Italian Radio in Rome. As you can hear on the CD transfer, Schwarzkopf sounds at odds with the rest of the cast. Her accent jars slightly; and her style is unFrench and over-sophisticated for the fragile, mysterious girl. Pelléas is taken by the Swiss tenor Ernst Haefliger who manages rather well although he has not the ideal *martin* voice for the role. The CDs are a curious record of Schwarzkopf in an inappropriate role and suggest why she sang no more stage Mélisandes.

Both Legges regarded Maria Callas as a friend: Legge as her record producer and Schwarzkopf because there was never any question of competition between them, although she always remained wary of the Greek-American diva. But even Callas felt she had something to learn from Schwarzkopf; and one evening towards the end of August 1954, she walked on her own into the Biffi Scala Restaurant in Milan, went straight to Schwarzkopf's table and demanded to be shown exactly how she was able to produce certain notes.

Schwarzkopf had just arrived back from Salzburg, which Callas knew because she was recording *La Forza del Destino* with Legge just across the road. It was not going well and she was apprehensive after hearing rumours that she might be replaced as Leonora. Callas was having trouble with certain passages in the score during recording, and one can imagine Legge saying, 'Ask Elisabeth how she does that: she'll tell you.' So Schwarzkopf was roped in to give Callas a private lesson, in public, prodding her while she sang, then demonstrating how *she* achieved the particular sounds which Callas was after. 'Yes, I think I've got it,' Callas said, thanked Schwarzkopf and walked out,[6] satisfied that she had learned something useful. Perhaps because of her very short sight, Callas seemed entirely oblivious of her uninvited audience in the restaurant, who gasped in astonishment and were able to regale their friends for months afterwards with a description of the Schwarzkopf–Callas singing lesson in Biffi Scala.

Nineteen fifty-four was a fantastic year for Schwarzkopf's operetta and opera recordings, which took priority over public appearances because Legge was intent upon capturing on disc as much of her voice as he could while it was in full bloom. She made five complete works during May and June, beginning with *Der Zigeunerbaron* (*The Gipsy Baron*), *Wiener Blut* (*Vienna Blood*) and *Eine Nacht in Venedig* (*A Night in Venice*), all under Otto Ackermann, the eminent Romanian-born Swiss conductor who had come up with a solid *Kapellmeister* training and whose work Legge greatly respected. Then they made *Ariadne auf Naxos* and *Così fan tutte*, both under Karajan. A memorable recording of the Verdi Requiem under De Sabata came between the operettas and the operas, dismissing the claims of those who believe that singers work much harder in the 1990s than they did in the 1950s.

Apart from a few individual songs, the operettas were the first works to display Schwarzkopf in lighter mood, as well as in leading roles that she had not sung on stage. These recordings are cast with singers who utter in authentic tones, perfectly supported by Ackermann, who directed these delicious bonbons as nobody had done since Clemens Krauss. Schwarzkopf was very proud of her operetta recordings, although, like Lotte Lehmann, she never braved them on either of the Viennese stages, despite her Austrian citizenship. In Vienna they are extremely particular about idiomatic accent and inflexion, which have to be absorbed with mother's milk.

There are several mysteries connected with roles that Schwarzkopf did not sing. At one time, Walter Legge said, 'She hankered after Desdemona and Strauss's Ariadne but no theatre could give her both the three weeks' rehearsal and the conductor we wanted . . .'[7] Schwarzkopf's performance in the *Ariadne* recording suggests that she would have made a great success of it on stage: her few lines as the haughty prima donna of the Prologue still raise a chuckle after all these years.

In the Opera, her vocalization is magnificent. Her admirably controlled breathing, ethereal tone-colour and her gift for tragedy are all in evidence. The one low A♭, which she just manages in the Lament, might have given rise to anxiety on an off night but, surprisingly, she sang this long aria at concerts on three consecutive nights under Karajan in Berlin in 1956.[8]

Rita Streich's very accomplished Zerbinetta and Irmgard Seefried's delightful Composer go a long way towards offsetting some of the disadvantages in this unevenly produced recording. There is a less than godlike Rudolf Schock as Bacchus and some careless mismatching of ambience in the Haushofmeister's (Major-domo's) declamations, about which Legge was sensitive afterwards; when it was mentioned he exclaimed, 'Oh, you *would* bring that up!'[9]

Arabella was another disappointment for Straussians – and Schwarzkopfians too – who hoped she might proceed farther than the inviting recorded excerpts; she made no more, and never assumed the role on stage despite encouragement from Lotte Lehmann, Clemens Krauss and Viorica Ursuleac, all of whom had been involved in *Arabella* premières. She refused to respond to their blandishments which may not have been altogether sincere anyway. When asked what Schwarzkopf had against these two Strauss heroines, Legge replied that they are both very unattractive and stupid women with whom his wife found little affinity.[10]

Around and between all the many recording sessions in these years, Schwarzkopf found time to give recitals, and one bright Sunday afternoon in March 1954 she and Fischer-Dieskau, with Gerald Moore at the piano, gave a memorable all-Schumann concert. He began it with the *Dichterliebe* cycle, and then Schwarzkopf sang the *Frauenliebe und -leben*, a less distinctive cycle (as the *Times* critic noted) and one in which she produced 'exaggerated intonations and emphases, as if determined to put forward a good case for a cycle with which she had no great sympathy'.[11]

In June 1954, Legge set up recording sessions for the Verdi Requiem with De Sabata which turned out to be his last studio adventure as his health was already declining. The performance is a thrilling one, from the awed whisper of 'Requiem' at the start, to the savagery of his 'Dies irae', when the chorus members violently spit out their words.

We can also admire Schwarzkopf's very beautiful contribution. She gives the impression of possessing a larger voice than she actually had; and who else, except perhaps Renata Tebaldi, was able to float those long, high phrases so exquisitely?

Both De Sabata and Legge wanted Callas to sing the solo mezzo in this most dramatic of Requiems. The mezzo may be considered to have greater importance than the soprano, whose only solo is the last number of all. Notwithstanding, Callas firmly declined. She was never going to take the *second* line, not even to Schwarzkopf. Whatever would her fans say? And what a time the press would have.

It was this Requiem's casting that came near to causing strife between Callas and the Legges. Callas always believed she would eventually quarrel with all her friends and told Legge how dreadful it was going to be when they had their set-to: they now knew so much about one another that the hurt was going to be very deep on both sides. Callas never completely forgave Legge for resigning from EMI when he did, because she insisted, very foolishly and entirely wrongly, that he did so deliberately to spoil her recording career.[12]

These tiffs apart, the Legges used to attend and support as many of Callas's stage occasions as they could; and they witnessed both the celebrated walk-out after Act I of *Norma* at La Scala on New Year's Day 1958 and her enormously successful and prestigiously attended Paris première in the same year. Callas did not consider herself and Schwarzkopf as *primae inter pares* because she thought only of herself and the role she was singing, and nobody else in the world of sopranos concerned her unless there was a possibility of her losing fees. If another singer replaced her for any reason, usually that of her nervous indispositions, Callas did not regard that soprano as anything more than a substitute, certainly not a rival.

Three international festivals came close together in the late summer of 1954. At Salzburg, in August, Schwarzkopf was Donna Elvira again in the Furtwängler *Don Giovanni*, of which a live performance was recorded, offering an ideal example of her voice at this time. She sang in Beethoven's 'Choral' under Furtwängler in Lucerne, then went straight to Edinburgh. The inspired choice of the Scottish capital as a festival city is believed to have been Rudolf Bing's, because its skyline reminded him of Salzburg. The Glyndebourne management had helped found the first Festival in 1947, with Bing as its director. He knew that to get the best international artists, Edinburgh must wait until Salzburg was over.

Schwarzkopf and Hans Hotter led otherwise British forces at Edinburgh in a Verdi Requiem that was given *in memoriam* Kathleen Ferrier, who had died the previous October. The mezzo on this occasion was Constance Shacklock, who had been the regular Octavian to Schwarzkopf's Sophie in the Covent Garden Opera Company. The Hallé Orchestra's lovable and understanding conductor was Sir John Barbirolli, no stranger to Schwarzkopf, and the British soloists included Richard Lewis, Schwarzkopf's intended Troilus in the Walton opera. Barbirolli provided the Italianate impulse, and Schwarzkopf's character-istic purity of tone was evident as she negotiated those soaring phrases with the greatest of ease. She was without doubt the star of the occasion. Barbirolli's Italian ear had perceived how right Schwarzkopf's voice was for this work when he engaged her for the performance on 26 May 1951 in London, at the new Royal Festival Hall.

The Legges were championing Karajan in his love affair with Eliette Mouret, who was now pictured on the Edinburgh Festival programmes advertising expensive woollen jumpers. They were all up in Edinburgh together because Karajan was engaged to give three concerts with the Philharmonia. The Glynde-bourne Opera was also there, performing *Così*, *Le Comte Ory* and *Ariadne* with several old colleagues from Vienna: Sena Jurinac as Fiordiligi, and Alda Noni as Despina; Murray Dickie, Sesto Bruscantini and Carl Ebert, their producer, as well, so there was much laughter and merriment in German and Italian at the Caledonian Hotel.

Karajan's second concert, all orchestral Beethoven, fell on a free day for Schwarzkopf. She attended the closed rehearsal at ten o'clock that morning in the Usher Hall, and Eliette Mouret, who was with her, brought along a man friend from London, to tease Karajan, just as she had done at another of his rehearsals at the Royal Festival Hall, with the same man, a few weeks before. He sat with Eliette and the Legges, and Karajan looked round inquiringly at them from time to time. By now the Philharmonia Orchestra was perfectly familiar with his handling of Beethoven's Fourth and 'Eroica' Symphonies, but this rehearsal was intense, all the same. Twice Legge called 'Noch einstimmen, Herbert!' ('Retune!'), with which the conductor instantly complied.

During the day there was usually time for the artists to hear other concerts and to visit the Festival attractions, and this year the Diaghilev Exhibition had been brought up from Forbes House in London, again sumptuously mounted by Richard Buckle. So that afternoon, while Karajan was resting, the Legges, Eliette Mouret and the Englishman visited the exhibition. Schwarzkopf was intrigued by the original costumes and décor, the designs and the whole mood which Buckle had caught so well. Eliette's friend was 'faschinated' by Eliette (her word) but Legge was more intrigued by pictures of those who had worked closely with Diaghilev. When they reached a showcase of photographs with the impresario's most intimate friends and lovers, he exclaimed, 'Just look, they've all got the same face: Nijinsky, Massine, Lifar, Dolin, Markevitch and – and Boris Kochno, but nobody quite knows whether he . . . er . . . well . . . um!'

Because the concert was sold out, Eliette's friend, by this time rather more than a hanger-on, was told he had to sit among the Philharmonia's second violins that evening, even though he had tickets for another Festival event.

Legge said, 'You've been to the rehearsal, so of course you'll be at the concert,' and wouldn't take no for an answer.

Karajan walked briskly on to the platform in front of a packed house and, briefly acknowledging the applause, turned to the orchestra, gave a deep breath, and as though in prayer, waited for complete silence. Then, with hands out-stretched, head still down and eyes shut, he willed the orchestra to launch Beethoven's 'Egmont' Overture into the air, seeing the printed page in his mind and thereafter seldom opening his eyes. At rehearsals he rarely spoke either, so that each word counted; nor did he raise his voice, whatever the circumstances, and that made the players listen to him more carefully. At concerts it was an unseeing contact between composer, conductor and musicians, a joint effort in which his will was supreme and he almost visibly became the conduit through which the sound passed. Only when there were singers present, or if he sensed that something was about to go wrong, did he maintain eye-contact with the artists.

Schwarzkopf was finding the situation amusing, perhaps because Eliette's 'tease' was still being perpetuated in front of Karajan throughout the concert. Two or three times, when she caught the eye of this non-playing member of the orchestra, Schwarzkopf laughed and pointed at him.

Afterwards Legge took his party of six, which now included Jane Withers, the Philharmonia Orchestra's manager, to dine at the fashionable Aperitif Restaurant. Karajan joined them, having changed and recovered Eliette, but was in a moody and argumentative frame of mind. 'Beethoven's Fourth Symphony is probably the most difficult of them all to bring off satisfactorily,' he announced. His audience waited to be told why, especially in view of the added complexities of the 'Choral' Symphony; but Legge was not in the mood for esoteric discussions and cut him short with the wine list.

There was a curious review of Karajan and the Fourth Symphony the follow-ing day, when one music critic noted: 'While Karajan remained ice-cold and in unbelievably complete control, there was always in addition to prodigious power a warmth and at times a quite ethereal beauty about the playing.'[13] Herbert von Karajan claimed different levels of admiration and detestation, but Schwarzkopf always championed him in his lifetime, claiming that while some people disliked his manner at concerts when he made grandiose gestures, he behaved in precisely the same way at rehearsals where there was no audience. Another of Karajan's many remarkable musical senses she noticed was his ability to return to exactly the same tempo after an interruption in rehearsal. She respected his capacity for fierce concentration, which can easily be confirmed by anybody who has sat facing him at a concert. As for his pianism, she acknowledged that it possessed great feeling.[14] Once, in the early 1950s, he had accompanied her on a short Lieder recital tour in North Africa, and before the war had played piano jazz in Aachen. But Schwarzkopf's admiration for Karajan's personality and his music-making did not last for ever. When she and Karajan were together, she seemed to regard him benignly, rather as a woman might a much younger man; but in fact Karajan was seven years older. Walter Legge cherished him as one of his most prized possessions, but nevertheless treated him in the same firm, courteous manner he would show to *any* first-class conductor he employed.

Legge and Karajan were businessmen, out to achieve their own ends; and so long as their association was acceptable – and profitable – they maintained their special relationship. Legge had willingly engaged and worked with both Karajan and Furtwängler despite the latter's feeling for his Austrian 'opponent'. Once, in Salzburg, Legge had appeared to be conscientiously trying to bring them together, but this had failed completely, as he had no doubt calculated that it would. Seeing himself as Europe's musical emperor, Legge did not discourage rivalry between the two conductors. Several times Legge had actually worked against Furtwängler, as in 1951 when his whole cast for the Salzburg Festival *Zauberflöte* was handed over to Karajan for him to record and it took several years for Furtwängler to get over this affront.

Karajan was tremendously ambitious, which Legge fully realized, and he knew that their present fruitful partnership, still a kind of honeymoon, would come to an end one day when the conductor had outgrown the Legge–Philharmonia–Schwarzkopf entente. While it continued though, Schwarzkopf mattered very much to Karajan, who found her ever willing to take the roles he planned for her and in which he groomed her.

If she was asked to take offers from outsiders, Karajan expressed no interest at all. One such was Cressida, in the world première of William Walton's opera at Covent Garden, a characterization stillborn for Schwarzkopf in 1954, although she has left a recorded memento of what might have been. Composition of this opera had taken Walton seven years, because he always worked slowly; and when the time came for singers' contracts for *Troilus and Cressida* to be drawn up, Schwarzkopf withdrew, protesting that she did not want to sing in English again and, in any case, the anticipated date by which the score should have been completed had passed, and she had been obliged to make alternative arrangements. In fact she had only a few recitals in North America which ended a month before the first night.

According to Edward Greenfield,[15] who came to know Walton, Legge advised Schwarzkopf against singing the role because he had always intensely disliked Christopher Hassall's libretto and had frequently decried it to Walton. Other received reasons are that Legge forbade his wife to accept Cressida because her English was not good enough. But Schwarzkopf's English had always been considered perfectly acceptable at Covent Garden; and ironically, the pronunciation of the soprano who replaced Schwarzkopf was far less idiomatic.

Finding another Cressida at this late stage was no easy matter. Leading sopranos, including Maria Callas, Renata Tebaldi and Eleanor Steber were considered, even canvassed, but with no success, and the eventual choice fell on the Hungarian soprano, Magda Lászlo, beautiful in appearance but cold of voice. Walton accepted her reluctantly because Schwarzkopf's very different timbre had been in his mind all along. Lászlo used to tease him at rehearsals too, which he found irritating.

On the first night at Covent Garden in December 1954, with Schwarzkopf and Legge among the audience, the general public and older critics liked the opera for its easy, romantic idiom; but mutterings about Hassall's work being 'Novello-ish' were also heard, simply because, in addition to serious verse and poetic plays, he had been a successful lyricist for seven of Ivor Novello's musicals and plays with music.

When *Troilus* was staged at La Scala, Milan, it had even less success. 'They'll understand it better in another fifty years,' said Walton,[16] but considering the new directions which opera composers were, and still are taking, this seems to have been no more than a pious hope, especially as the 'understanding' of *Troilus* requires relatively little effort.

Afterwards, Schwarzkopf agreed to record some excerpts, perhaps to assure Walton that his music had indeed been very suitable for her, perhaps merely as an exercise in self-justification. She has majority participation as Cressida on the CD and sings it very well indeed; a vibrant and virile Richard Lewis is Troilus, Monica Sinclair is Evadne; and Peter Pears's marvellously rich and comic characterization of Pandarus has been rescued from elsewhere in a telling fragment.

These are mementi of Walton's ideal cast and he conducts them. Schwarz-kopf's real tragic nobility and ardour in the love scene make her absence from the stage cast all the more frustrating, especially as her presence might have changed the whole future of this opera. As Lord Harewood later commented:

> . . . a subsequent revival of *Troilus and Cressida* convinced me that this . . . is a rewarding work, on any terms a successful opera, a bit unlucky perhaps in its initial timing in that it was born under what amounted to a low-brow star.[17]

Despite his serious mien, Sir William Walton's dry Lancastrian wit was never far away, even on important occasions. Sir Michael Tippett relates with some astonishment how he once dined with Walton and Legge during the composition of *Troilus*:

> Imagine my amazement when Willie announced that he was going to include a musical representation of heterosexual copulation – there would be the

greatest orgasm in music since Wagner's *Tristan* – and the two of them spent the greater part of the meal working out the rhythmic patterns of sexual intercourse![18]

They seemed to have overlooked *Der Rosenkavalier*.

On 30 November 1954 Wilhelm Furtwängler died of pneumonia at the relatively early age of sixty-eight. Schwarzkopf had been on friendly terms with him since the end of the war, and he had done much to help her career with the Lucerne concerts and then at Salzburg. There existed between them a special kind of affection which Schwarzkopf enjoyed as much as Furtwängler. Each admired the other's personality and artistry.

His death signalled a change in the whole balance of musical power in Europe. Karajan was in Rome on the night in question and received an anonymous telegram from Vienna: 'The king is dead, Long live the king.' He had already been approached secretly by Wolfgang Stresemann for the Berlin Philharmonic Orchestra, and had agreed to accept their invitation to become its conductor – something he had passionately wanted since 1938 when he first stood in front of them. Karajan was about to direct and stage a new production of *Der Ring* at La Scala, so this had to be cleared with their intendant, Antonio Ghiringhelli, who was completely understanding and willingly released Karajan from his contract there in order to take up such a vital appointment.

There were other considerations and complications to be overcome before Karajan finally found himself director for life of Europe's richest orchestra. Karl Böhm had just taken over the Vienna State Opera, who had participated in each Salzburg Festival since 1921. With the main impediment to his working in Salzburg now removed by Furtwängler's death, Karajan was on the verge of realizing his ambitions.

Meanwhile, here he was in Rome, in early December 1954, with a concert and two broadcast operas to perform by Christmas Day. In spite of his apparent lack of interest in French opera, remembering those doubtful Mélisandes under Rodzinski at La Scala, he had decided that Schwarzkopf should sing her again in a studio broadcast of *Pelléas* from Rome on 19 December. This is the only performance that has been preserved and allows us to judge her Mélisande for ourselves on the last occasion she sang it.

A week later, on Christmas Day, Karajan gave a concert performance in Milan of *Hansel and Gretel*, in which Schwarzkopf sang Gretel for the last time (and in Italian). So ended Karajan's spate of operatic experiments with Elisabeth Schwarzkopf in three highly unlikely roles. From now on, his interest in her career would begin to decline.

Recordings
1955–1959

Schwarzkopf had not sung the *Figaro* Countess for more than a year when, in March 1955, Otto Ackermann directed her in two performances of the opera in Monte Carlo. He had also accompanied her sympathetically in the first (mono) version she made of Richard Strauss's *Four Last Songs* the previous year, after what was apparently her first public performance, under Fritz Reiner at a concert in Chicago. Though more often associated with operetta, Ackermann was nevertheless 'a very serious opera conductor . . . he had this instinct for knowing what the singer does, guiding, but not giving too much away, but still giving way and having the lilt and feel for the Viennese freedom . . . It was liberty but governed, reined by taste.'[1]

Immediately afterwards, she appeared at the Royal Festival Hall, billed as the 'only recital this season', yet two months later she gave a joint recital there, with Irmgard Seefried, in connection with a recording that they had just made.

> The recital of vocal duets . . . presented a delightful form of music that is more often heard in the home than in public. With two singers of the quality of Miss Elisabeth Schwarzkopf and Miss Irmgard Seefried mutually attuned to a nicety and accompanied by Mr Gerald Moore, the duets by Monteverdi, Carissimi and Dvořák sounded fresh and lovely, for the singers' art concealed the artifice of the Italians' pastoral verse and revealed the naïvety of Moravian duets in the folk manner. The singers' voices blended as flute and clarinet. Miss Elisabeth Schwarzkopf taking the top line in the Italian pieces, the lower in some of the Dvořák duets.[2]

Schwarzkopf had been making the glorious recording of *Die Fledermaus* where she has a whale of a time, not as Adele but as Rosalinde, another of Legge's castings which could scarcely have been bettered at the time.

Schwarzkopf is not readily associated with Sibelius, but in June she went to Helsinki to take part in two concerts devoted to the Finnish master's works in his ninetieth year. This was a brave gesture because she recorded only a handful of his songs. Apart from Schwarzkopf's North American forays, Legge was making her concentrate more than ever on Lieder; consequently she did not encounter Karajan again until July. In the course of the Philharmonia's tour in 1955, Legge took them to Vienna with concerts and a recording date, which initially caused surprise among the resident Philharmonic Orchestra. The London players were at their peak of excellence, with the best strings in Britain at the time, but no one could pretend they rivalled the lustre of the Vienna Philharmonic. Legge knew this perfectly well, but he had made his point and showed his orchestra off to advantage. The Gesellschaft der Musikfreunde were delighted to provide their chorus for a new recording of Beethoven's 'Choral' Symphony with the Philharmonia under Karajan for which, apart from Schwarzkopf, there was a new generation of singers since their first commercial recording in Vienna eight years before.

In Canada that August Schwarzkopf gave a Lieder recital at Stratford, Ontario that was repeated in Toronto a few days later, with a concert in between. Paul Ulanowsky, who had so often accompanied Lotte Lehmann, was Schwarzkopf's able companion on both occasions. The Festival Concert Hall

> looked like a huge barn, was totally unventilated and the temperature on stage was 106°. After the orchestral concert she 'held court' outside the stage entrance of the big skating rink where the concert had taken place.
>
> Scherman, the conductor, asked her: 'How is Irmgard these days?'
>
> 'Irmgard!' she replied. 'You mean Madame Seefried? We both appear in the same house – in Vienna – occasionally, but we're very different persons. It's strange, although I was born in Germany, I was always, by nature, Viennese. She, on the other hand, has remained German . . . It's remarkable how far she's come, considering her peasant background.'[3]

Considering that the *grande dame* had been making the duet recording and singing in a London concert with Seefried only three months before, her response is striking. A few days before this incident in Stratford she had sung 'a great, all Hugo Wolf recital. At one point, a fly landed on her ample cleavage and even though she kept trying to blow or push it away, the fly continued to plague her through several Lieder. When we mentioned this "fly-routine" to our host, Sir Tyrone Guthrie, his comment was unprintable.'[4]

There were no Salzburg or Lucerne Festival dates in 1955 and very few opera performances until the autumn. But on 5 September Schwarzkopf sang what turned out to be her last Promenade Concert with Sir Malcolm Sargent and the BBC Symphony Orchestra. It was devoted to popular items by Mozart and Strauss. She sang the concert aria with piano obbligato 'Ch'io mi scordi di te' and afterwards three of the Strauss orchestrated songs: 'Wiegenlied', 'Morgen!' and 'Ständchen'.

That autumn she went to San Francisco for her American stage début as the Marschallin. Kurt Herbert Adler had been wise to grab her before the Met and, from Schwarzkopf's point of view, it was a useful introduction to North

American opera audiences. She gave two Marschallins and two Donna Elviras to packed and enthusiastic houses. They booked her to appear there again in the following year in other roles, although this was no slight on her first season's performances. Then it was back to Milan for five performances of *Die Zauberflöte* at La Scala in December, this time in German and far happier for that. Nicolai Gedda was an ideal Tamino.

Schwarzkopf stayed in Milan because, at the end of January 1956, she was given her first opportunity to sing Fiordiligi on the stage of the Piccolo Teatro. Guido Cantelli was to conduct eight performances of *Così fan tutte* and the director was to be Giorgio Strehler, a highly temperamental Italian and man of the theatre, who had already exerted a profound influence on dramatic and operatic staging, soon to extend through Europe. He had founded the little theatre of La Scala the previous year, mainly for experimental purposes, but now, as soon as he set eyes on Eugene Berman's 'murky décor for the production, he stormed out of the theatre belching clouds of quadrilingual obscenities'.[5]

There was now no alternative for Cantelli but to conduct and stage the opera himself, and he scored a notable success in this perilously difficult work. Schwarzkopf got on well with him. But his volatile, Italian temperament was the scourge of many orchestral musicians because, like his *'padre'* Arturo Toscanini, he would not accept the second-rate and demanded that they all paid meticulous attention to what the composer had written. The young maestro was being nominated as musical director of La Scala in early 1957, which looked like the beginning of a brilliant new career with the strong prospect of starry performances under a strong and dedicated hand.

In early July Schwarzkopf followed Cantelli's stimulating January *Così* production with two performances of the Verdi Requiem in London, which blazed with passion, drama and religious fervour, Cantelli drawing playing of rare beauty and intensity from the Philharmonia Orchestra. Schwarzkopf again took her place naturally among three Italian soloists, Ebe Stignani, Ferruccio Tagliavini and Giuseppe Modesti. She

> excelled in the quieter soprano music, and cleverly simulated the big style the 'Libera me' demands . . . what made it moving as well as exciting was the manner in which all the performers captured the deeply questioning quality with which the agnostic Verdi peered into the chasm of death.[6]

So wrote Peter Heyworth, all too prophetically: Cantelli was killed in a plane crash at Orly Airport the following November, at the age of only thirty-five. He was mourned by the entire musical world, though Arturo Toscanini was too ill to be told that his protégé, whom he loved as a son, had already preceded him into the next world. A memorial performance of the Verdi Requiem was held in honour of the young genius at the Royal Festival Hall, London in June 1957. The Philharmonia Orchestra played under Argeo Quadri but Schwarzkopf did not take part, although she was in London. Had Cantelli lived, it would have been fascinating to compare his progress with that of his older contemporary, Karajan. Both conductors possessed great personal dynamism. Would they have clashed?

A phrase used by Peter Heyworth to describe Schwarzkopf's singing in Cantelli's performances of the Verdi Requiem is worth consideration: she 'cleverly simulated the big style'. Her consummate technical mastery, her experience and ability to 'simulate' enabled her to continue her career for the next twenty years, when the bloom was gradually fading from her voice.

Shortly before Cantelli's unforgettable pair of Requiems in London, Schwarzkopf was there with Karajan in a concert which turned out to be his last as conductor of the Philharmonia Orchestra, due to his imminent move to the Vienna State Opera. This performance of the *Four Last Songs* was issued on CD in 1990, Schwarzkopf's seventy-fifth birthday year, to which she strongly objected, saying quite simply that it was a bad performance.

She returned to Salzburg in July for five *Figaro* Countesses under Böhm and a recital of mixed Lieder from Bach to Wolf. Then it was on to the delights of Lucerne, to sing songs from Wolf's *Italian Liederbuch* with Fischer-Dieskau, now an acknowledged partner in Lieder recitals.

Schwarzkopf was involved in a spate of major recordings in the latter half of 1956: first she took the grateful role of Margiana in Cornelius's *Barber of Baghdad* with Gedda and Prey, conducted by Erich Leinsdorf. According to Walter Legge, it is seldom a success with the public,[7] and although its recording may have been something of a vehicle for Schwarzkopf, its re-emergence on CD, after many years, shows it to be highly entertaining. The same is true of Carl Orff's *Die Kluge* (The Clever Girl), a characteristically *Plattdeutsch* one-acter with a role that also suited Schwarzkopf very well, although this cynical work has found limited appreciation by non-German audiences.

After a recital at the Royal Festival Hall in February 1957, the *Times* critic, William Mann, wrote a review of Schwarzkopf in which he extolled her gifts as a Lieder singer:

> A LESSON IN INTERPRETATION . . . a triumph in conveying every nuance of expression. . . . She possesses the vital ability in a singer of songs to seize the essence in the first bars and hold emotion of them to the last note and beyond, into the pianist's postlude . . .[8]

Schwarzkopf's next recording venture was a similar triumph: Alice Ford in Karajan's account of Verdi's *Falstaff*, with Tito Gobbi in the title role, Fedora Barbieri as Mistress Quickly, Luigi Alva as Fenton and Rolando Panerai as

Ford. The recording is said to hold a secret that has still not been divulged: at what point does Schwarzkopf speak for one of the other singers? There was once a similar mystery in the famous old *Rosenkavalier* set of 1933, when Elisabeth Schumann interpolated, 'Ja, ja!' for Lotte Lehmann, but we have known the answer to that for many years.

Schwarzkopf went on to sing her first staged Alice Ford on the West Coast of the United States during September 1956, with its première in San Francisco; then she sang *Così* again, now more confidently in her repertoire after the eight performances under Cantelli in Milan. The San Francisco management was delighted with her assumptions, and invited her back for 1957 to repeat Fiordiligi and her Marschallin.

The definitive *Rosenkavalier* recording had long been one of the Legges' ambitions and now, in December 1956, Legge had assembled his ideal cast. The intention had never been to follow Decca's example and record every note in Strauss's score (as they had done under Kleiber and were to do again with Solti) but to make the stage cuts so that the result would be familiar to those who already knew the work in the opera house.

Legge was employing Professor Heinrich Schmidt as musical coach to the singers because he had worked closely with Strauss on productions of his operas in Vienna and Munich and was said to have been 'the most insistent-on-accuracy coach in German-speaking Europe'.[9] During the love duet between Octavian and Sophie in Act II, there is a short trumpet solo, echoing the second part of a melody heard in the section beginning 'Wo war ich schon einmal . . .'[10] It is played differently here from the way it is heard in British opera houses or in any other recorded *Rosenkavalier*. During the war, so Professor Schmidt told Legge, Strauss always played the 'surprise note' at performances in exactly the way that Karajan agreed to do here (though not in his later recording for DG). In Vienna, however, it is entirely up to the conductor how he wants it played and musicians' parts are marked with names and the note each requires, either E♭ or E natural. A new conductor at the Vienna Staatsoper has to make his wishes known at the rehearsal – if he gets one.

The 1956 stereo LP *Rosenkavalier* was a tremendous success and acted as an eloquent ambassador for Schwarzkopf. The young Christa Ludwig emerged as a Legge–Karajan favourite with her Octavian. As Sophie, Teresa Stich-Randall's 'white' voice is ideal, though the characterization lacks that radiance which Elisabeth Schumann imprinted on Miss Faninal in the old selection and which Schwarzkopf herself gave us in the 1947 recording with Seefried as Octavian from Act II.

Shortly after Schwarzkopf had resumed authorized performances in Vienna, during the Occupation, she found a number of unfamiliar conductors on the rostrum. On two occasions for *Don Giovanni* in 1947 one of these strangers had been the towering Otto Klemperer, whose gruff manner was occasionally relieved by devastating flashes of dry wit. Now, at the beginning of 1957, Schwarzkopf found herself singing Bach and Mozart under his direction in Amsterdam; then, in May, three performances at the Amsterdam Concertgebouw of the Beethoven *Missa Solemnis*, a work she had not looked at for seven years.

As Klemperer was being considered for the Philharmonia Orchestra, he had been conducting sessions for Legge who thought he would be best employed in the larger, serious works of Bach, Beethoven and Brahms, and of Mahler too, whose disciples both he and Bruno Walter had been. Klemperer conducted three performances of the Beethoven *Missa Solemnis*, characteristic in their rugged grandeur, on alternate days at the 1957 Holland Festival in Amsterdam with Schwarzkopf, Nan Merriman, Heinz Rehfuss (baritone) and the Hungarian tenor Josef Simándy, who was not well known in Western Europe. Klemperer had recently been music director of the Budapest Opera where Simándy was the proficient leading tenor. In all these sacred works, Schwarzkopf's voice is clean, pure and cool, the tonal colouring subtly and imaginatively varied.

La Scala audiences were keen to hear the by now famous *Falstaff* production, and Schwarzkopf sang four performances there between her dates with Klemperer. The Italian music critics, as usual, wrote nothing, or next to nothing, about the singers and the performance.

The hybrid Berlioz work, *La Damnation de Faust*, cropped up again for Schwarzkopf in London (for the first time since 1950) with one concert performance. It was sung in French, conducted by the Florentine Massimo Freccia, with Michel Roux the only native; other members of the cast were Owen Brannigan, a Geordie, David Lloyd from the United States and Schwarzkopf herself. 'Gretchen's part is small but glorious; one wished for more, so exquisitely did Mme Schwarzkopf mould the lines "D'amour, l'ardente flamme", so pathetically murmur Marguerite's final "hélas!" '[11]

Schwarzkopf was again a favourite in Vienna, as she had been in the late 1940s. Now, as super-principal soprano, she was drawing this kind of review for performances of, among others, the *Figaro* Countess:

> The cast [Seefried, Ludwig, Kunz, Wächter] was worthy of the Staatsoper and, almost without exception, ideal: above all the enchanting, splendidly sung Countess of Elisabeth Schwarzkopf who sang her arias with genuine Mozart feeling, and aroused memories of Lotte Lehmann. We cannot believe that there is a more perfect presentation of this part on the stage today.

and

> We heard some magnificent Mozart evenings, especially a Figaro under

Karajan (Schwarzkopf, Gueden, Ludwig, London, Kunz) ... Perhaps Schwarzkopf ought to be singled out as the star among the stars: no matter what she does, she is always enchanting, sings beautifully, looks radiant.[12]

At Salzburg, Schwarzkopf took the same role again with Fischer-Dieskau as the Count, Seefried as an enchanting Susanna and Böhm conducting. Then came the amazing production of *Falstaff*, an opera not heard at Salzburg since 1939 when Tullio Serafin conducted Mariano Stabile in the role. Afterwards, Karajan took the majority of his cast on to Vienna for another four performances, where they were again received with delight and enthusiasm.

In September, Walter Legge set up sessions in London for the first LP studio recording of Richard Strauss's last opera, *Capriccio*, in anticipation of Schwarzkopf's stage performances of the Countess Madeleine. Legge had great plans for this stereo production: the studio floor at Kingsway Hall had been marked out to indicate where the singers were to move at specified moments, all carefully worked out in advance so as to gain a real effect of depth and latitude in the sound. It was going to outstrip the only other version of the work, a private mono recording with some of the original singers, made in 1944 after all theatres in Germany had been closed under the Third Reich.

There was great enthusiasm among the artists: Wolfgang Sawallisch was to conduct the Philharmonia Orchestra, while the handpicked cast was, as usual, the finest that could be assembled anywhere. Legge had even included Karl Schmitt-Walter, Schwarzkopf's Berlin benefactor of 1941, for the Haushofmeister (Major-domo).

Yet for all the artistry in the finished recording, the event was marked from the start by two misfortunes. When the orchestra and cast assembled for the first session, it was under the depressing cloud of Dennis Brain's death. Brain was a tremendous motoring enthusiast who always had a copy of *Autocar* or some such magazine on his music stand, and his colleagues were aware that he drove long distances after concerts, and always at speed. Driving back from the Edinburgh Festival the previous night, he had gone to sleep at the wheel only a few miles from home, and smashed into a tree. This terrible tragedy affected the whole cast, for Dennis was everybody's friend, and the gloom had to be lifted by a pep talk from Walter Legge, along the lines of 'the show must go on'. Alan Civil, promoted to first horn, would now undertake the *Nachtmusik*, the long, legato solo near the end of the opera, and his masterly playing in the recording can be heard as his personal dedication to Brain.

Hans Hotter, who had been the poet Olivier at the opera's première at Munich in 1942, was singing the taxing, bass-baritone role of the theatre director, La Roche, while Dietrich Fischer-Dieskau was now taking Olivier. Almost as soon as they had begun to record the first scene, he became unnerved by the volume of sound that Hotter was producing. Nicolai Gedda, as the poet Flamand, also displayed an impressively easy vocal production; but Eberhard Wächter, the unmusical Count in the story and another baritone, upset Fischer-Dieskau most of all by his very free top notes, all too clearly evident as he vocalized beforehand.

Finding himself with Gedda and Hotter in the gentle opening scene, Fischer-Dieskau felt overwhelmed by the other voices, and suddenly accused Legge and his technical staff of favouring his colleagues to his own disadvantage and detriment. Legge, well used to such interruptions, called a break and invited the baritone to make tests on every microphone in the building. Fischer-Dieskau was still not satisfied and hissed loudly at Wächter, who was not immediately concerned in any case: 'Herr Kollege! Wir wissen alle dass Sie eine gute Höhe haben aber Sie brauchen nicht nur damit zu protzen!'[13] ('We all know that you've got a good top to your voice, but there's no need to show off about it!')

The technicians said that they could not work under these conditions, and Legge came to the conclusion that the only way to get things moving again was to cancel the stereo and ask all the singers to stand in a row with individual microphones. So the first studio recording of *Capriccio* remains in mono.

Schwarzkopf spent the last two months of 1957 in North America, first in San Francisco with the two operas as promised, and then with recitals on the West Coast, in New York and Montreal. Back in Europe in the early New Year of 1958, she and Raucheisen made a return visit to Berlin. Apart from the three concerts there with Karajan in 1956, this was her first intimate public appearance since 1943, and the first of a number of sentimental journeys. In this case, her (rebuilt) *alma mater*, the Hochschule für Musik welcomed her in a recital that began and ended with two groups of Wolf, and some Richard Strauss in between, and finally three English songs, including what the programme dubbed a *Volkslied*, 'Drink to me only with thine eyes' – as if Schwarzkopf wanted to impress her new nationality on the Berlin audience.

A concert in London on 16 January 1958 featured a young Australian, Charles Mackerras, something of a specialist in both Mozart and Janáček, who was working as a staff conductor at Sadler's Wells. He had already conducted and recorded an agreeable programme of Christmas music with Schwarzkopf the previous spring. The concert began with Haydn's magnificent 'Scena di Berenice', 'a concert aria so abounding in original invention and in pathetic expression, to which Madame Schwarzkopf responded generously that one was inclined to forget the squally, coalescent singing with which she began'.[14]

On this occasion Schwarzkopf substituted the *Figaro* Countess for Cherubino, ending with a heavily ornamented version of 'Voi che sapete' that was rapturously received. It had followed the rarely heard 'Al desio', which Mozart composed as a substitute for Susanna's 'Deh vieni', 'exquisitely florid and adorned with blissful instrumental dialogue, notably for basset and French horns', continued William Mann.

> She ended with a brilliant demonstration of eighteenth-century gracing in Mozart: the aria was Cherubino's 'Voi che sapete' whose melodic line must have been familiar to almost everyone in the audience. One can imagine that many ambitious singers of Mozart's day blurred and distorted such a line, and it would be difficult to imagine other modern singers who would give as clean, flexible and sympathetic an exposition of the little runs and rhythmic variations in this version as did Mme Schwarzkopf. The favourite aria took on new life (or was it only rejuvenation?) because it was being treated as Mozart intended. Simplicity of line in Mozart is a myth: the audience recognized as much and cheered until Mme Schwarzkopf and her colleagues repeated their delightful performance.[14]

Karajan, now well established in Vienna, invited Schwarzkopf to sing there fairly frequently, first of all taking over her former January dates from La Scala in the two principal roles of Donna Elvira and the *Figaro* Countess. In Vienna he brought back *Falstaff* for the last time in Schwarzkopf's career. She also sang Fiordiligi for the first time there, under Karl Böhm, who had a much closer affinity with *Così fan tutte* than Karajan did.

Now an undisputed operatic *grande dame*, Schwarzkopf received the accolade of the BBC in July 1958 by recording her requests and potted autobiography for Roy Plomley's *Desert Island Discs* programme on the Home Service. But even Plomley, with all his experience in dealing with celebrities, must have been astonished by her selection: her own voice featured on seven of her discs, and the eighth, the Act I Prelude to *Der Rosenkavalier* conducted by Karajan, is an orchestral evocation of the Marschallin Elisabeth's love-making with Count Octavian Ludwig. Karajan conducted five of her choices; and the only other conductor to get a look in was Otto Ackermann with the *Wiener Blut* waltz duet. There were two ensemble numbers, the *Meistersinger* quintet and the *Falstaff* final fugue, Mozart's *An Chloë*, accompanied by Gieseking, and Wolf's 'Elfenlied' with Gerald Moore at the piano. Wilhelm Furtwängler was notably absent.

Kirsten Flagstad's diary comments on her own castaway requirements make a telling contrast with Schwarzkopf:

> I said NO ten times to the BBC people but they insisted. 'Please, please, won't you do it for us?' So I gave in. So far I have chosen only one record for my desert island: Mendelssohn's *Midsummer Night's Dream* music, as conducted

by Sir Thomas Beecham. I won't have any of my own records, if you don't
mind!¹⁵

Schwarzkopf's justification for her own programme was that it enabled her
to relive her life through her records and 'hear again the many wonderful
colleagues'¹⁶ with whom she had sung. In any case, this famous *Desert Island
Discs* broadcast has gone down in legend, immediately identifying Schwarzkopf
for many who had never previously heard of her.¹⁷

In the autumn of 1958 Schwarzkopf appeared in San Francisco and Los Angeles,
but nowhere else, in an English version of Smetana's *Bartered Bride* when she
was known as Marie rather than Mařenka. It had been nearly nineteen years
since she had last sung the small part of Esmeralda in Smetana's delightful piece
at the Deutsche Oper. Now, with pigtails and a saucy peasant dress, she had
graduated to the heroine, although she did not enjoy it: 'One ghastly experience
I had was to sing *The Bartered Bride* in San Francisco, in English – it was terrible.
To get through a thick orchestra with the "th's"; you can sing but not be
heard.'¹⁸

Despite her own views, Schwarzkopf was greatly applauded for her four
performances opposite Richard Lewis, but they were all she ever gave of the
role. (She had, incidentally, recorded the 'Endlich allein' *scena* in German at
the end of 1956.) In the San Francisco Opera House programme her Czech
rustic bride was juxtaposed, slightly incongruously, with the *Figaro* countess.

Her next quasi-operatic appearance was a single concert performance at
Carnegie Hall of Cleopatra in Handel's *Giulio Cesare*, prelude to the imminent
Handel bicentenary celebrations in Europe. For Schwarzkopf these began in
Milan at the end of December with *Hercules*, described by Handel as a musical
drama, though not intended to be staged. Herbert Graf, the director, and
Lovro von Matačič, the conductor, decided otherwise, and gave four staged
performances in Italian at La Scala. Schwarzkopf took the role of Iole, the
captive princess falsely accused of infidelity by Hercules' wife, in a classical,
sculpted white wig. She has some marvellous music, ranging from her tragic
opening aria through acceptance to her final happy union with Hercules' son
Hyllus. A first-class cast included Fedora Barbieri as Dejanira, the jealous wife
of Hercules; Franco Corelli (the only time Schwarzkopf sang with him) as
Hyllus (Illo); Ettore Bastianini as Lichas (Lica) and Jerome Hines as Hercules
(Eracle) himself.

A reasonable idea of the performance can be gained from an indifferent,
unofficial off-the-air recording from Milan. Act II gives Schwarzkopf great
opportunities in the confrontation scene with Barbieri, where, with their sharply
contrasted voices, they really strike sparks off each other.

Schwarzkopf also sang excerpts from *Belshazzar* in London and later a concert performance in Stockholm of *Judas Maccabaeus*, although nothing of this performance has survived. Another celebration of Handel, in London on 18 January 1959, was notable for a world première:

> Madame Elisabeth Schwarzkopf forsook the repertory of German songs which is her speciality, and with the aid of Harry Newstone and the R.P.O. paid tribute to Handel on the occasion of his approaching bicentenary . . . After the interval, the orchestra departed and Mr Gerald Moore joined her in two groups of Lieder: Three Youthful Songs by Richard Strauss which had been lost since the time of their composition. The third, 'Begegnung', is the most effective[19] and will be welcome as a good song to raise the roof at the end of a group.[20]

She gave another unusual concert in April, in London, under the baton of Heinz Wallberg from the Bremen Opera who

> proved a lively and punctual accompanist . . . Madame Schwarzkopf was not disposed to play the profound interpreter of Mozart in Fiordiligi's two great arias, and in the more jocular 'È amore un ladroncello' for Dorabella. She concentrated on the feminine allure in her singing with insinuating attention to words, girlish tenderness and the vocal equivalent of the *moue* . . . it could be felt that Madame Schwarzkopf was setting her sights too low.
>
> It was otherwise in the closing scene from *Capriccio*: here the singer, the role and the vocalization were at one – human, intent on truth and beauty and truly interpretative for with each inflexion and phrase, Mme Schwarzkopf brought the musicological meditations of the Countess Madeleine to springing, stimulating life . . . Here, rather than in the Mozart arias, was characterization on the concert platform.[21]

Schwarzkopf did not appear at Salzburg in 1959, when Mozart was represented solely by *Così* and *Die Zauberflöte*. Seefried was the Fiordiligi and Della Casa, Pamina; none of the other operas performed that year contained a suitable role for Schwarzkopf.

After a few performances of the Countess and Fiordiligi in Vienna during June, she had no engagements during the summer except for two appearances at Lucerne.

Schwarzkopf sang in only three performances of Handel's *Messiah* in the whole of her career. The first and second had been at Lucerne, in 1950; and now, in August 1959, came a far more riotous affair. This was under the baton of Sir Thomas Beecham, who had commissioned Eugène Goossens to 'realize' a new arrangement of the sacred oratorio. First given in New York, it did not have the status it enjoyed in Britain as a national musical monument.

Beecham did not like the Goossens arrangement so it was re- (or as Legge described it 'dis-') arranged once more, possibly by Beecham himself. There is a story, no doubt coloured over the years, that Beecham was in especially jovial mood, on account of his recent third wedding which the *Lausanne Tribune* critic referred to as his *'juvénile mariage'*. He became carried away by his own exuberance during a final chorus rehearsal, when it was obvious that the sopranos were at odds with the tenors and basses. Putting down his baton gently but emphatically, he said quite quietly,

> I would like, if I may, to point out the aptitude of No. 26, 'All we, like sheep, have gone astray' so let us look at that, shall we? No. 26. If you please. Got it? All right then, and if the ladies will open their parts . . . thank you . . . and examine them carefully, they should be able to discern, without any difficulty, exactly where the gentlemen enter.

As a coda to this episode, a Swiss music critic wrote that Wilhelm Pitz, the Philharmonia's chorus master, should be absolved from any blame for the tenors' false entry.[22]

Beecham tempered his high spirits during the performance, but his flamboyant irreverence greatly displeased Schwarzkopf, accustomed as she was to the far more dignified behaviour of Karajan and Furtwängler. The principals occupied one green room in the Lucerne *Kunsthaus* and, in the interval, Schwarzkopf used the only telephone to speak to her husband, who was in Italy. She was irritated and, in a voice that was bound to be heard, she unburdened herself, declaring, 'I shall *never* sing again for this clown!'[23] She kept her word, as she always did after professional decisions such as this.

Beecham's antics had upset Schwarzkopf, and after the concert the critics were less than ecstatic about her, reminding her of deficiencies in her high tessitura, perhaps caused by fatigue. But it was not quite the end of the relationship. Shortly before Beecham's death the Legges went round to see him during the interval of a Royal Philharmonic concert in London. He and Walter had worked a lot together and a certain professional affection remained, even though they were given to acid verbal sniping behind one another's backs. On this occasion, Beecham was expansive and friendly, and towards the end of the interval he said to them, 'Well now, you really must allow me to go out and join my orchestra; we are about to delight our audience with what is known as the Buggerall from *Samson and Delilah*. Goodnight!'[24]

That was the last time they saw him.

~ 14 ~

Consolidation
1959–1964

Sir Thomas Beecham's wit and showmanship always went hand in hand with dedicated, often inspired music-making, and his own orchestras relished his style. He conducted the Philharmonia only once, at their inaugural concert, then tried to take them over and turn them into the RPO. Legge put a stop to that: he was not going to be squeezed out.

Schwarzkopf and Legge had a sad personal engagement in July. Their old friend and benefactor Ernest Newman was dying. His mind was as keen as ever, though old age had shrunk his body to the size of a child's. On Saturday, 4 July, a very hot day, a group of five people had gathered round Newman's bedside in Tadworth. Apart from Legge and Schwarzkopf, there were Peter Andry of EMI and his brother Robert, who was a doctor of medicine, and Felix Aprahamian, deputy music editor of the *Sunday Times*, who had worked closely with Newman until his retirement in 1958. On seeing the sick man's condition, Robert Andry murmured, 'Twenty-four hours,' but Newman lasted until the Monday. Legge at once began thinking about the memorial concert.

Concert performances of two Mozart operas were already planned to take place at the Royal Festival Hall in September and October, with *Figaro* first. Schwarzkopf was to sing the Countess

> as a pendant to a new recording . . . By the time the concert begins there will have been at least 160 hours of intensive rehearsal – 16 three-hour recording sessions with orchestra, 20 recording hours of recitatives with harpsichord, 12 hours of chorus rehearsals, 80 hours of piano rehearsals with soloists and ensembles, and two full rehearsals in the Festival Hall.[1]

Even in 1959, this was unusually extravagant and far beyond the purse of any other London orchestra. It demonstrates, if nothing else, Walter Legge's constant endeavour to achieve perfection in every performance.

Figaro was followed by *Don Giovanni*, equally well cast, with Schwarzkopf as Donna Elvira. The *Figaro* passed off well after the lavish rehearsal time devoted to it; but there was a sensation over *Don Giovanni* when Klemperer sprang a high temperature and cancelled. Legge asked Giulini to take over, but conflicting dates and disobliging foreign managements prevented his release, so Klemperer's place was taken at short notice by the thirty-two-year-old Colin Davis, who had attended the rehearsals and knew the opera well after recently conducting it successfully at Sadler's Wells.

The Times reported:

> A superb conductor of Mozart declared himself last night at the Festival Hall
> . . . Mr Davis seized the opportunity and conducted a reading of *Don Giovanni*
> worthy of the splendid cast that had been assembled . . . Mr Davis had the
> benefit of the Philharmonia Orchestra . . . Mme Elisabeth Schwarzkopf,
> in beautiful though rather restrained voice, gave an eminently dignified
> performance of Donna Elvira . . .[2]

There were repeat concert performances in London of these two operas two years later, this time with Giulini conducting, but with changed casts except for Schwarzkopf.

Such international casts in live performances were brief challenges to David Webster, who fielded only home casts in these operas – when they were in the repertory. Now, at the end of 1959, almost a decade had passed since Schwarzkopf's last appearance in Floral Street and Webster was looking forward to welcoming her back. He regarded with gratitude her pioneering work in the early years of his struggling young opera company and had taken some personal pride in her outstanding career since then.

She was invited to sing the Marschallin in a strongly cast production, though still with the same, tired old 1947 Ironside sets which Schwarzkopf remembered so well from her Sophie days. The conductor was to be Georg Solti, making his operatic début at the Royal Opera House. In the summer of 1938 he had been an assistant conductor for Colonel De Basil's Russian Ballet there; but now he was being considered for the post of musical director in Floral Street, and the result of these *Rosenkavalier* performances was critical for him.

The first night was a great success for Solti but a huge disappointment for Schwarzkopf, whose sixteen stage performances of the Marschallin and the recording behind her made her feel perfectly secure about presenting the role in London. With her natural beauty and her fame as a profoundly musical recitalist, her Marschallin at Covent Garden in December was keenly awaited.

Between 1949 and 1955, Sylvia Fisher had been most frequently cast in the role there, but no Marschallin of international standard had been heard until 1958, exactly a year before Schwarzkopf's performances, when Claire Watson, 'who had studied with Elisabeth Schumann and Otto Klemperer, was able to bring an aristocratic interpretation to the part of the Marschallin, which she sang with feeling and sincerity'.[3] Régine Crespin had been the Marschallin at Glyndebourne in May 1959, to celebrate that house's twenty-fifth anniversary performance, but the event was slated by *The Times*, and Walter Legge, pre-dictably and none too privately, tore Crespin's performance to pieces.

Der Rosenkavalier provoked extreme views whenever it was produced at the end of the 1950s. Many of those who were, however optimistically, expecting another Lotte Lehmann to reveal herself at Covent Garden, were disappointed by Schwarzkopf when she failed to radiate the warmth and sincerity that had been the hallmark of Lehmann's Marie-Thérèse. Instead, she presented a skittish young woman in Act I, and in Act III one that a later critic was to describe as 'bitter'. The character was also hard-faced. Von Hofmannsthal's creation must surely have a more generous disposition if the whole renunciation theory is not to fall apart.

Schwarzkopf's singing and acting were too often marred by exaggerations and technical tricks that tended to deprive the performance of its expected spontaneity. Among other weaknesses in her performance, she sometimes indulged in that near-crooning which can be heard in her Lieder singing, and gave rise to that most hated criticism of 'arch'.

Desmond Shawe-Taylor, who had heard Lotte Lehmann's Marschallin more often than any living London critic, admired in the *Sunday Times* both Schwarz-kopf and the production: a few others were politely lukewarm, but several critics were downright hostile. The *Financial Times* remarked on Schwarzkopf's 'artificiality in her interpretation . . . that she seems almost a trivial woman, not substantial as great Marschallins should be'.[4] William Mann of *The Times*, one of Walter Legge's staunchest supporters and friends, considered that

> The chief difficulty in the overall presentation of this romantic, risqué comedy is to get the age and the class distinction entirely right. In this respect the concentration was right. Miss Schwarzkopf's Marschallin was feasible by reason of a certain archness in her start as a young woman, and the transition to early middle life in the course of the act was beautifully done.[5]

Damned with faint praise? Harold Rosenthal felt it was 'a case of art failing to conceal art, and one must regretfully register a major disappointment'.[6]

What they reported was succinctly paraphrased by Hermione Gingold in one of her 'poisoned ivy' barbs. 'Arch, dear? She's more Arch than the Admiralty!'

The general thrust of criticism appeared to underestimate the remarkable contributions by other members of the team who had been assembled by Webster. In addition to Georg Solti and Hans Busch, the producer, there was Kurt Böhme as Ochs and Sena Jurinac and Hanny Steffek as the young lovers. In fairness to Schwarzkopf, the reactions of most of those in the Royal Opera House on that first night, including this writer, were more positive than many of the reviews.

After such an unfavourable reception, Legge felt obliged to make amends to

Schwarzkopf on behalf of the Royal Opera House. He was a far from popular member of the Covent Garden Board, a fact which may have had something to do with the whole situation, as this reminiscence indicates:

'He was an extremely dangerous man. Widely experienced and with impeccable taste in music, he possessed a certain coarse charm and wit, but was nevertheless arrogant, unreliable and with a contempt for other people easily aroused.'[7]

Nevertheless, Legge attempted to reassure his wife that his and her view of the Marschallin was the right one and quite different from that of the British public, who probably think of her as a 'mother figure' – which she was not. That line of argument got Legge nowhere at all. Schwarzkopf was furious. The six performances of *Der Rosenkavalier* were all she had been offered at Covent Garden, and she swore she would never again set foot on the London opera stage – a promise she kept except for spots in charity shows, and one special Lieder recital, but she was heard in *Der Rosenkavalier* elsewhere with increased frequency until the end of her operatic career. It was as if she wanted to show the British critics what she thought of them, and resulted in a great loss to British opera-goers.

Three days after her last London Marschallin, Schwarzkopf returned to the Vienna Opera for a single Eva in *Die Meistersinger* which she had never sung there before. Her last Eva had been in London under Krauss in 1953, thought to have been her farewell to the part; now this really was the last time that Schwarzkopf–Eva placed the laurel wreath on Sach's brow. From the strength of her success at Bayreuth in 1951, and again in London, it is perhaps surprising that Eva did not become an enduring role. Her Vienna performance, though, was coolly received: 'Elisabeth Schwarzkopf sings Ev'chen,'[8] followed by the opera casts for the coming week, was all one leading critic was prepared to say, and one might assume that he was being kind.

The Viennese correspondent for *Opera* magazine was more forthcoming:

Miss Schwarzkopf was pretty as a picture and had great moments – she is one of the few Ev'chens able to carry vocally the beautiful quintet – but much of her singing wasn't up to the extremely high standard which she has set for herself, and there were disturbing sudden crescendos as if she couldn't make up her mind how to sing certain phrases . . . It was an artful performance but not a convincing one . . .[9]

With Schöffler in his greatest role of Sachs, Hotter as Pogner, imposing artists like Carl Dönch, Alfred Poell, Peter Klein and Ira Malaniuk in the other main roles, and Hollreiser conducting, Schwarzkopf was certainly in the right company. But it was perhaps unreasonable to expect an isolated performance to show her to maximum advantage when the other singers were well run in.

Having cancelled several scheduled performances of the Marschallin in Vienna during the summer of 1959, she now sang it for the first time there on New Year's Day 1960, to mixed reviews:

> Heading both the work and the stage, and drawing on a wealth of detail, the figure of the Marschallin was sung and portrayed perfectly by Elisabeth Schwarzkopf. Who can approach her singing of the Trio (the most splendid ensemble after the *Meistersinger* Quintet) or the shattering 'In Gottes Name' after it? Since Lotte Lehmann sang it we have seen no more convincing portrayal of this endlessly moving representative of the ancien régime.[10]

Joseph Wechsberg, for *Opera* again, thought otherwise:

> Miss Schwarzkopf has vocal virtuosity and can do subtle little parlando things that I've never heard before, and again there were moments when . . . no other Marschallin could touch her . . . so that one almost felt she was sincere. Almost. Unfortunately this is a part in which even the most skilled artist cannot pretend warmth and feeling that aren't there; and while Miss Schwarzkopf was as attractive as a Hollywood star and has a beautiful voice, her Marschallin never moved me, and sometimes irritated me when she was trying too hard. She was cute and coy in the first act, which is wrong, and catty and bitter in the last, which is even more wrong . . . Her Act I monologue was sung without any fault, and without any feeling. I can read the test of a successful Marschallin in the eyes of some ladies at the end of the first act . . . a good one . . . always brought tears to their eyes. This time there wasn't a tear in the house except perhaps a hidden tear of regret to see another illusion gone. Miss Schwarzkopf's failure made the whole opera meaningless . . .[11]

No other notice was as negative as this: and it was another slap in the face following those she had received from the London critics. For such epithets as 'catty and bitter' to be thrown at Schwarzkopf does seem uncharitable; and the criticism that she lacked the ability to raise the odd tear from female spectators again implies a performance relying largely on technique: flying on automatic pilot, as it were. This was hardly Schwarzkopf's way of performing. Since 1945 she had been far too conscientious, too experienced, too much the professional ever to remain uninvolved.

In early January 1960 Schwarzkopf went back to Vienna to sing the Marschallin at Karajan's invitation, though not under his direction. She did, however, give a single performance of *Figaro* with him in which she sang the Countess, as a kind of prelude to the State Opera's visit with the same opera to Wiesbaden in May.

Meanwhile, she had been to the United States for three Lieder recitals, with the ever-accommodating George Reeves, and for three concerts in San Francisco, before returning to London for a performance of the *Four Last Songs* of Strauss under Giulini's baton, one that seems not to have survived for posterity.

Schwarzkopf gave her first public performance of Countess Madeleine in *Capriccio* at San Francisco under Böhm, in May 1960. This was to be the last of her five principal roles, one to which she was ideally suited, drawing on the experience gained from the 1957 recording under Sawallisch.

Böhm had often discussed the opera with Strauss during the war, and although he did not direct its world première in 1942 (that was given by Clemens Krauss), Böhm was the first to conduct it in Vienna at the Theater an der Wien in 1951. Thereafter he held as fond a feeling for *Capriccio* as he did for the two earlier Strauss operas, *Die schweigsame Frau* and *Daphne*, whose world premières he had given in Dresden before the war.

Three days after her highly praised début as Madeleine in *Capriccio*, Schwarzkopf gave a Wolf recital in the Musikverein, Vienna, known as the 'Large Hall'. The usual preparations did not seem to have been carried out before her concert. This was not altogether surprising, in view of all her engagements, but it was unusual. A critic signing himself 'Kr' blamed faulty concert management for causing disadvantages to the singer:

> A song recital in the Large Hall, especially one devoted to Hugo Wolf's subtle lyrical treasures, is an open capitulation of artistic reason over economics. . . . Even as great an artist as Elisabeth Schwarzkopf cannot overcome the external circumstances, even she is involuntarily influenced and hampered by the false dimensions: she too involuntarily begins to force and exaggerate, to 'make points' and to over-stress nuances. A measure of hectic and nervous presentation was evident, to the detriment of charm in the shaping of her singing.
>
> Is the small increase in profit worth so much loss of artistic value? . . .
>
> Despite loss of atmosphere, Elisabeth Schwarzkopf sings enchanting songs, points Hugo Wolf charmingly and wittily and always has something special to give. She has great personality, some of which is expressed in every song, but there is no need to explain or praise this all over again. . . .[12]

Had the Musikverein been engaged for Schwarzkopf in order to net greater receipts, as the critic implies, it was certainly a false economy. He was far from unfavourably inclined towards her in his review, because such deficiencies as he noticed were largely the result of the sheer size of the auditorium.

Eleven days later there was a particularly emotional occasion in Vienna when Bruno Walter made his farewell concert appearance. Despite enforced political absence, he had been closely connected with the city and its music since he first went to Vienna in 1901 as assistant to Gustav Mahler at the Court Opera. Lotte Lehmann used to see him in the United States during, and especially after, the war when she gave him a glowing account of Schwarzkopf's abilities.

In any case, as none of Walter's soprano contemporaries was still singing, Schwarzkopf seemed the ideal choice. She sang 'Ich atmet' einen linden Duft', 'Wo die schönen Trompeten blasen' and 'Ich bin der Welt abhanden gekommen' from the Rückert group in an all-Mahler concert that ended with a performance of the Fourth Symphony.

The citizens of Salzburg were already preparing for the opening of their new opera house in the summer of 1960. It had been designed by the distinguished architect Clemens von Holzmeister, and built to Herbert von Karajan's specifications with an enormous proscenium opening and the largest stage in the world, almost 50 metres wide and over 25 metres deep. For Mozart? That was the question many people asked, and already the news had been leaked – then strongly denied – that Karajan was going to promote Wagner there. This would eventually prove true, and it signalled a radical change in the future of the Summer Festivals which, committee or no committee, were now completely in the hands of Salzburg's illustrious son, conductor and impresario.

Neither Mozart nor Wagner but Strauss and *Der Rosenkavalier* opened this enormous, £3.5-million Festspielhaus on 26 July 1960. Lisa Della Casa, now in the ascendant among Karajan's leading sopranos, sang the Marschallin on the opening night and gave four more of the total of six performances. Schwarzkopf sang only the third, but it was she, not Della Casa, who played the Marschallin in the film which followed.

As we have seen, Schwarzkopf had expected to take the role of Elvira in Salzburg's 1954 colour film of *Don Giovanni* because she had sung all six staged performances that season under Furtwängler. Instead, Lisa Della Casa was cast as Elvira, but now Legge ensured that the *Rosenkavalier* film was set up in Schwarzkopf's favour, well in advance. He believed her to be a bigger 'name' than Della Casa, and the best Marschallin of the day, both vocally and visually. Della Casa's supporters considered this monstrously unfair, but rationalized the situation by convincing themselves that Karajan now preferred their idol for *Der Rosenkavalier*, giving him the benefit of the doubt over his unusual inability to veto contracts made some two years earlier.

Besides the all-important film, Schwarzkopf had an additional, private role to play when she accepted an invitation to attend the first Karajan daughter's baptism during the Festival. This was at the home of a Salzburg industrialist, where five members of the Vienna Philharmonic accompanied Schwarzkopf while she sang 'Ave Maria' to the infant Isobel.[13]

As for the film, Dr Paul Czinner, the Hungarian director, had his own methods. He placed three cameras at strategic points and let them roll for the complete performance. The singers had to act convincingly, using half-voice, and when they needed to sing out, they altered their facial expressions by miming full voice. In the course of filming, Schwarzkopf became aware of a gap in her technique when the real singing, recorded at separate sessions on to a sound track, was put together with the action after miles of film had been edited. During the dubbing, Elisabeth Bergner, Czinner's wife and an experienced cinema actress, gave Schwarzkopf an invaluable tip to 'watch the transitions', to think ahead from one phrase to the next. Schwarzkopf called it 'difficult cross-thinking all the time. But it worked.'[14]

A review of the film in *Opera* went some way towards redressing the magazine's opinion of Schwarzkopf's first stage performance in Vienna:

> This is, in fact, a film of the Salzburg Festival production of two years ago. At the beginning of each act we see Herbert von Karajan walk through the ranks of the orchestra to take his place, amid applause, on the conductor's rostrum . . . Now this, in terms of honesty, is fake . . . but the fake is an artistic one, that is, it is aimed to give the impression of an opera performance in an opera house, and this is subtly and superbly done . . . Miss Schwarzkopf is in superb form; although film might be supposed 'remoter' than live opera, I have never found the end of the first act more moving than here.[15]

There was an occasion at one of the live *Rosenkavalier* performances in Salzburg when Karajan – unusually for him – was upstaged by another conductor with a flair for brilliant timing and showmanship. As the auditorium lights began to go down before the first act, Karajan entered the orchestra pit, as he does in the film, but had scarcely become visible when the unmistakable figure of Leonard Bernstein strode into a following spotlight that accompanied him all the way to his carefully chosen seat, stealing all the applause and leaving Karajan, barely acknowledged, to climb on to the rostrum and give the downbeat.

The two men had been introduced as early as 1947 by Bernstein's manager. They were polite to one another, as acquaintances rather than friends, but they remained diametrically opposed in their lifestyles and ways of making music. When Bernstein later announced that he was writing a big musical (*Candide*), Karajan replied that he was about to write one too, but of course he never did. Broadway is the place for new musicals, and Bernstein had New York sewn up. They were both good pianists and both played piano jazz, though never together. They seldom met, probably by choice; but Karajan's second wife, Anita, succumbed to the American's charms and became a confirmed Bernstein fan.

The *Rosenkavalier* film by Czinner and Karajan travelled to New York, and was seen and enjoyed by Schwarzkopf's admirers there and throughout major cities in the United States. Now available on video, it is an interesting realization of the Hofmannsthal–Strauss masterpiece. For older viewers, it holds its place among the proliferation of opera videos by later generations of singers, even though it embodies the traditional stage cuts. In style the film is essentially of the early 1960s and looks dated to modern eyes; but it is an invaluable guide to the kind of singing and staging in vogue at Salzburg when Karajan was in the ascendant as conductor and director in the new house.

Kurt Herbert Adler of the San Francisco Opera had cleverly grabbed Schwarzkopf for the Marschallin, when the role had been proved an ideal vehicle for her US stage début in 1955. This was shortly before her fortieth birthday, quite a good time of life for this role. Even if it had not been the success she had expected in London or Vienna, there seemed every reason to suppose that sooner or later she was going to be properly received as the Marschallin at the Met because she was already well known and liked on the New York concert platform. But no invitation was forthcoming.

Without naming names, Martha Mödl recalls:

> Rudolf Bing amused me. I remember him discussing the hiring of a famous soprano, who had been for a long time persona non grata to him because of her reported Nazi sympathies. With his dry wit he said: 'I can forgive her for having worn a Nazi uniform and for taking an American colonel as a boy friend right after the war, but I cannot swallow the fact that she then married a Jew.'[16]

Bing had already vetoed engagements for a number of 'suspect' European singers, including Gottlob Frick whose murky wartime history delayed his appearance at the Met until 1962. He had taken risks over a number of other artists believed to have had political pasts, and was only being prudent in avoiding possible criticism by delaying Schwarzkopf's engagement during his early years at the Met. There is another suggestion, though – more authoritative if less pungent – as to why it took so long for Schwarzkopf to sing at the Met during Rudolf Bing's stewardship. He was trying to build up a company of singers with an eye to sensible economy through the minimum of duplication in their roles. Eleanor Steber and Lisa Della Casa were Bing's reigning Marschallins and he was able to manage with the two of them.[17]

European star singers enjoy going to the San Francisco Opera which is financially well-endowed, friendly and hospitable, and they are always expected to give a few performances in Los Angeles and San Diego as well. This is what Schwarzkopf did. She sang the Marschallin again in San Francisco, this time under the Swiss conductor Silvio Varviso, appeared elsewhere on the West Coast, visiting Lotte Lehmann in Santa Barbara, and then went down to Dallas where she took part in an internationally cast *Don Giovanni*, with Joan Sutherland singing a vocally outstanding Donna Anna. Schwarzkopf's 'Donna Elvira was a model of style and emotional impact, and was fervently cheered'.[18]

Right Venice 1951. Stravinsky congratulates Schwarzkopf on her creation of Anne Trulove in *The Rake's Progress*; Nicholas Nabokov looks on

Below With Maria Callas in Milan *c.* 1954

Above As Donna Elvira with Cesare Siepi as Don Giovanni, February 1956 (*Opera* magazine)

Left With Guido Cantelli at the dress rehearsal for *Così fan tutte*, Piccola Scala, Milan, January 1956

A romantic and humorous Alice Ford in *Falstaff*, San
Francisco Opera, September 1956 (*Opera* magazine)

Affectionate souvenir!

With Leontyne Price as Donna Anna in *Don Giovanni*, Salzburg, August 1960

Otto Edelmann (Baron Ochs), Schwarzkopf (Marschallin), Sena Jurinac
(Octavian), *Der Rosenkavalier* Act I, Covent Garden, December 1959
(*Houston Rogers/British Theatre Museum*)

Left As Countess
Madeleine in the jinxed
Capriccio, Opéra
Comique, Paris,
February 1962

Below With Walter
Legge: anguish over
Lieder interpretation,
Kingsway Hall,
London, *c.* 1967

Lieder recital, December 1976 (*Opera* magazine)

Displaying her insignia as a Dame Commander of the Most Excellent
Order of the British Empire, 1992 (*Camera Press*)

The American Opera Society of New York had been made aware that the role of Iole in Handel's *Hercules* was familiar to Schwarzkopf. They invited her to take part in a single concert performance in English under Nicola Rescigno's baton, in December 1960. Dejanira, her new adversary in the opera, was now sung by Christa Ludwig, and Walter Berry was Hercules. They

> all contributed some distinguished and even memorable singing on this history-making occasion ... as the work's American première ... Miss Schwarzkopf used the score throughout. Her singing seemed somewhat externalized and she was not in top form as the opera began. However, she sang affectingly the aria about her father's death and thereafter, except for a lapse or two in the cadenzas, contributed measurably to the evening's enjoyment.[19]

It was Karl Böhm the faithful supporter, rather than Herbert von Karajan the instigator, who gave Schwarzkopf a single Marschallin in Vienna on Boxing Day 1960, as the first of a number which he was going to promote – four at La Scala in May, three Viennese performances scattered throughout the year, and then six at the Salzburg Festival, where Böhm also directed her as Fiordiligi in *Così*.

A Hugo Wolf Lieder recital with Gerald Moore completed Schwarzkopf's total of ten appearances in Vienna that season. There were also plans for Böhm to direct a new recording of *Così*. As she said of Böhm:

> Apart from George Szell ... he was the easiest to work with. With Böhm we never even had a single discussion. One never even had to look down at the conductor, and there were never any discrepancies. It was as though we had been doing it for a hundred years. With Karajan you had to be on your toes all the time.[20]

When Herbert von Karajan became conductor of the Berlin Philharmonic Orchestra after Furtwängler's death in 1954, he was no longer giving concerts with the Philharmonia, though he continued to make records with them until September 1960. In the selective autobiography dictated to Franz Endler, Karajan spoke about the difference between the Philharmonia and the two main Berlin and Vienna orchestras. While the British orchestra began in a way that was 'technically perfect from the word go', they played with great enthusiasm at all the rehearsals but advanced no further at the performance in the evening. But with the German and Austrian performance, 'there is always something extra that I could not hear and could not sense at the rehearsal. They then play with precisely those nuances which I never heard in London.'[21] Karajan also describes 'more important reasons why I finally parted company with the London orchestra. [I wanted] an orchestra that was like a wall I could always lean against. Legge knew that that was something he couldn't offer me. We went our separate ways but remained friends.'[22]

Legge now had to ensure the safety of the Philharmonia Orchestra in the hands of a new, regular conductor. Giulini, whom Legge was employing for Mozart and Verdi, was too busy in Italy to take on the job full time, but he gave two more concert performances of Mozart operas at the Royal Festival Hall in February 1961, first *Figaro* and then *Don Giovanni*. They both drew capacity houses and were the last opportunity for London audiences to hear Schwarzkopf as the Countess and Donna Elvira in the flesh.

Then the Giant arrived. Otto Klemperer, with over half a century's experience in the opera house and in the concert hall and a special affinity for Beethoven, Bruckner and Mahler, had given two guest performances with the Philharmonia during the Festival of Britain in 1951. After the concluding Jupiter Symphony at the Royal Festival Hall on 29 June, Marie Wilson, former leader of the BBC Symphony Orchestra and now at the second desk of the Philharmonia's first violins, gasped to Legge as she came off the platform in tears, 'I feel like a tart taking money from you for making music with that man.'[23] An utterance like that, from a practising musician, means a great deal.

After Bruno Walter, Klemperer was the eldest of that élite whose musical training had been in the traditional German manner, from thorough instruction at the piano to chorus master and then *Kapellmeister* in smaller opera houses, until he was appointed first conductor at Cologne. Despite Klemperer's proneness to illness and accidents, Legge knew that this sixty-six-year-old conductor was the man for his orchestra and had, for a start, signed him up with Columbia Records.

Schwarzkopf took part in several famous recordings under Klemperer, including Bach's *St Matthew Passion*, Handel's *Messiah* and Mahler's Second and Fourth Symphonies. But before these came the Brahms Requiem, preceded by a performance at the Royal Festival Hall on 3 March 1961. Fischer-Dieskau was the baritone soloist. According to *The Times*, it 'didn't quite come off'. The soloists, though, were 'on excellent form, bringing to their music all the intensity of expression that was missing elsewhere'.[24]

The recording certainly does come off, in a manner probably 'closer to Brahms's intentions than most we shall hear in London'.[24] This version of the Requiem is entirely different from the one Schwarzkopf made with Karajan in 1947. That underlined the work's drama, nowhere more strikingly than in the first baritone solo where Karajan brings out the ominous timpani and pizzicato basses. Schwarzkopf's 'Ihr habt nun Traurigkeit' is vocally less free under Klemperer and she has to snatch breaths more often than she did with Karajan whose tempi, curiously enough, are slightly broader throughout than Klemperer's. Schwarzkopf now sounds as though she is having to think about the technical difficulties of her solo, failing to project the words of comfort as serenely and effortlessly as she did for Karajan, where her fresh, youthful timbre was ideal.

The following month, Schwarzkopf again sang for Klemperer in a Mahler concert whose programme was almost a facsimile of Bruno Walter's farewell in Vienna two years before, except for one work: Klemperer began with the Adagio from Mahler's unfinished Tenth Symphony, and the concluding Fourth Symphony was later recorded in the studio. Schwarzkopf and Klemperer did not give performances of opera together after 1945 in Vienna; nor did Klemperer conduct at Salzburg after 1947 or record any opera for EMI until 1964. His working association with Schwarzkopf was always fruitful, but remained spasmodic.

There were four *Figaros* at the Holland Festival in July, conducted by Giulini, then six Marschallins and four Fiordiligis in Salzburg, all under Böhm, together with a Hugo Wolf recital when Schwarzkopf was partnered by the inimitable Gerald Moore. But in October Schwarzkopf surprised her audience at her annual Liederabend in the Royal Festival Hall by introducing an Australian, Geoffrey Parsons, who had been in London since 1950. Gerald Moore had not yet retired, but was so busy that he was not always available, even to Schwarzkopf, and for some time Legge had been on the lookout for a reliable successor. Schwarzkopf sang an attractive programme of Brahms, Strauss and Wolf, beginning with Schubert's 'An die Musik'. The *Times* critic wrote frostily:

> Mme. Schwarzkopf declaimed the first words of Schubert as soon as she and Geoffrey Parsons had taken the platform at the Royal Festival Hall as if she were John Wesley addressing one of his vast congregations in a Welsh valley. This incongruity is a ready intruder when songs intended for the drawing room are performed in a large hall . . . There were some harsh and unintegrated tones in her singing, at times, when she found it necessary to magnify some confidence or subtlety to within the range of the hall's furthest limit. In characterization and in verbal inflexion she did not fail.[25]

Schwarzkopf herself was well aware of the conflict between the need for intimacy and the necessity of projection into a large auditorium:

> I have sometimes been reproached for a certain excess of refinement in concerts. People are surprised that an opera singer, accustomed to dominate the orchestra, does not command a louder voice . . . The Marschallin's monologue in the first act of *Der Rosenkavalier* tires me no more than one of Hugo Wolf's Lieder. You may, if you will, call it a different technique, a different atmosphere – but not a greater strain. Then I would point out that intimacy is essential to the interpretation of Lieder and, when I sing the cycles of Schubert, Schumann and Brahms, I endeavour to remain within the

limitations of chamber music. The problem is how to get this aesthetic conception across in the great halls of today. Yet I hate little halls.[26]

Lotte Lehmann disagreed. Photographs of her at Lieder recitals in the 1930s show the audience crowding round her so closely that it looks more like a large drawing room than a concert hall. Of course she could speak personally to, and almost touch, individual listeners from a few feet away, creating a physical contact. Some artists cannot bear it, and need to preserve their distance.

Schwarzkopf crossed the Atlantic again for recitals in New York, making her presence felt once more in the shadow of the Metropolitan Opera, then went on to San Francisco and to Chicago in November 1961 for two perform- ances of Donna Elvira and two of Fiordiligi. There should have been three Elviras but Schwarzkopf, still suffering from London flu, had to be replaced on the opening night. Lisa Della Casa stepped in, she

> of the silent cinema disposition, delivered Elvira's music ably considering the terms of her last-minute employment. Miss Schwarzkopf recovered suf- ficiently to sing Elvira on November 8 and 11 . . . Finally, no performance of *Don Giovanni* can be taken quite seriously in the frightfully durable décor of Schenck von Trapp dating from 1926 . . .[27]

Schwarzkopf had recovered in time to sing in *Così* which

> was a delicious musical performance staged with restraint and taste . . . The Fiordiligi of Miss Schwarzkopf . . . became for once a vivacious stage figure, beautiful to gaze upon and always in theatrical accord with the now definitive Dorabella of Christa Ludwig . . . Mr Maag's conducting, however, and the elegant airborne performance he summoned, were most impressive of all.[28]

In early January 1962, the year when the *Rosenkavalier* film was to be released, only Paris and Salzburg were interested in casting Schwarzkopf as the Marschal- lin. After the reviews of her 1959 and 1960 performances in London and Vienna, managements might hesitate to book such a controversial interpretation within a year. But even after the release of the film, they failed to come running to her. There may, of course, have been no immediate call for her because there were already sufficient sopranos with the Marschallin in their repertoire. She may also have arrived on the scene at an inopportune moment in opera house planning. But with hindsight there were mutterings that Karajan had propelled her into the role at La Scala, with or without Legge's conviction, before she was ready for it.

In February Schwarzkopf appeared at the Paris Opéra for the first time since 1941, when she was a member of the combined Berlin Opera Companies' visit. With Paris achieved and the Met promised, some of the international bastions seemed to be coming down. She sang four Marschallins in the ideal setting of the Palais Garnier, interleaved between two performances of a new production of *Capriccio* at the Opéra Comique. Some understandable criticism arose because the opera was being given in German instead of in Gustave Samazeuilh's French translation made for its Parisian première in 1957. But then it is unlikely that Schwarzkopf was to be prevailed upon to sing it in any other language but the original. She received great applause, although the orchestra, stretched by the unfamiliar score, and the French singers not quite at home with the idiom and the language, were less successful.

The production gave rise to two incidents in the course of one evening which offended Schwarzkopf's professional dignity. There is a romantic scene near the beginning of the opera in which the Count, brother to the central figure of a young, widowed Countess, reads a love poem in the form of a sonnet to the actress Clairon, in the presence of the Countess. Her brother has distinct designs upon the great actress (a historical figure) and the sonnet forms an integral part of the opera's plot and score. In this performance the baritone who sang the Count had omitted to bring the sheet of paper with the words on stage with him, and he had not got them by heart. He was obliged to go off and retrieve the all-important hand prop. As the orchestra is *tacet* during the reading, there was silence from Georges Prêtre in the pit, stagnation on the stage and shuffling amongst a puzzled audience. After some delay, which as always felt like hours, the unfortunate singer returned and read the love poem to Clairon. *Capriccio* continued.

That in itself was enough to upset Schwarzkopf, to whom any such carelessness was anathema; but worse was to follow. Towards the end of the opera, when Clairon and the Count are about to leave for Paris together (the sonnet has had the desired effect), Clairon entered wearing a lovely Erté hat, with – the audience gasped in disbelief – a nondescript duster on top of it. All efforts to communicate with the bewildered singer failed, and she was at a complete loss to understand the reason for subdued laughter from the audience and facial contortions by the other singers. The duster remained in place until she bade her farewells to the Countess (Schwarzkopf), Flamand, Olivier and La Roche, then made her exit – willingly.[29] Sabotage?

Schwarzkopf never again sang the Countess Madeleine in Paris, and the official register of performers and operas (up to 1962) gives *Der Rosenkavalier* with no mention of *Capriccio*. What cast-lists do mention, however, among the names in the chorus of eight male servants for this pair of performances, is that of a young Belgian bass-baritone, just twenty-one years old – José Van Dam.

The familiar production of *Così* at Salzburg in 1962 also fared less well than usual. Schwarzkopf and Ludwig were the sisters in this Rennert–Böhm confection which, according to the critic Martin Bernheimer, was beginning to get stale after three consecutive summers with the same cast and the same production . . . mannerism, routine and exaggeration have crept into a production once dominated by sparkle and inspiration . . . Schwarzkopf, in less than top form, overstressed coyness, perhaps to compensate for vocal deficiencies. Graziella Sciutti [Despina], Ludwig, and Dönch [Alfonso] are, if anything, even better in their parts now than they were in 1960.[30]

This censure can hardly have applied to Böhm, whose direction of the work was always masterly. Schwarzkopf had made a mono recording of *Così* with Karajan in 1954. Now, eight years later and immediately after the Salzburg performances, Böhm came straight to London to conduct a new recording in stereo at Kingsway Hall with the Philharmonia Orchestra. No sooner was this in the can than the cast gave a concert performance of *Così* at the Royal Festival Hall on 19 September, the only time that Schwarzkopf was heard as Fiordiligi in London.

The *Times* critic wrote:

The distinguished cast [Ludwig, Steffek, Kraus, Taddei and Berry] did everything that was humanly possible to transcend the formality of evening dress, and little of the humour of the text and the gaiety of the music was wasted. As Fiordiligi, Miss Schwarzkopf was just as much a tower of strength as her 'Come Scoglio' would suggest . . . Perhaps one or two of the lower notes in this cruelly taxing aria lacked resonance, perhaps her quick vibrato at times made her tone sound a little tremulous. But for the most part her singing combined masterful tact, control and persuasive charm of characterization.[31]

In October 1962, with sets borrowed from Dallas, Franco Zeffirelli produced a *Don Giovanni* that included Schwarzkopf as Donna Elvira, Victoria de los Angeles as Donna Anna, Richard Lewis as Don Ottavio, Geraint Evans as Leporello (of course), and Giorgio Tozzi as the Don. These four performances in and around San Francisco were the only occasions, apart from La Scala in 1951, when de los Angeles and Schwarzkopf sang together in this opera. It was a magnificent cast conducted by Leopold Ludwig and produced with great understanding by Paul Hager who brought out 'the tensions and the demonic character of the drama in a most extraordinary way, uncovering dramatic subtleties in it that one had never known were there'.[32]

At the very end of 1962, on her return to Europe, Schwarzkopf began a fruitful association with the Théâtre Royal de la Monnaie, the Opera House in Brussels (so named because it stands on a site next to the former Mint) when she sang five Marschallins with particular success.

Then it was over to Paris, at the beginning of January 1963, where she was confronted with yet more trouble. She was due to sing the Marschallin again, not at the Opéra but at the reconstituted Salle Favart where she arrived early in order to rehearse for a new production of *Così*. The producer was Marcello

Cortis, a former baritone who, for the past twelve years, had been specializing in the staging of Mozart's operas. In an uncharacteristic display of anger, Schwarzkopf walked out of the rehearsals, claiming that Cortis's conception was 'clownish' (her favourite word of disapproval), because he was trying to reduce the operatic characters to marionettes. Admittedly, *Così* is always tempting fare for a producer with a theory; and Cortis went absurdly far in expecting his singers, including Schwarzkopf, to behave like puppets. It is in the characters' very human qualities that both the charm and friction of the opera lie. Schwarzkopf knew that only too well and, as a result of her firm refusal to 'debase' Fiordiligi, she, and Jane Berbié as her sister Dorabella, made their three performances as vivid and natural as they were able. After that, no more opera for Schwarzkopf in Paris, where the events surrounding both *Capriccio* and *Così* conspired against her. But she was to return there many times as a recitalist.

In the early 1960s Schwarzkopf began to widen her repertoire with operetta, both in the recording studio and at concerts. The five 'core' operas took hold, of course, but in 1963 Willi Boskovsky was brought into the picture to conduct Viennese operetta in London and in the United States. He was an outstandingly capable violinist, having been co-leader of the Vienna Philharmonic throughout the war. His proficiency in the Viennese style, with its pronounced use of portamento, earned him a personal following; and he was always welcome among the various Strauss Family Societies round the world. So too was Schwarzkopf, who willingly unbent from her prima donna stance, and she entered delightedly into a more frivolous idiom.

Willi Boskovsky was an amusing dinner companion and raconteur after a concert, but with a baton in his hand he was an altogether different proposition. Orchestral musicians did not find it easy to understand what he was trying to convey to them; and his ideas would change between rehearsal and performance. He took up his violin from time to time and played solo with the band à la Johann Strauss, which always proved very popular. Despite the enigmatic beat and his unpredictable temper Boskovsky was incomparable in the Viennese light music field.

On 4 March 1963 Schwarzkopf joined him as soloist at the Royal Festival Hall in an operetta programme. This time there was no misunderstanding about her. The *Times* critic found that she lent

> the charm of her personality and the distinction of her art to the proceedings. To everything she performs, she brings a rare musical intelligence, taste and great vocal artistry so that her programme last night was sheer delight.[33]

Schwarzkopf easily managed the songs from *Opernball*, *Vogelhändler* and *Obersteiger*; she had sung Adele in *Fledermaus* at the Deutsche Oper (nowhere else) when she had disposed of Ida, but had never sung Rosalinde until the recording in 1955. Now it was felt that, in the live performance, she was outparted by the Czardas which, the same *Times* critic considered, 'demands a more dramatic voice and a more abandoned, racy delivery'.

In 1963 she made her second recording of Verdi's Requiem, this time under Carlo Maria Giulini, one of his specialities now that his mentor, Victor De Sabata, had gone. It turned out to be Schwarzkopf's last recording of a major work. This Requiem is an introspective un-theatrical reading, broadly paced and often attaining a visionary intensity. As a religious man Giulini seemed to be deeply moved by the performance he drew from his forces. Schwarzkopf's fellow soloists for the recording were Ludwig, Gedda and Ghiaurov, all Legge favourites. But her voice combined with theirs less successfully than with De Sabata's all-Italian cast in 1951.

During the usual public performance connected with the recording, at the Royal Festival Hall, only the soprano, chorus and orchestra were the same. A familiar BBC announcer hyped it up in the television interval which was 'occupied with interviews of a reverential, plaudatory order that can be thought equally embarrassing'.[34] On the assumption that none of the viewers had heard Verdi's Requiem, or attended church very often, it was a big talk-down by a quorum of straight faces among whom only one person, the publisher Victor Gollancz, made a perceptive remark: 'Verdi's Requiem', he said, 'gives more of an impression in a hall than in a church, because it is a consecration of the secular.'[35] This was more a consecration of the announcer, with Elisabeth Schwarzkopf, Grace Bumbry, Sándor Konya and Rafael Ariё (again no Italians) tagging along somewhere behind.

Nineteen sixty-four was a significant year for Schwarzkopf, Legge and Karajan. For them all, in fact, it proved a professional watershed. It was also the centenary year of Richard Strauss's birth, celebrated widely in concert, recital and in print. Karl Böhm gave his early tribute to the composer at the Royal Festival Hall in January with the Philharmonia Orchestra in 'Don Juan' and 'Ein Helden-leben'; to end the first half of the programme, Schwarzkopf joined them for the closing scene from *Capriccio*, as the Countess Madeleine, wearing her exquisite costume from the Vienna State Opera. *The Times* gave a dissertation on 'trivial', her penultimate word, and concluded: 'Moved we were not, but sumptuously regaled!'[36]

Marschallins in Geneva, Marseilles and Vienna and Lieder recitals accompanied abroad by Jacqueline Robin were preludes to the Berlin Strauss centenary concerts under Karajan on 5 and 6 May, when Schwarzkopf sang the *Four Last Songs* between the Oboe Concerto and 'Ein Heldenleben'. Three months later, on 15 August, Schwarzkopf and Karajan performed the *Four Last Songs* at the Salzburg Festival, in what turned out to be their last concert together.

The sheer size of the programme at the 1964 Salzburg Festival was spectacular: four plays, seven operas (three by Strauss), four ballets (including the rare *Josephslegende*) and ten orchestral concerts of which half contained Strauss works. The 1964 Festival also marked a change in Karajan's activities. He had found it impossible to continue his battle with the Vienna Staatsoper – one of the few occasions when he failed to emerge the victor. Egon Hilbert had supported Furtwängler while running the Salzburg Festival. Now, as Karajan's co-director in Vienna, Hilbert had no difficulty in making it impossible for the joint administration to work. Karajan was stretching himself too far and had lost his normal equanimity. Rushing to and fro between Vienna and Berlin, he was reliving Richard Strauss's own predicament of 1919. Although Karajan was Austrian, he was not from Vienna and he hated what he saw as the excessively casual Viennese attitude to work. During the 1964 Festival, he was elected to serve on its Committee of Management, which was exactly what he wanted. So from the end of that 1963/64 season, he resigned his appointment as artistic director and director of the Vienna State Opera, leaving himself completely free to concentrate his activities in Berlin and Salzburg.

Schwarzkopf had sung only twenty-three times with Karajan since 1959, less than four appearances a year, with only single performances in 1959, 1961 and 1962. In this period the Marschallin predominated in their association at Salzburg, and when she came to sing her third Marschallin of the 1964 Festival for him on 29 August, they were making their last public appearance together.

It is impossible to determine when Karajan decided that the 1964 Salzburg Festival was going to be Schwarzkopf's last. It cannot have come as a surprise to the Legges, when no contracts arrived as usual a year to a year and a half beforehand. Walter Legge naturally made inquiries, but Karajan never discussed such matters personally with artists or their managers, and once he had made up his mind on a major change of singer, there was nothing that even Legge could do to alter the casting. In his position as the wily executive director of the Festival, who always managed to get his own way with the official committee, Karajan had wider issues to settle.

The 1965 Salzburg Festival was to move away from Mozart, embracing *Boris Godunov* and *Macbeth* (neither heard there before) and *Elektra*. There was nothing suitable for Schwarzkopf in any of these operas, and although *Così* stayed in the programme, the American soprano Evelyn Lear had been preferred as Fiordiligi. As the more typically 'Schwarzkopf' operas came back in the following years, Sena Jurinac as well as the younger voices of Claire Watson, Teresa Zylis-Gara and Gundula Janowitz were all chosen by Karajan ahead of Schwarzkopf.

Schwarzkopf had, in fact, reached the time for taking stock. Martha Mödl was one soprano who had overridden the age barrier by singing character roles, but that was not Schwarzkopf's way. She was emphatically the prima donna, often *assoluta*.

The 1965 season was more than half settled, and Karajan's mind was on his next major ambition, the Wagner Easter Festival at Salzburg. He had secured heavy endowments from the town because such an enterprise would obliterate a 'dead' season for trade and greatly increase annual income to Salzburg. But Wagner was not Schwarzkopf's métier. The time had now come to bid both Salzburg, where she had appeared since 1948, and its latest inspiration, Herbert von Karajan, a sad *Ade*.

PART III

~ 15 ~

After Karajan
1964–1968

Schwarzkopf's voice had gradually lost something of its bloom, though by the
end of 1960 she was only forty-five and had long acquired the means of
husbanding her resources. But the Karajan spate of leading operatic roles in the
middle 1950s had taken their toll, and Legge knew it.

In the early days of the triumvirate Karajan was very much one of the family,
as Legge declared in 1953: '. . . Karajan chooses to stay in the comparative
discomfort of our spare room whenever he is recording in England'.[1] But all
the time he was laying his plans and creeping slowly but surely up the ladder
of power, away from Legge and the Philharmonia to La Scala, Salzburg and
Vienna, until he reached the Berlin Philharmonic. Legge knew that in order
to keep himself and Schwarzkopf in the swim, they must fall in with at least
some of Karajan's plans, a reasonable explanation for those unsuitable roles
which Schwarzkopf was persuaded to sing and with which her anxious husband
was often reluctantly obliged to agree. Legge's resignation to Karajan's demands
came from his inability to challenge him, and was coupled with an impetuosity
and lack of foresight whatever else may be implied in *On and Off the Record*.

There had been little prior indication of radical change about to take place
in London's musical politics when, in June 1963, Walter Legge gave one year's
notice of his resignation from EMI. He had, though, already ensured his own
supervision and production of every future session for Schwarzkopf, one of
EMI's most valued artists. Legge had established his Philharmonia Orchestra
immediately after the war as a recording orchestra and it had always depended
largely on income from EMI for its survival. Once Legge had resigned from EMI
they declined to use the Philharmonia for recordings as long as he controlled it;
and as there were not going to be enough concerts to keep them solvent, Legge
had no alternative but to abandon his cherished orchestra.

He knew he had lost two jokers but imagined that he still had the King and
the Queen in his hands. But he was wrong. King Karajan went his own way
and Legge was now in great difficulties. Immediately, all those enemies he had
vanquished during his years of power went on the offensive, brandishing their
aces and ensuring that he never played another hand in the music business again.

By the summer of 1964, the Legge–Schwarzkopf partnership with Karajan had broken up; and Legge was the main casualty.

When they came to take a tally of the years since the end of the war, Schwarzkopf acknowledged that Karajan had done a great deal to help advance her career but that in the course of their collaboration he had involved her in too many near-failures. Many of the roles she had learned at his say-so during 1953–4 were clearly unsuitable, for all the artistry she brought to them. Schwarzkopf's Leonore, in the Swiss concert performances of *Fidelio*, makes for an intriguing companion with Maria Callas's premature tackling of the same role ten years earlier. Callas lore has it that the nineteen-year-old Maria learned Leonore perfectly in one day, before singing the entire role several times in Athens.[2] Although she already had a great voice, she had very little experience at that time, yet she was persuaded to sing it under difficult wartime conditions, with a local cast and orchestra of dubious quality.

Schwarzkopf, on the other hand, had enormous experience but simply not the right type of voice; she gave thoroughly professional performances with a first-class conductor, orchestra and cast, but in spite of her technique and years of singing, the voice lacked the depth and body of tone required to do full justice to Beethoven. It was experience for her, but of a negative kind; with hindsight, Karajan must take much of the blame for having forced her into this and other inappropriate roles.

With a concentration on La Scala, Vienna and Salzburg, her successes had amounted only to Donna Elvira, the gradually deepening *Figaro* Countess and an emerging Marschallin. She may have tackled the latter two roles too soon; but once firmly in her repertoire, they stayed. She herself declared that this was because they had been jointly inspired by Karajan and Legge:

> The Marschallin came at the right time of my singing career. Sopranos who sing Mozart also have the possibility of singing the Marschallin sooner or later . . . It was Karajan who said to me after so many Countesses[3] and Sophies, 'Now, my dear, it is time for you to do it. You are the type, you have the mind for it, and you have the vocal inflections of a true Lieder singer.' I can hear Walter saying too, 'You need a conductor who keeps the orchestra so far down that even a light voice can get those inflections through.' So they persuaded me.[4]

Legge's dream of recording the best *Rosenkavalier* of all time was inconceivable for him without Schwarzkopf as the Marschallin.

Among her three other major roles, Karajan had not been involved with establishing Schwarzkopf's Donna Elvira, although he promoted it very frequently afterwards; he made a studio recording of *Così* (the first time she had sung Fiordiligi) but he never conducted her in a stage performance – never conducted it again in the theatre after 1937 in Aachen. Nor did Karajan direct or record a performance of *Capriccio* in Schwarzkopf's time. Later, he made a recording of the final scene with Anna Tomowa-Sintow; and when he cast her as the Marschallin in his last *Rosenkavalier* at Salzburg in 1984, he announced: 'Even the famous Schwarzkopf is surpassed by Tomowa-Sintow. She is a real discovery. When I first heard her I said, "This is a woman we must develop." '[5]

Karajan's often ruthless treatment of singers once they had fulfilled his purpose is confirmed by Sena Jurinac:

> I had a twenty-year musical love-affair with Karajan. But at the end, I felt he acted badly. When he was through with me, he was through. That was that. No one even came to my dressing room after the last performance . . . What is wrong if after twenty years you cannot send a letter? Or take fifteen minutes to say face to face that you have decided to take someone else? But it was fantastic to sing for him.[6]

While there is truth in this observation, Jurinac's reason for making it may have been coloured by Karajan's casting of Galina Vishnevskaya as Marina in his recording of *Boris Godunov*, after Jurinac had sung the role successfully in every stage performance at the three Salzburg Festivals of 1965/6/7. Irmgard Seefried was another soprano casualty at this time. She had been Böhm's favourite Fiordiligi in Vienna and Salzburg, indeed his overall favourite, until her last performance there in 1959, when Schwarzkopf took over. A few Lieder recitals were to come; but she too had to say farewell to Salzburg in 1964.

In the post-Schwarzkopf–Seefried era, those who impressed the Maestro sufficiently to be taken on board the SS *Karajan* included Leontyne Price, Anna Tomowa-Sintow, Gundula Janowitz, Claire Watson, Anneliese Rothenberger, Teresa Zylis-Gara (as Donna Elvira for two seasons), while, in the lower *Fach*, he espoused Grace Bumbry. People who worked with Karajan said he was already able to *hear*, even to *see* them in his ear and his mind's eye, in the roles he had chosen for them. As he had already done so many times in Schwarzkopf's case, he may well have engaged them to satisfy his own imagination.

Schwarzkopf's first engagement after the 1964 Salzburg Festival was in San Francisco in September with *Der Rosenkavalier*, conducted by Erich Leinsdorf, only a fortnight before her Met début in the same part, which, on paper at any rate, looks a little provocative. The Marschallin had previously proved an ideal début vehicle for her in San Francisco and Los Angeles, and even if she had not enjoyed the success she had expected on her return to Covent Garden, or in Vienna, there seemed every reason to anticipate a favourable reception in the role at the Met, an engagement which she had accepted in 1962.

At last she was singing the Marschallin for the 'Golden Horseshoe'. But the voice was no longer quite what it had been, or quite what the New Yorkers had expected.

> Last night her performance was never less than admirable and often it was deeply moving. Constantly projecting the most minute dramatic details suggested by the text in terms of vocal phrasing and coloration and of facial and bodily expression.
>
> If these never seemed artificial there were times when the emotions swept by so quickly and easily that one was a little uneasy in their presence . . .
>
> Vocally Miss Schwarzkopf is no longer the fresh, pure-voiced artist she used to be. The voice has grown larger. At times it is more shrill; at times it has its old blandishments and she can still manage lovely high pianissimos.[7]

Schwarzkopf was now far more sensitive to adverse criticism than before, however many extenuating 'buts' and 'althoughs' graced the newsprint.

She sang seven Marschallins at the Met in her début year, with a very strong cast that included Otto Edelmann as Ochs, as in London, Lisa Della Casa as Octavian and Anneliese Rothenberger as Sophie. They gave an additional performance of Act I at a gala on 29 November, for the benefit of the Met's Welfare and Pensions Fund, when Tebaldi and Bergonzi followed with Act I of *La Bohème* and Joan Sutherland sang Act I of *Lucia di Lammermoor*. Renata Tebaldi was the longest-established of the three ladies at the Met, having sung there consistently since 1954. Joan Sutherland's impact as Lucia in 1961 had established her as another favourite; but Schwarzkopf was still an unknown quantity, and when the Met gala was being planned she was accorded the least prestigious position in the evening's running order.

She was invited back for the next season for Donna Elvira, but not the Marschallin. There is more than a faint similarity between Schwarzkopf's and Lotte Lehmann's relations with the Met. Lehmann had reached it in a blaze of glory with her Sieglinde in 1933, yet in spite of a number of great successes over a decade, she never felt at home there, nor did she and Bing care for one another. Carnegie Hall, on the other hand, was glad to welcome Schwarzkopf again; and she was joined by Dietrich Fischer-Dieskau between *Rosenkavalier* performances in a rare, joint recital of the Wolf *Italian Song Book*, which was ecstatically received. This may well have helped the remaining Met audiences to a more favourable appreciation of her.

Nineteen sixty-five began for Schwarzkopf at the Vienna Opera, with a whole month's stay in the city and eight comfortably spaced performances of her major roles that opened with a single Countess Madeleine in *Capriccio*. During Böhm's absence, this performance was under Robert Heger, who had become identified with the opera in Munich[8] and handled it comfortably. There were also three Marschallins and four *Figaros*, in which Gundula Janowitz, a striking new Cherubino, sang with Schwarzkopf for the first time.

Schwarzkopf crossed the Atlantic several times that year: back to Carnegie Hall in April for a mixed Lieder recital on the 9th with Geoffrey Parsons. It was brought to a premature halt when she inhaled some grit or dust, began to cough violently and had to leave the platform. She went back to her dressing room where the attack persisted for about fifteen minutes, but by that time her throat and vocal cords had become far too sensitive for her to resume, so the recital was abandoned.[9]

In the summer, Schwarzkopf gave four recitals in Scandinavia before her planned series of operetta and Viennese concerts at Ravinia (a suburb of Chicago), some with Willi Boskovsky and also in the huge New York Lewisohn Stadium as well as in the Hollywood Bowl with him. She and Boskovsky were to give return concerts, four years later, at the request of the delighted audiences who loved the Viennese idiom and encored *Vienna, City of my Dreams* over and over again.

Now Schwarzkopf was to sing for the first time under the awesome George Szell, a very different proposition from Boskovsky. He directed her in a concert at the Royal Festival Hall, London, in September, immediately following an important series of recording sessions in Berlin which included five Strauss Lieder in their orchestral versions as well as Schwarzkopf's last and most celebrated version of his *Four Last Songs*. Szell was a perfectionist, with a fiery temper and a chilling line in sarcasm, and was widely feared as an orchestral tyrant. A Hungarian Jew who had been trained in Vienna, in 1915 he had made an extraordinary début as piano prodigy, composer and conductor with the Berlin Philharmonic Orchestra. He trained in opera houses and with orchestras from the beginning of the First World War in the rigorous, traditional manner, from the ground up. Nothing annoyed Szell more than the merest hint of slovenliness, and he was formidably proficient in anything he tackled, even cooking.

By 1965 it was obvious that Schwarzkopf's future lay primarily with Lieder. Before the Szell sessions in Berlin she had recorded Schubert, Schumann and Wolf-Ferrari songs with Moore; and between 1965 and 1967 she completed a recording of Wolf's *Italian Song Book* with Fischer-Dieskau and Moore. But it was Geoffrey Parsons who joined Schwarzkopf at the Salle Pleyel, Paris on 22 November, the first time they had worked together since her coughing fit in New York. Then back to Carnegie Hall, New York, in January 1966, for two Lieder recitals in close succession, the first with Parsons, the second with the inspired maverick Canadian, Glen Gould.

Schwarzkopf had sung with Gould once before in Amsterdam, when they planned to record some Strauss together. Legge thought they would make an intriguing partnership; and so they did, but not quite as expected. The three rapid, spiky *Ophelien-lieder*, difficult for both singer and accompanist, have words in German translation from Shakespeare's *Hamlet*, expressing the mad Ophelia's thoughts. Gould entered into the spirit of the songs in his own idiosyncratic way, substituting piano improvisations for the printed notes. Strauss was known to improvise too, inserting references from his operas and other compositions, especially in piano postludes, although none of his improvisations have survived. Nor have Gould's similar efforts for Schwarzkopf, which is a pity. Legge found Gould's playing astonishing, but considered it unacceptably eccentric, which perhaps is why Gould receives no mention in *On and Off the Record*. Legge abhorred improvisation; in his philosophy, every detail had to be scrupulously planned beforehand. This time, at Carnegie Hall in January 1966, Gould played the same songs brilliantly, and with Strauss's actual notes, as can be heard on the recording.

Schwarzkopf's next engagement was at the Met, her second season there, in January 1966. On finding that the conductor for *Don Giovanni* was to be Joseph Rosenstock, Legge complained bitterly, protesting that however efficient and experienced Rosenstock might be, he was hardly of the calibre to be found in the major European houses.[10] To add insult to injury, the sets and production were both long past their best. After the first performance, it was given out that Schwarzkopf was ill and could not continue; but Geraint Evans, the Leporello to Cesare Siepi's Don, remembers differently. Evans had been surprised that the Met had not mounted a new production around Schwarzkopf's now world-famous Elvira. He recalls that when they were rehearsing the Act I Catalogue Aria scene, there was an interruption by Legge

> who came on stage to dispute with the director Elvira's movements at certain moments during my aria. I kept out of it, not knowing that everything on stage could be heard over the intercom in Rudolf Bing's office. A few minutes later, Bing appeared and asked Legge to leave the stage. The rehearsal went on as before but after the first night Schwarzkopf cancelled the rest of her performances.[11]

This was to be her very last Donna Elvira, as well as her last appearance at the Met. Her silent valediction may well have been along the lines of 'You kept me waiting long enough. Now I've been here, I far prefer San Francisco, thank you. So goodbye!'

She accepted an invitation from the Paris Opéra in June 1966 for three performances of the Marschallin, which turned out to be her last operatic performances there too, although she returned four years later to give a single Lieder recital. Schwarzkopf had sung her last *Capriccio* Countess at the Vienna State Opera the previous January, and her last *Figaro* Countess at Monte Carlo in March. Donna Elvira had now also 'died', whether Schwarzkopf was aware of that or not; and her operatic roles on offer were limited to the Marschallin and Fiordiligi. But the Théâtre de la Monnaie in Brussels were staunch supporters and wanted her back there to sing the Marschallin as often as possible.

Schwarzkopf sang at the Liceo Theatre, Barcelona for the first time during the opera festival in December 1966, when her three Marschallins

> looked ravishing and [she] moved with enchanting grace. Unfortunately her voice had not the firm line the part requires, and her stage presence (particularly in Act I) had a coquettish, 'skittish' quality more suitable to the young Resi than to the mature Marschallin.[12]

The critic here was Gilbert Price, yet another to object to Schwarzkopf's 'skittishness' in Act I. In fairness to Schwarzkopf, one can argue that she was consistent in her performance, however much it failed to appeal in detail, and that the skittishness was an integral part of her characterization from the start. Schwarzkopf indisputably possessed the 'firm line' when she made the recording twelve years earlier.

In February 1967 there was to be a celebratory concert the like of which had never been heard and seen in the Royal Festival Hall, London. The sixty-seven-year-old Gerald Moore was on the point of retiring; and it was Legge's idea that on this occasion he would be 'accompanied' by his three favourite singers: Elisabeth Schwarzkopf, Victoria de los Angeles and Dietrich Fischer-Dieskau.

A month before the concert, however, on the morning of a Schwarzkopf recital in Zürich, Legge suffered the first of a series of severe heart attacks. He was immediately taken into intensive care 'while I sang the recital about which I remember nothing,' she records.[13]

Legge was not to be deterred from completing preparations for Gerald Moore's concert, and his hospital ward in Zürich was turned into what soon looked like a branch of the local music library. In spite of his condition, Legge was firmly putting the discomfited nurses in their place while he got on with his work. The Swiss doctors had forbidden him to move but, a few days before the concert, he took the train back to London so that he might oversee the printed programme and souvenir booklet that went with it, and implement in person his usual strict methods before a concert.

The event guaranteed a full Royal Festival Hall, and there were queues of disappointed people outside on the night, hoping for returns. Nobody who was in the auditorium could possibly forget the occasion, which was recorded live. There were short groups of Lieder by each artist; two numbers by Mozart for two sopranos and a bass; and the sensational 'cat' duet, once attributed to Rossini.[14]

Wherever possible the emphasis was put on Gerald Moore, as when two words in a Haydn vocal trio were altered to 'O! wollte *Gerald* nun weiter spielen!' (Oh, that *Gerald* would go on playing!'). There were songs serious and merry, songs little known and songs very familiar, like Schwarzkopf's beautiful delivery of Wolf's 'Kennst du das Land?' in perfect partnership with Moore. At the end, Moore played his own arrangement of 'An die Musik', which almost said it all. But not quite. After a standing ovation, something hardly ever seen in the Royal Festival Hall, he managed to quell the applause and invited the clamouring audience: 'Pray be seated!' The speech he went on to give was witty, humorous and heartfelt.

Schwarzkopf and Legge were staying at the Savoy Hotel in order to be as near as possible to the Festival Hall, and very early the following morning they left together by ambulance for the hospital where Legge had been persuaded to have rest and treatment. He was suffering chest-pains but did not seem to care. What mattered to him were the rave reviews of his concert in that morning's papers.

Within a week Schwarzkopf had to be in Los Angeles, and then it was on to Chicago and New Orleans for Lieder recitals. Rather curiously, she also gave two concert performances of Gluck's *Orpheus and Eurydice*, in English, at the Carnegie Hall, the only time she sang Eurydice in her entire career.

Walter Legge had recovered by April and accompanied Schwarzkopf to Scandinavia for well-attended Lieder recitals, followed by her very last appearance with Gerald Moore in London in May. They had pre-recorded a television programme for the BBC which went out after the Farewell, but now, as a final flourish, they gave their last conventional recital together at the Festival Hall in May.

'SCHWARZKOPF'S NEW RECITAL PERSONALITY,' proclaimed William Mann in a major article on the *Times* arts page, and went on:

> an attentive and enthusiastic audience was quick to enjoy points of humour and were unusually noisy in applause but, at the end of 'Ruhe, meine Seele' they maintained an impressive silence after the soft postlude until some time after the last notes had died away. Geoffrey Parsons slowly withdrew his hands from the keyboard.
>
> This was one of Schwarzkopf's most gratifying recitals of recent years. There were a few distorted vowels and constricted, uneven tones, but fewer than her regular audiences are used to hearing and no gustiness of tone production. Contrariwise, she performed some thrilling feats of breath control . . .[15]

One of these included what Mann described as 'an exquisite *messa di voce*' (a rising and then a diminishing of volume on a single note) which occurred on the last word of 'Farewell to the World', the fourth of Schumann's *Maria Stuart*

Songs. Mann's observation that she was 'singing less cautiously, with a new and winning boldness of delivery' indicates how much at home she was in this recital of German and – by extension to her repertory – Russian songs (although Mann did suggest that she should have sung these in the original language).

In July and August, the Legges went on a short tour of Parsons's homeland of Australia, then Schwarzkopf returned to London and sang at the Royal Festival Hall in the autumn, with 'The President's Orchestra' on a European tour. This organization is properly called the Washington National Symphony Orchestra under Howard Mitchell. It was undoubtedly regarded as an honour for Schwarzkopf to be the only non-American on the platform; and between works by two American composers, Morton Gould and Samuel Barber, and Shostakovich's Fifth Symphony, she sang five of Richard Strauss's orchestrated songs. William Mann was again impressed by her:

> Mme Schwarzkopf, after a foggy start, sang radiantly in the opulently generous music that displays her new-found vocal freedom perfectly. She almost stole the evening's honours, though whether more by her artistry or by her stunning attire (blonde pageboy coiffure and a psychedelic pink tent-style gown) might be disputed.[16]

Three days later she was back at Covent Garden to take part in a gala concert conducted by Edward Downes. She sang one Wolf Lied, merely as a display of her willingness to be associated with the occasion.

In 1962 and 1965 Schwarzkopf had sung the Marschallin in Brussels, and had established a good relationship with the company there. She went back in December 1967 to perform the same role, which she still managed relatively comfortably. Her 'Lieder voice' was being produced with discretion and minute attention to the subtleties newly discovered in Marie-Thérèse. If she no longer commanded her former strength of voice and security of line in the role, she was still seeking further refinements of detail.

Schwarzkopf was to be joined by Dietrich Fischer-Dieskau and accompanied by the London Symphony Orchestra under Szell for a celebrity concert at the Royal Festival Hall in March 1968; and recording sessions with the same conductor and orchestra were scheduled before a repeat of the concert three days later, arranged in order to fulfil the huge demand for seats. A few days before the first concert, there was a demonstration of the typical Szell tantrum he was known to throw in order to test people's resilience. This particular spectacle took place without any warning on Waterloo Bridge, between the Royal Festival Hall and the Savoy Hotel where he was staying, when he began stamping about and shouting, so that his face turned purple. He demanded from the London Symphony Orchestra's administrator a far larger body of strings than usual for Mozart's 'Jupiter' Symphony, and first principal players for rehearsals, performances and recording. If his demands were not met, and he was fobbed off with any but the best woodwind principals in particular – and he named every one of them – he threatened to go straight back to Cleveland. Knowing his ways, the management had advised these very players beforehand, and the extra strings were duly booked too. In the event, Szell gave a remarkable performance of the 'Jupiter', combining richness of sonority, exceptionally clean articulation and a firm sense of line. After the interval Schwarzkopf and Fischer-Dieskau sang twelve of Mahler's fourteen settings from 'Des Knaben Wunderhorn' (omitting 11 and 12). Stanley Sadie remarked in *The Times*:

> Mme Schwarzkopf produced some beautiful tender singing. She had started too uncertainly, making her points too obviously . . . [her] warm phrasing of the long lines in 'Des Schildwaches Nachtlied' was a joy. The songs lie a little low for her but her tone in this mezzo register was rich and fine-drawn, her singing never less than grateful.[17]

～ 16 ～

Diminuendo
1968–1979

After Schwarzkopf's last London orchestral concert, with Szell and the LSO in March 1968, she now undertook more and more provincial engagements in Britain. After a recital at Cardiff, where she was delightedly received, she sang at a boys' school in Monmouth, then went straight to Tokyo, rapidly followed by engagements in Scandinavia and the United States. This was hardly careful planning, and some of these dates had probably not been booked early enough to allow for a reasonable schedule. Certainly, in future years there were fewer exhausting journeys of this kind.

In the late 1960s Schwarzkopf's voice had not quite lost its former youth and freshness. But the discerning listener was increasingly aware of the astonishing technique that enabled her to control the instrument so as to give *the impression* that her voice was unaltered. Of course she was still a great singer and an even more skilful one, technically speaking. Whereas the line had always been firm, the phrases beautifully controlled and coloured, there was now less ease. True, it could not be mistaken for any other voice, but the details had changed: the line might falter – only a shade, but it was not as secure; phrasing was generally as elegant, but its details were now very slightly smudged. A forcing of the tone was noticeable as well, and this became more evident as time went on. On top of everything else, the familiar adjectives of 'arch' and 'mannered' perpetually afflicted Schwarzkopf in the press because she was obliged to use almost every device in her sophisticated vocal armoury to compensate for vocal frailties.

Still, to go with an open mind to a Schwarzkopf recital in the late 1960s was to become immediately disarmed and enraptured (if not her instant and willing slave!) by her appearance, and before she had sung a note. Joan Chissell noted this at the Memorial Concert in London to honour Ernest Newman's centenary of birth.[1] Both Joan Chissell and William Mann were favourably disposed to her as a singer, and Mann especially went out of his way to praise her, even when he had to add the qualifying 'buts'.

Legge and Mann got on well together and Legge frequently commissioned him to write programme notes, including English translations of Lieder both for recitals and for recordings. The two of them used to spend many agreeable hours over their wine, weighing the values of German and English words and splitting philological hairs, often with bawdy overtones; and as Schwarzkopf knew that there were times when her husband preferred male company, she did not intervene.

From now on, with few exceptions, Schwarzkopf's professional life consisted of recitals at the less glamorous, provincial halls, though whatever the venue, each programme was beautifully built and tailored by Legge. He was still a master of presentation, and possessed a more intimate knowledge of German Lieder than many great artists who had devoted a lifetime to singing them. Legge always carefully matched his wife's programmes to the particular audience, their expectations, and the properties of each hall where she sang; and he rehearsed her and Parsons valiantly, sometimes pitilessly.

In the old days, before 1964, he was also running the Philharmonia Orchestra autocratically, as was his way. He nursed his section leaders and other vital players, and was generally inclined to be more sympathetic towards those whose extra-musical interests coincided with his own. Legge used to cheer those players who left the Philharmonia with the exhortation that, having worked for him, they were going to have no difficulty in finding a job with *any* other orchestra.

In his heyday as a senior recording executive at EMI, Walter Legge had to travel to hear concerts given by major artists, and not only those under his control; he formulated policies and met everyone concerned with them, which others called scheming; he kept himself closely informed of events in the music business, on both public and personal levels, and he was famous for throwing his weight about. The one occupation in which he revelled most was the management of Elisabeth Schwarzkopf; but now this was all he had.

By the early 1970s Legge was increasingly frustrated at having less and less to do. The pent-up energy, the grand schemes which went round and round inside his head, could not be put into operation because nobody wanted to hear about them.

When Geoffrey Parsons began to play regularly for Schwarzkopf, he was thirty-eight and Legge, at sixty-one, was far more bullish at rehearsals than had been possible with Moore, whom he had known and worked with since the 78 days. 'There's only one arse I can kick these days,' he said miserably, 'and that's Geoffrey's!'[2]

Legge was driving himself towards the grave: no orchestra, no regular work in the recording studio, no concerts to plan and supervise other than Schwarz-kopf's, no international circuit on which he could display his beautiful and talented wife. Even at Salzburg, where Karajan had reinforced his position unassailably with the establishment of the Easter Festivals in 1967, Legge was reduced to the capacity of a mere spectator. But convincing himself that he still had a part to play, he could not resist offering advice as though he still belonged. James Levine was one of his Salzburg favourites in the last years,[3] and he immediately recognized the young American's enormous potential after he had conducted *La Clemenza di Tito* in Jean-Pierre Ponnelle's vigorous 1976 production.

Some of the sopranos who came and went at Salzburg met with Legge's approval, others he positively disliked and told them so, especially if they were English. He was so entirely convinced that Schwarzkopf's way of handling a phrase or making a move on stage was the right one that he instructed his wife's successor in the role accordingly, whether he had been asked for advice or not. Sometimes it was gratefully received, but Legge's impossibly dictatorial attitude more often found no favour.

He was deeply hurt when managers and artists who used to fall over themselves to defer to him all over the world now ignored him. He had ceased to be of any use to them – and they let him know it. Probably the unkindest cut came from Karajan himself. It had been more and more difficult for Karajan to meet his old friend as had been customary in the past when Schwarzkopf was singing at Salzburg. The Maestro now had no time to listen to Legge's views on singers and programmes; nor was there any question of Legge and Schwarzkopf breezing into Karajan's office without an appointment. Instead, they had to put up with messages from one of the entourage: 'Not today, perhaps tomorrow; no, not this week after all, he's exceptionally busy at the moment, but I'll see what I can do for you in the last week of the Festival before he leaves town.'

It was painful for Legge to accept that Karajan was casting him aside, after all they had done together, and especially after all that Legge had done for him. It was also a bitter pill for Schwarzkopf, whose faith in her husband's authority had not wavered for a quarter of a century. But she continued to undertake her concert engagements with the same intensive care as ever, and to submit willingly to Legge's constant criticism.

A fair impression of Schwarzkopf's art in her later years can be gathered from this review of a San Francisco recital in 1972:

> Schwarzkopf's diction is becoming more and more mushy. Vowels are distorted and swallowed in her increasingly covered vocal production, making the German texts frequently unintelligible . . . The voice, still iridescent, has lost one or two of its hues, and many moods are illustrated almost as much by the soprano's plastic features as by her tonal manipulation . . .
>
> But the more declamatory songs were delivered with great enthusiasm, and Schwarzkopf still works her old magic with subtle rubato . . .[4]

Four years later Karl Löbl wrote this review of her last Vienna recital, on 13
October 1976, under the title 'Time Is Cruel':

She is sixty-one [in fact sixty] and still looks fabulous when the bright light
of the spots shines on her. The applause on her entry makes her both embar-
rassed and happy. Gratitude is in this applause, also love and respect.

Gratitude for countless great evenings in the opera and on the concert
platform. Respect for a singer who formed a style. And the love is from old
affection.

'That makes me even more afraid,' said the blonde lady in the red evening
gown as the applause died down, 'she knows and we know that the great
concert evenings were some time back.'

Then the recital begins: Elisabeth Schwarzkopf sings Hugo Wolf.

'Unless I am mistaken, it was roughly ten years ago that Schwarzkopf took
her leave of the opera stage without much ado.

'Parting from the concert platform is harder for her since here, as she says,
it is easier to hide the ageing in the voice.'

Four years ago, when I first heard Schwarzkopf, I thought so too. Today
I am no longer of the same opinion, because what we heard in the sold-out
Brahmssaal, despite the delighted audience, sounded full of fear, exertion,
and cramped, like the memory of a once-precious voice. Like its shadow.

Why, I ask, does Elisabeth Schwarzkopf want to spoil this memory?

And so I went home in the interval and played a record: a Wolf recital of
hers from the summer of 1953 with Furtwängler at the piano. And I am
impressed again – like then, when all the art, the presentation and the musi-
cality of this singer seemed incomparable.[5]

Harsh as Löbl's views seemed, they echoed what many people had increasingly
felt since the early 1970s.

Legge interested himself for a short time in the so-called 'Million Pound Orchestra',[6] a scheme devised by the Arts Minister in James Callaghan's Labour government. The Exchequer was offering to support a National British Orchestra
recruited from the very best available players, not necessarily all British. The
idea was being canvassed, but it was causing much anxiety, except among the
world's principal conductors and instrumentalists, and a few managers who
fancied their chances in London. Such a body would have disturbed the
country's delicately balanced, if not actually creaking, disposition of orchestras
far more than did the *ad hoc* National Philharmonic Orchestra, assembled solely
for recordings.

Had Legge still been in control of the Philharmonia, he would have vigorously opposed such an innovation; for although he knew himself to be too old
for the direct orchestral control he would dearly have liked to retain, he made
himself available for consultation and advice to those angling for the job of

supremo. The whole idea of this orchestra was an inappropriate proposition for Britain at the time, but, having disappeared as suddenly as the government which sought to promote it – to the immense relief of all established orchestral managements in Britain as well as the Musicians' Union – it later re-emerged as part of one of the Arts Council's contradictory plans in 1993.

Yet there were still a few people about who still regarded Legge's abilities highly enough to offer him a job. In particular, those abroad, to whom the name of Legge still spelled magic, probably had little realization of what they might be letting themselves in for. His sights were always set very high in the direction of excellence, so that projected budgets were not going to suffice; any more than the man's abrasive attitude was going to be acceptable.

In all these activities – suggested, considered, investigated and aborted – Legge expected Schwarzkopf to have a place. She was living uncomfortably with a husband who made life miserable for everybody around him. She knew that if he would only settle down to something definite, no matter what (within reason), and keep his mind on it, it would be altogether easier for them both.

The best suggestion so far advanced, which became a firm offer until the scheme capsized, was for Legge to direct the cumbersomely titled French National School of Style and Interpretation in Singing.[7] Schwarzkopf was to play a distinct and distinguished part in this, with other celebrated artists including Maria Callas, Renata Tebaldi and Peter Pears; three renowned piano accompanists; and Günther Rennert and Peter Brook for stage direction. It had got as far as confidential correspondence, with all Legge's demands for doing the job properly set out in a memorandum. The French were taking it entirely seriously, had earmarked a sensible budget, and were already planning to alter and soundproof one of the older Paris theatres, so that the school would be ready to open in October 1976. It had all the makings of a wonderful idea, and the Legges were perfectly prepared to move to Paris or near by, when suddenly one night – overnight in fact – the French government fell and the Minister for Cultural Affairs with the power to put the scheme into operation vanished without trace. The next government immediately abandoned the project.

After that severe disappointment, Legge became attracted to the idea of running the Wexford Festival, a job which he actually accepted, but then had to drop on account of his deteriorating health. Another offer of a lavish artistic directorship came from Puerto Rico, where a new music festival was planned. But Legge rejected it because, having done some quiet research, he found that the organization was unlikely to be able to afford anything like the acceptable material or support that he would require. Anyhow, it was too far away from the centre of his world.

There was no relaxation in preparation for Schwarzkopf's appearances, however. She and Legge always paid minute attention beforehand to every detail in every hall where she was going to give a recital, especially if it was a new one. The positioning of the piano was vitally important, and they had it moved about to get the best sound from the acoustic. Sometimes the conditions were far from ideal. On one occasion her accompanist found the loud pedal stuck down so that the strings stayed undampened.[8] Lighting also played a crucial part because Schwarzkopf liked to have a bright spot (known as a 'blinder') directed into her face so as to isolate her. Not only could she hold the different character of each song more easily this way, it also prevented distraction from fidgeters in the audience.

At the end of May 1973 she was giving a Lieder recital in Vienna and Legge, as usual, was fussing her beforehand with last-minute reminders. Geoffrey Parsons was waiting outside the Green Room door to see her, and was surprised when it flew open and a rather sheepish Legge shot out saying: 'Ich bin ausgeschmissen!' ('I've been chucked out!') Apparently, such a thing was unprecedented; the relationship had developed a new twist.

That evening was also the occasion of another unexpected incident. Parsons, who had recently been recording with Hans Hotter for Decca, had asked representatives of that company whether they would consider a session with Schwarzkopf if he approached her and Legge about it. As EMI no longer seemed to be interested in her, Decca told Parsons to go ahead. After the recital Schwarzkopf, Legge and Parsons met one of the Decca team in the Imperial Hotel and they agreed on plans for what was to be Schwarzkopf's last Lieder recording, under the title *For My Friends*. It was the best thing that could have happened to ease the atmosphere that night after the dressing-room scene.

But their disagreements were not at an end. For one thing, they had different ideas about where they were going to live after Legge's 'retirement'. He needed a warm climate for his weakening heart and opted for California: but that did not appeal to Schwarzkopf at all. She preferred German-speaking Switzerland, and had already bought a house in Zumikon, near Zürich. Legge could not possibly live there because of the local dry and gusty wind, called the *Föhn*. 'Preparing to change roofs is hell,' Legge said, 'especially when you and your spouse cannot even agree on the same continent!'[9]

There they were, man and wife, with possessions half-packed, and many indecisions about what to store and what to keep – mostly books. Indecision had never previously been part of Walter Legge's luggage, but he was still able to pun whimsically on the title of a Wolf Lied: 'Wandl' ich traurig von Book to Book'.

He gave a curious account of the disposal of his lifetime collection of gramophone records when he and Schwarzkopf were living in Geneva. These 78s and LPs included many private pressings, not only of his own unissued studio work, but also whole *Ring* cycles and other operas from the two Covent Garden seasons when he had been Beecham's artistic director. There was a total of some 10,000 records, many of them unique. It was essential that they should be preserved as a collection. So Legge offered them to the director of a Swiss library in expectation of an immediate and delighted acceptance but, after considerable delay, the response was to the effect that in order to relieve the library's foundation of an additional financial burden, the collection must have a substantial annual endowment, in Swiss francs, before it could become acceptable.

'There's the bloody Swiss for you!' was Legge's immediate response, as he smashed the lot and threw them into Lake Geneva.[10] This is a similar story to one told by Kirsten Flagstad when she declared that she threw her unwanted records out of the window of her house in Norway on to rocks far below.

Legge's account is less credible: for one thing it must have taken him weeks to destroy his acknowledged huge collection in such a way. And what about pollution? Did the acetates float or sink? Somehow it does not ring true. That fabulous collection, or the bulk of it, must still be carefully stored away somewhere in Switzerland.

Nineteen seventy-eight was the last full year of the Legges' life together and they spent it travelling extensively, always by air, too, which was not necessarily good for his heart. SwissAir was the only airline which still regarded Legge as a VIP, so obviously that was the one they chose when the flights tied in with their schedule.

It had now become obvious to them both that Schwarzkopf must soon retire. And then? Farewell recitals were planned for New York, London and her new homeland of Switzerland which Legge still resisted. Their joint masterclasses in America had been very successful; and with Legge to direct them and Schwarzkopf to demonstrate from her large repertoire, they soon became regular events elsewhere. Schwarzkopf enjoyed this public partnership but swore she would never present the masterclasses alone.

Her last pair of Wigmore Hall recitals in September 1978 had been rehearsed with the same infinite care as she would have lavished on them twenty years earlier. But the public knew, as Schwarzkopf knew, that the time had come to call a halt. Agonies of indecision contributed to Legge's severe heart attack on 16/17 March 1979 as he, Schwarzkopf and Geoffrey Parsons were preparing for the last concert of all on the 19th, in what she had determined was to be her future home-town of Zürich. Legge was absolutely determined to attend and, in the same way as he had snubbed his doctors and nurses before the Gerald Moore concert in London, so he again made a final effort, with a dangerously self-imposed recovery, as his last tribute to Schwarzkopf.

'You know, you're a bloody marvel!' he said to her, with a huge grin, the moment after she had taken her final curtain. Now, with all concert-giving at an end, they returned to the house in Cap Ferrat. Schwarzkopf had given more than four hundred Lieder recitals in her life, and it would have been surprising if she had not now experienced a feeling of emptiness. Still, the many bookings for their popular joint masterclass tours and lectures ahead were a partial compensation. However, they had not yet reached a decision about where they were going to live – or even whether it was to be together or separately.

Those questions turned out to be hypothetical. Three days after his wife's final concert, on 22 March 1979, Walter Legge was dead.

~ 17 ~

After Walter Legge

Walter Legge had been on the brink several times before. But his death came as a profound shock to Schwarzkopf, who had been anticipating a comfortable transition to a more relaxed existence. Less than a week after her farewell recital she was faced with the painful task of communicating the news to members of his family and all their close friends before it became common knowledge. One of the first she spoke to was Karajan, who uncharacteristically burst into tears.[1] Then there were Legge's last wishes to be fulfilled. He wanted his ashes to be put to rest near Hugo Wolf's grave in Vienna's Central Cemetery, and this was done following his cremation in Zürich on 25 March. Afterwards there were practical arrangements to attend to, such as clearing up and shutting down for ever the Cap Ferrat house and its beloved garden.

On 6 June a distinguished gathering of musical and artistic friends met at Legge's memorial service in St James's Church, Piccadilly. At the very end of the service, a recording of Schwarzkopf singing *Träume*, accompanied by Gerald Moore (who was present) floated over the heads of the congregation – one might say invited 'audience', because there was something eminently theatrical about it all. Schwarzkopf came down the aisle and out into the sunshine, looking quietly relaxed and as beautiful as ever on the supportive arm of her old friend Peter Andry, one-time record producer for EMI and now a senior executive there. The service was followed by a cheerful party at the Connaught Hotel, where Legge's absence struck the only incongruous note. An opinion voiced outside afterwards, not exactly in the best of taste, was to the effect: 'They hadn't been making a go of it lately, that's been obvious, but you see: she'll *canonize* him!'[2]

Life with Legge had not always been fun; indeed it had often been uncomfortable and sometimes unpleasant. He bore certain similarities to Antonio Ghiringhelli at La Scala (except for his suave appearance) and, much as he protested his love for Schwarzkopf, he tended to regard her as his neophyte and often as an inferior. He was quite capable of humiliating or insulting her in public when she said or did something of which he disapproved, like his previously mentioned crude rebuff at the Bayreuth party after her Lieder Recital in 1951 (see page 116). On the autobiography-cum-masterclasses video he sharply contradicts her about the position of the Café Mozart *vis-à-vis* the Vienna State Opera, and there is no joke made of it, no smile on his face. Instead, his tone implies that she often makes silly mistakes such as this, for he is always right and she had better realize the fact.

As soon as her widow's duties had been accomplished in England and France, Schwarzkopf became a permanent resident of Zumikon, near Zürich, and began to plan for a less active life ahead. She came to London quite often, sometimes to find out what EMI were doing for her, also to appear and lecture, give classes and sponsor events. EMI had arranged special issues of CDs for her seventy-fifth and eightieth birthdays, all of which needed her approval when it came to the request for issue of previously vetoed material that had been kept back in order to preserve her reputation.

At the EMI studios in Abbey Road they played her, from time to time, the tapes of those performances which had not been transferred to CD, and in some cases had never been issued on LP. She listened very carefully, then gave entirely dispassionate criticisms with remarks like 'That's rather good!' or 'That's not so good!' or 'Yes, that's a very good piece of singing!' Schwarzkopf was a vitally important pillar of the EMI edifice, for she and Maria Callas were still their best-selling sopranos and she wanted it kept that way. Her eightieth year was to see a new collection of three discs in the French *Références* series, containing recorded material that had still not been issued on CD. Two of them are with piano-accompanied works and the third is with orchestra. There are exceptions: a few of her LP recordings will not, in accordance with Schwarzkopf's own wishes, reappear. These include the 1974 recording of 'Frauenliebe und-leben', with Parsons, which had been pretty unfavourably received when it first appeared.

In June 1979 Schwarzkopf went back to San Francisco to hold the Merola masterclasses in connection with the Opera House, as she and Legge had done together in 1978. She had sworn then that she would never undertake them alone: but now she changed her mind. The fact that she had retired from the concert platform seemed to make her even more attractive to schools and to sponsors of such events, and she received many requests, by no means all of which she accepted. However, she did appear at the Mannes College of Music, New York in 1983, and took some of their classes, following in the footsteps of Lotte Lehmann and Maria Callas among others.

The flavour of a Schwarzkopf masterclass can be gathered from a biographical film made in 1989. We see her in Aldeburgh giving a lesson on 'O wär' dein Haus' from Wolf's *Italian Song Book* to an English girl called Fiona Rose, who displays plenty of confidence but little of the yearning which the Lied requires.

Throughout the film, the way Schwarzkopf blinks and crinkles her eyes indicates her disapproval of the pupil. When Fiona Rose begins, she gets only as far as the end of the first phrase before Schwarzkopf swiftly accuses her of singing huskily, to which the girl replies, 'Oh, did I?'! When she continues, and gets a little further, Schwarzkopf again interrupts with criticism of 'n's and 'm's that are not properly articulated, and Miss Rose is never allowed to get into the Lied. Instead, we are shown an early piece of film of Schwarzkopf singing the same song; and Miss Rose's efforts are, of course, eclipsed once and for all. When the film returns to the masterclass, Schwarzkopf is then preoccupied with the two words 'ohn' Unterlass', and the correct placing of the 't'. 'You killed it with your chin!' Schwarzkopf tells her, then congratulates her when she manages the awkward corner. How much further Miss Rose was allowed to go we are not shown; but as far as the film reveals, she has the words and the notes but little else.

There is a different lesson to be seen elsewhere on this film. Schwarzkopf's audition piece for Legge in Vienna, 'Wer rief dich, denn?', also from the *Italian Song Book*, cropped up from time to time in her concerts. Its difficulty lies primarily in the rapid changes of verbal colours as the singer rebukes her lover for showing up when he (if it is a he) evidently prefers the company of a rival. On her own recordings Schwarzkopf demonstrates different ways of achieving varied effects despite Legge's contention that the main change comes on the last word of all ('Wer hat dich herbestellt?' – 'Who sent for you?')[3] At this climax, Schwarzkopf suddenly reveals her sorrow at losing the object of her apparent wrath by a heartbroken last syllable. Her constant variations in tone colour throughout the song's 1 minute 20 seconds or so are spellbinding. On the film we also see Schwarzkopf working on the song with an exotic Japanese girl called Taemi Kohama; and her instructions correspond pretty well with her own recordings. The pupil seems to have found favour with her teacher, though her painstakingly built interpretation, not surprisingly, falls a long way below the kaleidoscopic brilliance of Schwarzkopf's own, and reinforces the impression that the Professor tends to work, whether consciously or not, towards a reproduction of her own reading. It may leave the student feeling more confident, but does little to encourage the belief in a 'school of Schwarzkopf'.

In May 1981 Schwarzkopf attempted something altogether new when she directed a production of *Der Rosenkavalier* at Le Monnaie in Brussels, which was greeted with respect rather than rapture. It was in this theatre and with this company that she had bidden farewell to the stage in December 1971, with a series of Act I of *Der Rosenkavalier*, and she had enjoyed going back to Le Monnaie. Now she was able to share with the young members of the Belgian company the experience acquired during those years when she had sung the first Noble Orphan, Sophie, and, finally and most famously, the Marschallin. Elisabeth Söderström was singing the Marschallin at Le Monnaie. In her time she had taken all three principal soprano roles in the opera, and already had her own ideas about the character of Marie-Thérèse. Relations between director and leading lady were cool. Söderström admired Schwarzkopf from a distance. But the younger members of the cast certainly gained from their director's wisdom.

Schwarzkopf was initially reluctant to take on private pupils. 'Why give away our secrets?' she said to her friend and colleague from Berlin, Rita Streich, who was now teaching in Vienna and at the Salzburg Mozarteum. But Schwarzkopf did change her attitude, and took on a small number of talented young singers, many but not all of them lyric sopranos. Three British sopranos who have at one time or another been Schwarzkopf students are Jane Eaglen, Alison Hagley and Joan Rogers, all of whom now have international reputations; while a promising Polish soprano, Dorota Jorda, has on Schwarzkopf's strong recommendation received grants for further study in Zumikon.

At times, though, Schwarzkopf found teaching a frustrating experience. When singers came to her unprepared, as they too often did, she expressed her disappointment at the standard of vocal education and training today. A typical comment was 'If I ask for a head voice from young singers today, they won't know what I'm talking about.'[4] And she lamented a frequent lack of discipline and application, and a reluctance to acquire a thorough knowledge of a wide range of music – a far easier task than when Schwarzkopf was a student, for she did not even have a wind-up gramophone.

Schwarzkopf made some fascinating comments about singing during a radio interview broadcast by the BBC in 1994, in appreciation of Maria Ivogün whose voice and technique Schwarzkopf was able to discuss and demonstrate from a selection of 78 rpm records. She paid the highest tribute to her teacher's art by expressing the view that nobody today, including her own students and ex-students, can match Ivogün's technique. As she demonstrated, Ivogün's fast-moving runs were invariably legato; there was no pushing with the larynx or inserted 'h's, as so often happens with singers today. Her transitions into and out of chest voice, middle voice, head voice and *supracuti* were all managed with such ease that there was no hint of a change in register. Such consummate technical skill, Schwarzkopf implied, is virtually unknown in today's young singers.

Herbert von Karajan was also critical of the lack of a really secure technical grounding amongst the post-war generation:

I am always hearing young singers, and each time I think that many of them still need working intensively before they are let loose on the circuit, which destroys them far too quickly . . . And there are of course far too few young artists who are themselves sensible enough to choose a slow, natural career for themselves. They all allow themselves to be led astray by seductive offers, so that their voices are very soon ruined, or else they never even reach the point of beginning to develop properly.[5]

Though it's hard to disagree, this does read curiously, coming from Karajan. How many of his finest singers did he allow to 'choose a slow, natural career'? Too often a 'seductive offer' persuaded his chosen artists to accept leading roles under his direction before they were ready for them.

During the 1980s Schwarzkopf kept in touch with the progressively ailing Karajan, usually at long range. But his death, on 16 July 1989, provoked this strange outburst:

Not that I like Karajan, I have no reason to like him at all . . . I do have to say, Karajan was an utterly bad character. In my case and in the case of my husband it was utterly awful. Although he was a great conductor, the behaviour of Karajan was such that we have no reason, even after his death, to say he was a great man. He was not.[6]

This was all the more unexpected in view of their close association over many years, both on and off the stage. On the face of it, he had done a great deal to further her career. But she never forgave his 'abandonment' of Legge; and perhaps she had come increasingly to resent the way in which Karajan had dominated her operatic career in the early 1950s, persuading her to accept a number of unsuitable roles. Her contrasting attitude to Karajan's predecessor at the Berlin Philharmonic is revealing: 'About Furtwängler I can say only good things because he was the first one to really help me in my career.'[7] Here Schwarzkopf was thinking particularly of their early Lucerne Festival collaborations and their international concerts after the war in oratorio and works like the 'Choral' symphony.

If Karajan masterminded Schwarzkopf's operatic career with mixed results when she was in her prime, Legge always called the tune where Lieder were concerned. And whatever her detractors might say about Legge's encouragement of an over-sophisticated, over-detailed approach to much of the repertoire, his role in nurturing one of the three or four greatest post-war Lieder singers cannot be overstated. His knowledge, insight and sheer expertise as a recording producer ensured that much of her vast song repertoire was superbly captured on disc and that her art will survive for future generations.

Schwarzkopf has received many awards and decorations, beginning in 1955 with the golden Orpheus of Mantua, a new prize for the five best singers. In

1974 the Deutsches Grosses Bundsverdienstkreuz came from the land of her
birth; and as a tribute from her adopted nation she received an honorary
Doctorate of Music from Cambridge University in 1977. Six years later she
was awarded the highly coveted *Pour le Mérite*, an order originally founded by
Frederick the Great in 1740, and in the same year she became a life member
of the Vienna State Opera and was granted honorary Austrian citizenship.
To crown these accolades, on New Year's day 1992 she was created Dame
Commander of The Most Excellent Order of the British Empire (DBE) by
Queen Elizabeth II, on ministerial recommendation. Only five other singers
have been similarly honoured in recent times: Kiri Te Kanawa, Janet Baker,
Joan Sutherland, Gwyneth Jones and Margaret Price. Of these, Te Kanawa has
specialized in exactly the same Mozart–Strauss operatic repertoire as Schwarz-
kopf, though there the similarities end.

Today, at eighty, Schwarzkopf lives comfortably and relatively quietly in the
house that she bought near Zürich, visited by friends and a few pupils. She
occasionally likes to appear in public, which, after all, is what she has been
doing all her life.

PART IV

Elisabeth Schwarzkopf: Opera Singer
1938–1970

'I am not really an opera singer, I am a Lieder singer,' Schwarzkopf once remarked.[1] There is ample evidence, on disc and video, as well as from memory of her live performances, that she was being unduly modest. On another occasion she said, 'At Bayreuth, when I sang Eva in *Die Meistersinger*, I was taken for an operatic [dramatic] soprano. In fact I am a lyric soprano.'[2]

Schwarzkopf's career embraced seventy-four roles in fifty-three operas (all listed in Appendix A), most of which have already been mentioned. She had been cast in several small *travesti* parts at the beginning of her career in Berlin, later graduating to light lyric and coloratura roles. She never sang Cherubino, though invited by Clemens Krauss to do so (he had taken a fancy to her in 1942); yet she later recorded a passionate 'Non so più' and sang an ornamented version of 'Voi che sapete' in concert. Schwarzkopf carried forward only four of her Berlin roles to Vienna: Zerbinetta, Musetta, Blondchen and Susanna. Zerbinetta was put aside after a single performance, Musetta gave way to Mimi and Blondchen to Konstanze, but Susanna proved surprisingly durable.

In the early 1950s Eric Blom wrote Schwarzkopf's entry in the Fifth Edition of *Grove's Dictionary of Music and Musicians*. He declared that she 'made her reputation as a recitalist and oratorio singer, giving her talent a more solid musicianly foundation than if it had been exclusive to the stage.'[3] Blom is unlikely to have known the extent of her operatic work in Berlin during the war, and so this comment was not entirely accurate, but it does throw an interesting gloss on the importance to her of three of the four main areas in which she was involved.

During the peak years of her operatic career, Schwarzkopf concentrated on five roles, three Mozart and two Strauss, which entered her repertoire in the following order: Donna Elvira in *Don Giovanni*, the *Figaro* Countess, the Marschallin in *Der Rosenkavalier*, Fiordiligi in *Così fan tutte* and the Countess Madeleine in *Capriccio*. One is put in mind of the golden rule which the great baritone Titta Ruffo once expounded to Walter Legge: the way for a singer to succeed is by concentration on five roles. No more, otherwise a singer whose sole aim is perfection will find herself wanting.

Schwarzkopf sang her first Donna Elvira at the Theater an der Wien on 19 January 1947, when she was thirty-one. Paul Schöffler was the Don, Helena Braun, Donna Anna, Irmgard Seefried, Zerlina; and during her first month of singing the role she worked under no fewer than four different conductors, including Otto Klemperer. After further repetitions in Vienna, she gave what was only her ninth performance with the State Opera on the opening night of their visit to Covent Garden in September 1947. That night, Schwarzkopf's Elvira created a very favourable impression indeed with the public, the critics and especially the management of the Royal Opera House.

During the nineteenth century Donna Elvira was regarded as a subsidiary role, a lesser figure than both Donna Anna or Zerlina. Edward J. Dent's study of Mozart's operas, published in 1913, did much to change this established view:

> Donna Elvira is by far the most interesting character in the opera after Don Giovanni himself. She is really the central female figure of the opera: she is always in the thick of the plot and almost deserves the tragic aria 'Mi tradi' . . . She is as tragic a personality as Gluck's Armida or Verdi's Amelia but . . . she is forced to conform to the general *opera buffa* standard set by Don Giovanni himself.[4]

In any production where Schwarzkopf was the Elvira, this was certainly true. In 1965, when she sang at La Scala, the soprano Rosanna Carteri produced an interesting thought in remembering Schwarzkopf 'whose Elvira was so divine in looks and delivery it made no sense that the Don was always running away from her.'[5] One should not necessarily look for logic in opera, and least of all perhaps in *Don Giovanni*; but, after all, Donna Elvira's aim is to make the Don return to her, so she tries to appear alluring in looks and voice: this was all too easy for Schwarzkopf.

However much Elvira is mocked and humiliated, she always appears a noble figure, which Donna Anna and Don Ottavio recognize when they first see her confronting Don Giovanni:

> 'Cieli, che aspetto nobile!
> Che dolce maestà!'

> 'Heavens! How noble a bearing,
> What dignity and sweetness!'

Schwarzkopf's Elvira already possessed nobility and dignity, together with a suggestion of the tragic manner.

The only example of her early Elvira that has been preserved on disc is the big Act II *scena*, 'In quale eccessi o Numi! . . . Mi tradi', that Legge very sensibly arranged for her to record under Krips at the Abbey Road Studios in London during the day, before her evening performances with the Vienna State Opera in 1947. Here her vocalization is exemplary and her characterization movingly emphasizes Donna Elvira's vulnerability and pathos.

Wilhelm Furtwängler conducted *Don Giovanni* in July 1950 at Salzburg, having given *Die Zauberflöte* there in the previous year. This now famous production of the *Don* was cast from strength: Tito Gobbi as the Don and Erich Kunz as Leporello, Ljuba Welitsch as Donna Anna and Anton Dermota as Don Ottavio; Elisabeth Schwarzkopf as Donna Elvira; Irmgard Seefried as Zerlina and Alfred Poell as Masetto. Schwarzkopf's Elvira is now more forceful and more grandly voiced than three years earlier, though it still possesses an ideal flexibility; in particular, her coloratura in 'palpitando il cor mi va' is beautifully executed. Furtwängler's interpretation fully merits the over-used adjective 'incandescent'; and he accompanies Schwarzkopf with unfailing sensitivity round the role's many difficult corners.

The opera was not played again at Salzburg until 1953, when Furtwängler returned to conduct. Cesare Siepi was well cast as the Don with an inkier voice than Gobbi's; Elisabeth Grümmer's Donna Anna was firm-voiced but rather less fierily dramatic than Weltisch's. A complete, unauthorized recording of the first night on 27 July finds Schwarzkopf as Donna Elvira in imperious voice, and giving an even more searching characterization than in 1950. The Act I quartet, in which Donna Elvira begins with 'Ah! ti ritrovo ancor, perfido mostro!', and what follows after the Don's exit, is projected with unsurpassed tension, while the sound balance allows one to relish Furtwängler's orchestral subtleties without short-changing the voices.

The 1953 production of *Don Giovanni* was repeated at the 1954 Salzburg Festival with the same cast, except for the Commendatore, and is available on CD in very decent sound. Schwarzkopf's arias and concerted numbers are more subtly coloured and expressed than ever, and her vocal production sounds wonderfully easy. She portrays an even stronger, more determined Elvira, burning with resentment at her treatment by Giovanni. Furtwängler's tempi varied very little between 1950 and 1954 with an invariably magisterial control of the score.

In October 1959, immediately following his studio recording of *Figaro*, Carlo Maria Giulini had been engaged by Legge to make a *Don Giovanni* in London with the Philharmonia Orchestra and a star cast. This included Eberhard Wächter as a dangerous, feline Don, Graziella Sciutti as a delicious Zerlina and Joan Sutherland as Donna Anna, an unexpected choice but one calculated to enhance sales following her recent *éclat* as Lucy of Lammermoor. Sutherland sings Donna Anna with rare technical aplomb and an appealing vein of pathos, though her characterization is not quite determined or assertive enough. Commenting on this, Philip Hope Wallace suggested that the recording should have been called *Donna Elvira* for 'Miss Schwarzkopf has the knack of making herself the leading lady of opera . . . the part has, so to speak, always belonged to her.'[6]

Giulini, who had learned *Don Giovanni* specifically for the recording, gives a filigree performance, lighter of touch than Furtwängler's, with finely wrought orchestral playing. The exciting finales to both acts unfold with an ideally judged crescendo of dramatic intensity. When Karajan watched Giulini at work for the first time (watched him 'like a lynx' according to Legge[7]) he congratulated Giulini and offered any help he might need. Karajan was quick to recognize a dedicated craftsman – and no real competitor.

Schwarzkopf had further strengthened her interpretation of Donna Elvira; and her voice was still in superb shape in 1959. Both the commercial CDs of *Don Giovanni* that feature Schwarzkopf, the 1954 live performance from Salzburg under Furtwängler and the 1959 Giulini studio recording are excellent. The Giulini set inevitably scores on sound quality, though it cannot quite match the spontaneity, passion and dramatic flair of the live Furtwängler recording. There is one more 'pirate' recording to consider. Schwarzkopf sang Donna Elvira at Salzburg for the last time in 1960, having not appeared there since 1954. Eberhard Wächter is again the Don and Graziella Sciutti Zerlina. Leontyne Price makes a fine Donna Anna, nearly as fiery and implacable as Welitsch, although the black soprano is more secure technically and provides an ideal vocal foil to Schwarzkopf whenever they are together. Conducted by Karajan, who directed Schwarzkopf in over twenty stage performances, it is a tougher conception of the opera than Giulini's, and is preserved in fair sound. Like the Furtwängler and Giulini recordings of *Don Giovanni*, it eloquently demonstrates why many consider Schwarzkopf to have been the finest Donna Elvira, vocally and dramatically, since the War.

The smouldering revolutionary atmosphere discernible in *Don Giovanni* is not far below the surface of *Figaro* either, even if it is called, simply, an *opera buffa*; '*Figaro* is a masterpiece of comedy in music such as had never been seen before.'[8] Countess Almaviva, the second of Schwarzkopf's main roles, is a complex character. The young minx Rosina, who relished playing tricks on people, is still there; but her gaiety and ebullience are now tempered by the sadness of a woman who has been spurned by her husband in favour of her own maid.

Schwarzkopf progressed to Rosina via Barbarina (the gardener's daughter) and Susanna at the Deutsche Oper in Berlin; and continued to sing Susanna in German after the war in Vienna, where she gave her last Susanna in June 1948 under Karl Böhm, one of the great *Figaro* conductors. Schwarzkopf's début as the Countess was at the 1948 Salzburg Festival under the persuasive Herbert von Karajan. But after only five performances there, and two at La Scala, she returned to singing Susanna in London, in English, during the next two years. Webster in fact asked whether she would sing the Countess instead; but as there was no market for the role in English, except in London, she declined.

It is unfortunate that, as with her Barbarina, Schwarzkopf's Susanna has not been preserved in its entirety, yet 'Giunse alfin il momento . . . Deh vieni, non tardar', made in the studio in 1952 (when she was already singing the Countess on the stage) displays a sophisticated, pert Susanna, obviously more than a match for the Count or anyone else. She recorded the Countess's 'Dove sono' at the same time and, just to confuse the issue, Cherubino's 'Non so più' and 'Voi che sapete', which as mentioned earlier she never sang in staged performances. These sessions were sensitively accompanied by John Pritchard.

Schwarzkopf's first recording of the Countess was in mono, made in Vienna under Karajan in 1950. She was especially praised for her vivaciousness in this recording, which was generally highly regarded and is available on a pair of CDs. It has two principal drawbacks: all the *secco* recitatives are cut; and Karajan's fast tempi often makes life difficult for the singers. Though she sings it beautifully, Schwarzkopf seems to have found the tempo in her Act III soliloquy, 'Dove sono', particularly uncomfortable. It requires the purest legato after the short phrases a 'di quel labbro' and again at 'la memoria di quel bene'. Perfect breath-control, and broad, clean phrasing are essential; but at several points Schwarzkopf is clearly taxed by Karajan's reluctance to allow her elbow-room. John Pritchard's accompaniment of operatic arias mentioned above is far more sympathetic; and Schwarzkopf gives a creamy-voiced, utterly poised account of the aria, her characterization now enhanced by her subsequent experience of the role on stage.

Before and during the War Wilhelm Furtwängler had been overwhelmingly associated with Wagner in the opera house. Anxious to modify his operatic image in the post-war political climate, he returned to conducting Mozart in three operas, *Die Zauberflöte*, *Don Giovanni* and *Figaro*, at Salzburg between 1949 and 1954. His first Salzburg *Figaro* was at the 1953 festival; and after his Italian-language *Don* it came as something of a surprise when Furtwängler decided that *Figaro* was to be sung in German, as it always had been at Salzburg until 1937, and again from 1941 until after the War. He conducted only four performances, which afforded precious memories to those who heard them. An unauthorized recording of one performance, always difficult to find as an LP, re-emerged on three elusive CDs. It was always a question of tempi, and although Furtwängler's conducting is often notably broad, he has an extraordinary way of sweeping the work inexorably and magnificently along. Schwarzkopf is clearly more comfortable with his spacious tempi than she had been under Karajan, and her characterization now ideally balances vivacity with nobility and pathos.

The first of five *Figaros* that Schwarzkopf sang at Salzburg in the summer of

1957 (again in Italian) was issued on a pirate CD under Karl Böhm, with whom she seemed to have found a genuine rapport. Böhm's understanding and command of Mozart inspired Schwarzkopf to her finest performance of the Countess to be heard on disc. The Act II cavatina 'Porgi amor', perfectly controlled and coloured, is deeply affecting, while Böhm finds the ideal tempo for the opening section of 'Dove sono', giving Schwarzkopf ample space but conveying a strong sense of forward motion. Seefried is a perfect Susanna and Christina Ludwig an ardent Cherubino. Fischer-Dieskau gives a powerful, highly sophisticated reading of the erring Count; and Schwarzkopf certainly makes him grovel to her at the end. Add Erich Kunz's endearing portrait of Figaro and the result is a very special account of the opera indeed, with the voices exceptionally well matched but invariably distinctive in ensemble.

By 1959 Walter Legge decided that it was time for Schwarzkopf to make her definitive recording of the Countess. He certainly felt that they could both improve upon the Karajan version of 1950 and, in any case, he wanted to encourage Giulini and to beat the pirates who were proliferating. Legge set up the ideal cast in London which, with its attendant difficulties, has already been mentioned on page 154; and the concert that followed the sessions was the first of only two occasions when Schwarzkopf sang as the Countess in London.

In *Figaro* the hectic action is constantly controlled by Susanna. In this recording, however, one feels that Countess Schwarzkopf is very much the dominant force, overshadowing Anna Moffo's Susanna, and consequently distorting the balance between these two characters. Did Legge have a hand in this? There also seems to be something missing in Giulini's performance, for all its tautness and distinction – that flair and spontaneity which marked the live performances under Furtwängler and Böhm and to which Legge always aspired.

Giulini is again the conductor of a live *Figaro* performance from the 1961 Holland Festival. Five singers are of international standing and the rest are local, but Schwarzkopf is below par, sometimes shrill and strained, occasionally sounding tentative, as if daunted by the role's technical demands. There is, however, a remarkable bonus on the third disc: ten solo highlights from the excellent 1957 Salzburg performance under Karl Böhm, which includes most of Schwarzkopf's role and rather tactlessly underlines the imperfections in the complete Giulini performance.

By now, although she did not know it, of course, Schwarzkopf was only three years away from saying farewell to the role she had performed so sympathetically and nobly throughout the 1950s.

Hugo von Hofmannsthal had intended his libretto for *Der Rosenkavalier* to be his and Strauss's answer to Mozart's *Figaro*. To a certain extent, they succeeded. There are evident similarities between the Countess and the Marschallin on the one hand, and between Susanna and Sophie on the other. And in both operas Schwarzkopf graduated from commoner to aristocrat. She found the role of Sophie satisfying enough; but Schwarzkopf had long wanted to perform the Marschallin, learning it slowly and carefully, listening to many recordings of its great interpreters from Margarethe Siems onwards, and working diligently at her interpretation under the guidance of both Legge and Karajan.

She also sought advice from Lotte Lehmann, who was still considered the pre-eminent living interpreter of the role, although some Viennese opera-goers preferred Maria Reining, just as there are those who preferred Gueden's, Loose's or Della Casa's Sophie to Schwarzkopf's. By this time, Lehmann had become rather grumpy, took imagined slights far too easily, and was offended when anybody ignored her advice: 'Schwarzkopf makes errors of judgement in Act I!'[9] she pronounced.

Just as she had been working at Anne Trulove in *The Rake's Progress* for Milan while singing Eva at Bayreuth, Schwarzkopf was now preparing to sing her first Marschallin in Karajan's new 1952 production of *Der Rosenkavalier*, during the Italian performances of *The Rake* at La Scala.

In October 1995 a hitherto unknown live recording of Schwarzkopf's first Marschallin (January 1952) appeared on CD. The quality is variable to poor, but the unmistakable voice emerges to display an emotionally fragile Maria Thérèse. Vocally, there are no exaggerations: it is a delightful, pure-toned performance. Her experienced colleagues are Della Casa, Jurinac and Edelmann.

Schwarzkopf particularly enjoyed the intellectual challenge of the Marschallin's role. Her radical development across the interval between two very different acts led her to observe that '*Rosenkavalier* is about coming to grips with life';[10] and she believed the Marschallin's most important dramatic utterance to be those six words before the Trio in Act III, which are not sung at all, but spoken:

> *Ich weiss auch nix, gar nix.*

There are occasions elsewhere when

> Stauss's conversational passages have to be sung in Lieder style – they have
> to seem like conversations with colourings as in Lieder singing . . . Then
> there is 'Die Zeit, die ist ein sonderbar Ding' in Act I which with Karajan I
> could whisper, barely suggesting the notes.[11]

Providing the singer knows when to use full voice and is working with an understanding conductor, she can ride the orchestra without effort and achieve fascinating, detailed effects.

Richard Strauss, a consummate master at writing for the soprano voice and orchestra, composed a role that is virtually singer-proof, although it is only the most intelligent and musical of sopranos who can do full justice to the Marschallin.

Schwarzkopf sang the part only six times more in the following three years; then not again until the studio sessions in December 1956.[12] Among studio recordings of *Der Rosenkavalier*, this version with Schwarzkopf sits between two from Decca that offer the complete score, whereas Legge deliberately does not. The first Decca *Rosenkavalier*, in mono, was superbly conducted by Erich Kleiber, with Maria Reining as the Marschallin, once glorious in the role but slightly faded by 1953. The second Decca recording, conducted by Georg Solti, has Régine Crespin giving a distinctly Gallic interpretation, with 'an aristocratic, rather melancholy elegance of style and a delicate mastery of nuance, both vocal and dramatic.'[13]

In between these, chronologically, stands Elisabeth Schwarzkopf, recorded when she was in her best voice, with a fine cast, handpicked by Legge, and performed with the familiar stage cuts. Karajan, Legge and Schwarzkopf laid down the groundplan for her Marschallin and presented it on disc after surprisingly little practical experience of the role. Her finished and perceptive performance belies this, and compared with her other available record-ings, the 1956 interpretation sounds crisply, and refreshingly, unmannered. One of the striking aspects of Schwarzkopf's Marschallin is the way in which she refined the nuances in her performances, adding subtle inflexions in the course of a total of 114 stage appearances, far more than she gave in any other role.

After the one and only studio recording came the famous Salzburg film, now available on video. Many years later, in the television biography, Schwarzkopf herself said that her monologue in this film was 'something quite unique; and it was very – *very* – good singing'. We must agree with her on that although, some forty years later, her facial expressions sometimes seem almost comically exaggerated.

In 1964 came another unauthorized recording of a Salzburg performance, conducted by Karajan. Four months later, Schwarzkopf appeared at the Met under Thomas Schippers and this has been available on CD. Schwarzkopf had an idiosyncratic way of forming an 's' so that it sounded like 'sh' or 'sch'. In Act I of the studio recording, 'Du bisht mein Bub', du bisht mein Schatz' comes over very clearly, sounding appealingly feminine. Then at the end of the opera, in reply to von Faninal's mundane comment about young people, her 'Ja, Ja!' becomes 'Scha, Scha!' though this aspirate is a way of ensuring that the consonant is heard. At Salzburg in August 1964 there was no 'sh' but an absolutely perfect 'Scha, Scha!' as before; and in the Met performance four months later we can hear that the 'sh' has disappeared altogether and Schwarz-kopf makes a bite at the first 'Ja' in Act III to deprive it of any sibilant.

She was generally considered to have been less successful before the Levée in Act I than after it. The skirmishes and skittishness with Octavian the morning after, and her coyness with Baron Ochs, struck an unconvincing note with many critics. In the 1964 recorded performance there is some elegant horseplay with Octavian—Jurinac at the beginning of the act; then, at the end of the Levée, the Marschallin has the sudden intuition that Octavian is lost to her. Apparently realizing their disparity in ages for the first time, it comes as such a shock, and she resorts to blaming Hippolyte, her hairdresser, for making her look old, then brusquely dismisses the assembled scroungers.

In 1965 Schwarzkopf muses gently on the wretched Ochs after he has gone. 'Da geht et hin, der aufgeblasne schlecte Kerl' is said wryly, not angrily at first; but when she reaches 'und einen Pinkl Geld dazu' the tone is scornful and bitter. Philosophically she reflects that this is, after all, the way of the world and settles down to her first soliloquy.

In the Salzburg performance of 1964, by contrast, she heavily dramatizes the discovery of what Hippolyte has done, gasping and pausing at 'altes', sung in a frightened-sounding *sotto voce*. Then, when she is left alone, she vents all her spleen on the absent Baron Ochs in her first line, getting into a rage on 'schlechte Kerl' when she uses chest voice for added weight and emphasis. She immediately lightens her voice affectionately for the 'hübsche junge Ding', and returns to a further attack on Ochs before the soliloquy.

At the Met later that year she is less demonstrative to Hippolyte but is audibly stunned by the situation: whether this is true or contrived is not clear. She is angry about Ochs at the start of the solo scene and again uses chest voice (a little roughly) for 'Kerl'. After this she is more resigned than relaxed when left alone to soliloquize on her new preoccupation with time. In each of her recordings these monologues are beautifully sung.

The three different ways in which Schwarzkopf managed these telling moments, all with the same Ochs (Otto Edelmann), made each very effective in its own way. The studio version is the most convincing because it is supremely aristocratic in expression and gives no hint that the Marschallin can foresee the effect on Sophie of either Octavian or Ochs. In the first filmed Salzburg stage performance of 1960, Sena Jurinac is ideal as the boy; and Schwarzkopf's tender treatment of him evokes memories of their performances together in London.

Sena Jurinac has the edge over Della Casa, who in her career alternated between singing Octavian and the Marschallin, and also over Christa Ludwig, the Octavian in the studio recording. In every case, though, Schwarzkopf's solicitous treatment of the 'boy' is most endearing. After Schwarzkopf's retirement from the stage Ludwig was also to sing the Marschallin.

When the Marschallin reappears two-thirds of the way through Act III, she remains centre-stage throughout and commands the action. Schwarzkopf's mingled poise, authority and tenderness in the Trio have been a model for many later interpreters of the role. She also invented a piece of business which may now be found in prompt books at the point when the Marschallin leaves with Faninal. Schwarzkopf did not turn round to look at Octavian, but extended her arm backwards in his direction, as if to say 'To be continued, mein Leib'!'

Donna Elvira and the Marschallin, certainly the Countess Almaviva and another Countess still to come, are a social notch above Fiordiligi in *Così fan tutte*, in which the sisters Fiordiligi and Dorabella have apparently travelled about 500 miles from Ferrara, with only a young and flighty maid as chaperon, in order to meet their fiancés in Naples. Musically this is 'the opera of ensembles and artificial comedy of the best'[14]; is more comically witty (not least in its orchestration) than anything else by Mozart. The two sisters, Fiordiligi (soprano) and Dorabella (mezzo), both begin as rather silly, vacuous creatures; but after their lovers return disguised as 'Albanians' they become increasingly sharply differentiated, the vulnerable, emotionally complex Fiordiligi contrasting with the more frivolous, practical Dorabella. It is their characters, rather than those of their two male lovers, Guglielmo and Ferrando, that subtly change and develop. The close of *Così* has always remained problematic. Are we meant to believe that all concludes happily, or is the ending uncomfortably ambivalent?

Schwarzkopf first sang the role of Fiordiligi in the recording studio. In 1954, Herbert von Karajan was principal opera conductor with the Philharmonia Orchestra for recordings, although he had only once before been connected with *Così*, directing stage performances in Aachen at the end of 1937.[15] Legge had now collected a first-class cast for a new version, and was determined that Karajan should conduct it. He agreed; but, interestingly, he never touched the work again.

Karajan's immaculately controlled reading of the opera tends towards extremes of tempo, and emphasizes the score's brittle, sardonic aspects at the expense of its charm and humour. Schwarzkopf's Fiordiligi is essentially serious, vocally assured throughout; she is uncomfortably prissy and affected at the opening of her first scene with the excellent Nan Merriman as Dorabella. And her minutely detailed approach leads to mannerism elsewhere. Her veiled tone at the start of 'Come scoglio', for instance, seems exaggerated, though Schwarzkopf manages the latter sections of the aria brilliantly, the coloratura beautifully even and precise. In her Act II aria, 'Per pietà', she brings an impeccable legato to the slow section (done very slowly indeed), though the rather 'cooing' tone she uses here is not to everyone's taste. The unusually wide intervals of this aria (culminating in a leap from D♯ below the stave to G♯ above it at 'al tuo candor'), are accomplished with impressive smoothness.

Eighteen months later, in January 1956, Schwarzkopf was given her first opportunity to sing Fiordiligi on stage at the intimate 600-seat Piccolo Teatro in Milan to celebrate Mozart's bicentenary. It was also Giudo Cantelli's début as an opera conductor. His personality, power and musicianship instantly attracted Legge, who fully supported the venture by 'planting' his own artists in the production; and the experience Schwarzkopf and Nan Merriman had gained in tandem during the Karajan recording paid dividends in their duet. The '*due dame ferrarese e Sorelle*' (two ladies – sisters from Ferrara) were definitely the linch-pins of the production. Graziella Sciutti (Despina), Luigi Alva (Ferrando) and Franco Calabrese (Alfonso), were unfamiliar with the opera; only Rolando Panerai had sung his role, Guglielmo, before. But all responded magnificently to Cantelli's inspiring direction. Legge described this *Così* as 'an exquisite, unaffected performance'[16] and Schwarzkopf remembered how Cantelli

> was fearfully nervous about it. When I hear it I think it's the best *Così* we have, of the ones I did. It is so good musically, it was so well rehearsed and he had such an incredible view of the music . . . He had a very dramatic approach, but at the same time a very chamber music and very symphonic view of everything, and his tempi were all so right to each other . . . He was very, very clear and *he battled for those tempi*, to keep them, to get those transitions right. He had great difficulties and was never satisfied with himself . . .[17]

An unofficial LP recording of the first Piccolo Teatro performance on 27 January 1956 was of very poor quality, said to have been taken from a single in-house speaker. Since then, a CD version has appeared; despite a harsh acoustic and an obvious effort to create an artificially quiet background, the close orchestral sound is decently caught. There are many unusual felicities in Cantelli's reading: the beautifully judged string crescendo and diminuendo in the women's first scene, the unusual attention given to the violas throughout, and the telling emphasis on the cellos in Don Alfonso's 'Barbara fato' and his following aria 'Vorrei dir'.

Cantelli sets a well-judged tempo for the *terzettino* 'Soave sia il vento', but Franco Calabrese's voice as Don Alfonso dominates at the expense of Schwarz-kopf and Merriman, and his 'Ai nostri desir' is unduly emphasized. Schwarzkopf finds his deliberate tempo comfortable for 'Come scoglio', which she sings confidently and more directly than under Karajan; the closing section is surpris-ingly contemplative until 'audaci ancor', which she accents heavily. The open-ing of 'Per pietà' is beautifully done (none of the 'cooing' heard in the Karajan recording), the top G$\sharp$ managed with exemplary poise. Cantelli displays pro-found understanding throughout this battle of the sexes, wit and tenderness ideally balanced, with an Italian flair and spontaneity in this most Italian of Mozart's operas.

Schwarzkopf has, not surprisingly, generally rejected pirated recordings, since they tend to be poorly balanced and atrociously recorded – possibly, too, because she earns no royalties from them. But the Cantelli *Così* recording is an exception. It is her favourite recording of the opera and, quite apart from its artistic merits, remains a memento of the exhilaration she and the rest of the cast experienced from working with him.

Also in the pirate category is an interesting disc of extracts from three broadcast concerts in Naples and Turin between 1958 and 1961. It includes a very good performance of 'Per pietà' with its recitative 'Ei parte!' from Naples in 1961, conducted by Carlo Franci. Schwarzkopf's voice is fresh, expressive and free of exaggerated tonal colouring. In all her performances of 'Per pietà' complete opera recordings display a slight loss of energy round 'A chi mai mancò di fede', as though she is gathering her vocal resources for the final furlong. In the performance under Franci the energy is maintained throughout; and she cleanly articulates the two bars of '–cò di fede', which Karajan, especially, allowed her to gloss over.

As something of a curiosity, this disc also includes Dorabella's 'E' un amore ladroncello' sung by Schwarzkopf, from the same concert. It is taken at a furious pace by Franci, sometimes making it impossible for her to articulate cleanly (the *acacciature* suffer particularly in this respect). There is also a structurally damaging cut of thirty-one bars in the central section, from 'Porta dolcezza, dolcezza e gusto'.

There are many unofficial tapes of Karl Böhm conducting Salzburg performances of *Così* with Schwarzkopf as Fiordiligi; and, in 1962, he was in charge of her second studio recording, the only one in stereo and, so far as recorded quality is concerned, a distinct improvement on the Karajan version. In the same year Nan Merriman forsook Schwarzkopf to team up with Seefried in a new *Così* recording under Eugen Jochum.

Schwarzkopf's new Dorabella is Christa Ludwig; and together they form a partnership which is as successful on disc as it was at many performances of the opera. Böhm's tempi are rather more spacious than Cantelli's, while Schwarzkopf's Fiordiligi is now more thoughtful and introspective. She is in fine voice throughout, and her lower register has grown stronger, paying particular dividends in 'Come scoglio'. At the start, the voice is slightly veiled, as it was for Karajan, and one notices a few idiosyncrasies: 'reshta' for 'resta' and 'ancoo' for 'ancor', with the second 'morte sola' sounding crudely; but these are small considerations in what is a thoroughly distinguished piece of singing. Böhm colours the accompaniment wonderfully. As always, in 'Per pietà' the voice is very (perhaps too) closely miked; and the second precipitous descent (top G♯ to middle C♯) is not as cleanly accomplished as before. Böhm encourages the Philharmonia's regal wind section whenever appropriate and is scrupulously supportive of Schwarzkopf, who has clearly profited from her twenty-odd stage performances under him.

Nevertheless, there are places in the score where both Cantelli and Karajan have the edge on Böhm. The crucial duet 'Fra gli amplessi' when Schwarzkopf-Fiordiligi (almost) yields to Luigi Alva-Ferrando is superbly realized under Cantelli, where Schwarzkopf is audibly trembling on the threshold of . . . what? Fulfilment? Disaster? It leaves one in suspense, as it should do. Karajan, too, makes it an exciting moment and again Schwarzkopf sings it very beautifully (in partnership with Leopold Simoneau), but without the intensity of feeling that Cantelli achieved. Böhm's reading, at a slower tempo, is distinctly sober by comparison. For all the mastery and subtlety of her Fiordiligi in this famous Böhm recording, Schwarzkopf's own preference for her inspired performance under Cantelli is understandable.

The Countess Madeleine in *Capriccio* was the last of Schwarzkopf's five major roles, of which she sang eighteen performances between 1960 and 1965. *Capriccio* is a romantic adventure bound up with a discourse about the supremacy of words or music in opera. A young, widowed countess is the central figure; as the subject of a sonnet set to music she cannot decide whether she is more in love with the poet or the composer who have together created it. This was Richard Strauss's last opera, and he anticipated that it would please only the musical intelligentsia; fortunately, however, he misjudged the post-war public's appetite for *Capriccio* and following his death in 1949 it has become increasingly popular.

Schwarzkopf was the first to record the complete role of the Countess Madeleine in the studio, though Viorica Ursuleac, the creator of the part, had sung the Countess in a 1944 live radio broadcast which may still surface in its entirety. Legge's London sessions hardly passed off smoothly, and the recording was made only in mono, as described in Chapter 13; but the result certainly challenges its two modern successors.

Böhm held the opera in great affection and was the conductor at the four 1950 Salzburg Festival performances with Della Casa, as he was for Schwarzkopf in Vienna in 1960–1, having coached her in the role for her first six performances at the Staatsoper. Schwarzkopf's recorded interpretation of the Countess Madeleine is almost ideal, although she declared the role far less interesting than the Marschallin because 'the opera hasn't much to do with the development of character. You can treat it emotionally, but it isn't *real* emotion. *Capriccio* deals with the question of a singer's profession (words or music?)[18] She catches perfectly Madeleine's cool, aristocratic poise, with the voice perceptibly warming as she responds to the advances of Flamand and Olivier. If she underplays the role's sensuality, the suggestion of intense latent physical passion, her quiet, subtle humour is delightfully evident throughout the recording.

Schwarzkopf recorded the final scene of *Capriccio* in 1953, four years earlier than her recording of the complete opera. Otto Ackermann conducted superbly, with beautiful pellucid textures. This was in mono, has been reissued on CD and reveals her in lighter voice and sounding more feminine and vulnerable than others do in subsequent recordings.

Schwarzkopf's eighteen live performances were given in Vienna, Stuttgart, Paris and on the west coast of the United States, with her final scene in concert at the Royal Festival Hall in 1964. That was especially touching, particularly her 'O! Madeleine, Madeleine!' to the looking glass, part in admonition, part in wonderment. The final question as to which of the two men she will choose, and the Major-domo's surprise at his employer's unusually capricious attitude as she goes to dinner alone, leaves the answer deliciously hanging in mid-air.

As a brief pendant to Schwarzkopf's five major roles, her highly diverting Alice Ford in Verdi's *Falstaff* must be mentioned. This was a part she sang only twenty times on stage. As with Fiordiligi, Schwarzkopf's first Alice Ford was in the recording studio with Karajan and, apart from a few performances with William Steinberg in the United States, Karajan conducted all her stage performances. His first encounter with the Fat Knight had already taken place some time previously, in May 1941 at the Aachen Opera, but he had not renewed his acquaintance until the famous 1957 production at La Scala.

Karajan's recording has not attracted universal plaudits. The late Harold Rosenthal, for instance, found that it

> is overpolished and lacks heart. The conductor's meticulous approach has distilled the humanity out of the work . . . [and] . . . Elisabeth Schwarzkopf is more Frau Fluth than Mistress Ford, though she sings in a refined, aristo-cratic style and bubbles over with good humour.[19]

If by 'more Frau Fluth [in Nicolai's *Merry Wives of Windsor*] than Mistress Ford' Rosenthal meant that Schwarzkopf was too soubrettish in timbre (rather than in style), we cannot agree with him. Alice is one of her most delectable recorded performances, from the very first 'Meg!' at the start of Scene 2, when she pounces on her cue, urging on gleefully throughout the scene, with its segues from one Merry Wife to the other while they are hatching Alice's plot. Throughout Schwarzkopf sings with verve, charm and guileful humour, while vividly conveying Alice's mettle as she orchestrates the anti-Falstaff faction. The final fugue was one of her *Desert Island Discs* (see page 150), a clear indication how much *Falstaff* meant to her. In every one of her appearances during the opera, it is evident that she is enjoying herself enormously, for in no other role since Susanna or Sophie has Schwarzkopf been able to give vent to such a sense of fun. She was, with little doubt, the best Mistress Ford to be heard anywhere during those three brief years.

Elisabeth Schwarzkopf: Lieder Singer
1941–1979

Being an opera singer is certainly a glamorous occupation, and it had always been very important to Schwarzkopf in securing huge audiences whenever she appeared in *stagione* performances. By contrast, each of her song recitals was a 'one-off', though eventually it became clear to her that Lieder singing, as a fully expressive lyric soprano, was her true forte. Long before she had arrived at this vocal state there had been a bumpy journey – and a lot of good luck. Lula Mysz-Gmeiner, after all, had got it entirely wrong. Maria Ivogün began to put it right, though under the most difficult circumstances while Schwarzkopf was singing at the Deutsche Oper nearly every night. Ivogün's husband, Michael Raucheisen, helped to build it and Schwarzkopf worked extraordinarily hard at it. Then Walter Legge came along and pursued it with vigour until he had made her realize her true destiny.

Schwarzkopf gave a joint and mixed Lieder recital in Berlin in June 1941, accompanied by Michael Raucheisen, the 'living encyclopedia of German song'.[1] On 9 May 1942 she gave her first solo recital, with Raucheisen again, in the Berlin Beethovensaal. Billed 'Of Spring and Nightingales', it was sold out. There was no review, merely an announcement in one of the few Berlin newspapers to report on the arts.[2] It was in any case unusual – and inadvisable – for adverse criticism to be directed towards artists in view of Goebbels' decree that 'the critic should always emphasize what was good'.[3]

This May 1942 recital was the first known occasion when Schwarzkopf sang a Wolf Lied in public; indeed, she claims that Raucheisen introduced her to the composer's songs, although they were in the mainstream of German Lieder already. Schwarzkopf is well represented in the wartime collection issued under the title *Raucheisen Lied Edition*.

The singers in this long series were chosen from among the most eminent of their time, despite criticism of some interpretations and technical reproduction: Schwarzkopf has told[4] how she was often hustled into the studio, even during an air raid, for a broadcast or a recording, not knowing whether it was going out immediately, being kept for future transmission, transferred to 78, or simply wiped. From the evidence here, Schwarzkopf was already singing Strauss Lieder, especially, with style and affection. She infects 'Hat gesagt, bleibt's nicht dabei', for instance, with her real sense of fun; and this Lied was to remain near the top of her Strauss bill throughout her career; then again, in the dreamy 'Morgen!', she floats a beautifully sustained line.

Schwarzkopf's wartime recitals were complemented by the concerts she gave for German troops, sponsored by the Propaganda Ministry, which comprised items like Strauss waltzes, Solveig's Song from *Peer Gynt*, and 'Summertime' from Gershwin's *Porgy and Bess* (an opera which Goebbels castigated as 'decadent' because of its black cast). These concerts were often broadcast by Berlin Radio to German and Italian troops in the Mediterranean, which is how Schwarzkopf's voice came to be heard by British soldiers in the same theatre of operations; even more significantly, Walter Legge first made a note of the name Schwarzkopf after some of his colleagues in uniform had reported to him in England on distinguished 'enemy' musicians.[5]

Schwarzkopf's Lieder singing undoubtedly became more subtle and sophisticated after she had come under Legge's influence. After a concert she gave in London with Gerald Moore in May 1965, *The Times* likened her 'sincere kind of naïveté in 'Das Lied im Grünen', to 'walking across country meadows in the most fetching kind of town shoes.'[6]

Schubert's 'Seligkeit' was a favourite encore piece of Schwarzkopf's, as it had been of Elizabeth Schumann. No fewer than seven Schwarzkopf versions have appeared on CD; but probably earlier than any of these is her performance of the first and last stanzas in the autobiographical television film first shown in 1992.[7] This version of 'Seligkeit' is the most effervescent and charming of them all, the fresh, beautifully produced voice complemented by Schwarzkopf's wonderfully vivacious delivery which captivated Walter Legge – and many others too – in those days immediately after the war.

Schwarzkopf's first version on record of 'Seligkeit' was made with Karl Hudez in the Brahmssaal, Vienna, in October 1946. It is a rather more careful interpretation than we hear on the film, though still admirably free from artifice. With its coupling 'Die Forelle', it proved to be her first commercial success on record. One of Schwarzkopf's warmest admirers, John Steane, finds it is

> where one hears pretty singing, not very much more. Or yes, look at it with the wisdom of hindsight and there *is* more: a firm placing of the delicate tone . . . and a smile that can make its way through the wax. She doesn't tell the story, doesn't arrest attention, doesn't make contact with the unseen audience . . .[8]

At the same time as Legge was supervising the young Schwarzkopf's recordings in Vienna in 1946, he was also encouraging Irmgard Seefried on the same label. Seefried had recorded two Schubert Lieder ('Heidenröslein' and the famous 'Wiegenlied', D.498) immediately before Schwarzkopf's 1946 'Seligkeit'; and there are over a dozen Mozart, Schubert, Wolf and Strauss Lieder recorded by both sopranos where their different approaches are revealing.

Steane does not consider Seefried to have been a 'connoisseur's singer' because of a want of 'a sort of perfection and virtuosity which [she] hardly offers and may well not be interested in'.[9] This is confirmed when listening to her recording of 'Seligkeit' with Erik Werba. She is not always in the middle of the note, and twice in each stanza negotiates uncomfortably the interval of B to E on '*hi-er*'. There is an affecting and joyful simplicity in her singing, but no attempt to vary the tone; and she makes one less aware of the words than Schwarzkopf does, with her clear and pointed enunciation. Even in her 1946 recording, Schwarzkopf is by some way the more technically finished singer of the two.

In Schwarzkopf's 1965 Carnegie Hall début recital she closed her Schubert group with a blithe, buoyant 'Seligkeit', a delectable performance. She takes it faster than before, with a slight rallentando before the last strophe. In contrast, two versions of 'Seligkeit' from 1960 are less successful. A performance with Jacqueline Robin at the Strasbourg Festival in June 1960 is distinctly fast, with a balance that emphasizes the piano's bass notes – particularly unfortunate in this, of all frothy pieces. Two months later, Gerald Moore was Schwarzkopf's accompanist in one of their regular *Liederabende* at the Salzburg Festival. He lacks delicacy here, and Schwarzkopf is by no means at her best, singing with distinctly raw tone and a strangely detached air. It is a pity that we do not have a better memento of Schwarzkopf and Moore in 'Seligkeit'; for they often gave it as an encore.

Schwarzkopf's last recording of 'Seligkeit' comes from a recital at Nohant in June 1969, in which Aldo Ciccolini is a brilliant, rather over-demonstrative accompanist. In this song her perfect partner was Geoffrey Parsons. There have been two versions on CD, the first from a public concert at Ancona in October 1967. Parsons performs delicately, affectionately and with a sense of humour, and draws a like response from Schwarzkopf. 'Seligkeit' also featured as a final encore at Schwarzkopf's Festival Hall concert in December 1968 to commemorate Ernest Newman's centenary. In *The Times* Joan Chissell wrote of the occasion that Schwarzkopf

> looked radiantly beautiful and put everything across with all her customary charm, telling facial expression and expressive colouring of individual words, but sometimes less than her customary fullness of voice and evenness of line.[10]

Some of the numbers in this recital, for sure, betray the slight vocal unsteadiness which could affect Schwarzkopf's singing by 1968. But her 'Seligkeit' is fetchingly done, with her ever-present sense of spontaneous joy in this Lied. And another favourite Schubert song, 'Gretchen and Spinnrade', is one of the evening's highlights: subtly paced and shaped, with Schwarzkopf capturing perfectly Gretchen's mingled anxiety and ecstasy. In her 1973 studio recording with Parsons, Schwarzkopf's interpretation is more careful, less spontaneous; and it is hard to ignore the signs of wear in the voice.

Two decades earlier, in October 1952, Edwin Fischer had been persuaded by Walter Legge to accompany Schwarzkopf in studio recordings of Schubert. The results are now to be heard on a rather parsimoniously filled CD. She has never sung Schubert better, with an ideally youthful voice at this time of her life and in an entirely unsophisticated manner, all to match Fischer's elegantly romantic presence at the keyboard. The programme is mainly familiar, and includes exceptional, inspiring renderings of 'Ganymed' and 'Der Musensohn'. It also contains Schwarzkopf's best-sung recorded performance of 'Gretchen' (although the 1968 live recording is more impassioned). The tempo is faster than usual, the accelerando imperceptibly accomplished by both artists. She performs the remarkable feat of sounding inquiringly virginal and sexually excited at the same time; and her final 'Meine Ruh' ist hin' interestingly leaves this physical question mark in the air without a hint of the sorrowful wonder that marks other interpretations.

During the 1950s Schwarzkopf was in great demand for recitals in Italy, when her accompanist was usually Giorgio Favaretto. She gave her first-ever all-Schubert recital with him in Rome in February 1952. It included both the familiar 'Die Forelle' and 'Ungeduld' and the rarer 'Suleika I'. The recital was repeated a few days later in Milan, and part of it was issued on CD. 'Die Forelle' suffers by comparison with her delightfully alert, uncomplicated 1946 reading with Karl Hudez. Perhaps under Legge's influence, her account is over-refined, a shade listless, too, with a tempo that is hardly *etwas lebhaft*.

In the 1950s, with her voice in its absolute prime, Schwarzkopf was one of the finest Mozart singers in the world and gave several recitals devoted entirely to Mozart's songs, most of them still rarities in the concert hall. In the 78 era she recorded a charming version of the relatively familiar 'Abendempfindung', accompanied in exemplary fashion by Gerald Moore.

A few years later, in 1955, Schwarzkopf recorded a whole clutch of Mozart's songs with Walter Gieseking in the Abbey Road studios. 'Abendempfindung' is wonderfully sensitive in phrasing and colouring, singer and accompanist in ideal accord. Less successful, however, is 'Das Veilchen' where Gieseking's crisp, clean tone is rather at odds with Schwarzkopf's coy, prissy delivery of the text. But she finds the desired simplicity for 'An Chloë' (magically supported by Gieseking); and she gauges ideally the comedy of 'Die Alte', the tedious old woman who forever complains about how much better things were in her day, with Gieseking adding his own gentle, witty inflexions.

Richard Strauss's extensive output of Lieder has been fully explored on disc by Dietrich Fischer-Dieskau; Schwarzkopf, surprisingly for a singer with such affinity with this composer, attempted relatively few of them, and never gave a complete recital of Strauss songs. Twenty, at most, appeared in her programmes. The humorous 'Hat gesagt, bleib's nicht dabei' and 'Schlechtes Wetter' were favourite encores, superseded in later years by 'Zueignung' and 'Morgen!'

In 'Morgen!' and 'Ruhe, meine Seele' Schwarzkopf generally exerted a profound magic, especially when she was partnered by Geoffrey Parsons, and she declared that of all the accompanists she had known, he was the only one guaranteed to maintain complete silence in the audience during the postlude to 'Morgen!'. No recording of either Lied survives with Schwarzkopf and Parsons. But both are included in their orchestral versions made by Szell and the LSO in 1968. 'Ruhe, meine Seele', Strauss's pessimistic revision of the Lied he composed fifty-four years earlier, is given a marvellous fervour and dramatic intensity.

The London première of Strauss's *Four Last Songs* by Kirsten Flagstad in 1950, and Schwarzkopf's early encounter with them are described on pages 102–3. Otto Ackermann conducted Schwarzkopf's first recording in September 1953. She sings 'Frühling' with a wonderful freshness and sense of discovery. In 'September' she achieves a haunting sensation of dreamy timelessness during the long phrase 'sterbenden Gartentraum', the whole six bars sung in one breath; though at the close of the song her last word 'zu' is covered by Dennis Brain's first note of the postlude. There is an ideal colour in Manoug Parikian's violin solo in 'Beim Schlafengehen', with its reminiscences of *Der Rosenkavalier* and *Ariadne*, though Schwarzkopf's technique easily supports those expansive, arching phrases, with their ebb and flow beautifully judged. She sings this song with deep feeling, and finds an even greater intensity for the mystical contemplation of death in 'Im Abendrot' – though the measured tempo here stretches her at the phrase 'So tief im Abendrot'.

Twelve years later Schwarzkopf made a stereo recording of the *Four Last Songs* with George Szell and the Berlin Radio Symphony Orchestra. Tempi throughout are consistently slower than before, though Szell's accompaniment is a model of consideration. No wonder she adored singing with him: he once told her: 'My dear, breathe as you please: you are not a gasometer!'[11] And she certainly takes more breaths than before – though, interestingly, under Szell she takes the last 'deine selige Gegenwart' in 'Im Frühling' in a single breath, whereas she had broken after the first syllable of 'Gegenwart' under Ackermann.

Her top register is less pure than it had been twelve years earlier, and she transposes 'Frühling' down a semitone. Here and there the tone is slightly curdled, and there are occasional exaggerated vowel-sounds. Schwarzkopf's interpretation is, as you would expect, more mature, more autumnal, with more depth of tone in the lower register. At times the expressive effects seem studied, and we are intermittently aware of her consciously husbanding her resources. But this 1965 recording has a wisdom and insight that have understandably made it many people's favourite version of the *Four Last Songs*.

Nine years earlier, in 1956, Karajan gave the *Four Last Songs* with Schwarzkopf at the Royal Festival Hall, but the performance, though recorded, was not issued until the Schwarzkopf seventy-fifth birthday celebrations in 1990 when she grudgingly agreed to the disc's release. When it appeared, she said in an interview that it was 'a very nasty performance of the *Four Last Songs* with Karajan. I could hardly produce a sound, it is fearful. It happens, and you regret it ever afterwards. In general I was against it . . .'[12] She sings 'Frühling' at pitch, as in 1953 and in three of the songs, Karajan's tempi are a good deal faster than Ackermann's and Szell's (the exception is an extremely expansive 'Beim Schlafengehen'). The performance is far from 'nasty', of course; and part of her distaste for it may stem from Karajan's change of sequence to 'Frühling', 'Beim Schlafengehen', 'Im Abendrot', 'September'.

Many eminent conductors have often given Strauss's most famous orchestral songs (Furtwängler never did after the première) and so have other sopranos; but the achievements of Schwarzkopf, Ackermann and Szell have established, through their recordings, an extraordinarily high standard of performance in which the voice and the orchestra speak intimately to any sensitive listener.

It was in the Lieder of Hugo Wolf, with their unique embracing of words with music, that Schwarzkopf exhibited her 'art taken to its subtlest peak' (as a *Times* critic once put it.[13]) As she herself remarked, in Wolf the singer has to devise a way of finding one vocal colour for the words, and another for the music, until they merge into the sung sound that Wolf required. It was not until she was thirty-four that Schwarzkopf devoted an entire Lieder recital to Wolf, in April 1950 at the Brahmssaal in Vienna, a building still haunted by the tragic composer's unquiet spirit.

> After a long, long interval Elisabeth Schwarzkopf has found her way back to Vienna, making a fine gesture with her Hugo Wolf recital. Her blossoming, pure and endlessly flexible instrument, a genuine 'voix blanche', has gained further in tonal beauty and intensity of expression. All technical matters – and the songs she chose were among the technically most demanding . . . were mastered in an almost playful manner. The advantage of her light,

coloratura soprano and her character were, of course, most evident when she chose the delicate, cheerful, even boisterous genre . . .

The deep meditativeness and intimacy of the first Mörike songs, like 'Schlafendes Jesuskind', or especially the passionately glowing religious songs of the *Spanish Song Book* . . . are less suited to her cheerful nature and the colour of her voice; and when she tries to underline the extreme plasticity and fine details of Wolf's word painting with gestures, then she remains in thrall to the stage when she is only on the platform. Nevertheless, a beautiful evening received with great warmth by the audience.[14]

Schwarzkopf was much loved in Vienna as an opera singer (though by 1950 she was hardly a 'light coloratura'), and had last appeared there in April of the previous year as Gilda – scarcely 'a long, long interval'.

The Mörike Lieder mentioned by the Viennese critic are so called because Eduard Friedrich Mörike wrote the poems. They remained central to Schwarz-kopf's Wolf repertoire and she recorded twenty-one of them, some, like 'Im Frühling' and 'Elfenlied' several times. She also included seven more Mörike Lieder at various recitals.

Wolf composed his fifty-one settings of poems by Goethe in a typically feverish outburst between October 1888 and February 1889. Like other sopranos, Schwarzkopf was drawn above all to the five settings from the novel 'Wilhelm Meister' suitable for female voice: the four songs sung by Mignon, that sad, mysterious creature searching for the secret to her forgotten past; and the flippant 'Philine', sung by the actress of that name. In her all-Wolf 1959 studio recording with Gerald Moore, her rendering of 'Philine' is distinctly self-aware, though her live 1958 Salzburg performance is deliciously spon-taneous and paints the flighty, cynical creature to the life. This Salzburg Wolf recital was aptly described by the critic of the *Salzburger Nachrichten* as 'a blissful ("beglückenden") experience of the purest art of song'. It also contains a glorious reading of the final Mignon song, 'Kennst du das Land?', catching all the waif's ruminative, questioning ache and opening out thrillingly on the impassioned climax of each verse.

Schwarzkopf often ended her recitals with the last song in this collection, that enchanting female answer to Mozart's Catalogue Aria, 'Ich hab' in Penna'. The piano postlude, with its witch-like laughter in the last two bars, is liable to be an awkward moment for the accompanist, though he may chance to reflect on the fact that the composer always caught and played it perfectly *ff feurig* as marked. It is virtuoso song for both artists.

Five years earlier, in August 1953, Schwarzkopf had given another all-Wolf recital in Salzburg, this time with Furtwängler at the piano. The whole recital was broadcast, and can be heard complete on CD, an absorbing experience, but desperately flawed from Schwarzkopf's point of view, as she recalls:

we landed a performance where everything was miles too slow, so slow it wasn't true. But in spite of the slowness he gave them magic. He was a composer as well as a conductor, and when he played a wrong note he could rescue it and fill in and do things which only somebody who knows how to compose and conduct can do. He had an overall view, a broader view, but he was known to be very slow in those years, partly because he was beginning to go deaf. . . I can't say that was the problem with the songs, he just couldn't play them fast enough . . .[15]

Her criticism is understandable because Furtwängler, marvellous musician though he was, with his velvety keyboard touch, had little practical experience as a pianò accompanist. In virtually all of the songs here, Furtwängler is far slower than other accompanists on disc, and often favours rich, sostenuto textures at odds with the printed notes: in the Goethe 'Blumengrüss', for example, he plays through the crucial quaver rests, scrupulously observed by Gerald Moore in the 1958 recital by lifting his hands from the keyboard and his foot from the sustaining pedal; Furtwängler seems to leave his there. In his performance, Furtwängler's textures are heavy, even muddy, the tempo distinctly lugubrious, and the *ff* at 'Hören muss ich' threatens to drown Schwarzkopf. Often we can sense her urging him along; and her final 'Ach, nein!' might almost be meant for him! Again, the 1958 Salzburg recital with Moore offers a delectable performance of this song: sensuous, playful and exquisitely timed.

Schwarzkopf sang only a few songs from Wolf's *Spanish Song Book* at *ad hoc* recitals. But she and Fischer-Dieskau performed the complete Song Book together at Lucerne in 1956 and at Carnegie Hall, New York in 1964. In 1967 they recorded for Deutsche Grammophon (Schwarzkopf's sole excursion on that label) what is probably the supreme version of this collection and Moore is again a masterly accompanist. Schwarzkopf can occasionally be too self-consciously girlish (as in 'Mögen all bösen Zungen'); but her range of colour and depth of understanding are supreme.

Schumann and Brahms were featured in Schwarzkopf's recitals far less frequently than Mozart, Schubert, Wolf or Richard Strauss. In her whole career Schwarzkopf sang no more than twenty-five of Brahms's Lieder, among which one has only to hear a few bars of her 1954 'Feldeinsamkeit' to be captivated. This is one of a group of eleven Brahms songs Schwarzkopf performed with Edwin Fischer at a recital in Rome in 1954[16]; and, as elsewhere, Fischer is an ideal accompanist. In the introduction of 'Von ewiger Liebe' the familiar melody is not, as so often, thudded out in the left hand, but delicately suggested; and how meltingly Schwarzkopf caresses the first words of 'Wie Melodien zieht es'! In 'Vergebliches Ständchen', a Schwarzkopf favourite, Fischer adds his humour to hers by beginning steadily; he then colours the key change, deftly calculates the false close, and makes a rapid accelerando just before the final rallentando, all of which enhances Schwarzkopf's own unexaggeratedly playful delivery.

Robert Schumann was featured more often than Brahms in Schwarzkopf's concerts, though very few of her Schumann interpretations are available on CD. 'Der Nussbaum' is well represented and can be heard in one studio and two pirate recordings. One of the latter, from a 1967 recital in Ancona, is magically accompanied by Geoffrey Parsons, who seems to be holding Schwarzkopf by some invisible thread: she floats on the piano sound, imperceptibly drifting towards the last bar until it all fades away after four minutes of delight.

They obviously relish the humour of 'Die Kartenlegerin' which follows, a favourite item in Schwarzkopf's recitals. But her 1973 studio recording of 'Der Nussbaum' with Geoffrey Parsons is far too slow, while the version with Aldo Ciccolini, recorded at the 1969 Nohant recital, finds Schwarzkopf in very affected mood, sounding as though her chin is on her neck, crooning and distorting vowels. She always sings 'er blättrig die Äste aus' in the second line, whereas the Hugo Pohle score gives 'er blättrig die Blätter aus' which is what Richard Tauber, Karl Erb and Elisabeth Schumann give us in their famous versions of the Lied. Their tempi are worth mentioning too. Without the least suggestion of hurrying, yet observing the prescribed ritenuto and rallentando, Tauber takes a few seconds more than three minutes, Erb and Schumann take about ten seconds less – around a minute less than Schwarzkopf in her Ancona recital with Parsons, though here, unlike in the still slower 1973 studio recording, the leisurely tempo is used to create a sense of dreamy timelessness.

During the 1970s Schwarzkopf sang Schumann's 'Frauenliebe und leben' in a few recitals, and also recorded it with Parsons. The result was frankly disappointing. Schwarzkopf gives a hypnotic account of the grief-stricken final song, but in the earlier part of the cycle her artful phrasing and inflexion and her ability to immerse herself in the mood of each song is offset by her vocal vulnerability. Schwarzkopf's final recording, 'Frauenliebe und-leben', was coupled with the Eichendorff *Liederkreis*, opus 39.[17] There are wonderful moments here: the ghastly unmasking of the witch in 'Waldesgespräch'; or the sheer range of subtle colouring in 'Auf einer Burg'. But again, we are too often aware only of vocal frailties. These cycles are best left on LP.

As a coda to the brief and necessarily selective survey of Schwarzkopf's art as a Lieder singer, we should mention a couple of forays into offbeat repertoire. She recorded, delightfully, a handful of Italian songs by Ermano Wolf-Ferrari, available on a CD entitled *Encores*, which also includes Swiss and Silesian folk songs, crowned by the famous encore "s Schätzli' that she originally learned from Maria Ivogün. Another unexpected venture was with the Russian *émigré* composer, Nicolas Medtner, who in 1950 accompanied Schwarzkopf in a recital of his German Lieder and Russian songs (sung in English translation); fourteen of them were issued on 78 and are now on CD. The singing is confident and characterful (though Schwarzkopf's English was not yet fully idiomatic), but Medtner's own accompaniments are over-demonstrative, sometimes threatening to overwhelm her. Writing of the concert, the *Times* critic observed:

> The music must be a delight to play but listening to it . . . makes one feel like a fly drowned in fruit juice. In the songs, the notes overwhelm the singer who is treated as a bystander offering explanatory observations on the tone poem that is pouring out of the piano.[18]

Schwarzkopf appeared three times in London in the fifties and sixties with several programmes, such as the Medtner concert, in which every one contained a surprise of one sort or another. In May 1966 she was presenting what was rumoured to be her last solo recital at the Royal Festival Hall with

> the most loyal and inspiring of her pianist-partners, Gerald Moore . . . She even walked off the platform behind his back, leaving him to take a solo call. Gerald Moore had done everything over the years to merit solo calls and Elisabeth Schwarzkopf has the humanity and musicianship to know it. Five encores and she shut the piano lid to send them home.[19]

Appendix A
Schwarzkopf's performances in chronological order

This appendix cannot claim to be a complete list of Schwarzkopf's stage and concert performances, but it is the most comprehensive one published to date.

Names of characters and of operas are given in the language of performance, which at the Deutsche Oper was invariably German. Thus *Il Trovatore* becomes *Der Troubadour*, *Le nozze di Figaro* becomes *Figaros Hochzeit*, and so on. Conductors' and accompanists' names are given after the solidus.

ABBREVIATIONS USED IN APPENDIX A

★ Schwarzkopf's first performance in named role
★★ Schwarzkopf in world première of named role

aG = appearance as guest artist   NP = new production   GP = German première
DSB = Deutscher Sender Berlin (Berlin Radio)

(Venues)

Aalborg	AH	Aalborg Hall	Boston	JH	Jordan Hall
Adelaide	TH	Town Hall	Bournemouth	WG	Winter Gardens
Aix-en-Provence	TA	Archbishop's Court Theatre	Brescia	TG	Teatro Grande
			Brussels	Expo	Exhibition Halls (1958)
Amsterdam	C	Concertgebouw		TRM	Théâtre Royal de la Monnaie
	S	Stadsschouwburg			
Baltimore	GC	Goucher College			
Barcelona	L	Liceo	Buenos Aires	TC	Teatro Cólon
Basel	MS	Musiksaal	Canberra	T	Theatre
Bath	AS	Assembly Rooms	Chicago	O	Opera
Bayreuth	FSH	Festival Opera House		OH	Orchestra Hall
			Chichester	FT	Festival Theatre
	MOH	Margrave's Opera House	Cincinnati	Z	Zoo
			Cleveland	SH	Severance Hall
Bergen	KP	Konsertpaleet	Copenhagen	OFP	Odd Fellow Palace
Berlin	BS	Beethoven Saal		OFPSS	Odd Fellow Palace Large Hall
	DO	Deutsche Oper			
	DSB	Deutschlandsender Berlin (Berlin Radio)		T	Tivoli Theatre
				TKSS	Tivoli, Large Concert Hall
	HfM	Hochschule für Musik (High School for Music)	Croydon	TR	Theatre Royal
			Detroit	FH	Fairfield Halls
			Eastbourne	FA	Ford Auditorium
	MS	Meistersaal	Edinburgh	CT	Congress Theatre
	P	Philharmonie (Philharmonic Hall)		FMH	Freemasons' Hall
				K	King's Theatre
Beverly Hills	HS	High School		UH	Usher Hall
Birmingham	TH	Town Hall	Florence	P	Teatro della Pergola
	TR	Theatre Royal		TComm	Teatro Communale
Bologna	Comm	Teatro Communale		TdeP	Teatro della Pergola

Geneva	GT	Grand Théâtre
	VH	Victoria Hall
Glasgow	CitH	City Hall
Göteborg	KH	Konserthuset
Hague	D	Diligentia
	R	Residentie
Hamburg	NWDR	Nordwest Deutsche Rundfunk (Radio)
	SO	State Opera
Helsinki	C	Conservatoire
	Univ	University
Innsbruck	GS	Grosser Stadtsaal
Ivrea	TG	Teatro Grande
Liseberg	KH	Concert Hall
Liverpool	PH	Philharmonic Hall
London	BBCMV	BBC Maida Vale Studio (MV1 = Maida Vale Studio 1)
	CTH	Camden Town Hall
	CG	Royal Opera House, Covent Garden
	G	Guildhall
	KH	Kingsway Hall
	RAH	Royal Albert Hall
	RFH	Royal Festival Hall
	WH	Wigmore Hall
Los Angeles	HB	Hollywood Bowl
	PA	Philharmonic Auditorium
Lyons	O	Opéra
Madrid	TZ	Teatro Zarzuela
Marseilles	O	Opéra
Melbourne	TH	Town Hall
Milan	C	Conservatorio Milano
	M	Cinema-Teatro Metropole
	PS	Piccola Scala
	RAI	Radio Italiana Studios
	S	La Scala
Minneapolis	NMA	Northrop Memorial Auditorium
Monte Carlo	sG	Salle Garnier
Munich	O	Bavarian Opera
Naples	TSC	Teatro San Carlo
New York	BAM	Brooklyn Academy of Music
	CH	Carnegie Hall
	HC	Hunter College
	LC	Lincoln Center
	LS	Lewisohn Stadium
	Met	Metropolitan Opera
	PH	Philharmonic Hall
	S	Stadium
	TH	Town Hall
	UN	United Nations Building
Odense	FFH	Fuen Assembly Hall
Palermo	TM	Teatro Massimo
Paris	FdD	Foyer de Danse
	O	Opéra
	OC	Opéra Comique
	RF	Radio France (Paris)
	SP	Salle Pleyel
	TC-E	Théâtre des Champs-Élysées
	TdeV	Théâtre de V
	UdeG	Université de la rive gauche (University of the Left Bank)
Perth (Australia)	GH	Government House
Perugia	TM	Teatro Morlacchi
Philadelphia	CC	Community College
Pittsburg	ML	Mount Lebanon
Portsmouth	G	Guildhall
Rome	O	Opera
	RAI	Italian Radio Studios
	SC	Santa Cecilia
	TA	Teatro Argentina
Rotterdam	D	De Doelen
Salisbury	CH	Civic Hall
Salzburg	FSH	Festspielhaus (Festival Theatre)
	LFSH	Little Festival Theatre
	NFSH	New Festival Theatre
	OFSH	Old Festival Theatre
	L	Landestheater (Provincial Theatre)
	M	Mozarteum
	R	Residenz
	StP	St Peter's Church
San Francisco	WMOH	War Memorial Opera House
Santa Barbara	ECC	El Camino College
Scheveningen	Circ.	Circus Theatre
Seattle	OH	Opera House
	PT	Palomar Theater
Stockholm	KH	Konserthus (Concert House)
	KT	Kungliga teatern (Theatre Royal)
Stresa	TPC	Teatro del Palazzo dei Congressi
Stuttgart	SO	State Opera
Sydney	TH	Town Hall
Toronto	EA	Eaton Auditorium
	MH	Massey Hall
Tours	GdeM	Grange de Meslay
Turin	C	Conservatorio
	RAI	Italian Radio Studios

Utrecht	GK	Groote Kerk		Sing.	Vienna Singverein
Venice	F	La Fenice		TadW	Theater an der Wien
Vienna	BS	Brahmssaal		VO	Volksoper
	GS	Large Hall	Washington	JFKC	J. F. Kennedy
	O	Old Opera House			Center
	Oper	State Opera	Zürich	GTS	Grosser
	R	Residenz or			Tonhallesaal
		Redoutensaal		OH	Opera House

Berlin Hochschule für Musik

1935 2 Bach Cantata duets with Carola Behr Reger's *Vier*
Schlichte Weisen / Busch   21 Nov
1 Hirt in Schütz's Weihnachtshistorie ('Christmas
Story') / Stein   20 Dec
1937 4 Italian Songs (Schubert) / Kusterer   17 Jun

Berlin Deutsche Oper
1937–38 season (stage début)

1938 *1 Blumenmädchen, 2 Gruppe in *Parsifal* / Rother   15, 16, 17, 18, 23,
(NP)   24 Apr
*Wellgunde in *Rheingold* / Dammer   26 Apr
*Wellgunde in *Götterdämmerung* / Dammer   4 May
*Lumpensammlerin (Rag Picker) in *Evangelimann*
(Kienzl) / Lutze   7 May
*1 Edelknabe in *Tannhäuser* / Dammer   17 May
*Esmeralda in *Vekaufte Braut* (*Bartered Bride*) / Lutze   20 Jun
*Ida in *Fledermaus* / Dammer   1, 2, 3 Jul, 21, 22,
                                                            23, 24 Aug

*Marie in *Der Waffenschmied* (*The Armourer*: Lortzing) /
Lutze   26 Aug
(Start of 1938–39 season at Berlin Deutsche Oper)
Marie in *Waffenschmied* / Lutze   9 Sep
Ida in *Fledermaus* / Schäfer   10 Sep
*Bertha in *Euryanthe* / Rother (NP)   14, 17 Sep
1 Edelknabe and *Junger Hirt (Young Shepherd) in
Tannhäuser / von Zallinger   18 Sep
Ida in *Fledermaus* / Schäfer   21 Sep
Bertha in *Euryanthe* / Rother   25 Sep, 1 Oct
*Pepa in *Tiefland* (d'Albert) / Dammer   5 Oct
Bertha in *Euryanthe* / Rother   6, 9 Oct
Wellgunde in *Rheingold* / Dammer   14 Oct
Bertha in *Euryanthe* / Rother   16 Oct
1 Edelknabe and Junger Hirt in *Tannhäuser* / Dammer   26 Oct
Bertha in *Euryanthe* / Rother   28 Oct
Ida in *Fledermaus* / Schäfer   29 Oct
*1 Edelknabe in *Lohengrin* / Dammer   30 Oct
Bertha in *Euryanthe* / Rother   7, 11 Nov
Pepa in *Tiefland* / Dammer   12 Nov
*Frasquita in *Carmen* / Rother (NP)   17 Nov
Pepa in *Tiefland* / Nettstraeter aG   20 Nov
Frasquita in *Carmen* / Rother   22 Nov
Ida in *Fledermaus* / Schäfer   25 Nov
Frasquita in *Carmen* / Rother   26 Nov
Bertha in *Euryanthe* / Rother   29 Nov
Frasquita in *Carmen* / Rother   2 Dec
*Inez in *Troubadour* / Lutze   6 Dec
Frasquita in *Carmen* / Rother   10 Dec

Bertha in *Euryanthe* / Rother	12 Dec
Frasquita in *Carmen* / Rother	13 Dec
Ida in *Fledermaus* / Schäfer	14 Dec
1 Edelknabe and Junger Hirt in *Tannhäuser* / Rother	17 Dec
Pepa in *Tiefland* / Zillig aG	19 Dec
Frasquita in *Carmen* / Rother	21 Dec
★Erika in *Schwarzer Peter* (*Black Peter*: Norbert Schültze) / Schültze	22, 23 27 Dec
★Valencienne in *Lustige Witwe* (*Merry Widow*) / Kölling	31 Dec

1939	Valencienne in *Lustige Witwe* (*Merry Widow*) / Kölling	1, 2, 3 Jan
	Frasquita in *Carmen* / Rother	6, 9 Jan
	Sang in presence of the Führer	12 Jan
	Erika in *Schwarzer Peter* / Schültze	16, 21 Jan
	Frasquita in *Carmen* / F. Rieger	22 Jan
	★1 Knabe in *Zauberflöte* (*Magic Flute*) / Rother (NP)	24, 28 Jan
	Frasquita in *Carmen* / Rother	29 Jan
	Valencienne in *Lustige Witwe* / Kölling	2, 3, 4, 5 Feb
	1 Knabe in *Zauberflöte* / Rother	7 Feb
	Bertha in *Euryanthe* / Rother	14 Feb
	Inez in *Troubadour* / Lutze	15 Feb
	Frasquita in *Carmen* / Rother	17 Feb
	1 Knabe in *Zauberflöte* / Rother	19 Feb
	Ida in *Fledermaus* / Schäfer	20 Feb
	1 Knabe in *Zauberflöte* / Rother	23 Feb
	Edelknabe and Junger Hirt: *Tannhäuser* / Zwissler aG	25 Feb
	★Edelknabe in *Rigoletto* / Schäfer	26 Feb
	Frasquita in *Carmen* / Rother	27 Feb
	1 Knabe in *Zauberflöte* / Rother	28 Feb
	★Musette in *Boheme* / Rother	2 Mar
	★1 Adelige Waise (Noble Orphan) in *Rosenkavalier* / Rother	3 Mar
	★Antonia in *Tiefland*	7 Mar
	1 Adelige Waise in *Rosenkavalier* / Rother	10 Mar
	1 Edelknabe in *Lohengrin* / Brückner	11 Mar
	1 Knabe in *Zauberflöte* / Rother	12 Mar
	Inez in *Troubadour* / Lutze	13 Mar
	Ida in *Fledermaus* / Schäfer	16 Mar
	Pepa in *Tiefland* / Dammer	21 Mar
	1 Adelige Waise in *Rosenkavalier* / Rother	22 Mar
	Pepa in *Tiefland* / Schmitz aG	23 Mar
	Musette in *Boheme* / Brückner	27 Mar
	Frasquita in *Carmen* / Brückner	28 Mar
	1 Knabe in *Zauberflöte* / von Tenner aG	3 Apr
	1 Blumenmä., 2 Gp. in *Parsifal* / Rother	7, 8, 9 Apr
	1 Blumenmä., 2 Gp. in *Parsifal* / Schmitz	10 Apr
	Esmeralda in *Verkaufte Braut* / Lutze	11 Apr
	Bertha in *Euryanthe*	17 Apr
	1 Edelknabe in *Lohengrin* / Pilowski aG	19 Apr
	1 Adelige Waise in *Rosenkavalier* / Rother	22 Apr
	1 Knabe in *Zauberflöte* / Rother	23, 24, 27 Apr
	Antonia in *Tiefland*	28 Apr
	1 Knabe in *Zauberflöte* / Rother	4 May
	Esmeralda in *Verkaufte Braut* / Lutze	7 May
	Frasquita in *Carmen* / Rother	8 May
	Musette in *Boheme* / Grüber (NP)	9, 12 May
	1 Knabe in *Zauberflöte* / Rother	13 May
	★★2 Page in *Katarina* (Kusterer) / Rother	14 May
	Inez in *Troubadour* / Grüber	15 May

2 Page in *Katarina* / Rother	17 May
1 Knabe in *Zauberflöte* / Rother	19 May
2 Page in *Katarina* / Kusterer	23 May
1 Adelige Waise in *Rosenkavalier* / Rother	25 May
Frasquita in *Carmen* / Grüber	28 May
*Alexei in *Katarina* / Kusterer	29 May
2 Page in *Katarina* / Kusterer	2 Jun
Edelknabe in *Rigoletto* / Schäfer	3 Jun
1 Knabe in *Zauberflöte* / Rother	5 Jun
Ida in *Fledermaus* / Schäfer	8 Jun
1 Edelknabe and Junger Hirt in *Tannhäuser* / Rother	10 Jun
1 Adelige Waise in *Rosenkavalier* / Rother	11 Jun
Musette in *Boheme* / Rother	12 Jun
Frasquita in *Carmen*	14 Jun
Esmeralda in *Verkaufte Braut* / Lutze	16 Jun
Musette in *Boheme* / Rother	17 Jun
*3 Brautjungfer in *Freischütz* / Schäfer	22 Jun
1 Knabe in *Zauberflöte* / Rother	24 Jun
1 Edelknabe and Junger Hirt: *Tannhäuser* / Rother	26 Jun
Frasquita in *Carmen* / Rother	28 Jun

(Start of 1939–40 season at Berlin Deutsche Oper)

1 Knabe in *Zauberflöte* / Rother	27 Aug
1 Edelknabe in *Lohengrin* / Rother	2 Sep
Musette in *Boheme*	3 Sep
*Lola in *Cavalleria Rusticana* / Lutze	7 Sep
1 Adelige Waise in *Rosenkavalier* / Rother	8 Sep
3 Brautjungfer in *Freischütz*	10 Sep
Inez in *Troubadour* / Lutze	14 Sep
1 Edelknabe in *Tannhäuser* / Rother	16 Sep
1 Knabe in *Zauberflöte* / Rother	17 Sep
Edelknabe in *Rigoletto* / Schäfer	18 Sep
Lola in *Cavalleria Rusticana* / Lutze	22 Sep
Esmeralda in *Verkaufte Braut* / Lutze	25 Sep
3 Brautjungfer in *Freischütz*	3 Oct
Lola in *Cavalleria Rusticana* / Lutze	6 Oct
1 Adelige Waise in *Rosenkavalier* / Rother	8 Oct
Esmeralda in *Verkaufte Braut* / Lutze	9 Oct
Pepa in *Tiefland* / Grüber	11 Oct
*Arsena in *Zigeunerbaron* / Schäfer and Voices of Spring Waltz in Act II	14 Oct
Arsena in *Zigeunerbaron* / Schäfer	17 Oct
Inez in *Troubadour* / Lutze	19 Oct
Junger Hirt in *Tannhäuser* / Rother	24 Oct
Inez in *Troubadour* / Lutze	29 Oct
*Serpetta in *Gärtnerin aus Liebe* (Mozart's *La Finta Giardiniera*) / Grüber	31 Oct
Inez in *Troubadour* / Lutze	1 Nov
Pepa in *Tiefland* / Grüber	4 Nov
Musette in *Boheme* / Grüber	6 Nov
Serpetta in *Gärtnerin aus Liebe* / Grüber	10 Nov
1 Edelknabe in *Lohengrin* / Grüber	12 Nov
1 Edelknabe in *Tannhäuser* / Rother	15 Nov
Arsena in *Zigeunerbaron*	16 Nov
Musette in *Boheme* / Grüber	17 Nov
*Ortlinde in *Walküre* / Rother	19 Nov
Marie in *Waffenschmied* / Lutze	21 Nov
1 Blumenmä., 2 Gp. in *Parsifal* / Rother	22, 25, 26 Nov
1 Waise in *Rosenkavalier* / Rother (NP)	6 Dec
Arsena in *Zigeunerbaron* / Schäfer	7 Dec

*Taumännchen (Dew Fairy) in *Hänsel und Gretel* /
Rother (NP)   8 Dec
*Gretchen in *Wildschütz* (Lortzing's *The Poacher*) /
Grüber   11 Dec
Pepa in *Tiefland* / Rother   13 Dec
*Barbarina in *Figaros Hochzeit* / Rother   15, 20 Dec
Ida in *Fledermaus* / Grüber   21 Dec
Taumännchen in *Hänsel und Gretel* / Rother   22, 23 Dec
1 Knabe in *Zauberflöte* / Rother   25 Dec
Arsena in *Zigeunerbaron* / Schäfer   26 Dec
Barbarina in *Figaros Hochzeit* / Rother   28 Dec
Taumännchen in *Hänsel und Gretel* / Grüber   29 Dec
Musette in *Boheme* / Grüber   30 Dec
Ida in *Fledermaus* / Schäfer   31 Dec

1940   Ida in *Fledermaus* / Schäfer   1 Jan
                1 Edelknabe and Junger Hirt in *Tannhäuser* / Rother   2 Jan
                Frasquita in *Carmen* / Grüber   4 Jan
                Taumännchen in *Hänsel und Gretel* / Grüber   6 Jan
                Gretchen in *Wildschütz* / Grüber (NP)   7 Jan
                Taumännchen in *Hänsel und Gretel* / Grüber   8, 10 Jan
                Ida in *Fledermaus* / Schäfer   11 Jan
                Arsena in *Zigeunerbaron* / Schäfer   13 Jan
                Frasquita in *Carmen* / Grüber   14 Jan
                Serpetta in *Gärtnerin aus Liebe* / Grüber   16 Jan
                1 Knabe in *Zauberflöte* / Rother   18 Jan
                Pepa in *Tiefland* / Grüber   19 Jan
                Barbarina in *Figaros Hochzeit* / Rother   20 Jan
                Arsena in *Zigeunerbaron* / Schäfer   21 Jan
                Frasquita in *Carmen* / Grüber   25 Jan
                Ida in *Fledermaus* / Schäfer   26 Jan
                Esmeralda in *Verkaufte Braut* / Lutze   28 Jan
                Frasquita in *Carmen* / Grüber   31 Jan
                *Marie in *Zar und Zimmermann* (Lortzing's *Czar and
                Carpenter*) / Lutze   3 Feb
                Barbarina in *Figaros Hochzeit* / Rother   6 Feb
                Arsena in *Zigeunerbaron* / Schäfer   8 Feb
                1 Edelknabe in *Lohengrin* / Grüber   9 Feb
                1 Knabe in *Zauberflöte* / Rother   10 Feb
                Musette in *Boheme* / Grüber   11 Feb
                Gretchen in *Wildschütz* / Grüber   15 Feb
                Arsena in *Zigeunerbaron* / Schäfer   16, 17 Feb
                1 Edelknabe and Junger Hirt in *Tannhäuser* / Rother   18 Feb
                Serpetta in *Gärtnerin aus Liebe* / Grüber   19 Feb
                Arsena in *Zigeunerbaron* / Schäfer   21, 23 Feb
                *Giannetta in *Liebestrank* (*L'Elisir d'amore*) / Lutze
                (NP)   27 Feb
                Esmeralda in *Verkaufte Braut* / Lutze   28 Feb
                Wellgunde in *Rheingold* / Rother   29 Feb
                Giannetta in *Liebestrank* / Lutze   1 Mar
                Lola in *Cavalleria Rusticana* / Lutze   3 Mar
                Ida in *Fledermaus* / Schäfer   5 Mar
                Arsena in *Zigeunerbaron* / Schäfer   11 Mar
                Wellgunde in *Götterdämmerung* / Rother   12 Mar
                Giannetta in *Liebestrank* / Lutze   13 Mar
                Frasquita in *Carmen* / Grüber   14 Mar
                Barbarina in *Figaros Hochzeit* / Rother   15, 20 Mar
                Inez in *Troubadour* / Lutze   21 Mar
                1 Blumenmä. in *Parsifal* / Rother   22, 23, 24 Mar

Giannetta in *Liebestrank* and *Lauretta in *Gianni Schicchi* / Lutze (NP)	30 Mar, 1 Apr
Barbarina in *Figaros Hochzeit* / Rother	3 Apr
Wellgunde in *Rheingold* / Rother	9 Apr
*Nonne (Nun) in *Palla de' Mozzi* / Marinuzzi (GP)	12 Apr
Arsena in *Zigeunerbaron* / Schäfer	13 Apr
Nonne in *Palla de' Mozzi* / Grüber	15, 18 Apr
Giannetta in *Liebestrank* and Lauretta in *Gianni Schicchi* / Lutze	19 Apr
Wellgunde in *Götterdämmerung* / Rother	20 Apr
Frasquita in *Carmen* / Grüber	21 Apr
Nonne in *Palla de'Mozzi* / Grüber	23 Apr
Esmeralda in *Zigeunerbaron* / Schäfer	24 Apr
Nonne in *Palla de'Mozzi* / Grüber	25 Apr
Arsena in *Zigeunerbaron* / Schäfer	26 Apr
Nonne in *Palla de'Mozzi* / Grüber	29 Apr
1 Adelige Waise in *Rosenkavalier* / Rother	30 Apr
*Adele in *Fledermaus* / Schäfer	1 May
Marie in *Zar und Zimmermann* / Lutze	2 May
Esmeralda in *Verkaufte Braut* / Schäfer	3 May
Nonne in *Palla de'Mozzi* / Grüber	4 May
Giannetta in *Liebestrank* / Lutze	5 May
Bertha in *Euryanthe* / Rother	6 May
Arsena in *Zigeunerbaron* / Schäfer	8 May
Nonne in *Palla de'Mozzi* / Grüber	9 May
1 Edelknabe and Junger Hirt in *Tannhäuser* / Rother	10 May
Giannetta in *Liebestrank* / Lutze	11 May
Adele in *Fledermaus* / Schäfer	12 May
1 Adelige Waise in *Rosenkavalier* / Rother	13 May
Wellgunde in *Rheingold* / Rother	14 May
1 Knabe in *Zauberflöte* / Rother	15 May
Nonne in *Palla de'Mozzi* / Grüber	17 May
Bertha in *Euryanthe* / Rother	18 May
Giannetta in *Liebestrank* / Lutze	20 May
Barbarina in *Figaros Hochzeit* / Rother	24 May
Wellgunde in *Götterdämmerung* / Rother	25 May
*Isabella in *Boccaccio* (von Suppé) / Lutze (NP)	26 May
Arsena in *Zigeunerbaron* / Schäfer	27 May
Nonne in *Palla de'Mozzi* / Grüber	28 May
Isabella in *Boccaccio* / Lutze	29 May, 1 Jun
1 Edelknabe in *Lohengrin* / Grüber	2 Jun
Esmeralda in *Verkaufte Braut* / Lutze	13 Jun
Isabella in *Boccaccio* / Lutze	21 Jun
Giannetta in *Liebestrank* / Lutze	25, 28 Jun
Isabella in *Boccaccio* / Lutze	1 Jul
Giannetta in *Liebestrank* / Lutze	2 Jul
Isabella in *Boccaccio* / Lutze	3 Jul
(Start of 1940–41 season at Berlin Deutsche Oper)	
Junger Hirt in *Tannhäuser* / Rother	11 Sep
Barbarina in *Figaros Hochzeit* / Rother	12 Sep
1 Knabe in *Zauberflöte* / Rother	13 Sep
Arsena in *Zigeunerbaron* / Schäfer	15, 16, 17, 18 Sep
*Zerbinetta in *Ariadne auf Naxos* / Rother (NP)	28 Sep
Zerbinetta in *Ariadne auf Naxos* / Rother	30 Sep
Giannetta in *Liebestrank* / Lutze	1 Oct
Arsena in *Zigeunerbaron* / Schäfer	4 Oct
Zerbinetta in *Ariadne auf Naxos* / Rother	5 Oct
Wellgunde in *Rheingold* / Rother	7 Oct
Ortlinde in *Walküre* / Rother	9 Oct

1 Knabe in *Zauberflöte* / Rother		10 Oct
Arsena in *Zigeunerbaron* / Rother		13 Oct
Zerbinetta in *Ariadne auf Naxos* / Rother		15 Oct
Giannetta in *Liebestrank* / Lutze		21 Oct
Barbarina in *Figaros Hochzeit* / Rother		22 Oct
Zerbinetta in *Ariadne auf Naxos* / Rother		24 Oct
Barbarina in *Figaros Hochzeit* / Rother		29 Oct
Musette in *Boheme* / Grüber		30 Oct
Giannetta in *Liebestrank* / Lutze		31 Oct
Zerbinetta in *Ariadne auf Naxos* / Rother		10 Nov
Antonia in *Tiefland* / Lutze		11 Nov
Giannetta in *Liebestrank* / Lutze		13 Nov
1 Adelige Waise in *Rosenkavalier* / Rother		17 Nov
Zerbinetta in *Ariadne auf Naxos* / Rother		18 Nov
1 Knabe in *Zauberflöte* / Rother		19 Nov
Lola in *Cavalleria Rusticana* / Lutze		19, 27 Nov
Barbarina in *Figaros Hochzeit* / Rother		1 Dec
Lola in *Cavalleria Rusticana* / Lutze		6 Dec
Antonia in *Tiefland* / Grüber		8 Dec
Zerbinetta in *Ariadne auf Naxos* / Rother		9 Dec
Lola in *Cavalleria Rusticana* / Lutze		12 Dec
Taumännchen in *Hänsel und Gretel* / Grüber		15 Dec
*Undine in *Undine* (Lortzing) / Grüber		16 Dec
Taumännchen in *Hänsel und Gretel* / Grüber		17 Dec
Lola in *Cavalleria Rusticana* / Lutze		18 Dec
Taumännchen in *Hänsel und Gretel* / Grüber		19 Dec
*Ännchen in *Freischütz* / Rother (NP)		20 Dec
Taumännchen in *Hänsel und Gretel* / Grüber		22, 23, 28 Dec
Ännchen in *Freischütz* / Rother		29 Dec
1941	Undine in *Undine* / Grüber	7 Jan
	Ännchen in *Freischütz* / Rother	9 Jan
	Antonia in *Tiefland* / Grüber	11 Jan
	Ännchen in *Freischütz* / Rother	16 Jan
	Barbarina in *Figaros Hochzeit* / Rother	20 Jan
	Lola in *Cavalleria Rusticana* / Lutze	23 Jan
	Junger Hirt in *Tannhäuser* / Rother	26 Jan
	Musette in *Boheme* / Grüber	28 Jan
	Barbarina in *Figaros Hochzeit* / Rother	1 Feb
	Ännchen in *Freischütz* / Rother	4 Feb
	Gretchen in *Wildschütz* / Schäfer	5 Feb
	Lola in *Cavalleria Rusticana* / Lutze	10 Feb
	Musette in *Boheme* / Grüber	12 Feb
Frankfurt am Main	Troop Concert for Hinkel	18 Feb
Worms	Troop Concert for Hinkel	19 Feb
Berlin DO	Ortlinde in *Walküre* / Rother	20 Feb
	Pepa in *Tiefland* / Grüber	24 Feb
	Ännchen in *Freischütz* / Rother	26 Feb
	Pepa in *Tiefland* / Grüber	7 Mar
	Zerbinetta in *Ariadne* / Rother (NP)	14 Mar
	Undine in *Undine* / Busch	18 Mar
	Gretchen in *Wildschütz* / Schäfer	1, 4 Apr
	Pepa in *Tiefland* / Grüber	7 Apr
	Gretchen in *Wildschütz* / Schäfer	9 Apr
	1 Knappe and 2 Blumenmä. 1 Gp. in *Parsifal* / Rother	11, 12, 13, 14 Apr
	*Oskar in *Maskenball* (*Un Ballo in Maschera*)	nd Apr
Lublin	Troop Concert for Hinkel	19 Apr
Warsaw	Troop Concert for Hinkel	20 Apr
Berlin DO	Barbarina in *Figaros Hochzeit* / Grüber	28 Apr

		Arsena in *Zigeunerbaron* / Rother	1 May
		Junger Hirt in *Tannhäuser* / Rother	2 May
		1 Knabe in *Zauberflöte* / Rother	7 May
		Ännchen in *Freischütz* / Rother	11 May
		Lola in *Cavalleria Rusticana* / Lutze	18 May
		Giannetta in *Liebestrank* / Lutze	21 May
		Junger Hirt in *Tannhäuser* / Rother	22 May
		Wellgunde in *Rheingold* / Rother	24 May
		Wellgunde in *Götterdämmerung* / Rother	29 May
		1 Knabe in *Zauberflöte* / Rother	30 May
	MS	Joint Recital / Raucheisen	7 Jun
	DO	Lola in *Cavalleria Rusticana* / Lutze	10 Jun
		Barbarina in *Figaros Hochzeit* / Rother	13 Jun
		★Leonore in *Alessandro Stradella* (Flotow) / Lutze	15 Jun
		Arsena in *Zigeunerbaron* / Rother	16 Jun
		Wellgunde in *Rheingold* / Rother	18 Jun
		Arsena in *Zigeunerbaron* / Schäfer	22 Jun
		Wellgunde in *Götterdämmerung* / Rother	24 Jun
		Barbarina in *Figaros Hochzeit* / Rother	7 Jul
(Start of 1941–42 season at Berlin Deutsche Oper)			
		Musette in *Boheme* / Grüber	8 Sep
Paris	O	Adele in *Fledermaus* / Grüber	17 Sep
Berlin	DO	Gretchen in *Wildschütz* / Grüber	1 Oct
		Barbarina in *Figaros Hochzeit* / Rother	8 Oct
		Giannetta in *Liebestrank* / Lutze	9 Oct
		Junger Hirt in *Tannhäuser* / Rother	10 Oct
		Junger Hirt in *Tannhäuser* / Grüber	26 Oct
		Ida (as Maria Helfer) in *Fledermaus* / Grüber	27 Oct
		[State Celebration for 15th Anniversary of Gauletiers]	
		Ännchen in *Freischütz* / Rother	31 Oct
		★Waldvogels Stimme (Woodbird's Voice) in *Siegfried* / Rother	1 Nov
		Ännchen in *Freischütz* / Rother	4 Nov
		Lola in *Cavalleria Rusticana* / Lutze	8 Nov
		Waldvogels Stimme in *Siegfried* / Rother	9 Nov
		Giannetta in *Liebestrank* / Lutze	13 Nov
		Junger Hirt in *Tannhäuser* / Rother	16 Nov
		Serpetta in *Gärtnerin aus Liebe* / Lutze	17 Nov
		1 Knappe (as Helfer) and 2 Blumenmä., 1 Gp. (as ES) in *Parsifal* / Rother	19, 20, 21, 23 Nov
		1 Knappe (as Helfer) and 2 Blumenmä., 1 Gp. (as ES) in *Parsifal* / Grüber	22 Nov
		Musette in *Boheme* / Lutze	30 Nov
		Serpetta in *Gärtnerin aus Liebe* / Lutze	7 Dec
		Gretchen in *Wildschütz* / Grüber	14 Dec
		Taumännchen in *Hänsel und Gretel* / Grüber	15, 17 Dec
		Lola in *Cavalleria Rusticana* / Lutze	19 Dec
		Taumännchen in *Hänsel und Gretel* / Grüber	21 Dec
		Waldvogels Stimme in *Siegfried* / Rother	22 Dec
		Taumännchen in *Hänsel und Gretel* / Grüber	23 Dec
		Junger Hirt in *Tannhäuser* / Rother	25 Dec
		Serpetta in *Gärtnerin aus Liebe* / Lutze	27 Dec
		Taumännchen in *Hänsel und Gretel* / Grüber	28, 29 Dec

1942

Berlin	DO	Adele in *Fledermaus* / Grüber	1 Jan
		Marie in *Waffenschmied* / Lutze	3 Jan
		Taumännchen in *Hänsel und Gretel* / A. Busch	4 Jan
		Lola in *Cavalleria Rusticana* / Lutze	5 Jan

		Barbarina in *Figaros Hochzeit* / Rother	8 Jan
		Gretchen in *Wildschütz* / Grüber	10, 13, Jan
		Marie in *Waffenschmied* / Lutze	20, 22 Jan
		Wellgunde in *Götterdämmerung* / Rother	25 Jan
		Marie in *Waffenschmied* / Lutze	27 Jan
		Taumännchen in *Hänsel und Gretel* / Busch	1 Feb (2 perf.)
		Pepa in *Tiefland* / Lutze	2 Feb
		*Susanna in *Figaros Hochzeit* / Rother	7 Feb
		Marie in *Waffenschmeid* / Lutze	14 Feb
		Arsena in *Zigeunerbaron* / Rother	15 Feb (1030h)
		Pepa in *Tiefland* / Grüber	15 Feb (1830h)
		Susanna in *Figaros Hochzeit* / Rother	21 Feb
		Gretchen in *Wildschütz* / Grüber	22 Feb
		Susanna in *Figaros Hochzeit* / Lange	24 Feb
		Pepa in *Tiefland* / Grüber	28 Feb
		Morgenveranstaltung zugunsten des KWHW (Special Morning Performance to promote Winter Help) 'Voices of Spring' Waltz; Gilda in Quartet from *Rigoletto* / A. Busch	1 Mar
		Namenfeier (NS artistic-political 'ritual')	1 Mar
		Wellgunde in *Götterdämmerung* / Rother	8 Mar
		Marie in *Waffenschmeid* / Lutze	13 Mar
		Arsena in *Zigeunerbaron* / Rother	18 Mar
		Marie in *Waffenschmied* / Lutze	25 Mar
		Gretchen in *Wildschütz* / Grüber	27 Mar
		Marie in *Waffenschmied* / Lutze	2 Apr
		1 Knappe (as Helfer) and 2 Blumenmä., 1 Gp. in *Parsifal* (as ES) / Rother	3, 5 Apr
		1 Knappe (as Helfer) and 2 Blumenmä., 1 Gp. in *Parsifal* (as ES) / Grüber	4, 6 Apr
		Susanna in *Figaros Hochzeit* / Rother	9 Apr
		Waldvogel in *Siegfried* / Rother	16 Apr
		Marie in *Zar und Zimmermann* / Lutze	17 Apr
		Marie in *Waffenschmied* / Lutze	3 May
	BS	Liederabend 'Von Frühling und Nachtigallen' (On Spring and Nightingales) / Raucheisen	9 May
	DO	Marie in *Zar und Zimmermann* / Lutze	11 May
		Serpetta in *Gärtnerin aus Liebe* / Lutze	12 May
		Susanna in *Figaros Hochzeit* / Rother	14 May
		Arsena in *Zigeunerbaron* / Rother	18 May
		Serpetta in *Gärtnerin aus Liebe* / Lutze	20 May
		Musette in *Boheme* / Grüber	24 May
		Gretchen in *Wildschütz* / Grüber	26 May
	BS	Lieder Recital with Piltti / Raucheisen	27 Jun
Vienna	O	Zerbinetta aG in *Ariadne auf Naxos* / Moralt	7 Oct
Berlin	DO	Leonore in *Alessandro Stradella* / Lutze	28 Oct
	BS	Lieder Recital / Raucheisen	11 Nov
Vienna	O	*Blondchen aG in *Entführung* / Böhm	16 Nov
Ostfront		Berlin Artists' Tour: Concert for Waffen SS	7 Dec
Prague		Berlin Artists' Tour	15, 16 Dec
Ostfront		Berlin Artists' Tour: Concert for Waffen SS	21 Dec
Berlin	DO	Adele in *Fledermaus* / Grüber	31 Dec

1943

Berlin	BS	Loewe Recital / Raucheisen	9 Mar
		Stunde der Musik (Pfitzner songs) / A. Morgenroth	17 Apr
		St Matthew Passion / Schneider	23 Apr

1944

Vienna	Oper	Blondchen in *Entführung* / Moralt	15 Apr
		Musette in *Boheme* / Moralt	21 Apr
		*Rosina in *Barbier* (Rossini's *Il Barbiere di Siviglia*) / Moralt	2, 13 May
		Ännchen in *Freischütz* / Perlea	21 May
		Musette in *Boheme* / Reichwein	28 May
		Ännchen in *Freischütz* / Reichwein	2 Jun
		Blondchen in *Entführung* / Moralt	10 Jun
		Blondchen in *Entführung* / Reichwein	21 Jun
	MVS	Lieder Recital / Graef	12 Dec

1945

Graz	Oper	*Konstanze aG in *Entführung* / Moralt	21 Sep, 7 Oct
Salzkammergut		'Modest Troop Concerts' with Lorenz and Böhm	nd
	VO	*Nedda in *Bajazzo* (*I Pagliacci*) / Loibner	12, 14, Dec

1946

Vienna	TadW	*Mimi in *Boheme* / H. Schmidt aG	23 Jan
	VO	Nedda in *Bajazzo* / Loibner	29 Jan
	TadW	Mimi in *Boheme* / Paulik	11, 14 Feb
		Mimi in *Boheme* / Moralt	28 Feb
		Rosina in *Barbier* / Moralt (NP)	3, 7 Mar
		Mimi in *Boheme* / Paulik	6, 15, 20 Mar

(Start of 1946–47 season at Theater an der Wien)

	TadW	Konstanze in *Entführung* / Moralt	20, 22 Oct
		Rosina in *Barbier* / Krips	29 Oct
		Konstanze in *Entführung* / Etti	3 Nov
		*Gilda in *Rigoletto* / Etti	5 Nov
		Rosina in *Barbier* / Krips	6 Nov
		Gilda in *Rigoletto* / Etti	14 Nov
		Konstanze in *Entführung* / Sedlak	18 Nov
		Rosina in *Barbier* / Etti	21 Nov
		Konstanze in *Entführung* / Prohaska	22 Nov
		Gilda in *Rigoletto* / Sedlak	27 Nov
		Konstanze in *Entführung* / Etti	1, 5 Dec
		Gilda in *Rigoletto* / Sedlak	12 Dec
		Konstanze in *Entführung* / Etti	13 Dec
		Gilda in *Rigoletto* / Etti	27 Dec
		Rosina in *Barbier* / Moralt	31 Dec

1947

	TadW	Konstanze in *Entführung* / Etti	4, 6 Jan
		Gilda in *Rigoletto* / Etti	10 Jan
		*Donna Elvira in *Don Giovanni* / Prohaska	19 Jan
		Elvira in *Don Giovanni* / Prohaska	22 Jan
		Susanna in *Figaros Hochzeit* / Moralt	27 Jan
		Gilda in *Rigoletto* / Etti	4 Feb
		Elvira in *Don Giovanni* / Jahoda	7 Feb
		Elvira in *Don Giovanni* / Moralt	13 Feb
		*Violetta in *Traviata* / Krips	27 Feb
		Gilda in *Rigoletto* / Etti	6 Mar
		Violetta in *Traviata* / Etti	12, 16, 18, 21, 24, 31 Mar, 2, 8 Apr
		Elvira in *Don Giovanni* / Klemperer	10, 12 Apr
		Elvira in *Don Giovanni* / Prohaska	21 Apr
		Rosina in *Barbier* / Krips	8 May
		Zerbinetta in *Ariadne auf Naxos* / Krips (NP)	13 May

		Rosina in *Barbier* / Etti	18, 29 May
		Konstanze in *Entführung* / Moralt	25 May
		Violetta in *Traviata* / Etti	24 Jun
		Elvira in *Don Giovanni* / Moralt	25 Jun
Salzburg Fest.	FSH	Susanna in *Nozze di Figaro* / Krips	28 Jul
Lucerne Fest.		★Brahms: *Deutsches Requiem* / Furtwängler	20 Aug
		Mozart: *Exsultate, jubilate* / Sacher	24 Aug
Vienna	TadW	Rosina in *Barbier* / Loibner	2 Sep
		Gilda in *Rigoletto* / Loibner	5 Sep
		Konstanze in *Entführung* / Loibner	9 Sep
London		(Visit of Vienna State Opera)	
	CG	Elvira in *Don Giovanni* / Krips	16, 20, 27, 29 Sep
		Marzelline in *Fidelio* / Krauss	17, 19 Sep
	CG	Concert with H. Konetzni, Tauber / Krips, Krauss	21 Sep
		Marzelline in *Fidelio* / Krauss	24 Sep
		Elvira in *Don Giovanni*, Tauber / Krips	3 Oct
Vienna	TadW	Mimi in *Boheme* / Moralt	11, 13 Oct
		Violetta in *Traviata* / Loibner	15, 28 Oct
		Rosina in *Barbier* / Moralt	17 Oct
		Elvira in *Don Giovanni* / Prohaska	1 Nov
	VO	★Agathe in *Freischütz* / Knappertsbusch	14 Nov
	TadW	Konstanze in *Entführung* / Moralt	24 Nov
		Violetta in *Traviata* / Loibner	10 Dec
		Mimi in *Boheme* / Sedlak	12 Dec
	VO	Agathe in *Freischütz* / Prohaska	18 Dec
	TadW	Konstanze in *Entführung* / Moralt	21 Dec
		Konstanze in *Entführung* / Loibner	23 Dec
		Elvira in *Don Giovanni* / Krips	25 Dec
		Mimi in *Boheme* / Moralt	28 Dec

1948

Vienna	TadW	Elvira in *Don Giovanni* / Krips	1 Jan
		Marzelline in *Fidelio* / Krauss	4 Jan
		Konstanze in *Entführung* / Loibner	9 Jan
		★Pamina in *Zauberflöte* / Krips	16 Jan
London	CG	Pamina in *Magic Flute* / Rankl	3, 13 Feb
		★Sophie in *Rosenkavalier* / Rankl	17 Feb
	RAH	Richard Tauber Memorial Concert	20 Feb
	CG	Pamina in *Magic Flute* / Gellhorn	1, 5, 22 Mar
		Violetta in *Traviata* / Goodall	6, 9, 15, 20, 24, 28 Apr, 4 May
		Pamina in *Magic Flute* / Rankl	7 May
Stockholm	KH	Concert	nd
London	CG	Sophie in *Rosenkavalier* / Gellhorn	19 May
		Violetta in *Traviata* / Goodall	24 May
		Pamina in *Magic Flute* / Gellhorn	27 May
		Violetta in *Traviata* / Goodall	1 Jun
Vienna	TadW	Gilda in *Rigoletto* / Loibner	13 Jun
		Elvira in *Don Giovanni* / Prohaska	15 Jun
		Violetta in *Traviata* / Fricsay	16 Jun
		Pamina in *Zauberflöte* / Prohaska	17 Jun
		Susanna in *Figaros Hochzeit* / Böhm	19 Jun
		Konstanze in *Entführung* / Prohaska	21 Jun
London	CG	Bach–Mozart Charity Concert / R. Austin	11 Jul
Salzburg Fest.	FSH	★Selige Geist (Blessèd Spirit) in *Orpheus und Eurydike* / Karajan	28 Jul, 2, 7, 10, 13, 16 Aug
		★Contessa (Countess) in *Nozze di Figaro* / Karajan	11, 14, 17, 21, 27 Aug
Lucerne Fest.		★Beethoven: Ninth Symphony / Furtwängler	28, 29 Aug

Vienna	TadW	Pamina in *Zauberflöte* / Prohaska	1 Sep
		Marzelline in *Fidelio* / Böhm	8 Sep
		Violetta in *Traviata* / Ferencsik	14 Sep
		Sophie in *Rosenkavalier* / Moralt	16 Sep
Perugia: Sagra Musicale		*Mozart: Requiem	26 Sep
London	CG	Pamina in *Magic Flute* / Gellhorn	30 Sep
		Sophie in *Rosenkavalier* / Rankl	1 Oct
		Violetta in *Traviata* / Goodall	12, 20, 26 Oct
		Mimi in *Bohème* / Rankl	15, 18, 30 Oct
Vienna	TadW	Elvira in *Don Giovanni* / Prohaska	4 Nov
		Violetta in *Traviata* / Ferencsik	7 Nov
London	CG	Violetta in *Traviata* / Goodall	12, 19 Nov
		*Eva in *Mastersingers* / Rankl	23 Nov
		Mimi in *Bohème* / Gellhorn	3, 10 Dec
		Violetta in *Traviata* / Goodall	7 Dec
		Marcelline in *Fidelio* / Rankl	9, 17 Dec
		Mimi in *Bohème* / Braithwaite	20 Dec
Milan	S	(Visit of Vienna State Opera) Contessa in *Nozze di Figaro* / Karajan	28, 30 Dec

1949

London	CG	Mimi in *Bohème* / Gellhorn	1 Jan
		Marcelline in *Fidelio* / Rankl	7 Jan
		Violetta in *Traviata* / Goodall	11 Jan
		Pamina in *Magic Flute* / Gellhorn	13 Jan
		Susanna in *Marriage of Figaro* / Rankl NP	22 Jan
		Mimi in *Bohème* / Braithwaite	23 Jan
		Susanna in *Marriage of Figaro* / Rankl	26, 28 Jan
Vienna	Sing.	Beethoven: Ninth Symphony / Karajan	19, 20, 21 Feb
	TadW	Gilda in *Rigoletto* / Loibner	21 Feb
		Violetta in *Traviata* / Moralt	24, 28 Feb
		Gilda in *Rigoletto* / Loibner	2 Mar
		*Liù in *Turandot* / Böhm	6, 16 Mar
		Pamina in *Zauberflöte* / Moralt	17 Mar
London	RAH	Brahms: *Deutsches Requiem* / R. Austin	25 Mar
Paris	TC-E	Susanna in *Nozze di Figaro* / Böhm	23, 26, 28, 29 Mar
Vienna	TadW	Violetta in *Traviata* / Moralt	3 Apr
		Gilda in *Rigoletto* / Loibner	4 Apr
Birmingham	TR	(CG) Opera on Tour) Susanna in *Marriage of Figaro* / Gellhorn	19 Apr
		Eva in *Mastersingers* / Goodall	21 Apr
		Mimi in *Bohème* / Gellhorn	23 Apr
London	CG	Susanna in *Marriage of Figaro* / Gellhorn	26 Apr
		Violetta in *Traviata* / Goodall	28 Apr
		Marcelline in *Fidelio* / Gellhorn	29 Apr
		Gilda in *Rigoletto* / Gellhorn	4 May
		Mimi in *Bohème* / Braithwaite	7 May
		Violetta in *Traviata* / Goodall	10 May
		Mimi in *Bohème* / Gellhorn	18 May
		Susanna in *Marriage of Figaro* / Gellhorn	20 May
		Mimi in *Bohème* / Gellhorn	23 May
		Violetta in *Traviata* / Goodall	26 May
		Marcelline in *Fidelio* / Gellhorn	27 May
Brussels	TRM	(Visit of Vienna State Opera) Sophie in *Rosenkavalier* / Böhm	20, 24 Jun
Amsterdam	S	(Visit of Vienna State Opera) Sophie in *Rosenkavalier* / Böhm	2 Jul
Sydney	TH	(Tour for Australian Broadcasting) Handel and Bach / Klemperer	11, 12, 13 Sep

Melbourne	TH	(Tour for Australian Broadcasting) Mozart and Mahler: Fourth Symphony / Klemperer	17, 19, 20 Sep
London	CG	Susanna in *Marriage of Figaro* / Rankl	13, 14, 21 Oct
		Sophie in *Rosenkavalier* / Rankl	15 Nov
		Mimi in *Bohème* / Braithwaite	17 Nov
		Susanna in *Marriage of Figaro* / Rankl	21 Nov
		Pamina in *Magic Flute* / Rankl	24 Nov
	RAH	Beethoven: Ninth Symphony / Karajan	25 Nov
	CG	Sophie in *Rosenkavalier* / Rankl	10 Dec
		Mimi in *Bohème* / Braithwaite	14 Dec
	WH	Wolf *Liederabend* / Moore	18 Dec

1950

London	CG	Marcelline in *Fidelio* / Gellhorn	3 Jan
		Pamina in *Magic Flute* / Rankl	5 Jan
		Violetta in *Traviata* / Goodall	19 Jan
		Madam Butterfly / Braithwaite	25, 28, 30 Jan
		Mimi in *Bohème* / Braithwaite	1 Feb
		Pamina in *Magic Flute* / Rankl	10 Feb
		Susanna in *Marriage of Figaro* / Gellhorn	14 Feb
		Madam Butterfly / Braithwaite	16 Feb
		Violetta in *Traviata* / Goodall	19 Feb
	RAH	Mozart: *Exsultate, jubilate* / Kubelik	20 Feb
	CG	*Madam Butterfly* / Braithwaite	22 Feb
		Violetta in *Traviata* / Goodall	24 Feb
		Madam Butterfly / Braithwaite	27 Feb
Florence	TComm	Concert / Kletzki	5 Mar
Vienna	BS	Hugo Wolf Recital / Nordberg	13 Apr
Edinburgh	K	(CG on tour) Pamina in *Magic Flute* / Rankl	18 Apr
		Violetta in *Traviata* / Goodall	20 Apr
		Susanna in *Marriage of Figaro* / Rankl	24 Apr
London	CG	Pamina in *Magic Flute* / Gellhorn	2 May
		Sophie in *Rosenkavalier* / Rankl	9 May
		Mimi in *Bohème* / Gellhorn	11 May
		*Manon in *Manon* / Braithwaite	18 May
	RFH	Lieder Recital / Moore	20 May
	CG	Pamina in *Magic Flute* / Gellhorn	22 May
		Manon in *Manon* / Braithwaite	24, 27, 31 May
	WH	'20C. Concert' with Medtner Songs	25 May
Florence	P	Lieder / Favaretto	3 Jun
Vienna	BS	*Bach: Cantata 51 / Hindemith	12 Jun
		*Bach: B minor Mass / Karajan	15 Jun
Milan	S	*Beethoven: *Missa Solemnis* / Karajan	29, 30 Jun
	S	Bach: B minor Mass / Karajan	2, 3, 7 Jul
Salzburg Fest.	FSH	Elvira in *Don Giovanni* / Furtwängler	27, 31 Jul, 4 Aug
		Marzelline in *Fidelio* / Furtwängler	5 Aug
		Marzelline in *Fidelio* / Furtwängler	11 Aug
	St P	*Mozart: C Mass / Paumgartner	12 Aug
	FSH	Marzelline in *Fidelio* / Furtwängler	14, 17 Aug
		Elvira in *Don Giovanni* / Furtwängler	18 Aug
		Marzelline in *Fidelio* / Furtwängler	22 Aug
Lucerne Fest.	KH	*Marguerite in *Damnation of Faust* / Furtwängler (concert)	26, 27 Aug
Edinburgh	FMH	Wolf Recital / Moore	5 Sep
London	RAH	Schubert: *Shepherd on the Rock* / Cameron (Prom)	12 Sep
Perugia	TM	Bach: B minor Mass / Karajan	24 Sep
London	CG	Violetta in *Traviata* / Gellhorn	20 Oct
		Mimi in *Bohème* / Gellhorn	26 Oct
		Manon in *Manon* / Braithwaite	28 Oct

		Pamina in *Magic Flute* / Rankl	1 Nov
		Sophie in *Rosenkavalier* / Rankl	4 Nov
	KH	Medtner Chamber Concert	6 Nov
	CG	Violetta in *Traviata* / Gellhorn	7 Nov
		Pamina in *Magic Flute* / Rankl	9 Nov
		Susanna in *Marriage of Figaro* / Rankl	11 Nov
		Mimi in *Bohème* / Gellhorn	13 Nov
		Manon in *Manon* / Braithwaite	15 Nov
	KH	Concert: Bach / Fischer	20 Nov
	CG	Marcelline in *Fidelio* / Rankl	21 Nov
		Sophie in *Rosenkavalier* / Rankl	23 Nov
		Pamina in *Magic Flute* / Gellhorn	25 Nov
		Susanna in *Marriage of Figaro* / Rankl	27 Nov
		Mimi in *Bohème* / Gellhorn	29 Nov
Turin	C	Lieder Recital / Favaretto	6 Dec
Milan	S	★Elisabeth in *Tannhäuser* / Karajan	27, 30 Dec

1951

Milan	S	Elisabeth in *Tannhäuser* / Karajan	6, 9, 14 Jan
London	CG	Violetta in *Traviata* / Gellhorn	10 Jan
Milan	S	Elvira in *Don Giovanni* / Karajan	15, 18, 21, 23, 28 Jan
London	CG	Violetta in *Traviata* / Gellhorn	29 Jan
Naples	TSC	Contessa in *Nozze di Figaro* / Böhm	3 Feb
London	CG	Pamina in *Magic Flute* / Rankl	7, 19 Feb
		Sophie in *Rosenkavalier* / Rankl	9, 22 Feb
	KH	*Liederabend* / Moore	12 Feb
		Brahms Folk Songs Recital / Matthews	26 Feb
	CG	Recital: Lieder and Opera arias / Moore	27 Mar
		Violetta in *Traviata* / Gellhorn	4 Apr
	RAH	Concert / Kletzki	9 Apr
	CG	Violetta in *La Traviata* / Gellhorn	19 Apr
	RFH	Beethoven: Ninth Symphony / Sargent	4, 8 May
Vienna		★*Four Last Songs* in Concert / Kletzki	9 May
London	CG	Mimi in *Bohème* / Gellhorn	15 May
		Marcelline in *Fidelio* / Rankl	16, 21 May
	RFH	★Verdi: Requiem / Barbirolli and Hallé	26 May
Bayreuth	FSH	Beethoven: Ninth Symphony / Furtwängler	29 Jul
		1st *Ring* Cycle / Knappertsbusch: Woglinde in *Rheingold*	31 Jul
	MOH	Lieder Recital / Max Kojetinsky	3 Aug
	FSH	Woglinde in *Götterdämmerung* / Knappertsbusch	4 Aug
		Eva in *Meistersinger* / Karajan	5, 8 Aug
		2nd *Ring* Cycle / Karajan: Woglinde in *Rheingold*	11 Aug
		Woglinde in *Götterdämmerung*	15 Aug
		Eva in *Meistersinger* / Karajan	16, 19, 21, 24, 26 Aug
Lucerne Fest.		Bach: B minor Mass / Karajan	1, 2 Sep
Milan	S	Verdi: Requiem / De Sabata	8 Sep
Venice	F	★★Anne Trulove in *The Rake's Progress* / Stravinsky	11 Sep
		Anne Trulove in *The Rake's Progress* / Leitner	13, 14 Sep
Copenhagen	TR	Countess in *Figaro* / Frandsen	22 Sep
Stockholm	KT	Countess in *Figaro* / Dobrowen	25 Sep
Copenhagen	OFPSS	*Sang Aften* / Kjell Olsson	28 Sep
Munich		Bach: Cantata 51, *Jauchzet Gott* Concert / Jochum	5 Oct
Milan	S	Anne Trulove in *Carriera d'un Libertino* (*Rake's Progress*) / Leitner	8, 10 Dec
Hague	D	Lieder Recital / J. Antonietti	11 Dec
Milan	S	Anne Trulove in *Libertino* / Leitner	22, 30 Dec

1952

Milan	S	*Marschallin in *Rosenkavalier* / Karajan	26, 31 Jan, 3, 6, 13 Feb
Rome	RAI	Schubert Recital / Favaretto	16 Feb
Milan	S	Marschallin in *Rosenkavalier* / Karajan	17 Feb
Monte Carlo	sG	Mimi in *Bohème* / Quadri	23, 24 Feb
Rome	TA	Lieder Recital / Favaretto	29 Feb
Florence	TComm	Beethoven: Ninth Symphony / Knappertsbusch	2 Mar
Milan	M	Lieder Recital / Favaretto	3 Mar
Geneva	VH	Bach: Cantata 51, *Jauchzet Gott*, and Stravinsky: Scene and Arias from *Rake* / Ansermet	5 Mar
London	RFH	Stravinsky: Scene and Arias from *Rake*, and Mozart / Blech	21 Mar
Stockholm	KT	Mimi in *Bohème* / Grevilius	15, 17 Apr
Copenhagen	OFPSS	Lieder Recital / Olsson	22, 24 Apr
London	KH	Lieder Recital / Moore	8 May
Turin	C/RAI	*Mozart: *Betulia Liberata* / Rossi	30 May
Amsterdam	C	Mahler: Fourth Symphony / B. Walter	5 Jun
Hague	R	Concert / Markevitch	11 Jun
London	CG	Mimi in *Bohème* / Capuana	20, 23, 25 Jun
	RFH	*Mozart: *Schuldigkeit des ersten Gebotes* (Obligation of the First Commandment) / Blech	3 Jul
Salzburg Fest.	FSH	Contessa in *Nozze di Figaro* / Moralt	26 Jul, 2, 8, 23, 29 Aug
		Verdi: Requiem / De Sabata	20, 21 Aug
Lucerne Fest.		*Messiah* / Denzler	30, 31 Aug
London		(Big studio recording programme)	Sep–Nov
Turin	RAI	Mozart Arias Concert / Rossi	1 Dec
Hamburg	NWDR	Operatic Arias / Schüchter	4 Dec
		Concert NDR Orch. / Schüchter	6 Dec
Turin	RAI	Beethoven: Ninth Symphony / Furtwängler	19 Dec

1953

Milan	S	*Elsa in *Lohengrin* / Karajan	10, 13, 17, 20, 25 Jan
		Elvira in *Don Giovanni* / Karajan	28, 31 Jan
		Elsa in *Lohengrin* / Karajan	1 Feb
		Elvira in *Don Giovanni* / Karajan	5, 8, 11 Feb
		Trionfi (Orff) (including **Afrodite in *Trionfo di Afrodite*) / Karajan	14, 16, 18 Feb
Turin	C	Lieder Recital / Favaretto	17 Feb
	C	*A Child of Our Time* / Karajan	22 Feb
Milan	M	Lieder Recital / Favaretto	23 Feb
	S	*Trionfi* / Karajan	24 Feb
Rome	TA	Lieder Recital / Favaretto	27 Feb
Milan	S	*Mélisande in *Pelléas et Mélisande* / De Sabata	1, 7, 19 May
Basel	MS	*Der Tod zu Basel* – 'A Grand Miserere' (Conrad Beck) / Sacher	22 May
Milan	S	Mélisande in *Pelléas et Mélisande* / De Sabata	29, 31 May
Vienna	Sing.	Marzelline in *Fidelio* / Karajan	5, 6, 7 Jun
Sparsborg		Lieder Recital	13 Jun
Copenhagen	T	Concert	16, 18 Jun
Göteborg	KH	Concert	17 Jun
London	CG	Eva in *Meistersinger* / Krauss	3, 6, 8, 10 Jul
Holland Fest.		Lieder Recital	14 Jul
Salzburg Fest.	FSH	Elvira in *Don Giovanni* / Furtwängler	27 Jul, 3, 8 Aug
		Gräfin in *Figaros Hochzeit* / Furtwängler	7, 11 Aug
	M	Hugo Wolf *Gedächtnisfeier* / Furtwängler	12 Aug

	FSH	Gräfin in *Figaros Hochzeit* / Furtwängler	14 Aug
		Elvira in *Don Giovanni* / Furtwängler	18 Aug
Munich	O	(Visit of La Scala Company) Elvira in *Don Giovanni* / Karajan	19 Aug
Salzburg	FSH	Elvira in *Don Giovanni* / Furtwängler	28 Aug
		Gräfin in *Figaros Hochzeit* / Furtwängler	29 Aug
Lucerne		Verdi: Requiem / Votto	30 Aug
London	RAH	Promenade Concert / Boult	9 Sep
Tangier and Tunis		Lieder Recitals / Karajan	nd Sep
Leeds	TH	Delius: *A Mass of Life* / Sargent	8 Oct
New York	TH	Lieder Recital / Sándor (US début)	25 Oct
Basel		*Leonore in *Fidelio* / Karajan (concert)	28 Oct
Geneva	VH	Leonore in *Fidelio* / Karajan (concert)	29 Oct
Zürich		Leonore in *Fidelio* / Karajan (concert)	30 Oct
Copenhagen	OFPSS	Lieder Recitals	18, 25 Nov
Rome	O	Elvira in *Don Giovanni* / Karajan	12, 15 Dec
Milan	RAI	Pamina in *Il Flauto Magico* / Karajan	19 Dec
Rome	O	Elvira in *Don Giovanni* / Karajan	20 Dec
	RAI	Bach, Sutermeister Concert / Karajan	21 Dec
	O	Elvira in *Don Giovanni* / Karajan	22 Dec

1954

Basel		Lieder Recital / M. Lipatti	15 Jan
Milan	S	Contessa in *Nozze di Figaro* / Karajan	4, 6, 9 Feb
		*Marguerite in *Faust* / Rodzinski	13 Feb
		Contessa in *Nozze di Figaro* / Karajan	14 Feb
		Marguerite in *Faust* / Rodzinski	16, 18 Feb
		Contessa in *Nozze di Figaro* / Karajan	20 Feb
		Marguerite in *Faust* / Rodzinski	24 Feb
Rome	RAI	Lieder Recital / Edwin Fischer	21 Feb
	TA	Lieder Recital / Favaretto	26 Feb
Palermo	TM	Lieder Recital / Favaretto	3 Mar
London	RFH	Schumann Lieder Recital with Fischer-Dieskau / Moore	7 Mar
Monte Carlo	sG	Lieder Recital / Gastaldi	25 Mar
		Marschallin in *Rosenkavalier* / Moralt	28, 30 Mar
London	RFH	Lieder Recital / Fischer	30 Apr
	BBCMV1	*Dvořák: Te Deum / Sargent; *The Spectre's Bride* (aria)	26 Mar
Bergen	KP	Lieder Recital / Levin	5 Jun
Copenhagen	OFP	Lieder Recital / Olsson	8 Jun
Aix-en-Provence	TA	Lieder Recital / Rosbaud	23 Jul
Salzburg Fest.	FSH	Elvira in *Don Giovanni* / Furtwängler	3, 6, 10, 13 Aug
	M	Hugo Wolf *Liederabend* / Moore	14 Aug
	FSH	Elvira: *Don Giovanni* / Furtwängler	18 Aug
Lucerne Fest.	KH	Beethoven: Ninth Symphony / Furtwängler	21, 22 Aug
Edinburgh Fest.	FMH	Lieder Recital / Moore	31 Aug
		Wolf *Liederabend* with Hans Hotter / Moore	2 Sep
	UH	Verdi: Requiem / Barbirolli	4 Sep
Pittsburg	ML	Lieder Recital / Sandor	16 Oct
Boston	JH	Lieder Recital / Sandor	24 Oct
Chicago	OH	4 LL in Strauss Concert / Reiner	28 Oct
New York	HC	Lieder Recital / Sandor	6 Nov
Toronto	EA	Lieder Recital / Sandor	7 Nov
Seattle	PT	Lieder Recital / Sandor	8 Nov
Rome	RAI	Mélisande in *Pelléas* / Karajan	19 Dec
Milan	RAI	*Gretel in *Hansel e Gretel* (concert perf.) / Karajan	25 Dec

1955

| Paris | | Concert / Sébastian | 18 Jan |
| Bordeaux | | Lieder Recital / M. Lipatti | 20 Jan |

Albi		Lieder Recital / M. Lipatti	23 Jan
Avignon		Lieder Recital / M. Lipatti	25 Jan
Marseilles		Concert / Audoli	26 Jan
Lyons		Lieder Recital / M. Lipatti	30 Jan
Bologna Comm.		Lieder Recital / Favaretto	27 Feb
Monte Carlo	sG	Lieder Recital / Ackermann	5 Mar
		Contessa in *Nozze di Figaro* / Ackermann	6, 8 Mar
London	RFH	Lieder Recital / Moore	13 Mar
Paris		Concert / Sébastian	3 Apr
London	RFH	Vocal Duets with Seefried / Moore	15 May
Oslo		Concert / Jordal	2 Jun
Bergen	KP	Lieder Recital / Levin	4 Jun
Oslo		Lieder Recital	6 Jun
Copenhagen	OFPSS	Lieder Recital / Olsson	8 Jun
Stockholm		Lieder Recital	10 Jun
Helsinki	C	Sibelius Chamber Concert and Recital / C. Szalkiewicz	11 Jun
	Univ	Sibelius Concert / T. Hannikainen	14 Jun
Grenade		Concert / Caracciolo	24, 27, 29 Jun
Aix-en-Provence	TA	Lieder Recital / Rosbaud	21 Jul
Stratford, Ontario		Lieder Recital / Ulanowsky	2 Aug
Toronto	EA	Concert: Hart House Orch. / P. Scherman	3 Aug
		Lieder Recital / Ulanowsky	5 Aug
Menton		Recital	13 Aug
		Concert / Ristenpart	14 Aug
Lucerne		Lieder / Fischer	16 Aug
London	RAH	Mozart–Strauss Prom / Sargent	5 Sep
Besançon Fest.		*Liederabend* / Bonneau	9 Sep
		Concert / Schuricht	11 Sep
San Francisco	WMOH	Marschallin in *Rosenkavalier* / Leinsdorf (US stage début)	20, 24 Sep
		Elvira in *Don Giovanni* / Leinsdorf	30 Sep, 6 Oct
New York	CH	Lieder Recital / Ulanowsky	22 Oct
Los Angeles	PA	Marschallin in *Rosenkavalier* / Leinsdorf	28 Oct
	PA	Elvira in *Don Giovanni* / Leinsdorf	5 Nov
New York	HC	*Liederabend* / Ulanowsky	26 Nov
Milan	S	Pamina in *Zauberflöte* / Karajan	10, 13, 18, 20, 22 Dec

1956

Milan	PS	*Fiordiligi in *Così fan tutte* / Cantelli	27, 29, 31 Jan, 3 Feb
	S	Elvira in *Don Giovanni* / Ackermann	8 Feb
	PS	Fiordiligi in *Così* / Cantelli	9 Feb
	S	Elvira in *Don Giovanni* / Ackermann	11, 13, 15 Feb
	PS	Fiordiligi in *Così* / Cantelli	19, 22, 26 Feb
		Concert / Tonini, Favaretto	27 Feb
		Lieder Recital / Favaretto	29 Feb
London	RFH	Lieder Recital / Moore	4 Mar
Monte Carlo	sG	Lieder Recital / Ackermann	22 Mar
		Elvira in *Don Giovanni* / Ackermann	25, 27 Mar
Paris		Concert / Kletzki	30 Mar
		Lieder Recital / Bonneau	17 Apr
Basel	MS	*Der Tod zu Basel* – 'A Grand Miserere' / Sacher	25 May
Zürich	GTS	*Der Tod zu Basel* – 'A Grand Miserere' / Sacher	27 May
London	RFH	Bach Concert / Dart	4 Jun
Paris		Lieder Recital / Bonneau	6 Jun
London	RFH	Concert: Philharmonia 4 LL / Karajan	20 Jun
	RFH	Verdi Requiem / Cantelli	1, 6, Jul
Salzburg Fest.	FSH	Contessa in *Nozze di Figaro* / Böhm	21, 28 Jul, 3 Aug
	M	*Liederabend* / Moore	7 Aug

	FSH	Contessa in *Nozze di Figaro* / Böhm	10, 21 Aug
Lucerne Fest.		Wolf: *Italienisches Liederbuch* with Fischer-Dieskau / Moore	28 Aug
Salzburg Fest.	FSH	Contessa in *Nozze di Figaro* / Böhm	30 Aug
San Francisco	WMOH	*Alice Ford in *Falstaff* / Steinberg	21, 27 Sep
		Fiordiligi in *Così* / Schweiger	2, 6, 14 Oct
Los Angeles		Alice Ford in *Falstaff* / Steinberg	23 Oct
San Diego		Fiordiligi in *Così* / Schweiger	25 Oct
Los Angeles	PA	Fiordiligi in *Così* / Schweiger	2, 6 Nov
Beverly Hills	HS	Lieder Recital / Novaes	10 Nov
New York	CH	Lieder Recital / Reeves	25 Nov
Cleveland		Lieder Recital / Reeves	1 Dec
Berlin	HfM	Concert (Ariadne's Monologue) / Karajan	8, 9, 10 Dec

1957

Paris		Concert / Dervaux	27 Jan
		Lieder Recital / Bonneau	4 Feb
Amsterdam	C	Bach, Mozart Concert / Klemperer	6, 7 Feb
		Bach Wedding Cantata / Klemperer	16 Feb
London	RFH	Wolf Recital / Sawallisch	24 Feb
Milan	S	Alice Ford in *Falstaff* / Karajan	11, 14, 16, 19 Mar
Sienna		Lieder Recital / Favaretto	28 Mar
Turin	C	Lieder Recital / Favaretto	1 Apr
Milan	PS	Lieder Recital / Favaretto	4 Apr
Brescia	TG	Lieder Recital / Favaretto	5 Apr
Paris	TC-E	Lieder Recital / Bonneau	nd Apr
Bordeaux		Concert	23 Apr
Copenhagen	TKSS	Lieder Recital / Olsson	24 Apr
		Concert	3 May
Aalborg	AH	Lieder Recital / Olsson	6 May
Amsterdam	C	Beethoven: *Missa Solemnis* / Klemperer	17, 19, 21 May
Bordeaux		Concert / Szell	23 May
London	RFH	Bach Concert / Dart	4 Jun
		Marguerite in *Damnation de Faust* / Freccia	25 Jun
Salzburg Fest.	FSH	Contessa in *Nozze di Figaro* / Böhm	30 Jul, 3, 8, 13, 24 Aug
		Alice Ford in *Falstaff* / Karajan	10, 14, 21, 27 Aug
	M	*Liederabend* Hugo Wolf / Moore	19 Aug
Vienna	Oper	Alice Ford in *Falstaff* / Karajan	15, 17, 20, 23 Sep
San Francisco	WMOH	Marschallin in *Rosenkavalier* / Leinsdorf	1, 3, 13 Oct
		Fiordiligi in *Così* / Leinsdorf	22, 24 Oct
Los Angeles	PA	Marschallin in *Rosenkavalier* / Leinsdorf	27 Oct
		Fiordiligi in *Così* / Leinsdorf	6 Nov
San Francisco		Lieder Recital / Reeves	10 Nov
Cleveland		Lieder Recital / Reeves	16 Nov
New York	TH	Recital	18 Nov
	BAM	Lieder Recital / Reeves	29 Nov
	CH	Strauss Concert, 4 LL / Previtali	5, 6, Dec
Montreal		Recital	8 Dec

1958

Berlin	HfM	Lieder Recital / Raucheisen	6 Jan
London	RFH	Opera Arias / Mackerras	16 Jan
Vienna	R	Contessa in *Nozze di Figaro* / Karajan	25, 27 Jan
		Elvira in *Don Giovanni* / Moralt	28 Jan
Aachen		Lieder Recital / Sawallisch	31 Jan
Paris		Lieder Recital / Bonneau	4, 18 Feb
London	RFH	Concert / Sawallisch	27 Feb
Berlin		*Liederabend* / Raucheisen	1 Mar

Basel		Lieder Recital / Raucheisen	4 Mar
Paris		Concert / Fournet	9 Mar
London	RFH	Lieder Recital / Demus (vice Fischer-Dieskau)	11 Mar
Paris		Lieder Recital / Bonneau	16 Mar
		Concert / Sébastian	3 Apr
Brescia	TG	Lieder Recital / Favaretto	10 Apr
Siena		Lieder Recital / Favaretto	13 Apr
Naples	RAI	Bach–Mozart Concert / V. Rapallo	15 Apr
London	RFH	Lieder Recital / Moore	13 May
Vienna	Oper	Contessa in *Nozze di Figaro* / Böhm	4 Jun
		Contessa in *Nozze di Figaro* / Karajan	7 Jun
		Alice Ford in *Falstaff* / Karajan	8, 10 Jun
		Contessa in *Nozze di Figaro* / Böhm	13 Jun
		Fiordiligi in *Così* / Böhm	16 Jun
Scheveningen	KH	Lieder Recital / F. de Nobel	23 Jun
Amsterdam		Bach–Haydn Concert/Goldberg	24 Jun
Brussels	Expo	Verdi Requiem / Votto	26 Jun
Amsterdam	C	Haydn and Bach Cantatas / Goldberg	nd Jul
Salzburg Fest.	M	Wolf *Liederabend* / Moore	27 Jul
	FSH	Contessa in *Nozze di Figaro* / Böhm	4, 14, 19, 23, 30 Aug
	R	Fiordiligi in *Così* / Böhm	11, 17, 24, 31 Aug
Lucerne		*Liederabend* / Moore	28 Aug
Vienna	Oper	Elvira in *Don Giovanni* / Böhm	10 Sep
		Fiordiligi in *Così* / Böhm	12 Sep
		Alice Ford in *Falstaff* / Karajan	14, 17 Sep
San Francisco	WMOH	*Marie in *Bartered Bride* / Ludwig	30 Sep
		Fol-de-Rol / Ludwig	2 Oct
		Marie in *Bartered Bride* / Ludwig	4, 12 Oct
		Contessa in *Nozze di Figaro* / Adler	21, 23 Oct
San Diego		Contessa in *Nozze di Figaro* / Adler	30 Oct
San Francisco		Lieder Recital / Reeves	2 Nov
Los Angeles	PA	Marie in *Bartered Bride* / Ludwig	5 Nov
		Contessa in *Nozze di Figaro* / Adler	9 Nov
Cleveland	SH	Mozart Concert / Szell	13 Nov
Cincinnatti		Mozart Concert / Szell	15 Nov
New York	CH	*Cleopatra in *Giulio Cesare* / Gamson (concert)	18 Nov
		Lieder Recital / Reeves	30 Nov
Milan	S	*Iole in *Hercules* / Matacic	29 Dec

1959

Milan	S	Iole in *Hercules* / Matacic	1, 5, 7 Jan
London	RFH	Handel, Strauss Concert / Newstone, Moore	18 Jan
Lyon		Concert / Fournet	10 Feb
Paris	RF	Concert / Vandernoot	12 Feb
		Mozart Chamber Concert / Rosenthal	3 Mar
		Concert du livre d'Or	nd
Innsbrück	GS	Lieder Recital / Rapf	10 Mar
Stockholm		*Concert: *Judas Maccabaeus* / Rosenthal	nd
London	RFH	Mozart, Strauss Concert / Wallberg	27 Apr
Copenhagen	OFPSS	Lieder Recital / Olsson	29 Apr
	TKSS	Concert	1 May
Odense	FFH	Lieder Recital / Olsson	3 May
Stockholm		Concert	5, 8 May
Oslo		Lieder Recital	11 May
		Concert	14 May
Paris		Lieder Recital	20 May
Vienna	Oper	Contessa in *Nozze di Figaro* / Karajan	27 May
		Elvira in *Don Giovanni* / Hollreiser	30 May

Prague		Lieder Recital	2 Jun
Vienna	Oper	Countess in *Figaro* / Böhm	4 Jun
		Countess in *Figaro* / Karajan	7 Jun
		Countess in *Figaro* / Böhm	13 Jun
		Fiordiligi in *Così* / Böhm	17, 21 Jun
Scheveningen	KH	Mozart Concert / Giulini	8 Jul
Lucerne		Handel: *Messiah* / Beecham	10 Sep
London	RFH	Countess in *Figaro* / Giulini (concert)	28 Sep
	RFH	Elvira in *Don Giovanni* / Davis (concert)	18, 20 Oct
New York	UN	Beethoven: Ninth Symphony / de Carvalho	24 Oct
Cincinnatti		Concert, 4 LL / Szell	5 Nov
Chicago		Fiordiligi in *Così* / Krips	9, 11, 14 Nov
London	CG	Marschallin in *Rosenkavalier* / Solti	4, 7, 10, 14, 17 Dec
Vienna	Oper	Eva in *Meistersinger* / Hollreiser	20 Dec

1960

Vienna	Oper	Marschallin in *Rosenkavalier* / Wallberg	1, 4 Jan
		Contessa in *Nozze di Figaro* / Karajan	6 Jan
		Elvira in *Don Giovanni* / Hollreiser	9 Jan
Detroit	FA	Lieder Recital / Wustman	18 Feb
New York	CH	Lieder Recital / Wustman	13 Mar
San Francisco		Concert / Jorda	16, 17, 18 Mar
Berkeley		Lieder Recital / Reeves	20 Mar
London	RFH	Lieder Recital / Moore	10 Apr
		Concert (including Strauss: 4 LL / Giulini	28 Apr
Wiesbaden		(Visit of Vienna State Opera) Contessa in *Figaro* / Karajan	1, 2 May
Vienna	Oper	Fiordiligi in *Così* / Böhm	3, 8 May
		*Madeleine in *Capriccio* / Böhm	15 May
	GS	Wolf Lieder Recital / Schmidt	18 May
	Oper	Madeleine in *Capriccio* / Böhm	20, 23 May
		Marschallin in *Rosenkavalier* / Hollreiser	27 May
	GS	Mahler Concert / Walter (his farewell)	29 May
		4 LL in Concert / Giulini	30 May
	Oper	Marschallin in *Rosenkavalier* / Hollreiser	3 Jun
		Madeleine in *Capriccio* / Böhm	9 Jun
Strasbourg		Lieder Recital / Robin	15 Jun
Holland Fest.		Vivaldi, Verdi Concert / Giulini	22 Jun
Grenade		Lieder Recital	27 Jun
Amsterdam	C	Mozart Concert / Giulini	5 Jul
Salzburg Fest.	L	Fiordiligi in *Così* / Böhm	27 Jul
	OFSH	Elvira in *Don Giovanni* / Karajan	3 Aug
	NFSH	Marschallin in *Rosenkavalier* / Karajan	6 Aug
	L	Fiordiligi in *Così* / Böhm	7 Aug
	NFSH	Elvira in *Don Giovanni* / Karajan	10 Aug
	M	Schubert *Liederabend* / Moore	13 Aug
	OFSH	Elvira in *Don Giovanni* / Karajan	17 Aug
	L	Fiordiligi in *Così* / Böhm	21 Aug
	OFSH	Elvira in *Don Giovanni* / Karajan	25 Aug
	L	Fiordiligi in *Così* / Böhm	27 Aug
	OFSH	Elvira in *Don Giovanni* / Karajan	29 Aug
Vienna	Oper	Madeleine in *Capriccio* / Böhm	2 Sep
		Elvira in *Don Giovanni* / Böhm	4 Sep
		Marschallin in *Rosenkavalier* / Cluytens	10 Sep
San Francisco	WMOH	Marschallin in *Rosenkavalier* / Varviso	29 Sep, 7, 16 Oct
		Fiordiligi in *Così* / Adler	15, 18 Oct
Chicago	O	Contessa in *Nozze di Figaro* / Krips	26, 29, 31 Oct
San Diego		Marschallin in *Rosenkavalier* / Varviso	3 Nov
Los Angeles	PA	Marschallin in *Rosenkavalier* / Varviso	5 Nov

		Fiordiligi in *Così* / Adler	9 Nov
San Francisco		Lieder Recital / Wustman	11 Nov
Dallas		Elvira in *Don Giovanni* / Rescigno	20, 23 Nov
New York	TH	Iole in *Hercules* (exc.) American Opera Soc / Rescigno	2 Dec
Vienna	Oper	Marschallin in *Rosenkavalier* / Böhm	26 Dec

1961

Vienna	Oper	Marschallin in *Rosenkavalier* / Hollreiser	3 Jan
		Madeleine in *Capriccio* / Swarowsky	5 Jan
London	RFH	Contessa in *Figaro* / Giulini (concert)	6 Feb
Paris		Operatic Concert / Prêtre	11, 12 Feb
London	RFH	Elvira in *Don Giovanni* / Giulini (concert)	20 Feb
Monte Carlo	sG	Concert / Frémaux (same prog. as 11 Feb)	25 Feb
Paris		Lieder Recital	27 Feb
London	RFH	Brahms: *Deutsches Requiem* / Klemperer	3 Mar
		Mahler Concert / Klemperer	24 Apr
Milan	S	Marschallin in *Rosenkavalier* / Böhm	20, 22, 29, 30 May
Vienna	Oper	Elvira in *Don Giovanni* / Böhm	10 Jun
	BS	*Liederabend* / Demus	16 Jun
	Oper	Madeleine in *Capriccio* / Böhm	19 Jun
		Fiordiligi in *Così* / Ludwig	21 Jun
		Marschallin in *Rosenkavalier* / Böhm	23 Jun
Holland Fest.		Contessa in *Nozze di Figaro* / Giulini	3, 6, 9, 13 Jul
Salzburg Fest.	NFSH	Marschallin in *Rosenkavalier* / Böhm	28 Jul
	OFSH	Fiordiligi in *Così* / Böhm	1 Aug
	NFSH	Marschallin in *Rosenkavalier* / Böhm	3 Aug
	M	Hugo Wolf *Liederabend* / Moore	5 Aug
	OFSH	Fiordiligi in *Così* / Böhm	8 Aug
	NFSH	Marschallin in *Rosenkavalier* / Böhm	12 Aug
	OFSH	Fiordiligi in *Così* / Böhm	14 Aug
	NFSH	Marschallin in *Rosenkavalier* / Böhm	18, 25 Aug
	OFSH	Fiordiligi in *Così* / Böhm	27 Aug
	NFSH	Marschallin in *Rosenkavalier* / Böhm	30 Aug
Vienna	Oper	Marschallin in *Rosenkavalier* / Böhm	7 Sep
		Marschallin in *Rosenkavalier* / Wich	23 Sep
		Contessa in *Nozze di Figaro* / Karajan	26 Sep
Amsterdam	C	Lieder Recitals / De Nobel	29 Sep
Stuttgart	SO	Madeleine in *Capriccio* / Leitner	6 Oct
Naples	TSC	Mozart Concert and Operatic Arias / Franci	10 Oct
London	RFH	Lieder Recital / G. Parsons	17 Oct
Chicago	O	Fiordiligi in *Così* / Maag	1, 3 Nov
		Elvira in *Don Giovanni* / Maag	8, 11 Nov
New York	HC	Lieder Recital / Wustman	25 Nov
Vienna	Oper	Fiordiligi in *Così* / Loibner	15 Dec
		Madeleine in *Capriccio* / Swarowsky	20 Dec
		Marschallin in *Rosenkavalier* / Böhm	25 Dec

1962

Paris	O	Marschallin in *Rosenkavalier* / Fourestier	26, 29 Jan, 5, 12 Feb
Paris	OC	Madeleine in *Capriccio* / Prêtre	2, 9 Feb
Detroit		Handel – R. Strauss Concert / Paray	18 Feb
Hanover		Lieder Recital / Reuther	2 Mar
Los Angeles	PA	Lieder Recital / Wustman	31 Mar
Copenhagen	OFP	Lieder Recital / Reuther	9 May
Oslo		Lieder Recital / Reuther	11 May
Stockholm		Lieder Recital / Reuther	14 May
Copenhagen	T	Concert	16 May
Vienna	Oper	Contessa in *Nozze di Figaro* / Swarowsky	2 Jun

		Marschallin in *Rosenkavalier* / Karajan	7 Jun
		Madeleine in *Capriccio* / Prêtre	19 Jun
		Elvira in *Don Giovanni* / Keilberth	22 Jun
Amsterdam	C	Lieder Recital / de Nobel	29 Jun
London	G	Lieder Recital / Moore	18 Jul
Salzburg Fest.	OFSH	Fiordiligi in *Così* / Böhm	8 Aug
	M	Concert, 4 LL / Kertesz	11 Aug
	OFSH	Fiordiligi in *Così* / Böhm	15 Aug
	M	*Liederabend* / Moore	17 Aug
	OFSH	Fiordiligi in *Così* / Böhm	21, 26 Aug
	RFH	Fiordiligi in *Così* / Böhm (concert)	19 Sep
San Francisco		Marschallin in *Rosenkavalier* / Ferencsik	27 Sep
Berkeley		Lieder Recital / Wustman	5, 8 Oct
San Francisco	WMOH	Marschallin in *Rosenkavalier* / Ferencsik	12 Oct
		Elvira in *Don Giovanni* / Ludwig	16, 20 Oct
Los Angeles	PA	Elvira in *Don Giovanni* / Ludwig	28 Oct
San Diego		Elvira in *Don Giovanni* / Ludwig	1 Nov
Los Angeles	PA	Marschallin in *Rosenkavalier* / Ferencsik	7 Nov
		Elvira in *Don Giovanni* / Ludwig	9 Nov
San Francisco		Lieder Recital / Wustman	11 Nov
Brussels	TRM	Marschallin in *Rosenkavalier* / Vandernoot	18, 21, 24, 27, 31 Dec

1963

London	RFH	Concert / Maazel	26 Jan
Paris	OC	Fiordiligi in *Così* / Baudo	6, 9 Feb
	O	Marschallin in *Rosenkavalier*	11, 15, 17 Feb
	OC	Fiordiligi in *Così* / Baudo	19 Feb
London	RFH	Viennese Operetta / Boskovsky	4 Mar
Milan	S	Elvira in *Don Giovanni* / Scherchen	28, 30 Mar, 2, 4 Apr
London	RFH	Lieder Recital / Moore	7 Apr
Milan	S	Elvira in *Don Giovanni* / Scherchen	9 Apr
Munich		Concert / von Zallinger	24 Apr
Hamburg	SO	Marschallin in *Rosenkavalier* / L. Ludwig	2 May
		Fiordiligi in *Così* / Kulka	5 May
Paris	TC-E	Lieder Recital / Robin	13 May
Vienna	Oper	Madeleine in *Capriccio* / Heger	16 May
		Countess in *Nozze di Figaro* / Wallberg	23 May
		Elisabeth in *Tannhäuser* / Karajan	29 May
London	RFH	Verdi: Requiem / Giulini	23 Jun
Los Angeles	HB	Viennese Operetta / Boskovsky	9 Jul
New York	S	Viennese Concert / Boskovsky	11 Jul
Ann Arbor		Operetta / Boskovsky	14 Jul
Salzburg	NFSH	Marschallin in *Rosenkavalier* / Karajan	31 Jul
	LFSH	Fiordiligi in *Così* / Böhm	8 Aug
	NFSH	Marschallin in *Rosenkavalier* / Karajan	10 Aug
	LFSH	Fiordiligi in *Così* / Böhm	14 Aug
	M	Hugo Wolf *Liederabend* / Moore	17 Aug
	LFSH	Fiordiligi in *Così* / Böhm	20, 25 Aug
	NFSH	Marschallin in *Rosenkavalier* / Karajan	29 Aug
Lucerne Fest.		*Liederabend* / Moore	6 Sep
Besançon Fest.		*Liederabend* / Moore	14 Sep
San Francisco	WMOH	Fiordiligi in *Così* / Ferencsik	19 Oct
		Madeleine in *Capriccio* / Prêtre	25 Oct
		Fiordiligi in *Così* / Ferencsik	29 Oct
		Madeleine in *Capriccio* / Prêtre	31 Oct
Los Angeles	PA	Madeleine in *Capriccio* / Prêtre	6 Nov
		Fiordiligi in *Così* / Ferencsik	8 Nov

Milwaukee		R. Strauss–Mozart Concert	26 Nov
Vienna	Oper	Marschallin in *Rosenkavalier* / Krips	26 Dec

1964

London	RFH	Strauss Centenary Concert / Böhm	16 Jan
Barcelona	L	Fiordiligi in *Così* / Eykman	19, 21 Jan
Innsbruck	GS	Lieder Recital / Fischer	31 Jan
London	RFH	Lieder Recital / Parsons	7 Feb
	BBCMV	Lieder Recital / Parsons (studio live)	10 Feb
Vienna	Oper	Marschallin in *Rosenkavalier* / Wallberg	12 Feb
Geneva	GT	Marschallin in *Rosenkavalier* / Vöchting	25, 27, 29 Feb
Marseilles	O	Marschallin in *Rosenkavalier* / Trik	6, 8 Mar
Paris	TC-E	Lieder Recital / Robin	18 Mar
Geneva	VH	Lieder Recital / Robin	21 Mar
London	RFH	Operetta Concert / Matacic	29 Mar
		Mozart Concert Arias / Giulini	9 Apr
		Concert	26 Apr
Berlin	P	4 LL in Strauss Centenary Concert / Karajan	5, 6 May
Vienna	Oper	Madeleine in *Capriccio* / Prêtre	5 Jun
		Contessa in *Nozze di Figaro* / Krips	9 Jun
		Marschallin in *Rosenkavalier* / Wallberg	13 Jun
Holland Fest.		4 LL in Concert / Szell	19 Jun
Amsterdam C		Lieder Recital / Parsons	23 Jun
Salzburg Fest.	NFSH	Marschallin in *Rosenkavalier* / Karajan	1 Aug
	LFSH	Fiordiligi in *Così* / Böhm	10 Aug
	NFSH	Marschallin in *Rosenkavalier* / Karajan	13 Aug
		4 LL in Strauss Concert / Karajan	15 Aug
	LFSH	Fiordiligi in *Così* / Böhm	16 Aug
	M	Hugo Wolf *Liederabend* / Moore	19 Aug
	LFSH	Fiordiligi in *Così* / Böhm	22, 26 Aug
	NFSH	Marschallin in *Rosenkavalier* / Karajan	29 Aug
San Francisco	WMOH	Marschallin in *Rosenkavalier* / Leitner	22, 24, 27 Sep
New York	Met	Marschallin in *Rosenkavalier* / Schippers	13, 24, 28 Oct, 2, 12 Nov
	CH	Wolf: *Italienisches Liederbuch* with Fischer-Dieskau / Reeves	22 Nov
Los Angeles		Marschallin in *Rosenkavalier* / Leitner	26 Nov
New York		Gala Perf. Act I *Rosenkavalier* / Schippers	29 Nov
		Marschallin in *Rosenkavalier* / Schippers	8, 19 Dec

1965

Vienna	Oper	Madeleine in *Capriccio* / Heger	10 Jan
		Marschallin in *Rosenkavalier* / Wallberg	13 Jan
		Contessa in *Nozze di Figaro* / Wallberg	16 Jan
		Marschallin in *Rosenkavalier* / Wallberg	21 Jan
		Contessa in *Nozze di Figaro* / Wallberg	24, 27 Jan
		Marschallin in *Rosenkavalier* / Ludwig	30 Jan, 2 Feb
Brussels	TRM	Marschallin in *Rosenkavalier* / Kraus	21, 24, 27 Feb
London	RFH	Lieder Recital / Moore	4 Mar
Monte Carlo	sG	Contessa in *Nozze di Figaro* / van Remoortel	14, 16 Mar
Paris		Lieder Recital / Parsons	24 Mar
New York	CH	Lieder Recital / Parsons (*Recital abandoned midway*)	9 Apr
London	RFH	Lieder Recital / Parsons	20 May
Copenhagen		Lieder Recital / R. Levin	26 May
Bergen Fest.		Lieder Recital	28 May
Stockholm	KH	Lieder Recital	31 May
Madrid	TZ	Marschallin in *Rosenkavalier* / Kraus	8 Jun
Chicago		Ravinia Fest. Concert / Boskowsky	17 Jul
New York	LS	Strauss and Mozart Concert / Rosenstock	21 Jul

		Operetta / Boskovsky	24 Jul
San Francisco		Operatic Arias / Ehrling	29 Jul
Hollywood Bowl		Viennese Night / Boskovsky	31 Jul
Paris	SP	Lieder Recital / Parsons	22 Nov
Lyons	O	Fiordiligi in *Così* / Peters	17, 19 Dec

1966

New York	CH	Lieder Recital / Parsons	8 Jan
		Lieder Recital / Gould	14 Jan
	Met	Donna Elvira in *Don Giovanni* / Rosenstock	29 Jan
Long Island		TV Recital / Moore	4 Mar
London	RFH	Lieder Recital / Moore	6 May
Drottningholm		Fiordiligi in *Così* / Koltay	10, 13 May
Stockholm	O	Marschallin in *Rosenkavalier* / Varviso	nd May
Paris	O	Marschallin in *Rosenkavalier* / Sebastian	3, 6, 8 Jun
Bath	AS	Lieder Recital	19 Jun
Divonne		Lieder Recital / Parsons	22 Jun
Paris		Lieder Recital / Parsons	nd
Lyons	O	Fiordiligi in *Così* / R. Peters	nd
		Lieder Recital / Parsons	30 Jun
New York	LC	Stravinsky and Mozart Concert / Foss	7 Jul
	PH	Lieder Recital / Wustman	13 Jul
Teesside Fest.		Lieder Recital / Parsons	16 Jul
Baalbeck		Lieder Recital / Parsons	23 Jul
Vichy		Concert / De Froment	30 Jul
Chichester Fest.		Lieder Recital	7 Aug
Harrogate Fest.		Lieder Recital	14 Aug
Flanders Fest.		Lieder Recital	26 Aug
Edinburgh Fest.		Lieder Recital / Demus	31 Aug
Stresa		Lieder Recital / Demus	5 Sep
Montreux		Mozart–Strauss Concert / Dorati	1 Oct
Paris	TC-E	Lieder Recital / Isepp	24 Oct
Stockholm	KT	Marschallin in *Rosenkavalier* / Varviso	2, 5 Nov
Brussels	TRM	Fiordiligi in *Così*	20, 23, 26, 29 Nov, 1 Dec
Barcelona	L	Fiordiligi in *Così* / R. Kraus	8 Dec
	L	Marschallin in *Rosenkavalier* / R. Kraus	11, 13, 15 Dec

1967

Zürich		Lieder Recital	nd Jan
Amsterdam		Fiordiligi in *Così* / A. Rieu	25, 27 Jan, 3, 5 Feb
London	RFH	Gerald Moore's Farewell with de los Angeles and Fischer-Dieskau	20 Feb
Los Angeles		Lieder Recital / Isepp	26 Feb
Chicago		Lieder Recital / Isepp	5 Mar
New Orleans		Lieder Recital / Isepp	11 Mar
New York	HC	Lieder Recital / Isepp	18 Mar
	CH	★Eurydice in *Orfeo ed Eurydice* / Perlea (concert)	4, 7 Apr
Stockholm		Lieder Recital	20 Apr
Oslo		Lieder Recital	23 Apr
Copenhagen		Lieder Recital / Olsson	25 Apr
Bergen	KP	Mozart and Strauss Concert / Bruland	27 Apr
London	RFH	Lieder Recital / Moore	6 May
Paris	TC-E	Lieder Recitals / Parsons	18 May
Bordeaux		Lieder Recital / Parsons	22 May
Bergen	KP	Lieder Recital / Levin	28 May
Paris	TC-E	Lieder Recital / Parsons	3 Jun
	SP	Mozart–Verdi Concert / Klobucar	7 Jun
Cincinnatti	Z	Marschallin in *Rosenkavalier* / Rich	5 Jul

Sydney	TH	Lieder Recital / Parsons	29 Jul
		Lieder Recital / Parsons	1 Aug
		Concert / Post	10 Aug
		Lieder Recital / Parsons	19 Aug
Melbourne	TH	Lieder / Parsons	nd
Perth	GH	Lieder / Parsons	nd
Ascona		Lieder / Parsons	6 Oct
London	RFH	Washington NSO Concert / Mitchell BBC and TV	13 Oct
	CG	Gala Concert / Downes	15 Oct
Birmingham		Lieder Recital / Parsons	17 Oct
Chichester	FT	Lieder Recital / Isepp	22 Oct
Paris	TC-E	Lieder Recitals / Parsons	6 Nov
Turin	C	Lieder Recital / Parsons	8 Nov
Paris	TC-E	Lieder Recital / Parsons	13 Nov
Lyons	O	Marschallin in *Rosenkavalier* / Gierster	24, 26 Nov
Brussels	TRM	Marschallin in *Rosenkavalier* / Kraus	24, 27, 31 Dec

1968

New York	CH	Mahler Concert / Steinberg	15 Jan
Chicago	OM	Lieder Recital / Parsons	21 Jan
New York	PH	Lieder Recital / Parsons	18 Feb
London	RFH	Mahler: Des Knaben Wunderhorn with Fischer-Dieskau / Szell	7, 10 Mar
Cardiff		Lieder Recital / Parsons	18 Mar
Monmouth Boys' School		Lieder Recital / Parsons	20 Mar
Tokyo		Lieder Recitals / Parsons	5, 8 Apr
Stockholm		Concert	12 May
Copenhagen		Concert	16 May
Oslo		Concert	21 May
Ravinia		Concert / Boskovsky	16 Jul
Cleveland		Strauss 4 LL in Concert / Szell	25 Jul
Blossoms Fest.		Mozart, Strauss 4 LL in Concert / Szell	28 Jul
Buenos Aires	TC	Lieder Recitals / Parsons	15, 18, 21 Aug
St-Jean-de-Luz		Lieder Recital / Tunnard	4 Sep
Glasgow	CitH	Lieder Recital / Parsons	13 Oct
Liverpool	PH	Lieder Recital / Parsons	15 Oct
Bournemouth	WG	Lieder Recital / Parsons	17 Oct
Turin	C	Lieder Recital / Parsons	6 Nov
London	RFH	Lieder Recital (In Memoriam Ernest Newman) / Parsons	2 Dec

1969

New York	LC	Lieder Recital / Parsons	2 Feb
Chicago		Lieder Recital / Parsons	3 Mar
Upland, Indiana		Lieder Recital / Parsons	17 Mar
Rotterdam	D	Lieder Recital / Parsons	21 Apr
Amsterdam		Lieder Recital / Parsons	23 Apr
Utrecht	GK	Lieder Recital / Parsons	26 Apr
Chicago	OH	Lieder Recital / Parsons	2 May
Paris	TC-E	Lieder Recital / Parsons	13 May
Prague		Lieder Recital / Parsons	23 May
Strasbourg Fest.		Concert / Stoll	6 Jun
Liseberg	KH	Concert / S. Westerberg	12 Jun
Lyons	O	*Liederabend* / Lamport	15 Jun
Birmingham	TH	Recital / Lamport	19 Jun
York		Recital / Lamport	22 Jun
Nohant		Lieder Recital / Ciccolini	29 Jun
Tours	GdeM	*Liederabend* / Lamport	4 Jul

Hollywood Bowl		Concert: A Night in Vienna / Paulik	26 Jul
		Operatic Concert / Ehrling	29 Jul
Ravinia		Viennese Night / Allers	3 Aug
Columbia, Maryl.		Viennese Concert / Allers	10 Aug
Meadowbrook		Strauss–Mozart Concert / Ehrling	23, 24 Aug
Rosehill, Cumberland		Lieder Recital	20 Sep
London	RFH	4 LL in Concert / Barbirolli	25, 28 Sep
Birmingham	TH	Concert / Frémaux	2 Oct
Marseilles		Concert / Giovaninetti	10 Oct
London	RFH	Lieder Recital / Parsons	20 Oct
New York	PH	Lieder Recital / Parsons	16 Nov

1970

Tokyo		Lieder Recital / Parsons	17 Jan
Toronto	CBC	Lieder / Newmark; arias with orch. / Rich	15 Feb
Pasadena		Lieder / Parsons	19 Feb
Toronto	EA	Marschallin in *Rosenkavalier* / Rich (concert)	22 Feb
	MH	Lieder Recital / Newmark	24 Feb
London	BBC TV	Lieder Recital / Moore	22 Mar
Torrance, Cal.		Lieder Recital / Parsons	26 Mar
Paris	TC-E	Lieder Recital / Parsons	12 May
Strasbourg Fest.		Mozart Arias	6 Jun
Lyons		Lieder Recital / Lamport	15 Jun
Tours		Lieder Recital / Lamport	4 Jul
Göteborg	KH	Concert	12 Aug
London	RFH	Lieder Recital / Parsons	17 Oct
Mill Hill		Recital for school	24 Oct
Birmingham		Recital / Parsons	27 Oct

1971

Turin	C	Lieder Recital / Parsons	20 Jan
Louisville		4 LL in Concert / Mester	6 Feb
Krannart		Lieder Recital / Wustman	15 Feb
Dayton, Ohio		Recital / Paul Katz	22 Mar
Canberra	T	Lieder Recital / Parsons	7 May
Adelaide	TH	Lieder Recital / Parsons	25 May
Sydney	TH	Lieder Recital / Parsons	27, 29 May
Versailles	TG	Lieder Recital / Ciccolini	30 Jun
Salon–de–Provence		Lieder / Ciccolini	19 Jul
Barcelona Fest.		Lieder Recital	31 Jul
Turku		Lieder Recital	20 Aug
		Crosière musicale à bord de Renaissance	15 Sep
Windsor		Lieder Recital / Parsons	28 Sep
Brighton Dome		Lieder Recital / Parsons	1 Oct
York		Lieder Recital / Parsons	9 Oct
Swansea		Lieder Recital / Parsons	12 Oct
London	RFH	Lieder Recital / Parsons	17 Oct
Glasgow		Recital	24 Oct
Manchester		Concert (Barbirolli Memorial) / Loughran	31 Oct
Paris	O	*Liederabend* / Parsons	12 Nov
Ivrea	TG	*Liederabend* / Parsons	23 Nov
Rome	SC	*Liederabend* / Parsons	26 Nov
Brussels	TM	*Homage à ES: Adieux à la scène* (Farewell to the stage)	17, 19, 22, 26, 28,
		Marschallin in *Rosenkavalier* Act I / Sébastian	31 Dec

1972

Tokyo		Lieder Recital / Parsons	27 Jan, 20 Feb
Yokohama		Lieder Recital / Parsons	5 Feb
San Francisco		Lieder Recital / Parsons	7 Mar

New Orleans		Lieder Recital/Parsons	11 Mar
New York	CH	Lieder Recital/Parsons	19 Mar
Snape, Maltings		Lieder Recital/Parsons	28 Apr
Paris	TC-E	Lieder Recital/Parsons	1 May
Vienna	BS	Lieder Recital/Parsons	31 May
Geneva		Lieder Recital/Lamport	13 Jun
Toulon Fest.		Lieder Recital/Lamport	15 Jun
Paris	TC-E	Concerts/Maazel	19, 21 Jun
Ciboure		Lieder Recital/Parsons	1 Sep
Newcastle		Lieder Recital/Parsons	1 Oct
Southport		Lieder Recital/Parsons	5 Oct
Grangemouth		Lieder Recital/Parsons	16 Oct
London	RFH	Lieder Recital/Parsons	21 Oct
Portsmouth	G	Lieder Recital/Parsons	24 Oct
Birmingham		Lieder Recital/Parsons	27 Oct
Cupertino, Cal.		Lieder Recital/Parsons	22 Nov
New York	CH	Lieder Recital/Parsons	3 Dec
Rochester	Univ	Lieder Recital/Parsons	6 Dec

1973

London	CG	Gala: Fanfare for Europe/Davis	3 Jan
Salisbury	CH	Lieder Recital/Parsons	5 Jan
Paris	FdD	Lieder Recital/Parsons	25 Jan
Manchester		Last Concert RPO/Groves	28 Jan
Croydon	FH	Lieder Recital/Parsons	1 Feb
Lyons	O	Lieder Recital/Lamport	5 Feb
Hong Kong		Lieder Recitals	1, 3 Mar
Rome	SC	Lieder Recital/Parsons	11 May
Paris	TC-E	Lieder Recital/Parsons	24 May
Prague		Lieder Recital/Parsons	27 May
Vienna		Lieder Recital/Parsons	31 May
Scheveningen	KH	Lieder Recital/Parsons	27 Jun
Vichy		Lieder Recital	20 Jul
St Jean de Luz		Lieder Recital/Ciccolini	8 Sep
Veves Château		Lieder Recital (Save Venice)/Ciccolini	15 Sep
Eastbourne		Lieder Recital	3 Oct
Northampton		Lieder Recital/Lamport	11 Oct
Sutton, Granada		Lieder Recital/Lamport	14 Oct
Cambridge		Lieder Recital/Lamport	19 Nov
London	RFH	Lieder Recital/Parsons	24 Nov
Nottingham		Lieder Recital/Parsons	28 Nov
Turin	C	Lieder Recital/Parsons	12 Dec
Naples		Lieder Recital/Parsons	17 Dec

1974

Hull		Lieder Recital/Parsons	24 Jan
New Haven, Conn.		Lieder Recital/Parsons	30 Jan
Chicago	OH	Lieder Recital/Parsons	3 Feb
Toronto	MH	Lieder Recital/Parsons	7 Feb
Oxford, Miss.		Lieder Recital/Parsons	11 Feb
Appleton, Wis.		Lieder Recital/Parsons	14 Feb
Carlisle, Penn.		Lieder Recital/Parsons	17 Feb
Glasboro, NJ		Lieder Recital/Parsons	20 Feb
Palm Beach, Fla.		Lieder Recital/Parsons	28 Feb
Waukegan, Ill.		Lieder Recital/Parsons	2 Mar
Philadelphia	CC	Lieder Recital/Parsons	5 Mar
Hemel Hempstead		Lieder Recital/Lamport	8 May

Paris	TdeV	Lieder Recital / Lamport	11, 12, 13, 14, 15 Jun
Nohant		Lieder Recital / Ciccolini	29 Jun
Aix-en-Provence		Lieder Recital / Parsons	29 Jul
Teesside		Lieder Recital / Parsons	8 Aug
Lisbon		Lieder Recital	16 Sep
Bucharest		Lieder Recitals	20, 23 Sep
Croydon	FH	Lieder Recital / Parsons	26 Sep
Eastbourne		Lieder Recital / Parsons	3 Oct
Harlow		Lieder Recital / Parsons	6 Oct
London	RFH	Lieder Recital / Parsons	12 Oct
Cologne		Lieder Recital / Parsons	20 Oct
Paris	TC-E	Lieder Recital / Parsons	25 Oct
Chiba, Japan		Lieder Recital / Parsons	25 Nov
Tokyo		Lieder Recital / Parsons	10 Dec

1975

El Camino Coll. Santa Barbara		Lieder Recitals / Parsons	2, 15 Jan
Vancouver		Lieder Recital / Parsons	18 Jan
Seattle	OH	Lieder Recital / Parsons	22 Jan
Berkeley, Cal.		Farewell Lieder Recital / Parsons	26 Jan
San Francisco		'Mozart's Birthday Marathon' / Parsons	27 Jan
Phoenix, Ariz.		Lieder Recital / Parsons	29 Jan
Torrance, Cal.		Lieder Recital / Parsons	1 Feb
Chicago	OH	Lieder Recital / Parsons	9 Feb
Ottawa		Lieder Recital / Parsons	12 Feb
New Orleans		Lieder Recital / Parsons	22 Feb
Minneapolis	NMA	Lieder Recital / Isepp	4 Mar
Toronto	MH	Lieder Recital / Isepp	6 Mar
Baltimore	GC	Lieder Recital / Isepp	16 Mar
Montreal	TV	Lieder Recital / Isepp	7 Apr
Washington	JFKC	Lieder Recital / Parsons	13 Apr
New York	CH	Farewell Lieder Recital / Parsons	27 Apr
Rome	SC	Lieder Recital / Willison	9 May
Milan	PS	Lieder Recital / Willison	13 May
Tours	GdeM	Lieder Recital / Richter	nd
Monte Carlo	sG	Lieder Recital / Lamport	2 Aug
Villach		Lieder Recital / Lamport	29 Aug
Stockholm		Lieder Recital / Parsons	20 Sep
Göteborg	KH	Lieder Recital / Parsons	23 Sep
Manchester		Lieder Recital / Parsons	2 Oct
Birmingham		Lieder Recital / Parsons	13 Oct
London	RFH	Wolf Lieder Recital / Parsons	18 Oct
Eastbourne	CT	Lieder Recital / Parsons	22 Oct
Florence	TdP	Lieder Recital / Parsons	25 Oct
Cambridge		Lieder Recital / Parsons	29 Oct
London	CG	Lieder Recital vice de los Angeles / Parsons	2 Nov
Vienna		Lieder Recital / Parsons	6 Nov
Paris		Interview Recitals / Parsons	10, 13, 17, 22, 24, 28 Nov

1976

Milan	PS	Last Milan Lieder Recital / Parsons	16 Feb
Brussels	TRM	Lieder Recital / Parsons	29 Apr
Bordeaux		Lieder Recital / Johnson	8 May
Helsingor		Lieder Recital	3 Jun
Cambridge Univ.		Lieder Recital / Parsons (hon. Mus. D.)	10 Jun
London	WH	Lieder Recital / Parsons	12 Jun

Luxembourg		Lieder Recital / Parsons	26 Jun
Edinburgh	UH	Lieder Recital / Parsons	23 Aug
Vienna		Lieder Recital / Parsons	13 Oct
Hamburg		Lieder Recital / Parsons	18 Oct
Paris	UdeG	Lieder Recitals	28 Oct, 23 Nov
Blois		Lieder Recital	11 Dec
Roubaix		Lieder Recital	14 Dec

1977

Stratford-on-Avon		Lieder Recital / Parsons	10 Jan
Turin	C	Lieder Recital / Lamport	18 Jan
Essen		Lieder Recital / Parsons	21 Jan
Reutlingen		Lieder Recital / Parsons	27 Jan
Stuttgart		Lieder Recital / Parsons	1 Feb
Amsterdam	C	Lieder Recital / Parsons	8 Feb
Witten		Lieder Recital / Parsons	12 Feb
London	CG	Lieder Recital / Parsons	20 Feb
Strasbourg		Lieder Recital / Parsons	26 Feb
London	CTH	Lieder Recital / Parsons	26, 30 Mar
Stockholm		Lieder Recital / Lamport	24 Apr
Göteborg	KH	Lieder Recital / Lamport	26 Apr
Uppsala		Lieder Recital / Lamport	28 Apr
Stockholm		Lieder Recital / Lamport	2 May
Geneva	GT	Lieder Recital / Parsons	25 May
Paris	TS-E	Lieder Recital / Parsons	31 May
Ann Arbor		Lieder Recital / A. Wustman	23 Jul
Harrogate		Lieder Recital / Parsons	27 Sep
Birmingham		Lieder Recital / Parsons	1 Nov
Sheffield	TH	Lieder Recital / Parsons	6 Nov
Glasgow		Lieder Recital / Parsons	13 Nov
London	WH	Wolf Lieder Recital / Parsons	19, 26 Nov
Cambridge		Lieder Recital / Parsons	30 Nov
Warsaw		Lieder Recital / Parsons	5 Dec
Poznán		Lieder Recital / Parsons	9 Dec

1978

Berlin	DO	Lieder Recital / Parsons	7 Jan
Milan	C	Lieder Recital / Lamport	10 Jan
Florence	P	Lieder Recital / Lamport	14 Jan
Turin	C	Lieder Recital / Lamport	18 Jan
Asolo		Schubert Lieder Recital / Lamport	1 Apr
Oslo		Lieder Recital / Parsons	9 May
Budapest		Lieder Recital / Parsons	18 May
Paris	TC-E	Lieder Recital / Parsons	13 Jun
Hohenems Fest.		Lieder Recital / Parsons	16, 17 Jun
Oslo		Lieder Recital / Parsons	21 Jun
Breslau		Lieder Recital / Parsons	6 Sep
London	WH	Farewell Lieder Recital / Parsons	23, 30 Sep

1979

Zürich	OH	Final Lieder Recital / Parsons	19 Mar

Appendix B
Schwarzkopf's roles for the Deutsche Oper

APPENDIX B I

See Chapter 4, page 47.

This is the list of her suggested roles which Schwarzkopf gave to Dr Maeder on 17 June 1942.

The marks before names of characters were made in pencil by Dr Maeder and can be taken as meaning:

− has already sung
+ could sing now

The marks after names of characters were possibly made by Rode:

○ not agreed because of her relatively junior status in the Company

Roles sung:	Afterwards sung at:
− Zerbinetta	Vienna
Konstanze ○	Vienna
−+ Gilda	Vienna and CG
Violetta ○	Vienna and CG
−+ Fluth ○	
−+ Rosina ○	Vienna
− Adele	
−+ Nedda ○	Vienna
+ Zerline	
+ Marcelline	Vienna and CG
Mimi ○ und − Musetta	Vienna and CG (Mimi)
Sofie ○	Vienna and CG
− Gretchen (*Wildschütz*)	
− Waldvogel	
− Ännchen	
− Serpetta (*Gärtnerin*)	
− Marie (*Waffenschmied*)	
− Marie (*Zar u. Zimmermann*)	
− Undine	
− Leonore (*Stradella*)	
− Lola	
− Hirt (*Tannhäuser*)	
− 1 Blumenmädchen	
− Wellgunde	
− Ortlinde	
− Arsena	

APPENDIX B2

See Chapter 5, page 58.

In June 1944, her health restored, Schwarzkopf sent this list to the Deutsche Oper, describing the various categories of roles she wanted to sing as a guest artist in Berlin, after she had signed her Vienna contract:

Familiar roles: Zerbinetta (*Ariadne auf Naxos*)
Adele (*Fledermaus*)
Undine (*Undine* by Lortzing)
Marie (*Waffenschmied* by Lortzing)
Marie (*Zar und Zimmermann* by Lortzing)
Gretchen (*Wildschütz* by Lortzing)
Musette (*Die Boheme*)
Ännchen (*Freischütz*)
Leonore (*Alessandro Stradella* by Flotow)
Waldvogel (*Siegfried*)
Shepherd (*Tannhäuser*)
Lola (*Cavalleria Rusticana*)
Wellgunde (*Rheingold, Götterdämmerung*)
Ortlinde (*Walküre*)
Arsena (*Zigeunerbaron*)

Not yet sung but ready for performance: ★Gilda (*Rigoletto*)
Frau Fluth (*Merry Wives of Windsor*)
★Rosina (*Barber of Seville*)
★Nedda (*Pagliacci*)
★Mimi (*La Bohème*)
★Sophie (*Rosenkavalier*)
★Konstanze (*Die Entführung*)
★Violetta (*Traviata*)

Being studied: Marie (*Daughter of the Regiment*)
Zerlina (*Don Giovanni*)
★Marzelline (*Fidelio*)

Of the eight roles in the second group, she was to be associated with seven, of which four are for lyric-coloratura soprano voice (Gilda, Rosina, Konstanze and Violetta) and were to be more important to her in London than Vienna. Of the 'roles being studied', she sang only Marzelline.

This indicates not so much how differently she was directed once Walter Legge had charge of her, but how she was already considering lyric roles before his arrival in her life.

Appendix C
Die Gottbegnadete Liste oder Liste der Himmlischen

Dr Goebbels had been issuing annual lists of the most prominent artists in the Reich since 1940 ('Those blessed by God'); but from August 1944, when Total War was the policy, he attempted to inspire all artists who were being drafted into munitions factories by 'enshrining' their names in his 'List B' so that, should they perish in the expected catastrophe, their memory would never die. There were 100 names in each branch of the arts and literature, of which these seventy-nine named individuals are from the music section:

Special List

Richard Strauss
Hans Pfitzner
Wilhelm Furtwängler

Conductors' List

Hermann Abendroth	Clemens Krauss	Oswald Kabasta
Karl Elmendorff	Paul Schmitz	Hans Knappertsbusch
Eugen Jochum	Carl Schuricht	Rudolf Krasselt
Herbert von Karajan	Karl Böhm	Hans Schmidt-Isserstedt
Joseph Keilberth	Robert Heger	Johannes Schüler

Singers' List under Theatre

Irma Beilke	Erna Schlüter	Max Lorenz
Erna Berger	Gerda Sommerschuh	Walther Ludwig
Helena Braun	Carla Spletter	Hans Hermann Nissen
Paula Buchner	(Goering's nomination)	Julius Patzak
Maria Cebotari		Prof. Julius Pölzer
Clara Ebers	Peter Anders	Jaro Prohaska
Liselotte Enck	Matthieu Ahlersmeyer	Hans Reinmar
(Goering's nomination)	Herbert Alsen	Helge Roswaenge
Trude Eipperle	Rudolf Bockelmann	Karl Schmitt-Walter
Marta Fuchs	Anton Dermota	August Seider
Lore Hoffmann	Willy Domgraf-Fassbaender	Horst Taubmann
Elisabeth Höngen	Eugen Fuchs	Ludwig Weber
Margarete Klose	Josef Greindl	Marcel Wittrisch
Hilde Konetzni	Josef Herrmann	Wilhelm Schirp
Tiana Lemnitz	Theo Herrmann	Paul Schöffler
Hildegarde Ranczak	Hans Hotter	Ludwig Suthaus
Maria Reining	Eduard Kandl	Franz Völker
Martha Rohs	Fritz Krenn	Erich Witte
Gertrude Rünger	Werner Kraus	Erich Zimmerman

Formerly on the list, but later omitted without explanation

Felicie Hüni-Mihacsek	Alda Noni	Elisabeth Schwarzkopf
Adele Kern	Erna Sack	Irmgard Seefried
Anny Konetzni		

Instrumentalists and complete orchestras were also included:

The Berlin and Vienna Philharmonic Orchestras; the Prussian, Bavarian and Saxon State Orchestras; the Leipzig Gewandhaus and Hamburg Philharmonic Orchestras; the Bruckner, Linz and Prague Orchestras.

Notes

Chapter 1: Upbringing in the Weimar Republic (1915–1938)

1 A. H. J. Nicholls, *Weimar and the Rise of Hitler* (London: Macmillan, 1970), p. 85.
2 DAP or German Workers' party. Its name was later prefixed with the letters NS, standing for National Socialist, and emphasis on four letters in the German spelling of NA*tional* SoZI*alistische deutsche Arbeiter Partei* produced the acronym *Nazi*.
3 Bernard Gavoty, (trans. F. E. Richardson), *Elisabeth Schwarzkopf* (Geneva: René Kister, 1958), p. 31.
4 WL told AJ (1978) that the League of Nations provided a scholarship for Schwarzkopf, but the League's archivist confirmed by letter in 1993 that the only scholarships given by the League in the 1930s were in connection with medicine.
5 St. Akad, H. für M. Jahr 55 (1933–4), pp. 18–21.
6 K. J. Kutsch and Leo Riemens (eds.), *Grosses Sängerlexikon* (Franke Verlag, Berne & Stuttgart, 1987), p. 2064.
7 Gavoty, op. cit., p. 31.
8 St. Akad. H. für M. Jahr 55, op. cit., p. 23.
9 NSD St B.: Nazional-Sozialisten Deutsche Studenten Bund (National Socialist German Students' Association) with No. 77802.
10 Stanley Sadie (ed.), *New Grove Dictionary of Opera* (NGDO), vol. 2, (London: Macmillan 1992) p. 884.
11 Tubeuf (ed.), *l'Avant-Scène l'Opéra*, Schwarzkopf Number, August 1983 (*l'Avant-Scène*, ES), p. 10.

Chapter 2: Opera Singer in Berlin (1938–1940)

1 Gisela Huwe (ed.), *Die Deutsche Oper Berlin* (Berlin: Quadriga Verlag, n.d.), p. 25.
2 Peter Heyworth, *Otto Klemperer: His Life and Times*, vol. 1, 1885–1933 (Oxford: OUP, 1983), p. 170.
3 Fred K. Prieberg (trans. C. Dolan), *Trial of Strength: Wilhelm Furtwängler and the Third Reich* (London: Quartet, 1991), p. 77.
4 WL–AJ, 1978.
5 George Clare, *Berlin Days* (London: Macmillan, 1989), p. 51.
6 Wiener Library Microfilm: PC4 Reel 47.
7 Irma Beilke, Ruth Jahnke, Margaret Pfahl, Tresi Rudolph.
8 Berlin Document Centre (Schwarzkopf File) [BDC (ES File)].
9 Arbeitsbuch No. 40/1 238 359; Party No. 7 548 960 in the Paulsen Group BDC (ES File).
10 Ibid.
11 Schultze's own 1979 recording of his opera is on CD.

Chapter 3: Rising Star (1940–1942)

1 Friedelind Wagner with Page Cooper, *The Royal Family of Bayreuth* (London: Eyre and Spottiswoode, 1948), pp. 99–100.
2 BDC (ES File).
3 Gisela Huwe (ed.), *Die Deutsche Oper Berlin* (Berlin: Quadriga Verlag, n.d.), p. 26.
4 ES–Tubeuf radio interview, 1994.

5 Huwe, op. cit., p. 26.
6 BDC (ES File).
7 Ibid.
8 Ibid.
9 Ibid.
10 Ibid.
11 Deutsche Oper Archive, Berlin.
12 BDC (ES File).
13 Huwe, op. cit., p. 27.
14 Ibid.
15 DO Archive, 1992.
16 Ibid.
17 *The Gramophone*, December 1990, p. 1174.
18 BDC (ES File), quoted by Oliver Rathkolb *Führertreu und Gottbegnadet: Kunstereliten im Dritten Reich* (Vienna: Osterreichischer Bundesverlag, 1991), p. 97.
19 George Clare, *Berlin Days* (London: Macmillan, 1989), p. 52.

Chapter 4: Opera, Cinema and Adversity (1942–1943)

1 NGDO, vol. 1 p. 81.
2 BDC (ES).
3 In Nicolai's *Merry Wives of Windsor*.
4 BDC (ES).
5 Ibid.
6 Ibid.
7 IB–AJ, Berlin, 1980.
8 BDC (ES).
9 Ibid.
10 BBC documentary film, *Goebbels, Master of Propaganda*, 1992.
11 *Deutsche Spielfilm Almanach*, p. 456.
12 *Goebbels, Master of Propaganda*, op. cit.
13 Hans-Otto Meissner (trans. Gwendolen M. Keeble), *Magda Goebbels* (London: Sidgwick and Jackson, 1980), pp. 116, 135, 137.
14 Fred K. Prieberg (trans. C. Dolan), *Trial of Strength: Wilhelm Furtwängler and the Third Reich* (London: Quartet, 1991), p. 217.
15 VU–AJ, 1981.
16 TL–AJ, 1981.
17 Heringdorf, Detlef Meyer zu, *Das Charlottenburger Opernhaus 1921–61* (Berlin: Deutsche Oper, 1988), pp. 70–1.

18 Gisela Huwe (ed.), *Die Deutsche Oper Berlin* (Berlin: Quadriga Verlag, n.d.), p. 27.

Chapter 5: Vienna, Sweet and Sour (1943–1945)

1 Tubeuf, *l'Avant-Scène*, ES, p. 37.
2 *Neues Wiener Tageblatt*, 9 October 1942.
3 Anton Dermota, *Tausendundein Abend Mein Sängerleben* (Munich: Deutscher Taschenbuch Verlag, 1989), pp. 176–7.
4 BDC (ES).
5 Lanfranco Rasponi, *The Last Prima Donnas* (London: Gollancz, 1984), p. 537..
6 Gisela Huwe (ed.), *Die Deutsche Oper Berlin* (Berlin: Quadriga Verlag, n.d.), p. 27.
7 Her illness was also attributed to the damp air raid shelters of Babelsberg.
8 Poprad Cultural and Health Office: letter of 14 May 1992 quoting post-war director of the Clinic, Dr Vašečka.
9 BDC (ES).
10 Ibid.
11 *Neues Wiener Tageblatt*, 4 May 1944.
12 BDC (ES).
13 Oliver Rathkolb, *Führertreu und Gottbegnadet: Kunstereliten im Dritten Reich* (Vienna: Osterreichischer Bundesverlag, 1991), p. 97.
14 *Encyclopedia Britannica* (1985), vol. 10, p. 519.
15 Hans Frank; *Das Diensttagebuch des deutschen Generalgouverneurs in Poten 1939–45* (Office Diary) (Stuttgart: Deutsche Verlagsanstalt, 1975), passim.
16 Karl Böhm (trans. J. Kehoe), *A Life Remembered: Memoirs* (London: Chatto and Windus, 1992).
17 Ibid.
18 Ibid., p. 106.
19 George Clare, *Berlin Days* (London: Macmillan, 1989), p. 106.
20 NGDO, vol. 2, p. 893.
21 Marcel Prawy, *The Vienna Opera* (London: Weidenfeld and Nicolson, 1969), pp. 168–9.

Chapter 6: Red Soldiers and Red Tape (1945–1946)

1 Marcel Prawy, *The Vienna Opera* (London: Weidenfeld and Nicolson, 1969), p. 169.
2 Stephen Gallup, *A History of the Salzburg Festival* (London: Weidenfeld and Nicolson, 1987), p. 34.
3 Karl Böhm (trans. J. Kehoe), *A Life Remembered: Memoirs* (London: Chatto and Windus, 1992), p. 109.
4 Norman Lebrecht: *The Maestro Myth: Great Conductors in Pursuit of Power* (London: Simon and Schuster, 1993), p. 107.
5 Gallup, op. cit., p. 120.
6 Böhm, op. cit., p. 107.
7 LWT Schwarzkopf film, 1992.
8 Headquarters US Forces in Austria, Information Services Branch [HFQ USFA ISB (ES File)].
9 Ibid.
10 Rudolf List, *Oper und Operette in Graz* (Graz: Landesverlag Ried, 1974), p. 84.
11 LWT film, op. cit.
12 In her ITV television interview of 1992, Schwarzkopf stated that she, Patzak and Weber again sang in *Die Entführung* at Innsbruck, but that opera house had not been reopened in September 1945 and no mention of such a production is to be found in its archive.
13 HQ USFA, op. cit.
14 Ibid.
15 George Clare, *Berlin Days* (London: Macmillan, 1989), p. 52.
16 Distinguished for having sung in world premières of *Lulu* and *Mathis der Maler* in Zürich.
17 HQ UFSA, op. cit.
18 Ibid.
19 Ibid.
20 Ibid.
21 Gallup, op. cit., p. 122.
22 HQ UFSA, op. cit.
23 Gallup, op. cit., p. 125.
24 *Parteigenoss* or Party member.
25 Gallup, op. cit., p. 133.

Chapter 7: Walter Legge

1 *Notting Hill Gazette*, August 1913.
2 Alf Levy was standing behind him and heard him say it.
3 WL–AJ, 1978.
4 Elisabeth Schwarzkopf (ed.), *On and Off the Record* (London: Faber and Faber, 1982), p. 156.
5 It has been reissued on CD under five different European labels.
6 Waldo Favre's *Favre Soloistenvereinigung* became the Favre Chorus after the war, recording operetta choruses for Polydor Records.
7 WL–AJ, 1978.
8 NC–AJ, 1993.
9 Entertainment National Service Association (affectionately known as 'Each Night Something Awful').
10 Basil Dean, *The Theatre at War* (London: Harrap, 1956), pp. 213–14.
11 Public Record Office File LAB 6/243.
12 WL–AJ, 1977.
13 Schwarzkopf, op. cit., p. 222.
14 WL–AJ, 1978.
15 The German is: *eine Katze im Sack kaufen* (to buy a cat in a sack).
16 Schwarzkopf, op. cit., p. 139.
17 Ibid., p. 85.
18 Ibid., pp. 64–5.
19 Alec Robertson; *More than Music* (London: William Collins, 1961), p. 221.

Chapter 8: The Great Partnerships (1946–1948)

1 Elisabeth Schwarzkopf (ed.), *On and Off the Record* (London: Faber and Faber, 1982), p. 222.
2 Ibid., p. 223.
3 Marcel Prawy, *The Vienna Opera* (London: Weidenfeld and Nicolson, 1969), p. 133.
4 Harold Rosenthal, *Two Centuries of Opera at Covent Garden* (London: Putnam, 1958), pp. 554–5.
5 Ibid., p. 591.
6 Werner Thärichen (exc. trans. H. Pleasants), *Paukenschläge: Furtwängler oder Karajan* (Zurich/Berlin: M & T Verlag, 1987), p. 5.
7 Herbert Hackenberger and Walter

Herrmann, *Die Wiener Staatsoper im Exil* (Vienna: Österreichischer Bundesverlag, 1985), p. 15.

8 *The Times*, 18 September 1947.
9 Ibid., 22 September 1947.
10 Schwarzkopf, op. cit., p. 141.
11 Ibid.
12 She was in Los Angeles that day.
13 Schwarzkopf, op. cit., p. 144.
14 *The Gramophone*, December 1990, p. 1175.

Chapter 9: Covent Garden, London (1948–1950)

1 *Neues Österreich*, 18 January 1948.
2 PG–AJ.
3 R. Temple Savage, *A Voice from the Pit* (Newton Abbot: David and Charles, 1988), p. 117.
4 *The Times*, 4 February 1948.
5 Harold Rosenthal, *Two Centuries of Opera at Covent Garden* (London: Putnam, 1958), p. 590.
6 Frances Donaldson, *The Royal Opera House in the Twentieth Century* (London: Weidenfeld and Nicolson, 1988), p. 114.
7 *The Times*, 18 February 1948.
8 Ibid., 7 April 1948.
9 Sir Geraint Evans and Noël Goodwin, *A Knight at the Opera* (London: Michael Joseph, 1984).
10 Evans, op. cit., p. 47.
11 FED–AJ.
12 The strong recommendations that had persisted, and Klemperer's wishes, resulted in Evans being cast as Figaro in the 1960 recording after Legge had left EMI.
13 *The Times*, 24 January 1949.
14 *The Observer*, 23 January 1949.
15 *The Gramophone*, December 1990, p. 1174.
16 *The Times*, 31 November 1949.
17 15 February 1950. The author was there.
18 *The Times*, 19 May 1950.
19 Howard Vogt: *Flagstad* (London: Secker and Warburg, 1987), pp. 225–6.
20 WL–AJ, 1978.
21 Eklipse Records CD15.
22 *Gazette de Lausanne*, 13 August 1950.

23 Debussy's *Nuages et Fêtes*; Franck's D minor Symphony; Ravel's *Rhapsodie Espagnole*, the Second Suite from *Daphnis et Chloë* and *Valses Nobles et Sentimentales*.
24 Legge, quoted by Roger Vaughan, *Herbert von Karajan* (London: Weidenfeld and Nicolson, 1986), p. 150.

Chapter 10: Callas, Wagner and Karajan (1951)

1 Roger Vaughan, *Herbert von Karajan* (London: Weidenfeld and Nicolson, 1986), p. 146.
2 Michael Scott, *Maria Meneghini Callas* (London: Simon and Schuster, 1991), p. 56.
3 Arianna Stassinopoulos, *Maria: Beyond the Callas Legend* (London: Weidenfeld and Nicolson, 1980), p. 69.
4 *Corriere della Sera*, 28 December 1950.
5 Bernard Gavoty (trans. F. E. Richardson), *Elisabeth Schwarzkopf* (Geneva: René Kister, 1958), p. 15.
6 *Neues Österreich*, 31 May 1963.
7 Elisabeth Schwarzkopf (ed.), *On and Off the Record* (London: Faber and Faber, 1982), pp. 194–5.
8 HDR–AJ.
9 *Daphne* was first given in London as a concert performance at the RFH, in September 1993 by the BBCSO under Andrew Davis.
10 BBCSO, LPO, LSO, Philharmonia, RPO. On 4 May, Beethoven's Ninth Symphony was prefaced by his First; on 8 May his *Choral Fantasia*, with Benno Moiseiwitsch as soloist, opened the concert.
11 Tietjen's note to Rode of 27 July 1942 in BDC (ES File).
12 Friedelind Wagner, with Page Cooper, *The Royal Family of Bayreuth* (London: Eyre and Spottiswoode, 1948), p. 41.
13 Lanfranco Rasponi, *The Last Prima Donnas* (London: Gollancz, 1984), p. 538.
14 WL–AJ, 1977.
15 Geoffrey Skelton: *Wieland Wagner: The*

Positive Sceptic (London: Gollancz, 1971), p. 99–100.
16 Ibid., p 98.
17 Ibid., p. 99.
18 John Culshaw, *Putting the Record Straight* (London: Secker and Warburg, 1981), p. 107.
19 WL–AJ, 1977.
20 Skelton, op. cit., p. 102.
21 *Opera*, October 1951, p. 557.
22 Geoffrey Skelton, *Wagner at Bayreuth* (London: Barrie and Rockcliff, 1965), p. 162.
23 Quoted in ibid., p. 94.
24 Ibid., p. 162.
25 Vaughan, op. cit., p. 146.

Chapter 11: Stravinsky, Tippett and Karajan (1951–1953)

1 LK–AJ, 1993.
2 Vera Stravinsky and Robert Craft, *Stravinsky in Pictures and Documents* (New York: Simon and Schuster, 1978), p. 407.
3 Ibid., p. 413.
4 Ibid., p. 362.
5 *CD Review*, April 1991, p. 32.
6 Spike Hughes, *Glyndebourne: A History of the Festival Opera* (London: Methuen, 1965), p. 194.
7 Elisabeth Schwarzkopf (ed.), *On and Off the Record* (London: Faber and Faber, 1982), p. 96.
8 The public dress rehearsal of *Danae* in 1944, with the chosen cast, and in Strauss's presence, was specially permitted to go that far, but no.jyfurther because all theatres in the Reich were closed. It is regarded, in some quarters, as the true première all the same.
9 *Gazette de Lausanne*, 2 September 1952.
10 Quoted in liner notes to CD recording.
11 Quoted in liner notes to CD recording.
12 Schwarzkopf op. cit., p. 86.
13 Sir Michael Tippett, *Those Twentieth Century Blues* (London: Hutchinson, 1991), p. 159.
14 Ibid., p. 159.
15 Ibid., p. 206.
16 *The Times*, 4 July 1953.

17 Not true; he conducted it all. JH–AJ, 1994.
18 From sleeve notes for LP of Wolf Concert.
19 WL–AJ, 1978.
20 *Gazette de Lausanne*, 1 September 1953.
21 *The Times*, 10 September 1953.

Chapter 12: Herbert von Karajan Supreme (1953–1954)

1 Elisabeth Schwarzkopf (ed.), *On and Off the Record* (London: Faber and Faber, 1982), pp. 88–9.
2 *Basler Nachtricht*, 29 October 1953.
3 Tubeuf, *l'Avant-Scène* ES, op. cit., p. 15.
4 Sergio Segalini, *Elisabeth Schwarzkopf* (Paris: Fayard, 1983), p. 72.
5 Schwarzkopf, op. cit., p. 141.
6 Ibid., p. 201.
7 Ibid., p. 142.
8 John Hunt, *Philharmonic Autocrat* (London: Hunt, 1993), p. 340.
9 WL–AJ, 1978.
10 Schwarzkopf, op. cit., p. 142
11 *The Times*, 8 March 1954.
12 Schwarzkopf, op. cit., p. 202.
13 *The Scotsman*, 8 September 1954.
14 Bernard Gavoty (trans. F. E. Richardson), *Elisabeth Schwarzkopf* (Geneva: René Kister, 1958), p. 12.
15 *Gramophone*, January 1994, p. 101.
16 CH–AJ, 1955.
17 Lord Harewood, *The Tongs and the Bones* (London: Weidenfeld and Nicolson, 1981), p. 157.
18 Sir Michael Tippett, *Those Twentieth Century Blues* (London: Hutchinson, 1991), p. 215.

Chapter 13: Recordings (1955–1959)

1 Schwarzkopf quoted in *Gramophone*, December 1990, p. 1175.
2 *The Times*, 16 May 1955.
3 IL–AJ correspondence 1992.
4 Ibid.
5 Elisabeth Schwarzkopf (ed.), *On and Off the Record* (London: Faber and Faber, 1982), p. 141.
6 *Observer*, 8 July 1956.
7 WL–AJ, 1978.

8 *The Times*, 25 February 1957.
9 WL–AJ, 1978.
10 Vocal Score, p. 173, one bar after fig. 31.
11 *The Times*, 26 June 1957.
12 *Neues Österreich*, 28 January 1958.
13 WL–AJ, 1978.
14 *The Times*, 17 January 1958.
15 Edwin McArthur; *Kirsten Flagstad* (New York: Knopf, 1965), p. 258.
16 *Gramophone*, December 1990, p. 1175.
17 Pre-recorded on 2 June 1958. Broadcast by Home Service between 1.10 p.m. and 1.40 p.m. on 28 July 1958.
18 *Gramophone*, December 1990, p. 1174.
19 The others are 'Die erwachte Rose' and 'Rote Rose'.
20 *The Times*, 19 January 1959.
21 *The Times*, 28 April 1959.
22 *Tribune de Lausanne*, 11 September 1959.
23 WL–AJ, 1978.
24 Ibid.

19 Ibid., March 1961, p. 103.
20 Hamilton, op. cit., p. 309.
21 Herbert von Karajan (trans. S. Spencer), *My Autobiography* (as told to Franz Endler) (London: Sidgwick and Jackson, 1989), p. 70.
22 Ibid., p. 71.
23 Elisabeth Schwarzkopf (ed.), *On and Off the Record* (London: Faber and Faber, 1982), p. 100.
24 *The Times*, 4 March 1961.
25 Ibid., 18 October 1961.
26 *Gramophone*, 1990, p. 1175.
27 *Opera*, November 1961, pp. 106–7.
28 Ibid., Festival issue, 1962, p. 105.
29 TC–AJ (TC was there).
30 *Opera*, Festival issue, 1962, pp. 24–5.
31 *The Times*, 20 September 1962.
32 *Opera*, January 1963, p. 30.
33 *The Times*, 5 March 1963.
34 Ibid., 24 June 1963.
35 VG's talk broadcast on Radio 3 BBC.
36 *The Times*, 17 January 1964.

Chapter 14: Consolidation (1959–1964)

1 *The Times*, 28 September 1959.
2 Ibid., 19 October 1959.
3 *Opera*, January 1959, p. 61.
4 *Financial Times*, 5 December 1959.
5 *The Times*, 5 December 1959.
6 *Opera*, January 1960, p. 67.
7 Frances Donaldson, *The Royal Opera House in the Twentieth Century* (London: Weidenfeld and Nicolson, 1988), p. 115.
8 *Neues Österreich*, 22 December 1959.
9 *Opera*, March 1960, p. 201.
10 *Neues Österreich*, 6 January 1960.
11 *Opera*, March 1960, pp. 201–22.
12 Heinrich Kralik in *Die Presse*, 20 May 1960.
13 Roger Vaughan, *Herbert von Karajan* (London: Weidenfeld and Nicolson, 1984), pp. 89–90.
14 David Hamilton (ed.), *Metropolitan Opera Encyclopedia* (New York: Simon and Schuster, 1987), p. 309.
15 *Opera*, February 1962, p. 102.
16 Lanfranco Rasponi, *The Last Prima Donnas* (London: Gollancz, 1984), pp. 540–1.
17 RT–AJ correspondence 1993.
18 *Opera*, February 1961, p. 112.

Chapter 15: After Karajan (1964–1968)

1 Elisabeth Schwarzkopf (ed.), *On and Off the Record* (London: Faber and Faber, 1982), p. 73.
2 Michael Scott, *Maria Meneghini Callas* (London: Simon and Schuster, 1991), pp. 22–3.
3 Not so many – only eight.
4 David Hamilton (ed.), *Metropolitan Opera Encyclopedia* (New York: Simon and Schuster, 1987), p. 308.
5 Roger Vaughan, *Herbert von Karajan* (London: Weidenfeld and Nicolson, 1986), pp. 243–4.
6 Ibid., p. 232.
7 R. Ericson in *New York Times*, 14 October 1964, quoted by Seltsam in 2nd supplement of *Metropolitan Opera Annals*.
8 Heger had given the London première of *Capriccio* at Covent Garden with the Bayerische Staatsoper in September 1953.
9 GP–AJ correspondence, 1993.
10 Joseph Rosenstock was an experienced musician. His career began in 1922. Expelled from Germany during the war,

he then became conductor and musical director of the New York City Opera between 1948 and 1955.

11 Sir Geraint Evans with Noël Goodwin, *A Knight at the Opera* (London: Michael Joseph, 1984), p. 144.

12 *Opera*, March 1967, p. 245.

13 Schwarzkopf, op. cit., p. 75.

14 Julian Budden believes that it was put together by a Danish musician called Humbold in the last century, and first given at a bishop's garden party as a joke. It contains a brief parody on the Kyrie and two misquotations from Rossini's opera *Otello*.

15 *The Times*, 8 May 1967.

16 Ibid., 14 October 1967.

17 *The Times*, 7 March 1968.

Chapter 16: *Diminuendo (1968–1979)*

1 *The Times*, 3 December 1968.

2 WL–AJ, 1978.

3 Elisabeth Schwarzkopf (ed.), *On and Off the Record* (London: Faber and Faber, 1982), p. 85.

4 *San Francisco Chronicle*, 24 November, 1972.

5 *Neues Österreich*, 16 October 1975.

6 WL–AJ, 1978.

7 Schwarzkopf, op. cit., pp. 233–4.

8 BL–AJ, telephone conversation, 1993.

9 WL–AJ, telephone conversation, 1978.

10 WL–AJ, 1977.

Chapter 17: *After Walter Legge*

1 Norman Lebrecht: *The Maestro Myth: Great Conductors in Pursuit of Power* (London: Simon and Schuster, 1993), p. 130.

2 Uttered by a stranger, overheard by AJ.

3 WL's notes with *Italienisches Liederbuch* CD.

4 LWT Schwarzkopf film, 1992.

5 Herbert von Karajan (trans. S. Spencer), *My Autobiography* (as told to Franz Endler) (London: Sidgwick and Jackson, 1989), p. 92.

6 Sam H. Shirakawa: *The Devil's Music Master* (Oxford: OUP, 1992), p. 381.

7 Ibid.

Chapter 18: *Elisabeth Schwarzkopf: Opera Singer (1938–1970)*

1 *Stuttgarter Zeitung* interview, (1970s, n.d.).

2 Bernard Gavoty (trans. F. E. Richardson), *Elisabeth Schwarzkopf* (Geneva: René Kister, 1965), p. 15.

3 Eric Blom (ed.), *Grove's Dictionary of Music and Musicians* (London: Macmillan, 1954).

4 E. J. Dent, *Mozart's Operas* (Oxford: OUP, 1946), p. 158.

5 Lanfranco Rasponi, *The Last Prima Donnas* (London: Gollancz, 1984), p. 566.

6 *Gramophone*, February 1961, p. 442.

7 Elisabeth Schwarzkopf (ed.), *On and Off the Record* (London: Faber and Faber, 1982), p. 101.

8 Dent, op. cit., p. 110.

9 LL–AJ, 1971.

10 David Hamilton (ed.), *Metropolitan Opera Encyclopedia* (New York: Simon and Schuster, 1987), p. 309.

11 Ibid.

12 Referred to as 1956 because it was made in that year, although the recording was not issued until late 1957.

13 Max Loppert in NGDO, p. 1006.

14 Dent, op. cit., p. 192.

15 John Hunt, *Philharmonic Autocrat* (London: Hunt, 1993), p. 266.

16 Schwarzkopf, op. cit., p. 141.

17 *Gramophone*, December 1990, p. 1174.

18 Hamilton, op. cit., p. 308.

19 Alan Blyth (ed.), *Opera on Record* (London: Hutchinson, 1979), pp. 332–3.

Chapter 19: *Elisabeth Schwarzkopf: Lieder Singer (1941–1979)*

1 *l'Avant-Scène*, ES, p. 70.

2 *Berlin Nachtausgabe* 10, May 1942.

3 Wiener Library PC4, Reel 47.

4 *Gramophone*, December 1990, p. 1174.

5 Elisabeth Schwarzkopf (ed.), *On and Off the Record* (London: Faber and Faber, 1982), p. 183.

6 *The Times*, 21 May 1965.

7 ITV biographical film, 1992.

8 J. B. Steane, *The Grand Tradition* (London: Duckworth, 1993), p. 348.

9 Ibid., p. 356.

10 *The Times*, 3 December 1968.

11 Clare Delamarche and François Lafor, *Le Monde de la Musique*, (Paris, 1988).

12 *Gramophone*, December 1990, p. 1175.

13 *The Times*, 21 May 1965.

14 *Neues Österreich*, 20 April 1950.

15 *Gramophone*, December 1990, pp. 1174–5.

16 The Brahms group has been on a 'pirate' CD coupled with six Schubert songs accompanied by Favaretto (Rome, February 1952), and four excerpts from *Il flauto magico* (Milan, December 1953).

17 Not Opus 24, as it says on the LP sleeve.

18 *The Times*, 7 November 1950.

19 *The Times*, 7 May 1966.

Bibliography

GENERAL

Abraham, Gerald, *Concise Oxford History of Music* (Oxford: OUP, 1988)
Bielenberg, Christabel, *The Past is Myself* (London: Chatto and Windus, 1968)
Böhm, Karl (trans. J. Kehoe), *A Life Remembered: Memoirs* (London: Chatto and Windus, 1992)
Christiansen, Rupert, *Prima Donna – A History* (London: Bodley Head, 1984)
Clare, George, *Berlin Days* (London: Macmillan, 1989)
   Last Waltz in Vienna (London: Macmillan, 1981)
Crozier, Eric, *Sadler's Wells Opera Books No. 2: 'Cosi fan Tutte'*. Essay by E. J. Dent on the opera's history (London: J. Lane, 1945)
Culshaw, John, *Ring Resounding* (London: Secker and Warburg, 1967)
   Putting the Record Straight (London: Secker and Warburg, 1981)
Dean, Basil, *The Theatre at War* (London: Harrap, 1956)
Dent, E. J., *Mozart's Operas* (Oxford: OUP, 1946)
Dermota, Anton, *Tausendundein Abend mein Sängerleben* (Munich: Deutscher Taschenbuch Verlag, 1989)
Donaldson, Frances, *The Royal Opera House in the Twentieth Century* (London: Weidenfeld and Nicolson, 1988)
Drogheda, Lord, *Double Harness: Memoirs* (London: Weidenfeld and Nicolson, 1978)
Evans, Sir Geraint, with Goodwin, Noël, *A Knight at the Opera* (London: Michael Joseph, 1984)
Frank, Hans, *Im Angesicht des Galgens* (Munich: Beck Verlag, 1953)
   Das Diensttagebuch des deutschen Generalgouverneurs in Poten 1939–45 (Stuttgart: Deutsche Verlagsanstalt, 1975)
Gaisberg, Fred, *Music on Record* (London: Robert Hale, 1946)
Gallup, Stephen, *A History of the Salzburg Festival* (London: Weidenfeld and Nicolson, 1987)
Gavoty, Bernard (trans. F. E. Richardson), *Elisabeth Schwarzkopf* (Geneva: René Kister, 1958)
Geissmar, Berta, *The Baton and the Jackboot* (London: Hamish Hamilton, 1944)
Goebbels, Joseph, *Tagebücher* (Munich: Bundesarchiv, 1987)
Haltrecht, Montague, *The Quiet Showman* (London: Collins, 1975)
Hamilton, David (ed.), *Metropolitan Opera Encyclopedia* (New York: Simon and Schuster, 1987)
Harewood, Lord, *The Tongs and the Bones* (London: Weidenfeld and Nicolson, 1981)
Hase, Hellmuth von (ed.), *Jahrbuch der deutschen Musik* (Leipzig: Breitkopf and Härtel; Berlin: Max Hesses Verlag, 1943)
Heringdorf, Detlef Meyer zu, *Das Charlottenburger Opernhaus (1912–61)* (Berlin: Deutsche Oper, 1988)

Heyworth, Peter, *Otto Klemperer: His Life and Times (1885-1933)*, vol. I (Oxford: OUP, 1983)

Hughes, Spike, *Glyndebourne: A History of the Festival Opera* (London: Methuen, 1965)

Huwe, Gisela (ed.), *Die Deutsche Oper Berlin* (Berlin: Quadriga Verlag, n.d.)

Jefferson, Alan, *The Lieder of Richard Strauss* (London: Cassell, 1971)
   Lotte Lehmann, (London: Julia MacRae, 1988)
   The Operas of Richard Strauss in Britain 1910–1963 (London: Putnam, 1963)
   Richard Strauss Operas: (New York: Discography Series XVII, 1975)
   Der Rosenkavalier (Oxford: OUP, 1985)

Karajan, Herbert von (trans. S. Spencer), *My Autobiography* (as told to Franz Endler) (London: Sidgwick and Jackson, 1989)

Kralik, Heinrich (trans. R. Rickett), *The Vienna Opera* (London: Methuen, 1964)

Lebrecht, Norman, *The Maestro Myth: Great Conductors in Pursuit of Power* (London: Simon and Schuster, 1993)

List, Rudolf, *Oper und Operette in Graz* (Graz: Landesverlag Ried, 1974)

McArthur, Edwin, *Kirsten Flagstad* (New York: Knopf, 1965)

Meissner, Hans-Otto (trans. Keeble, Gwendolen M.), *Magda Goebbels* (London: Sidgwick & Jackson, 1980)

Moore, Gerald, *Singer and Accompanist,* (London: Methuen 1953)
   Am I Too Loud? (London: Hamish Hamilton, 1962)

Newman, Ernest, *Hugo Wolf* (London: Methuen, 1907)
   (ed. F. Aprahamian) *Writings from The Sunday Times* (London, 1976)

Nicholls, A. J. H., *Weimar and the Rise of Hitler* (London: Macmillan, 1970)

Pleasants, Henry, *The Great Singers* (London: Macmillan, 1983)
   Opera in Crisis (London: Thames and Hudson, 1989)

Porter, Andrew, *A Musical Season* (London: Gollancz, 1974)

Prawy, Marcel, *The Vienna Opera* (London: Weidenfeld and Nicolson, 1969)

Prieberg, Fred K. (trans. C. Dolan), *Trial of Strength: Wilhelm Furtwängler and the Third Reich* (London: Quartet, 1991)

Rasponi, Lanfranco, *The Last Prima Donnas* (London: Gollancz, 1984)

Rathkolb, Oliver, *Führertreu und Gottbegnadet: Künstereliten im Dritten Reich* (Vienna: Osterreichischer Bundesverlag, 1991)

Reimann, Viktor, *Dr Joseph Goebbels* (Vienna: Verlag Fritz Molden, 1971)

Rémy, Pierre-Jean (trans. C. Atthill), *Maria Callas: A Tribute* (London: Macdonald & Jane's, 1978)

Robertson, Alec, *More Than Music* (London: William Collins, 1961)

Savage, R. Temple, *A Voice from the Pit* (Newton Abbot: David & Charles, 1988)

Schwarzkopf, Elisabeth (ed.), *On and Off the Record* (London: Faber and Faber, 1982)

Scott, Michael, *Maria Meneghini Callas* (London: Simon and Schuster, 1991)

Segalini, Sergio, *Elisabeth Schwarzkopf* (Paris: Fayard, 1983)

Sheean, Vincent, *First and Last Love* (London: Gollancz, 1957)

Shirakawa, Sam H., *The Devil's Music Master* (Oxford: OUP, 1992)

Shirer, William L., *Rise and Fall of the Third Reich* (London: Pan, 1964)

Skelton, Geoffrey, *Wagner at Bayreuth* (London: Barrie and Rockcliff, 1965)
   Wieland Wagner: The Positive Sceptic (London: Gollancz, 1971)

Stassinopoulos, Arianna, *Maria: Beyond the Callas Legend* (London: Weidenfeld and Nicolson, 1980)

Steane, J. B., *The Grand Tradition* (London: Duckworth, 1993)
   Voices: Singers and Critics (London: Duckworth, 1992)

Stravinsky, Vera and Craft, Robert, *Stravinsky in Pictures and Documents* (New York: Simon and Schuster, 1978)

Thärichen, Werner (exc. trans. H. Pleasants), *Paukenschläge: Furtwängler oder Karajan* (Zurich/Berlin: M&T Verlag, 1987)

Tippett, Sir Michael, *Those Twentieth Century Blues* (London: Hutchinson, 1991)
Vaughan, Roger, *Herbert von Karajan* (London: Weidenfeld and Nicolson, 1986)
Vogt, Howard, *Flagstad* (London: Secker and Warburg, 1987)
Wagner, Friedelind with Page Cooper, *The Royal Family of Bayreuth* (London: Eyre and Spottiswoode, 1948)
Walker, Frank, *Hugo Wolf: A Biography* (London: Dent, 1951)
Zweig, Stefan, *The World of Yesterday* (London: Cassell, 1943)

REFERENCE

Bauer, A., *Deutscher Spielfilm Almanach 1929–50* (Berlin: Filmblätter Verlag, 1950)
Blom, Eric, (ed.), *Grove's Dictionary of Music and Musicians* (5th Edition) (London: Macmillan, 1954)
Brosche, Dr G. (ed.), *International Richard Strauss Gesellschaft* Blätter (Tutzing), passim
Blyth, Alan (ed.) *Opera on Record* (London: Hutchinson, 1979)
Delamarche, Claire and Lafor, Francois, *Le Monde de la Musique* (Paris, 1988)
Gefen, Gérard, *Furtwängler: Une biographie par le disque* (Paris: Belfond, 1986)
Gourret, Jean, *Dictionnaire des Cantatrices de l'Opéra de Paris* (Paris: Albatros, 1987)
Hackenberger, Herbert and Herrmann, Walter *Die Wiener Staatsoper im Exil* (Vienna: Osterreichischer Bundesverlag, 1985)
Hase, Helmuth von, *Jahrbuch der deutscher Musik* (Leipzig & Berlin: Gemeinsamer, 1942)
Hunt, John (ed.), *The Furtwängler Sound* (3rd Edition) (London: Hunt, 1990)
  Philharmonic Autocrat, (Herbert von Karajan's sound, video, concert and opera register (London: Hunt, 1993)
  'Viennese' Sopranos (Discography) (London: Hunt, 1991)
Kaut, Josef, *Festspiele in Salzburg* (Munich: Deutsche Taschen Verlag, 1970)
Kutsch, K. J. and Riemens, Leo (eds.) *Grosses Sängerlexikon*, vols. 1 and 2 (Berne and Stuttgart: Franke Verlag, 1987)
Larue, C. Steven (ed.), *International Dictionary of Opera* (Detroit and London: St James Press, 1993)
Prendergast, Herbert C., *Internat. Richard Strauss Gesellschaft*, No. 32, March (Berlin: 1962)
Rosenthal, Harold (ed.), *Opera Annual 1955–6* (London: Calder, 1955)
Rosenthal, Harold, *Two Centuries of Opera at Covent Garden* (London: Putnam 1958)
Rosenthal, Harold and Warrack, John (eds.) *Concise Oxford Dictionary of Opera* (Oxford: OUP, 1990)
Sadie, Stanley (ed.), *The New Grove Dictionary of Opera* (London: Macmillan, 1992)
Scott, Michael, *The Record of Singing*, vol. 2 (London: Duckworth, 1979)
Seltsam, William H. (comp.) *Metropolitan Opera Annals* (New York: 1947)
  First Supplement: 1947–1957 (New York: 1957)
  Second Supplement: 1957–1966 (New York: 1966)
Slonimsky, Nicolas, *Baker's Biographical Dictionary of Musicians* (Oxford: OUP, 1984)
Smith, Michael and Cosens, Ian (comps.) *The Columbia Catalogue (Voices of the Past Vol. 8)*, (Oakwood Press, n.d.)
Ward, John Owen (ed.), *The Oxford Companion to Music* (10th edition) (Oxford: OUP, 1970)
Wolff, Stéphane, *L'Opéra au Palais Garnier* (Paris: Slatkine, 1983)
  Un Demi-Siècle d'Opéra-Comique (Paris: André Bonne, 1953)

Augustin, Siegfried (trans. D. Mason), 'Wilhelm Rode' (article in *The Record Collector* vol. 38 no. 3 (Chelmsford: 1993)
l'Avant-Scène l'Opéra: No. 69/70 *Les Introuvables d'Elisabeth Schwarzkopf* (Paris: 1983)
  No. 84 *Le Chevalier à la Rose* (Paris: 1984)
Bayreuther Festspielbuch (Bayreuth: 1951)

The Classical Catalogue 1–7 (Harrow: Gramophone Publications, 1990–3)
Salzburger Festspiele: 1937 und 1938 (Saltzburg: 1988)
Staatliche Akad. Hochschule für Musik in Berlin. Jahresbericht 55 and 56 (Berlin: 1933/4)

OFFICIAL SOURCES

Public Record Office, Kew:
F.O. 1020/1097
Lab 6/243

Berlin Document Center (US)
Reichskulturkammer File on
Elisabeth Schwarzkopf (1938–45)

United States Forces in
Austria. Information
Services Branch, Theatre & Music Section (1945–6)

Index